*Praise for* Defenders of the Faith

'Highly informative . . . extensive background'
Theo Hobson, *TLS*

'Fascinating, thorough and timely . . . [Pepinster] shines particularly in the task of sketching the faith of the Queen, about which, as she rightly remarks, the stacks of royal biographies make "barely a mention".'
*Daily Telegraph*

'The most valuable part of *Defenders of the Faith* shows how Queen Elizabeth II has responded to the vastly changed ecumenical and interfaith picture since the Second World War.'
*Church Times*

'It's a delight to walk the faith trail trodden by monarchs past, the monarch present and the monarch to come with the discriminating mind and poised pen of Catherine Pepinster as one's guide.'
Peter Hennessy

'A well-researched and accessible assessment of the monarchy's relationship with faith and religion over the past 500 years, and how that might develop in the future . . . [Pepinster] has authority and insight and great sensitivity that shows her deep understanding of faith.'
Peter Crumpler, *Preach Magazine*

# Defenders of the Faith

## The British Monarchy, Religion and the Coronation

CATHERINE PEPINSTER

HODDER

First published in Great Britain in 2022 by Hodder & Stoughton
An Hachette UK company

This fully revised edition first published in 2023

1



A CIP catalogue record for this title is available from the British Library

Paperback ISBN 978 1 399 80007 5
eBook ISBN 978 1 399 80008 2

Typeset in Bembo MT by Hewer Text UK Ltd, Edinburgh
Printed and bound in Great Britain by Clays Ltd, Elcograf S.p.A.

Hodder & Stoughton policy is to use papers that are natural, renewable and recyclable products and made from wood grown in sustainable forests. The logging and manufacturing processes are expected to conform to the environmental regulations of the country of origin.

Hodder & Stoughton Ltd
Carmelite House
50 Victoria Embankment
London EC4Y 0DZ

www.hodderfaith.com

# *Contents*

# *The British Monarchy*

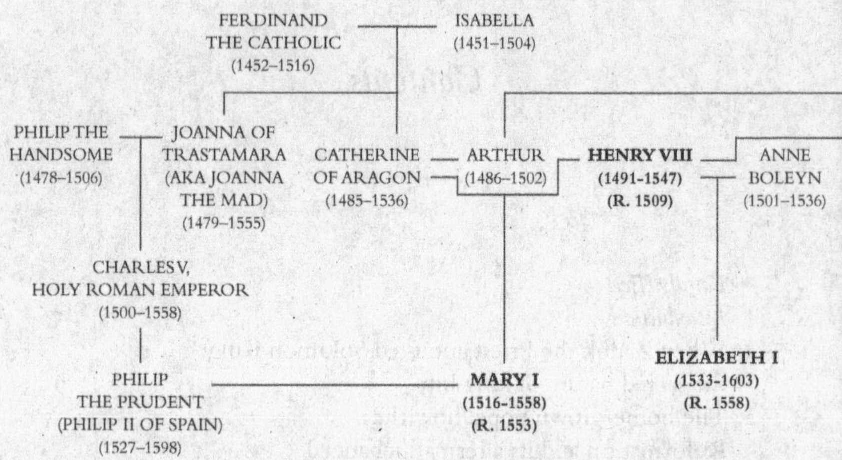

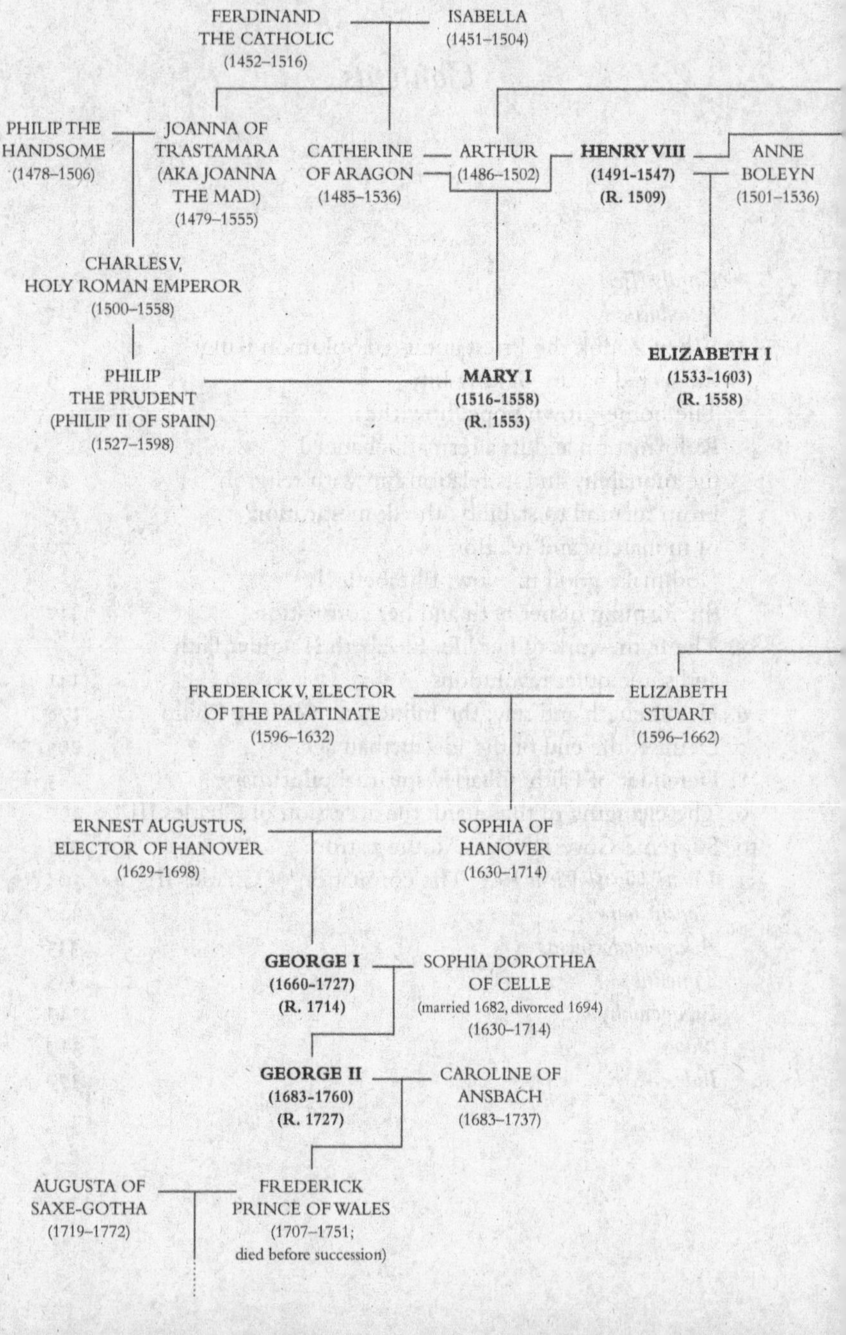

FERDINAND THE CATHOLIC (1452–1516)
ISABELLA (1451–1504)
PHILIP THE HANDSOME (1478–1506)
JOANNA OF TRASTAMARA (AKA JOANNA THE MAD) (1479–1555)
CATHERINE OF ARAGON (1485–1536)
ARTHUR (1486–1502)
HENRY VIII (1491–1547) (R. 1509)
ANNE BOLEYN (1501–1536)
CHARLES V, HOLY ROMAN EMPEROR (1500–1558)
ELIZABETH I (1533-1603) (R. 1558)
PHILIP THE PRUDENT (PHILIP II OF SPAIN) (1527–1598)
MARY I (1516-1558) (R. 1553)
FREDERICK V, ELECTOR OF THE PALATINATE (1596–1632)
ELIZABETH STUART (1596–1662)
ERNEST AUGUSTUS, ELECTOR OF HANOVER (1629–1698)
SOPHIA OF HANOVER (1630–1714)
GEORGE I (1660-1727) (R. 1714)
SOPHIA DOROTHEA OF CELLE (married 1682, divorced 1694) (1630–1714)
GEORGE II (1683-1760) (R. 1727)
CAROLINE OF ANSBACH (1683–1737)
AUGUSTA OF SAXE-GOTHA (1719–1772)
FREDERICK PRINCE OF WALES (1707–1751; died before succession)

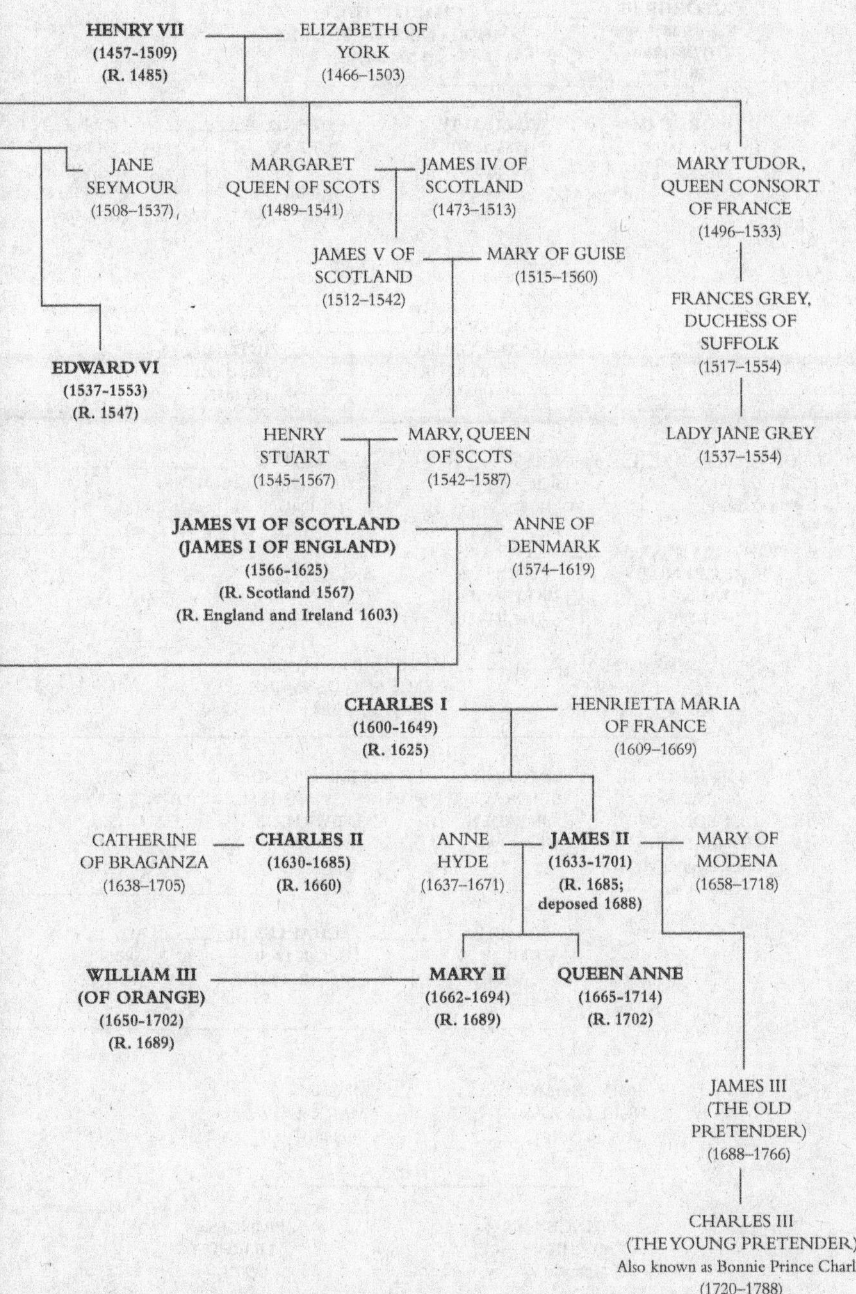
HENRY VII
(1457-1509)
(R. 1485)
ELIZABETH OF YORK
(1466–1503)
JANE SEYMOUR
(1508–1537)
MARGARET QUEEN OF SCOTS
(1489–1541)
JAMES IV OF SCOTLAND
(1473–1513)
MARY TUDOR, QUEEN CONSORT OF FRANCE
(1496–1533)
JAMES V OF SCOTLAND
(1512–1542)
MARY OF GUISE
(1515–1560)
FRANCES GREY, DUCHESS OF SUFFOLK
(1517–1554)
EDWARD VI
(1537-1553)
(R. 1547)
HENRY STUART
(1545–1567)
MARY, QUEEN OF SCOTS
(1542–1587)
LADY JANE GREY
(1537–1554)
JAMES VI OF SCOTLAND
(JAMES I OF ENGLAND)
(1566-1625)
(R. Scotland 1567)
(R. England and Ireland 1603)
ANNE OF DENMARK
(1574–1619)
CHARLES I
(1600-1649)
(R. 1625)
HENRIETTA MARIA OF FRANCE
(1609–1669)
CATHERINE OF BRAGANZA
(1638–1705)
CHARLES II
(1630-1685)
(R. 1660)
ANNE HYDE
(1637–1671)
JAMES II
(1633-1701)
(R. 1685; deposed 1688)
MARY OF MODENA
(1658–1718)
WILLIAM III
(OF ORANGE)
(1650-1702)
(R. 1689)
MARY II
(1662-1694)
(R. 1689)
QUEEN ANNE
(1665-1714)
(R. 1702)
JAMES III
(THE OLD PRETENDER)
(1688–1766)
CHARLES III
(THE YOUNG PRETENDER)
Also known as Bonnie Prince Charlie
(1720–1788)

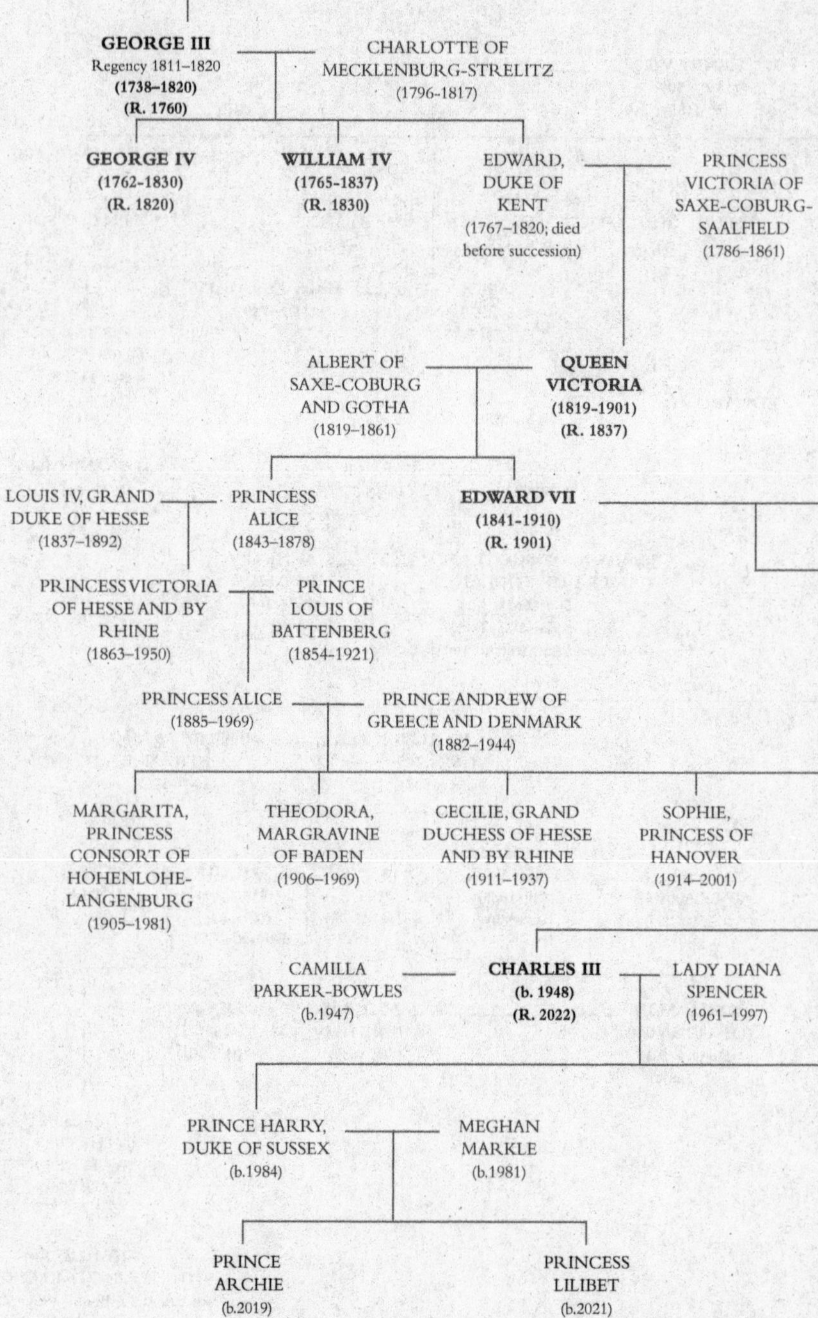
GEORGE III
Regency 1811–1820
(1738–1820)
(R. 1760)
CHARLOTTE OF MECKLENBURG-STRELITZ
(1796-1817)
GEORGE IV
(1762-1830)
(R. 1820)
WILLIAM IV
(1765-1837)
(R. 1830)
EDWARD, DUKE OF KENT
(1767–1820; died before succession)
PRINCESS VICTORIA OF SAXE-COBURG-SAALFIELD
(1786–1861)
ALBERT OF SAXE-COBURG AND GOTHA
(1819–1861)
QUEEN VICTORIA
(1819-1901)
(R. 1837)
LOUIS IV, GRAND DUKE OF HESSE
(1837–1892)
PRINCESS ALICE
(1843–1878)
EDWARD VII
(1841-1910)
(R. 1901)
PRINCESS VICTORIA OF HESSE AND BY RHINE
(1863–1950)
PRINCE LOUIS OF BATTENBERG
(1854-1921)
PRINCESS ALICE
(1885–1969)
PRINCE ANDREW OF GREECE AND DENMARK
(1882–1944)
MARGARITA, PRINCESS CONSORT OF HOHENLOHE-LANGENBURG
(1905–1981)
THEODORA, MARGRAVINE OF BADEN
(1906–1969)
CECILIE, GRAND DUCHESS OF HESSE AND BY RHINE
(1911–1937)
SOPHIE, PRINCESS OF HANOVER
(1914–2001)
CAMILLA PARKER-BOWLES
(b.1947)
CHARLES III
(b. 1948)
(R. 2022)
LADY DIANA SPENCER
(1961–1997)
PRINCE HARRY, DUKE OF SUSSEX
(b.1984)
MEGHAN MARKLE
(b.1981)
PRINCE ARCHIE
(b.2019)
PRINCESS LILIBET
(b.2021)

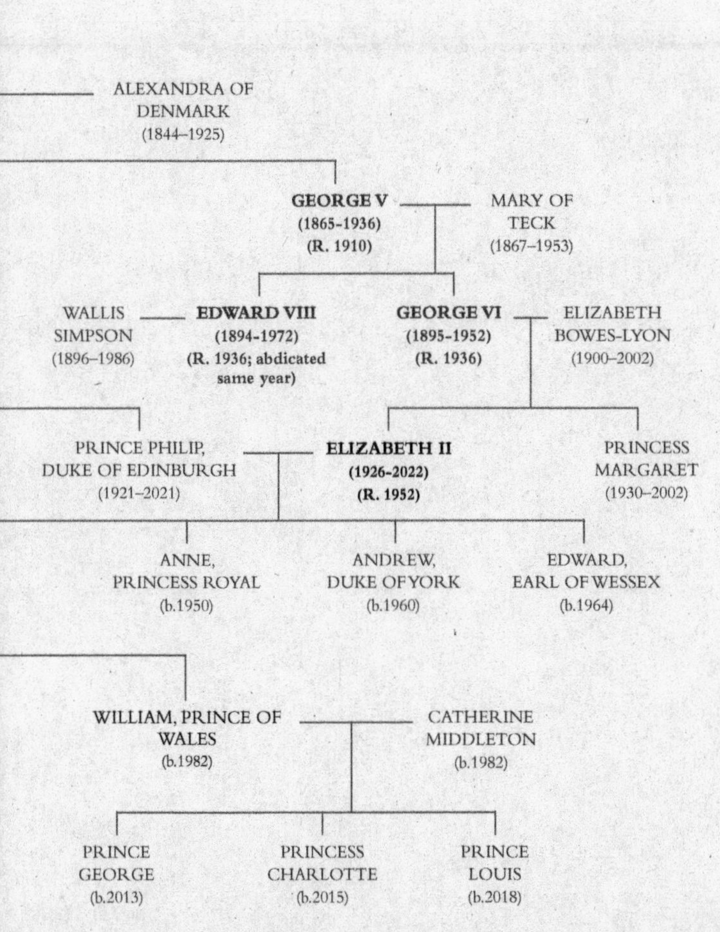

ALEXANDRA OF DENMARK (1844–1925)
GEORGE V (1865-1936) (R. 1910)
MARY OF TECK (1867–1953)
WALLIS SIMPSON (1896–1986)
EDWARD VIII (1894-1972) (R. 1936; abdicated same year)
GEORGE VI (1895-1952) (R. 1936)
ELIZABETH BOWES-LYON (1900–2002)
PRINCE PHILIP, DUKE OF EDINBURGH (1921–2021)
ELIZABETH II (1926-2022) (R. 1952)
PRINCESS MARGARET (1930–2002)
ANNE, PRINCESS ROYAL (b.1950)
ANDREW, DUKE OF YORK (b.1960)
EDWARD, EARL OF WESSEX (b.1964)
WILLIAM, PRINCE OF WALES (b.1982)
CATHERINE MIDDLETON (b.1982)
PRINCE GEORGE (b.2013)
PRINCESS CHARLOTTE (b.2015)
PRINCE LOUIS (b.2018)

# Introduction

IT WAS LUNCHTIME on Thursday 8 September 2022 when I received a phone call from the BBC. As someone on their books as a commentator on the monarchy, could I come into the studio, and how soon? I had no need to ask why. My mobile phone had been pinging with news alerts for at least an hour, telling me that the Queen's doctors were concerned for her health. It was an ominous message and suggested that a reign that had lasted a record-breaking seventy years might soon be coming to an end. Within half an hour or so I was in the studio, talking to the BBC's main news presenter, Huw Edwards, who was keeping some semblance of order over a fast-breaking story – and one of the biggest stories any of the journalists involved had ever worked on. But it was a tricky situation: there were the doctors' worries, but other than that little to go on. Yet everybody sensed something monumental was happening. What could be said? As Huw Edwards asked me for my thoughts, I reached for a suitable phrase: 'The tectonic plates are shifting, Huw.'

Something certainly shifted in Britain on that day, the day that saw the death of one monarch – Elizabeth II – and the immediate accession of another – Charles III. As huge numbers in person and millions more via television and online witnessed the ceremonial events that took place in the aftermath of what constitutional experts call the demise of the monarch, there was a sense that they were seeing history in the making.

One of the conflicted aspects of the British monarchical system is that death and newness are combined. There is grief at the loss of one monarch, but the supposed joy at another acceding to the throne is simultaneous. Not one day of unconfined mourning occurs.

These alternating emotions, which reflect both the change and the continuity of the system, were expressed in the events marking the passing of one sovereign and the succession of another. There were the processions, vigils, lying-in state, funeral and committal, juxtaposed with the new King's broadcast to the nation, the ceremony of accession and the proclamations of the new reign made across Britain.

What the obsequies and the succession also highlighted was how embedded religion is within the monarchy and constitution of Britain. The presence of the Imperial State Crown, sceptre and orb on the Queen's coffin, with their crosses and images of the world under Christ's dominion, were a reminder of the constant theme of British monarchy: that the sovereign is a servant of God. There were the announcements of, first, the late Queen's titles, and then the new King's, with their links to Christianity. The personal commitment and faith of the Queen was a constant during her funeral and committal – a faith that the new King also mentioned in his tributes to his mother and used as a means of signposting his own. His official connection to the Church of England and his role in upholding the Protestant religion was also highlighted.

In a country that is increasingly religiously diverse, yet also increasingly secular, the frequent references to Christianity during those weeks in September were striking. They were matched by nods to other faiths as well – and also to people of no faith.

So what are we to make of this imprint of religion on those remarkable days in September when Britain lost one sovereign and gained another? While it has always been a crucial part of the makeup of the British monarchy, it has often been taken for granted. Yet a clue to this connection is the pound in your pocket, or indeed any coin. The vast majority of them are still those of Elizabeth II, and surrounding the Queen's head you will see the acronyms *Elizabeth II, D.G. REG. FD: Elizabeth II, Dei Gratia, Fidei Defensor*, Latin for 'By the grace of God, Queen, Defender of the Faith'. Coins with the King's effigy will slowly be released – the first have been fifty pence pieces – and they will have the same, but masculine, legend: *D.G. REX. FD*: 'by the grace of God, King, Defender of the Faith'.

'Defender of the Faith' was the title first given to Henry VIII in 1521 by a grateful pope, delighted with the English King's endeavours to defend the Roman Catholic religion from the verbal onslaughts of Martin Luther. Just six years later, Henry clashed with the Pope as he sought to extricate himself from his marriage to Catherine of Aragon, marry Anne Boleyn and father a male heir. When the Pope refused to annul Henry's marriage, the King broke away from Rome and founded the Church of England. A Christian monarch, if no longer a Catholic one, Henry clung on to his title of Defender of the Faith, and all his successors have used it since, with the title always bestowed on them upon their accession to the throne.

Even before Henry was first honoured by the Pope, monarchy in the country was bound up with Christianity, and was heavily influenced by ideas of kingship found in the Bible. For a thousand years the coronations of our monarchs have been Christian services – their links to ancient text powerfully and dramatically expressed in the words of Scripture used at every crowning: Zadok the priest and Nathan the prophet anointed Solomon King. These words have been sung to the music of Handel at every coronation since George II's in 1727 and are due to be heard again at the coronation of King Charles III.

Evidence of the theological foundations of the British monarchy – or at least how they were interpreted by Elizabeth II – was signposted in February 2022 when, to mark the seventieth anniversary of her accession, she issued a statement. It ended with the words, written in her own hand, 'Your servant, Elizabeth'. King Charles stressed this service of his mother in the tribute he made to her on television the day after she died and again in his personal Accession Declaration on September 10. It was an approach that he indicated he would adopt, although he suggested it was something of a burden: 'In carrying out the heavy task that has been laid upon me, and to which I now dedicate what remains to me of my life, I pray for the guidance and help of almighty God'.[1]

The weight on the sovereign's shoulders was expressed at length by the Archbishop of Canterbury, Geoffrey Fisher, who crowned Elizabeth II. As the late Queen prepared for her coronation in 1953, Fisher gave a series of sermons about the service, explaining that he saw the Queen as called by God, that the sovereign had spiritual power through her character, example and convictions and so could unite and lead her people. This was not just about power, he said, but about sacrifice; she would be 'giving herself and being herself at all times'.[2] It is likely that seventy years ago, considerable numbers of people might have understood that sense of sacrificial duty, especially in a country that had fought the six long years of the Second World War. It was this duty that King Charles was hinting at when he spoke of his heavy task. But in 2023, will it make sense to the British people?

Attempts to explain that sacrifice were made during Elizabeth II's funeral, and references to it came thick and fast throughout the new King's speeches. So did a sense of Charles' personal faith. In this volume I attempt to analyse it, as well as that of his mother. The combination of her official role, including as Supreme Governor of the Church of England, and her personal beliefs were highlighted many times after the Queen died. They had not gone unnoticed elsewhere – to the extent that during a visit I made to Rome some years ago, she was described to me by a Vatican official as 'the last Christian monarch'.[3] In the coming months and years, people will debate whether that moniker was correct, or unfair to her son and heir.

In this volume I have attempted to examine the monarchs of England and later, Britain, from that first Defender of the Faith, Henry VIII, to King Charles III. It is not only the monarch's public role regarding religion that matters but also their spiritual life and faith, not just to those of us who are inquisitive journalists or curious historians but to everybody, because they often have a significant impact on how they reign. From Elizabeth I's delight in music, which enhanced the young Church of England's choral tradition and helped it veer away from the low church approach of other European Protestant traditions, to James II's intransigent Roman Catholicism which eventually lost him the Crown, to Elizabeth II's increasingly overt declamations of her personal faith through her Christmas broadcasts, it is worth considering just how deep a faith a particular monarch has and how it impacts on their reign.

As I write at the start of the new reign of Charles III, it is worth noting that his mother was unusual. Because she was the only sovereign that most people in Britain had ever known, until last September, many assumed that the strong faith she expressed so publicly was the norm. But Elizabeth II was a woman with what was akin to a religious vocation. The jury is out on her son. But as I indicate in the following pages, the signs are that the decades spent as Prince of Wales, engaging with different religions, are setting the tone for his reign.

The way in which the monarchy has been bound up with religion since the Elizabethan Settlement of 1559 has been most clearly seen in the role of Supreme Governor of the Church of England, a constitutional role that expresses Anglicanism's position as the established Church. Even in 1953, at the time of the last coronation, attendance at Church of England services was declining, but there were none of the regular challenges to its position by commentators, academics and secular pressure groups that there are today.

While those voices are heard more loudly, the Church still retains its position, and the King – the new Supreme Governor – his. Indeed, both might be said to be more visible than ever before. Since the age of Victoria, there have been increasing numbers of grand ceremonial, ecclesiastical occasions. Royal weddings, once mostly private occasions, have in recent times more frequently been church spectacles. Major monarchical anniversaries – called jubilees, after great celebrations described in the Old Testament's Book of Leviticus – have been celebrated by George III, Victoria, George V and Elizabeth II. For the past hundred years, Church, state and monarch have combined to remember the dead of world wars. The greatest ever liturgy to combine the connections between this triumvirate was undoubtedly the funeral of Queen Elizabeth II – or at least was until the coronation in May.

Since its foundation, the Church of England has been a means of expressing national identity, and its relationship with the monarchy has reinforced that role. But the monarchy's religious role has arguably become more important and goes beyond being Supreme Governor since the retreat of the Crown as a political power in the time of George III. Instead, it has become a symbol of the nation's values, whether standing for their defence, through the Royal Family's strong links with the armed forces, or for duty and for charity. Walter Bagehot described the monarchy as 'the head of our morality'.[4]

This puts an enormous burden on our monarchs – most evident in the crisis over the wish of Edward VIII to wed the twice-divorced

Wallis Simpson and the ensuing opposition. His critics argued this was unacceptable for a King who should stand for the values of the nation and set a particular example as both monarch and Supreme Governor of the Church of England.

Time and time again, the woes, including religious ones, of the monarchy have been bound up with marriages: marriages involving members of the barred Roman Catholic Church; marriages that did not produce heirs or ones who lived long enough to succeed; marriages that failed. Even Queen Victoria, who managed to fall in love with a Lutheran, enjoy a happy marriage with him and produce nine children, considered being Queen a burden, expressing her distress in religious language: 'I have worn a thorny crown and carried a heavy cross'.[5]

Since the time of George III, marriage and family life have been key to the way the monarchy expresses the values it stands for: the Royal Family has presented itself as the epitome of Christian values through its stable home life. Thus, when things have gone wrong, it has not just been an apparent challenge to the Church of England's teaching on divorce but also bad PR for the institution itself. More recently, in the final year of Elizabeth II's reign and the start of King Charles', the bad PR goes beyond marriage (although the fallout from the King's first marriage to Diana, Princess of Wales, still continues to ripple through the institution). It is also about fraternal issues – think of the impact on the monarchy of Prince Andrew's friendship with the paedophile Jeffrey Epstein and the bad blood between Princes William and Harry – and about father and son. These familial dramas need a Shakespeare to do them justice.

And yet, as the former Archbishop of York, John Habgood, so memorably said, 'Sovereigns are not required to be saints,' nor have they been.[6] What the following chapters examine is the extent to which, despite their flawed normality, they have stood for those values that are closely allied to monarchy and to Christianity: duty and sacrifice. It is also notable that as political power has waned from the monarchy, it is the person, not just as the embodiment of the Crown but also as an individual, who has become much more important. In other words, character matters, as does what shapes that character, such as beliefs. This is another reason why I explore in these pages the spiritual beliefs of different monarchs.

It was frequently repeated that the late Queen Elizabeth II insisted that she must be seen to be believed: monarchy won't work, the argument goes, unless it is visible among the people and alongside Church and state. The demands upon it in the era of twenty-four-hours media and multimedia are never greater, and the lives of its chief protagonists are constantly in the spotlight and dissected. While that is uncomfortable, it is much better than going unnoticed. In a Jubilee year, as 2022 was, and through landmark events such as a monarch's funeral and a coronation, there are opportunities for the monarchy to unite the nation, to reaffirm its covenant with the people, to link them with their history and, in a secular age, to be one of the most powerful voices for values in stark contrast to dominant materialist ones. What Frank Prochaska called the 'welfare monarchy'[7] has been one of the most successful reinventions ever of monarchy: extending the Crown's reach in all kinds of charitable endeavours and, in doing so, reaffirming its belief in Christian charity.

That reinvention had to happen because, however much monarchy stands for tradition, neither can it stand still if it is to survive. Its motto could well be 'always changing, always the same'. Queen Elizabeth II, her husband, the Duke of Edinburgh, and their son, King Charles III, have all understood this, with their varied encounters with Christian denominations beyond the Church of England, and with other faiths. They learned the significance of those faiths both in the Commonwealth and in Britain, something I explore in these pages, as well as their active pursuit of welfare monarchy. This clear interest and well-intentioned response of these individuals to these varying faiths makes the lingering institutionalised antipathy to Roman Catholicism, expressed through vehement oaths about upholding Protestantism, altogether bizarre and in need of reform.

Just how much all of these interests and values of King Charles III – of Christianity, other faiths, philosophies whether of the ancient Greeks or Eastern thinkers, as well as welfare monarchy – will be evident in a melting-pot coronation and in a reign that encompasses the early to middle years of the twenty-first century? It might well be tempting to opt for the apparent safety of tradition – or at least what passes for tradition, given the House of Windsor's consummate capacity to reinvent it. One of the greatest challenges of all for those planning the coronation of 2023 will be to find a way to have a religious service that appeals to those without faith at all. Might the sheer spectacle of its drama carry all before it? These pressing questions I will also address as I consider the future of the British monarchy and of the Defender of the Faith.

# I

# When Zadok the Priest anointed Solomon King: the sacred nature of kingship

Gold, frankincense and myrrh. Gifts fit for a king and given, according to tradition, by three kings drawn to a stable in Bethlehem to honour the infant Jesus. It is one of the most popular of the Christmas narratives of the Gospels, often cited as a reason why presents are so much a part of the festive season.

It is a Gospel story that the British monarchy has always taken very seriously. On 6 January, Feast of the Epiphany, the choir of the Chapel Royal at St James's Palace, dressed in their scarlet and gold-trimmed tunics, process to the church for the service to celebrate how those with earthly powers bowed down before the Christ Child. And at this service, the giving of gold, frankincense and myrrh is repeated once more, this time on behalf of the sovereign.

The ceremony is at least five hundred years old and at one time was attended by the sovereign in person who, until the time of George III, also carried the offerings in person. These are now carried on silver salvers by ushers led by the Serjeant of the Vestry and escorted by Beefeaters from the Tower of London. The Dean of the Chapels Royal, currently Dame Sarah Mullally, also Bishop of London, officiates.

The gift-giving of the monarch to the newborn Christ Child has layers of meaning, not least a sign that a sovereign has a role in leading his or her subjects in worship. But it also highlights that the British monarch is following in the footsteps of those ancient kings of the east by paying homage to this particular King, Jesus Christ, who rules both heaven and earth. Humility, therefore, is one of the attributes of a monarch.

The comforts of the material world and the grandeur of royalty enjoyed by monarchs are not what are commonly associated with Christianity, the religion founded by someone born in a stable, who knew poverty and advocated that his disciples give everything away to the poor, and who taught that it is harder for a camel to pass through the eye of a needle than for a rich man to enter heaven.[1] And yet there are constant reminders throughout both Old and New Testaments that kingship and majesty are key themes in the shaping of first Judaism and later Christianity. In turn they have played their part in forming the thinking of what monarchy means in this country.

The references to Christ's kingship come thick and fast in the Gospels' passion narratives and provide conflicting ideas of authority and power. Pontius Pilate, the Governor of Judea, is introduced as one who has been given the authority and power to act for the good of the Roman Empire, something that is often at odds with the good of the majority. He exercises his office with little concern for justice or for the importance of truth. Even though he finds no fault with the arrested Jesus, he does not release him, but as a pragmatist, chooses to hand over to the crowd the decision as to whether he should be freed.

Jesus does not deny his kingship when challenged about it by Pilate, but it is clear that it is not a majesty of this world. It is not one that derives from territory or power. This is a kingship of true authority that comes from God, that has been mandated by him. It is a kingship that has been woven through the Gospel narratives, revealed in how Jesus acts, not by flexing his oppressive muscles or revealing himself as a tyrant, but as a king who 'emptied himself, taking the form of a slave, and being born in human likeness'.[2]

This idea of the King as humble servant is seen earlier in the Old Testament, with the prophet Zechariah saying:

> Rejoice greatly, O daughter of Zion!
> Shout aloud, O daughter of Jerusalem!
> Lo, your king comes to you;
> triumphant and victorious is he,
> humble, and riding on a donkey,
> on a colt, the foal of a donkey.[3]

So in joining the procession of the kings at Epiphany, a monarch is humbling himself or herself before the King who has himself shown humility, in becoming human at all, in being laid in a manger – the eating receptacle of the ox and ass in the stable – who will come into Jerusalem not with a grand retinue but mounted on a donkey, as Zechariah foretold. He will become food himself through the Last Supper – as much spiritual nourishment as the hay and straw of the manger was food for the animals.

The writers of the Old Testament explored many aspects of human kingship, as well as the countercultural idea of kingly humility, and through it indicated how the monarchs of this earth might reflect the kingship of God. In this way they underlined the spiritual and sacred nature of monarchy, which has been key to the British concept of kingship for generations.

The Bible's early books record the history of the people of Israel, ruled in their early years by judges after their arrival in the land of Canaan, but their rule brought corruption and lawlessness. Kings were the solution to anarchy, bringing stability after years of unrest. The King became an intermediary between God and his people, ensuring that the covenant between them remained. Kingship in that part of the ancient world was vested in the gods, and those on earth were mediators, striving to ensure that the vulnerable, be they widows or orphans, were protected. The King to the Israelites was a guarantor of order, but also acted as a spiritual pointer to God's mercy, justice, faithfulness and righteousness by embodying those same qualities. As the psalmist put it:

> Give the king your justice, O God,
> And your righteousness to a king's son.
> May he judge your people with righteousness,
> And your poor with justice.[4]

Not that kingship got off to a good start for the Israelites. Samuel anointed Saul to be the first King, a military leader who would deliver them from their enemies. But he became disobedient and, rather than listening to God first, sought to do the people's bidding first, even if this meant not doing what God commanded.

The next King, David, fared better, and his rule is the dominant story of the Old Testament – more space is given to him than even to Abraham or Moses. Under David and his successor, Solomon, kingship became a dominant feature of Israelite society.

While David displayed as much military prowess as Saul, there were other significant developments in ideas of kingship during David's rule. This was a king who was also a healer, the poet psalmist and, of course, the representative of the little man, with his killing of the giant, Goliath.

David was also a shepherd, away looking after the sheep when Samuel went to find Israel's next king, directed by God, among Jesse's sons, and the early use of the shepherd as leader metaphor comes with the people repeating God's words: 'you . . . shall be shepherd of my people Israel, you . . . shall be ruler over Israel.'[5]

For Christians, this foretells the idea of Jesus the Good Shepherd – another King who leads his flock.

This is a king who provides stability for Israel, no longer a wandering tribe but settled, ruled over by the dynasty that comes after David. David was not without his failings: this is the King who committed adultery with Bathsheba and saw off his rival, her husband Uriah, by ensuring he was killed while he was away at war. But David was repentant – a king but still a flawed human being. He came before God, seeking forgiveness – another sign of the need among kings for humility.

Solomon, who followed after David, was the next King by reason of his being born of the house of David – a king through heredity because David had made a covenant with God: while David promised to build a permanent temple for God, the Lord promised that his descendants would inherit the throne.

God's promise is made explicit in the second book of Samuel: 'I will raise up your offspring after you, who shall come forth from your body, and I will establish his kingdom. He shall build a house for my name, and I will establish the throne of his kingdom for ever.'[6]

It is Solomon more than any other Old Testament monarch who matters to the British tradition of monarchy, as a byword for wisdom and a monarch who also stands for grandeur.

From the moment that his reign began, with his dream in which God asked what he wanted and he answered wisdom and knowledge,[7] Solomon was favoured by God, who approved of his desire for such gifts rather than wealth. Once more, it was the humility of the King that caused him to be much blessed and showered with treasures and triumphs over his enemies.

Solomon's reputation for wisdom – a gift believed to reflect God's own wisdom – began a tradition where wisdom was always connected with the gifts of kings. In the book of Wisdom of Solomon, supposedly written by him but probably written much later, in the first century BC, addressed to kings and advising the need for wise counsel, justice and virtue, it says that 'a sensible king is the stability of any people'.[8]

If wisdom, due to Solomon, was ever after seen as a necessary attribute of monarchs, so was anointing a sign of a monarch's right to rule, through its symbolising God's choosing this person for kingship and bestowing blessings.

The idea of anointing with oil to denote special blessings from God came early in Scripture, with Moses commanded by God to prepare holy oils with which to bless places and vessels for religious rituals.[9]

Coronations in the Old Testament involved priests, prophets and the respected elders of the community, as well as the people whose acclamation of the monarch was an essential part of the ceremony. Anointing – a sign of the sacred nature of kingship – was adopted into their coronations by the Jews from other societies around them, including the Syrians and the Egyptians.

The first book of Samuel records that when the elders asked the prophets to choose a king, it was the ritual of anointing that singled out Saul: 'Samuel took a phial of oil and poured it on his head, and kissed him; he said, "The LORD has anointed you ruler over his people Israel." '[10]

There are several references in the Old Testament to David's anointing by a priest – the moment when he passed from being a highly respected individual to someone touched by the divine. Psalm 89:20–21 says:

I have found my servant David;
with my holy oil I have anointed him;
my hand shall always remain with him;
my arm also shall strengthen him.

And it is also recorded that Samuel anointed David with a horn of oil and 'the Spirit of the LORD came mightily upon David from that day forward'.[11]

The horn of oil was also used at the coronation of Solomon – the ceremony that is the foundation of all coronations of English monarchs at Westminster Abbey and even before those ceremonies. The Old Testament verses of 1 Kings 1:39 and 1 Chronicles 29:22–23 notably refer to all the aspects of Christian coronation used since in Britain: from the choosing of the monarch to the religious service with its rituals, including the anointing of oil by a priest, then the acclamation of the people and finally enthronement.

The first recorded coronation to use the words of 1 Kings 1:38–40 was that of Edgar, the Saxon King crowned in 973 in Bath. The day chosen was Pentecost, the feast that marks the coming of the Holy Spirit upon the apostles – a sign that Dunstan, the Archbishop of Canterbury who led the ceremony, and his fellow churchmen, saw it as a moment of particular blessing for the monarch.

The account of Edgar's crowning, recorded in a life of St Oswald, Archbishop of York, recalls that Edgar prostrated himself before the altar and then made his sacred pledges to God that he would work for peace, justice and mercy.

Then came the moment of unction – the anointing of Edgar's head by the bishops with holy oil or chrism, poured from an animal's horn, accompanied by prayers invoking the Old Testament Kings as exemplars of the virtues that Edgar would be blessed with, and calling on the Holy Spirit to descend on the new King.[12]

The most solemn moment of all was the anthem *Unxerunt Salomonem*, with its words from 1 Kings 1:38–40 and, since the time of George II, sung at every coronation to Handel's music:

Zadok the Priest and Nathan the prophet anointed Solomon King.
And all the people rejoiced, and said:

God save the King!
Long live the King!
May the King live for ever,
Amen, Hallelujah.

At Elizabeth II's ceremony, Handel's music was played first and then, after she had been anointed with oil on her palms, breast and head, the words were invoked again, when the Dean of Westminster prayed:

And as Solomon was anointed King
by Zadok the priest and Nathan the prophet,
so be thou anointed, blessed, and consecrated Queen
over the Peoples, whom the Lord thy God
hath given thee to rule and govern.

As Roy Strong put it in his history of the coronation, 'All this, for over a thousand years has been re-enacted at every coronation . . . it is extraordinary to grasp that its roots lie as far back as the last quarter of the tenth century.'[13]

If anointing in the Old Testament symbolises the blessing of God and the trust he puts in the anointed one, then the King in turn is perceived as a source of blessings on his people, with continual references to kings as sources of wisdom, good judgement and righteousness, and upholding divine order through their human authority.

Of all the books that explore kingship – and they include Proverbs – it is the book of Psalms that offers the most insight into the idealised visions of kingship known to the Jews. The psalms highlight the King, as do the history books of the Old Testament, as a servant, as God's son and as someone with whom God has a covenant.

Some Old Testament scholars have also highlighted that some of the psalms may well have been written for enthronement ceremonies, while others were used for royal anniversaries, birthdays and other celebrations. At these moments, the connection would be made between God's kingship and human kingship.

John Eaton, in his discussion of kingship, suggests that the psalms were used to show that the King had been anointed and blessed to serve God: 'Through him God sends out justice, care and health to nature and society. It is God's laws that he must uphold. He witnesses to the world and preaches of God's sovereignty and faithfulness. To God he turns with all the burdens of his people.'[14]

It is a description akin to those of Christ as depicted in the Gospels: the rabbi who taught and continues to teach his followers, advocating God's love and his faithfulness.

The Gospels, though, depict Jesus as more than one type of king: a royal king in the line of David, a king recognised by his followers and a king derided by his enemies. The Gospels of Matthew and Luke both underline the importance of Jesus' role as the heir of David with their accounts of his genealogy, taking the reader through a family tree whose branches include Abraham, David and later kings of Israel. The angel of the Lord, who appears to Joseph in a dream to tell him Mary is to bear a son, calls him Joseph, son of David, while the angel who appears to the shepherds in the fields near Bethlehem speaks of a child born in David's town and of David's line. This King, like David, is born in a humble setting in Bethlehem rather than in the grandeur of Jerusalem.

If the shepherds – the lowliest members of the community – venerate this King born among them, then the kings who come to worship him show that this is someone who is to be the lord of all, both rich and poor. The gifts they bring are also a reminder that he is an heir to Solomon as well as David, reflecting the gifts of gold, spices and precious stones brought by the Queen of Sheba to Solomon.[15]

These tributes to Jesus' kingship are replicated in the Gospels by people acclaiming Christ as King. Nathanael, sitting beneath a fig tree, says, 'Rabbi, you are the Son of God! You are the King of Israel!' – a triumvirate of roles – a teacher, a divine lord and an earthly one. It is noticeable that he acclaims Jesus in this way after Jesus has said of Nathanael, 'in [him] there is no deceit', indicating he is straightforwardly telling the truth.[16]

But Jesus' kingship is celebrated in the most striking way when he enters Jerusalem, acclaimed by the crowd. It is a triumphal route, with his followers spreading before him their clothes and branches cut from the trees. It is significant that all four Gospel writers record these events, with Mark's narration including people crying out, 'Blessed is the coming kingdom of our ancestor David!', while Luke records that the disciples shouted out, 'Blessed is the king who comes in the name of the Lord!'[17] This is a quote from Psalm 118:25–26, and it is also mentioned in Matthew 23:39 and Luke 13:35 as part of the traditional festive Hallel, sung each morning by the temple choir during the Feast of Tabernacles, and therefore very well known to the Jewish people.

The Catholic theologian Edward Schillebeeckx says that both Matthew and Mark emphasise that Jesus has a hereditary claim to the throne of Israel through David, while Luke and John present him as already the King of Israel. But is this an earthly kingship, a threat to the Roman Empire, or something else – a spiritual kingship?[18]

It is certainly a kingship that the Gospel writers wanted to convince Christians had been foretold. The writers of the Synoptic Gospels record that Jesus enters Jerusalem on a colt, although Matthew mentions both a colt and a donkey, while John mentions a donkey. Both Matthew and John refer to the fulfilling of the prophecy of Zechariah 9:9, with Matthew writing it:

> Tell the daughter of Zion,
> Look, your king is coming to you,
> humble, and mounted on a donkey,
> and on a colt, the foal of a donkey.[19]

The historicity of this episode may be debatable – there are variations between the Gospel writers – but the procession's meaning is clear. This is a king acclaimed by the crowd and especially by his followers, and yet it is not entirely a predictable scene of triumph. Just as Zechariah foretold a king of humility on a donkey, so do the Gospel writers emphasise that Jesus is not an imperial warlord or a king to rival the Roman Empire, riding on a magnificent horse; rather, he comes into Jerusalem in what New Testament scholars Marcus Borg and John Dominic Crossan consider a 'counterprocession', unlike that of the Romans in charge in Jerusalem.[20]

So we have a sense in these accounts that the crowds recognise Jesus' majesty, but his understanding of his kingship – indeed, of kingship as a whole – is different from theirs. He chooses a donkey or ass, a sign of humility, rather than superiority. There is no account of his rejecting the people's acclamation, but their interpretation of what a king is does not match his. This is not a king who encourages pomp and circumstance but instead goes on to weep over Jerusalem and clear the money-changers from the Temple – a literal overturning of the tables that can also be taken as a metaphor for how Jesus will upend understanding of a kingly role.[21]

It is in the Passion narratives that Jesus the King most clearly emerges – and a king who is not only a person of humility, but also humiliated, in his efforts to sacrifice his life for humanity.

The narratives reveal Jesus being mocked as a king by those who seek to destroy him, but taken together they indicate a complex idea of what kingship is – not just in terms of what it means regarding Christians honouring their God, but it also can lead to a reinterpretation of what being a Christian monarch means.

Earlier in John's Gospel, he records an episode which indicates that Jesus is not willing to be a king on human terms; he has not come to be King of the Jews in the political sense, as an alternative to the occupying Romans. The moment comes after Jesus has fed the five thousand – something that fills the crowd with wonder, and they say, 'This is indeed the prophet who is to come into the world.'

But then John writes, 'When Jesus realized that they were about to come and take him by force to make him King, he withdrew again to the mountain by himself.'[22]

Instead, the King he was about to become was one who would be mocked and derided, but would also be a source of redemption. Rather than a king of glory and triumph, the Passion narratives describe a king who is more akin to the biblical scapegoat, cast out into the wilderness after the Jewish chief priest had symbolically laid the sins of the people upon it.[23]

It is Pilate – representative of the Roman occupying forces – who first asks Jesus, as this Passion drama moves relentlessly to its climax on Calvary, 'Are you the King of the Jews?' – a question recorded by Matthew (27:11), by Mark (15:2), by Luke (23:3) and by John (18:33). 'You say so,' is Jesus' response, throwing it back to Pilate. But in John's Gospel, he goes further, underlining that he is rewriting the rules of kingship: 'My kingdom is not from this world. If my kingdom were from this world, my followers would be fighting to keep me from being handed over to the Jews.' And then, as Pilate asks again, 'So you are a king?' he replies, 'You say that I am a king. For this I was born, and for this I came into the world, to testify to the truth. Everyone who belongs to the truth listens to my voice.' And Pilate asks him, 'What is truth?'[24]

Another idea of kingship – standing up for the truth – is introduced here. Pilate shows Jesus to the crowd, then calls him 'the King of the Jews', although whether he means the spiritual king that Jesus has described or a territorial king remains ambiguous as the Jews reject him, wanting Pilate to free Barabbas instead.

Then comes Jesus' mock coronation, with many of the elements familiar to crownings: the Roman soldiers dress him in a robe, they weave a crown out of thorns and, in Matthew's Gospel, hand him a reed to hold, as if a mock sceptre, symbol of a monarch's power and authority.[25] The Roman soldiers mock him with their cries of 'Hail, King of the Jews!'

The continuing tensions between Jesus' divine kingship and what those surrounding him perceive as his claim to earthly power continues with Pilate, now filled with foreboding about his part in this troubling man's downfall, presenting him to the crowd, which calls out, 'If you release this man, you are no friend of the emperor. Everyone who claims to be a king sets himself against the emperor.'[26]

The Jews know full well that this would be a capital offence, for the Romans would see Jesus as putting himself up against the puppet-king Herod, and therefore a threat to the Empire. And so the journey of Jesus continues to Calvary, where, nailed to the cross, a sign is placed above his head: *Iesus Nazarenus Rex Iudeorum* – Jesus of Nazareth, King of the Jews.

So who is this King? The theologian and church historian Ian Bradley suggests that Jesus is turning the world upside down: 'His statement [to Pilate] that his kingdom is not of this world suggests rather that it has a more radical quality, either being essentially spiritual and rooted in heaven rather than earth, or counter-cultural and opposed to the values of this world.'[27]

What is particularly evident in rereading the New Testament's account of kingship is that it is paradoxical. For it contains not only references to Jesus, heir to the kingship of David and therefore an actual king, and episodes that highlight Jesus as a prophet, standing for the truth, as well as a spiritual king, seated at the right hand of the Father after he ascends to glory. But we also have the emerging idea of the Servant King – a theology that has become more popular in recent years. It moved from academic circles to the mainstream with Graham Kendrick's 1989 hymn, 'The Servant King', which focuses on the idea of Christ coming to serve as much as to be worshipped, and to call his followers to do the same vocation:

So let us learn how to serve
And in our lives enthrone Him
Each other's needs to prefer
For it is Christ we're serving.[28]

In 2016, the Bible Society, together with two other organisations, produced a booklet to mark Queen Elizabeth II's ninetieth birthday. Its title was notable – *The Servant Queen and the King She Serves* – and it seems reasonable to presume that the Queen approved of it, given she wrote the foreword, in which she said, 'I have – and remain – very grateful to you for your prayers and to God for His steadfast love. I have indeed seen His faithfulness.'[29]

This suggests, therefore, that the late Queen made a strong connection between the theology of the Servant King and the idea of following in his footsteps as a royal sovereign, serving the people.

The idea of service is one that is expressed in the Feast of Christ the King, instituted by Pope Pius XI in 1925 in the liturgical calendar of the Roman Catholic Church, and adopted by many other denominations since, including the Anglican, Methodist and Lutheran Churches. Since 1969, Catholics celebrate the feast on the last Sunday of the liturgical year, before the start of Advent when they prepare for the coming of the King to Bethlehem.

The Collect, used for all three of the liturgical cycles, includes a prayer:

That the whole creation, set free from slavery,
May render your majesty service
And ceaselessly proclaim your praise.[30]

Year B's Gospel is John's account of Jesus' conversation with Pilate: 'You say that I am a king . . . for this I came into the world, to testify to the truth,' while Year C turns attention of the faithful to Luke's account of the cross – the mockery of the soldiers, saying, 'If you are the King of the Jews, save yourself!'; the inscription of 'Jesus of Nazareth, King of the Jews', and the thief, crucified beside Jesus, asking him, 'Jesus, remember me when you come into your kingdom.'[31] But it is the Gospel for Year A that makes the strongest connection between the King and the idea of service. Matthew records Jesus making the connection between the Son of Man and the King. The Son of Man, on judgement day, he reports Jesus saying, will be seated on his throne and will divide people as a shepherd separating sheep from goats. And to the sheep on his right, he will say, Jesus tells the disciples:

> For I was hungry and you gave me food, I was thirsty and you gave me something to drink, I was a stranger and you welcomed me, I was naked and you gave me clothing, I was sick and you took care of me, I was in prison and you visited me . . . Truly I tell you, just as you did not do it to one of the least of these, you did not do it to me.[32]

Fr Robert Gay, prior of the Priory of the Holy Spirit, Oxford, and a theologian at Blackfriars, Oxford, has written that the Feast of Christ the King helps people to reflect:

> The King's throne is always a symbol of his authority and power. But in this too Jesus turns the normal world order on its head. His enthronement is on Calvary, when he's lifted up on the throne of the Cross. In his pain, his nakedness and his vulnerability, he reveals the depth of God's love. He's shown as a king who doesn't exploit the weakness and frailty that weighs us down. Instead, he makes these things his own: he shares in our vulnerability, and then lifts us up through it . . .
>
> Christ's kingship is a crucial doctrine. It reveals to us who Jesus is and what he achieves for us. And it helps us to realise that we don't stand over and above others, but with others.[33]

Can this view that Christians do not stand over and above others but with others work as a philosophy or theological foundation for monarchy?

If that monarchy is patterned less on power and more on justice, wisdom, sacrifice and humility, then it can. In previous eras, there might have been more emphasis put on a king's grandeur, martial force and temporal power. A monarch would have turned to the reassuring words of St Paul: 'Let every person be subject to the governing authorities.'[34]

Or this advice of St Peter: 'For the Lord's sake accept the authority of every human institution, whether of the emperor as supreme, or of governors, as sent by him to punish those who do wrong and to praise those who do right . . . Honour everyone: Love the family of believers. Fear God. Honour the emperor.'[35]

This countercultural strand of Christian thinking – that the first should be last – has remained nevertheless a powerful one for this country's monarchy. It is powerfully articulated in the ritual of Maundy Thursday and the distribution of gifts by the monarch.

The word 'Maundy' derives from the *mandatum*, or command, that Jesus gave his followers at the Last Supper to love one another, while he also washed their feet: 'You call me Teacher and Lord – and you are right, for that is what I am. So if I, your Lord and Teacher, have washed your feet, you also ought to wash one another's feet. For I have set you an example, that you also should do as I have done to you.'[36]

A medieval tradition of bishops and abbots washing the feet of the poor, known as the *pedilavium*, after the Latin for washing feet, developed first, followed by a monarchical version of the ceremony.

The first king recorded as giving Maundy alms was John, who gave clothing, forks, food and other items to the poor in Yorkshire. Then in 1213, at a ceremony in Rochester, he gave thirteen pence to thirteen men, a number that was a reminder of the thirteen – Jesus and his apostles. Evidence exists that the practice continued in varied forms by other later monarchs, with Henry IV decreeing that the number of pence given should reflect the monarch's age.

Some monarchs took the ceremony very seriously. Mary I is recorded as washing the feet of forty-one women in 1556, the year of her forty-first birthday, as she knelt before them, and also gave them forty-one pence each plus other gifts of bread, fish and clothes, including her own gown.[37]

Not all monarchs endured the drawbacks of meeting the poor. When the plague made its way through the country, the monarch declined to attend, sending an official instead. According to historian Brian Robinson, others often washed the feet of the poor first so that the monarch avoided the smells and dirt of unwashed feet. But Charles II, after the Restoration, attended even during plague years in 1661 and 1663.

By the end of the seventeenth century, the involvement of the monarch was minimal, with the Lord High Almoner washing feet instead until 1737, and after that gifts such as clothing were distributed, and coins too – to the same number of people as the sovereign's age. While the Maundy ritual had first moved to churches close to where the monarch was residing – whether Greenwich, Windsor or Richmond – it finally took place every year at the Chapel Royal.

By the twentieth century, members of the Royal Family would attend, particularly Princess Helena, Queen Victoria's third daughter, and her own daughter, Princess Marie Louise. After Marie Louise's attendance in 1931, she suggested that her cousin, George V, should distribute Maundy money the following year. Although he agreed, it was the only time he did so during his reign, although his son, Edward VIII, carried out the distribution during the only year of his reign, 1936. His brother, George VI, whose reign was dominated by war, made the distribution in 1940 for the first time and then not again until 1944, with the Lord High Almoner carrying out the ritual on his behalf in other years.

It was Elizabeth II who was the most assiduous distributor of Maundy money, and she took the tradition around Britain to different cathedrals. In this sense the service became rather like a royal pilgrimage: it was the only occasion in the year when the recipients of an award did not travel to meet the Queen, but she travelled to them.

When the then Prince of Wales attended the Maundy Thursday service at St George's Chapel, Windsor, in April 2022, to represent his mother who was incapacitated, it followed the same rubrics as those of previous years. There are always two readings, of which the first is John 13:34 which contains the *mandatum* from which Maundy Thursday gets its name, and the second is the account of the Last Judgement, from Matthew 25:34–40, when people are challenged as to how they have treated others:

> Then the king will say to those at his right hand, 'Come, you that are blessed by my Father, inherit the kingdom prepared for you from the foundation of the world; for I was hungry and you gave me food, I was thirsty and you gave me something to drink, I was a stranger and you welcomed me, I was naked and you gave me clothing, I was sick and you took care of me, I was in prison and you visited me.' Then the righteous ones will answer him, 'Lord, when was it that we saw you hungry and gave you food, or thirsty and gave you something to drink? And when was it that we saw you a stranger and welcomed you, or naked and gave you clothing? And when was it that we saw you sick or in prison and visited you?' And the king will answer them, 'Truly I tell you, just as you did it to one of the least of these who are members of my family, you did it to me.'

Today, the gifts of food and clothing are long gone, and instead there are two gifts: a white leather bag containing special Maundy coins and a red leather one containing other money. A man and a woman are chosen for each year of the monarch's age, and the money also represents the years the monarch has lived. Six silver dishes are used to hold the gifts; one, the traditional Maundy Dish, forms part of the Royal Regalia and is held at the Tower of London when not in use. All six dishes date from the reign of Charles II. Anthems are sung by the choir of the Chapel Royal and the local choir while the Maundy gifts are distributed, ending with Handel's 'Zadok the Priest' – a reminder, each year, of the monarch's crowning and the links of this monarchy to Scripture and its profoundly influential ideas of kingship.

Today, in the twenty-first century, human kingship, founded on Christ the King, offers a Gospel interpretation of the role: a sense of service, a life of sacrifice, and gifts to be offered to Christ, as kings drawn to the stable of Bethlehem once brought gifts too.

Monarchy in Britain has undergone profound change over the centuries, yet its foundation has remained in Christian notions of kingship, shaped by Scripture. Faith is at the heart of monarchy, yet it has scarred it too. And nobody scarred it more than the first English monarch to be named Defender of the Faith, Henry VIII. The earthquake of his changes and those of the Reformation are what I shall turn my attention to next.

# 2

# The home-grown pope: how the Reformation and its aftermath changed the monarchy and its relationship with religion

In 1519, Henry VIII was considered one of the great Renaissance princes of Europe. A patron of the arts, a talented musician, with a fine physique and athletic prowess, the golden-haired King was also a devoted husband and father and an equally devoted Catholic. Religion and culture came together when he wrote *In Defence of the Seven Sacraments*, becoming the first English monarch since Alfred the Great to publish a book.

*In Defence of the Seven Sacraments* was Henry's riposte to Martin Luther, whose writings, including his *Ninety-Five Theses* – an attack on the Catholic Church's sale of indulgences – were circulating in England by then. The treatise delighted Pope Leo X, who awarded Henry with the title *Fidei Defensor*, Defender of the Faith, on its publication in 1521.

But within a few years, all would change. Henry's devotion to his wife, Catherine of Aragon, and delight in his daughter, Mary, born in 1516, would turn to frustration. Continually wary of rival countries and rival monarchs, especially those of France and Scotland, Henry was increasingly paranoid about his lack of a male heir to seal England's future as a Tudor redoubt. His wife, Queen Catherine, had been pregnant several times, including giving birth to a boy, Henry, in 1511, but he died after seven weeks.

By 1525 Catherine was thirty-nine – six years older than Henry – and it was seven years since she had last been pregnant, with a child who was stillborn. The fact that King Henry had only a Princess as his heir did not, it seems, disturb the Queen. As Tudor historian Tracy Borman puts it, 'As the daughter of Europe's great warrior queen, Isabella of Castile, Catherine did not see this as a disaster. But to her husband and his subjects, it was little short of a catastrophe.'[1]

To Henry, after sixteen years of marriage and with his wife heading to her fortieth birthday, it seemed that time was running out for him to have a legitimate heir. He had had other children with other women, including thriving sons, so he must have believed that the problem lay with Queen Catherine. And his wandering eye had also alighted on Anne Boleyn, who had arrived at court in 1522. The Boleyns were a family on the make, who had enjoyed, thanks to Anne's father Thomas, a rise from tenant farmers to gentry with titles and a court presence. They were also known to the King: Henry had fathered a child by Mary Boleyn, Anne's sister. Historians seem to agree that Anne was a more able tactician than her sister, holding out against the King's desire for a sexual relationship for some time, likely with her eye on a bigger prize.

If Henry was to discard Catherine, make Anne his queen and sire an heir, there were monumental diplomatic and theological hurdles to overcome. Henry's determination, supreme self-confidence, concern for the Tudors' destiny and obsession with Anne Boleyn was to change England and the monarchy's relationship with religion for ever. The Defender of the Faith was to become the destroyer of all that he had once held dear.

It would also mark a dramatic end to the relationship of English monarchs with the papacy, to whom they had owed allegiance for generations. They had fought the Crusades, defending Christianity against the infidels. They had built grand churches and chapels to honour their faith. Henry was to change all that.

However, ambition was not the sole province of the King. Others also yearned for prizes, and they were to be Henry's confidants as he strove to break his bond with first Catherine and then the Roman Catholic Church. The first was Thomas Wolsey, son of a butcher who shone at court, first made royal almoner in 1509, the year of Henry's succession and marriage to Catherine. This role gave him enormous power over Henry's financial and ecclesiastical matters, leaving the King time for his other interests, from jousting to banqueting. Wolsey was eventually appointed cardinal, a role that encompassed far more than Church matters and included what was effectively propaganda for Henry, including the showstopping Field of the Cloth of Gold in 1520. Created as a two-week event to celebrate accord between Henry's England and Francis I's France, it involved effort on the part of each monarch to outshine the other.

But organising showmanship was put to one side as Henry turned to Wolsey to make the King's case to Rome for an annulment of his marriage. The entire case rested on Catherine's previous marriage to Henry's late elder brother, Arthur, Prince of Wales. The Spanish Princess' marriage to the heir to the English throne was organised by her parents, Ferdinand and Isabella, and Henry VII as a political and diplomatic coup, sealing a deal between the two nations that would put France's nose out of joint, when Catherine was just three years old. She and Arthur married in 1501, when she was fifteen, at a spectacular marriage service in St Paul's Cathedral, where she was led into the church by a ten-year-old Prince Henry. The wedding was followed by a pageant at Richmond Palace, celebrating the union of England and Spain, and with one allegorical scene suggesting Henry VII was the equivalent of God the Father and Arthur as Christ.

But Arthur died just five months later, some suggesting that he was taken suddenly by a sweating sickness while others suggested that he was already ill. Catherine's doctor commented that at the wedding Arthur already looked ill, and that he had 'never seen a man whose legs and other bits of his body were so thin'. He later went on to claim that Arthur would have been too weak to consummate the marriage, something that Catherine herself was to claim and which would be key in her later dispute with her second husband, Henry, over the validity of their marriage.[2]

Arthur's death was both an emotional blow and a political one for Henry VII, and deeply problematic for this young girl, now cast adrift as a widow in England, albeit a royal one. A year after Arthur's death, his mother Elizabeth of York followed him to the grave, and Henry VII, grief stricken but also keen to salvage his alliance with Spain, offered to marry the widowed Princess of Wales. Catherine's parents were horrified that the elderly, white-haired King should take his daughter-in-law as his bride, and rejected the deal. Another deal then appeared on the table: for Catherine to marry her brother-in-law, Prince Henry. The negotiations over the marriage would take years, so long that the old King died before they were completed. On 11 April 1509, Henry VIII acceded to the throne; on 11 June he married Catherine, and they were crowned almost two weeks later.

The marriage to Catherine had not only involved lengthy disputations with Spain before it could go ahead. Henry, crucially for his future plans regarding Anne Boleyn, had also secured a papal dispensation. Eighteen years later, he asked for another papal dispensation, arguing that his marriage to Catherine had gone against Scripture, with its prophecy, 'If a man takes his brother's wife, it is impurity; he has uncovered his brother's nakedness; they shall be childless.'[3]

The existence of Princess Mary and the son who had lived little more than a week proved the couple was not childless. Catherine's argument was akin to her doctor's: her marriage to Arthur had not been consummated. Therefore she had not really been married to him, so Henry had not married his brother's wife at all.

Henry, however, was convinced this was his route out of marriage to Catherine. As the Queen's biographer, Giles Tremlett, puts it, 'The King's apparent attack of moral panic raised the question of who, or what, had stirred his suddenly troubled conscience.'[4]

But he had the means, he believed, to make use of this scriptural warning to solve his marital quandary. On 17 May 1527, a hearing was held in Cardinal Wolsey's town palace at York Place, Westminster, involving Wolsey, the King, the Archbishop of Canterbury and doctors of law in what was an ecclesiastical court. On trial was the King: given the evidence that he had gone against God by living with his brother's wife, he therefore had committed a terrible sin.

The trial was, of course, not a trial at all, but a farce, set up to find that the King had committed this awful sin and endangered his soul, and so this sin – marriage to Catherine – must be brought to an end. Meanwhile, the other party, Queen Catherine, was not made aware of this gathering of men convening to destroy her marriage.

Catherine had been living in isolation for some time. Her Spanish ladies had been expelled; her daughter had been sent away to live in the Welsh Marches and govern Wales; her husband was often away. Wolsey put her under the watch of spies and informants; she was only allowed to have meetings with her nephew, Charles V's envoy, Iñigo de Mendoza, if they were organised by Wolsey. She was increasingly isolated.

The difficulty for Henry and his decision to go down the ecclesiastical court route was that if it were to declare that Henry's marriage were sinful, it would effectively be saying that a previous pope, Julius II, had been wrong to give a dispensation to allow Henry to marry Catherine. Wolsey's court found this so thorny a problem that it did not make a decision but decided instead to further consult theologians.

Despite her isolation, Queen Catherine quickly found out about the secret sessions at York Place and was able to inform Spanish ambassador Mendoza. He in turn informed Charles V, the Holy Roman Emperor and Catherine's nephew. What they all knew was that Wolsey could not make the final decision; it would have to be the Pope's.

There was also the issue of public opinion. Catherine was a popular queen and mother of the one legitimate heir. Whispers began circulating about Henry's intentions. Surviving letters written by Mendoza describe what was happening in England: 'Not that the people of England are ignorant of the King's intentions, for the affair is as notorious as if it had been proclaimed by the town crier. They cannot believe that he will ever carry so wicked a project into effect.'[5]

Other family members were also involved in the dispute but did not play well for Henry. The current Pope, Clement VII, would have noted Henry until this time as a keen upholder of Catholicism – his cousin, Leo X, had given Henry his title of Defender of the Faith – and was unmoved by Henry's Leviticus arguments. They could be countered by a verse in Deuteronomy advocating the exact opposite – that it was the duty of a man to take his dead brother's wife.[6] He was also at the mercy of Charles V, whose troops occupied Rome itself in May 1527. Pope Clement sought refuge in the Castel Sant'Angelo, beside the Tiber. Powers in Europe were getting involved and their sympathies lay with the Aragon Princess, now threatened with becoming Henry's discarded Queen.

While spies had watched the Queen, other forces also made use of espionage. Love letters between Henry and Anne Boleyn and intercepted by Rome still exist in the Vatican archives, revealing a game of cat and mouse. They were dominated by Anne, who resisted the King's advances, indicating that they would displease God and the Queen. Henry would not be deterred and secretly proposed to Anne.

But the battle to make her his wife continued for six long years. As David Starkey notes, 'Not even Wolsey could change the reality of European power politics.'[7]

Pope Clement prevaricated, until he eventually made a concession to Henry – that the court case for the annulment should be heard in London, although it would be heard not only by Wolsey but also by another cardinal, Lorenzo Campeggio.

The idea emerged, backed by Henry, taken up by English bishops and indeed supported by Campeggio, that the whole problem could be solved if Catherine were to take herself off to a nunnery and live a life of chastity ever after. But the Queen showed an iron will: she would not cave in.

In November 1528, Catherine tested the waters of public opinion. The hearing moved from Rome to London and was to take place at the Dominican friary, Blackfriars, beside the Thames and close to the royal residence of Bridewell. Because the new palace had no chapel, there was a raised gallery connecting it to the friary, and as Catherine walked along it, crowds below cheered her. It was clear evidence that not only was Europe uneasy about Henry's moves against the Queen, but so were his own subjects.

Henry's response was to embark on a PR mission of his own, summoning dignitaries, including the Lord Mayor of London and his aldermen as well as judges, to hear him declare how troubled he was, how much he wanted to make England a place of peace, how he feared that he and the Queen should not continue to live together in adultery and how hurt he would be if the court were to rule that he would have to move aside his wife. It did not go down well.

Continual reasons for postponement held up the case. Campeggio appears to have been ordered by Pope Clement to drag things out, giving Catherine a chance to avoid the vigilance of Henry's men and get a letter to the Pope. The Queen might have been persuaded to enter a convent – some of the Pope's own advisers, including Cardinal Giovanni Salviati, thought she should for her own sake – but this was not just about her future. It was also about her daughter Mary.

The hearing eventually began in May 1529 with both the King and the Queen due to appear in court on 18 June. This was unlike anything seen before: the monarch and his consort would appear in a court, on opposing sides, in scenes worthy of the greatest playwrights. Placed on opposing sides of the court, the two cardinals representing the Pope were also seated there, as well as England's bishops. And squeezing in to watch the spectacle were ordinary citizens.

The most memorable moment of the trial came when Catherine rose to speak. She walked past the bishops to kneel at her husband's feet and told him – and the court, the Pope and the people:

> Sir, I beseech you for all the loves that hath been between us, and for the love of God, let me have justice and right, take of me some pity and compassion, for I am a poor woman and a stranger born out of your dominion, I have here no assured friend, and much less indifferent counsel: I flee to you as to the head of justice within this realm.

She went on to defend herself as a true wife and mother, not a childless woman:

> This twenty years I have been your true wife or more, and by me ye have had divers children, although it hath pleased God to call them out of this world, which hath been no default in me.

And she then put Henry up for judgement, hinting that the truth was she had married him a virgin:

> And when ye had me at the first, I take God to be my judge, I was a true maid without touch of man; and whether it be true or no, I put it to your conscience. If there be any just cause by the law that ye can allege against me, either of dishonesty or any other impediment to banish and put me from you, I am well content to depart, to my great shame and dishonour; and if there be none, then here I most lowly beseech you let me remain in my former estate, and receive justice at your princely hand.[8]

It was a remarkably powerful, clever speech, her tactics made all the cleverer by her appeal finally to Henry to give her permission to appeal directly to the Pope. Backed into a corner, he did so. Catherine then left the court, though she called back, denouncing it as biased. Without Catherine, the hearings continued, with Henry looking to his supine bishops to back him. One did not.

John Fisher had been close to the Tudor monarchs for decades. He had preached at the funerals of the Tudor dynasty's founding father, Henry VII, and his mother, Lady Margaret Beaufort. He was Prince Henry's tutor, and it is entirely possible that he advised him on his riposte to Luther, *In Defence of the Seven Sacraments*.

Some weeks later, after the *Defence*'s publication, Cardinal Thomas Wolsey processed through the churchyard of St Paul's Cathedral and, in front of a crowd of thirty thousand, ensured that Luther's books were consigned to the flames of a great bonfire. While Wolsey held the King's polemic in his hand, Fisher preached on the wrongs of the new ideas. Pope Leo X rewarded Henry with the title *Fidei Defensor* – Defender of the Faith.

Within five years of helping the King with his treatise, Fisher would no longer be a spiritual and theological mentor to Henry. Although not averse to theological challenge, he was concerned to work with Church teaching and develop it, rather than overturn it. He was also deeply sympathetic to Queen Catherine and became her most outspoken ally. He was not cowed by appearing in the legatine court.

Fisher's arguments went beyond protestations of Catherine's virginity when she married Henry. He was so convinced of what he knew was the truth that he was prepared to die for it. John the Baptist had said it was impossible to die more gloriously than in the cause of marriage, said Fisher, and this was even more true after Christ's death than it had been before. Fisher's reference to John the Baptist was not lost on the court, nor on Henry, for the King in John the Baptist's case – Herod – had John beheaded for questioning his change of wife.

Cardinal Lorenzo Campeggio wrote to his Italian masters to say that Fisher 'made his appearance to say, affirm, and with forcible reason demonstrate to them that this marriage of the king and queen can be dissolved by no power, human or Divine, and for this opinion he declared he would even lay down his life'.[9]

Campeggio was signalling that martyrdom was indeed a possibility. If such a martyrdom were to take place, it would be the first in many years for the Catholic Church. Fisher, however, was undaunted. He went on to preach against the divorce as well. His stance was duly noted. The red of his cardinal's garb later came to be more than just decoration and symbolism: it was the colour of the blood that really would be shed.

Fisher, of course, was not alone. Thomas More, too, was part of Queen Catherine's faction. He had a lengthy career serving the King and became his Lord Chancellor in 1529, the role that led to his involvement in the defence of the Church. His antipathy to those who sought Church reform was fierce, indeed aggressive. He saw Protestantism as heresy and a threat to society and was particularly vengeful towards those involved in translating the Bible into English. He was also, like Fisher, convinced of the authority of the pope as being greater than any other, even a king's.

By 1530, Henry would take steps that would have lasting significance not only for himself, but also for the future of the monarchy and England's relationship with Rome. He instructed his agents in Rome to tell the Pope that he should not listen to an appeal from Queen Catherine about her marriage and that if he did not grant the annulment, Henry would break from Rome. He stated, 'In [our kingdom] we are supreme and so rule that we recognise no superior.'[10]

Bit by bit, advised by his Archbishop of Canterbury, Thomas Cranmer, and Thomas Cromwell, who had succeeded as Henry's right-hand man following the fall from grace and death of Cardinal Wolsey, Henry asserted his authority and compromised that of the pope in England. In February 1531, Henry ordered Convocation, the parliament of the English Church, to recognise him as sole protector and supreme head of the Church in England. A year later, he ordered the clergy to no longer make payments to Rome and instead supply them to the King's own treasury – handy sums which made Henry one of the richest monarchs in Europe.

There was more: in 1533 the right to appeal to Rome in ecclesiastical cases was junked, and twelve months after that, it was ruled that the law of the Church would be dependent on the consent of the King. New laws meant the English could not criticise the marriages of the King, nor could they refuse to swear the Oath of Supremacy, which renounced papal authority. The Act of Succession of 1534 recognised Henry and Anne's children as lawful successors to the throne and required those asked for it to swear an oath endorsing this. And finally, the Act of Supremacy, of November 1534, recognised the King as 'the only Supreme Head on earth of the Church of England'.

It was the final curtain coming down on England's loyalty to Rome. It was done with, as far as Henry was concerned. What had begun as a desire for Henry to rid himself of one wife and take another and have a legitimate male heir had become a dispute over authority – authority of the pope versus authority of the monarch. Because the whole row began with a debate over the ultimate court of appeal in canon law, this assertion of England as a nation no longer beholden to the pope owed its origins to a dispute over who was chief magistrate.

At one point Henry was so confident that he would secure an annulment that he had married Anne in a private ceremony in Whitehall in 1533. It was not just about taking a wife; Anne, persuaded that marriage would be possible, had finally consented to a sexual relationship and was pregnant. Henry wanted to ensure his child would be his lawful heir. With this in mind, Cranmer and Cromwell worked to ensure that ecclesiastical appeals would be heard in England rather than Rome, and Cranmer would therefore have the right to hear the appeal for annulment. In May 1533, he pronounced Henry's marriage to Catherine null and void and Princess Mary therefore illegitimate.[11]

Pope Clement was outraged and ordered Henry to take back Catherine as his wife. Henry, for his part, responded with a ceremony full of pomp to crown Anne, who was visibly pregnant, as Queen. It was a tipping point for Thomas More, who was already refusing to take the planned Oath of Supremacy recognising the King's role as Supreme Head of the Church of England and refusing to recognise rejection of the authority of the pope. More refused to attend the coronation of Anne Boleyn as Queen.

In April 1534 More was arrested for treason and imprisoned in the Tower of London. His trial was held on 1 July 1535. The jury quickly found him guilty – a judgement that caused More to at last express his view to the court that he believed no temporal man could be head of spirituality. In other words, no earthly ruler could take the pope's place. He was executed on 6 July at Tower Hill and buried in an unmarked grave in the chapel of St Peter ad Vincula within the confines of the Tower. His head was displayed on a pike on London Bridge, replacing that of John Fisher who had been executed two weeks earlier.

Fisher, like Thomas More, had believed that speaking out maliciously was a dangerous thing to do and that instead there was safety in silence. Unfortunately, he was duped into thinking that it was possible to say in private what he really believed. He confirmed then that he rejected Henry as Supreme Head of the Church of England. By doing so he had effectively signed his own death warrant.

Something else determined Fisher's fate. In Rome, Pope Clement VII had died in 1534 and had been succeeded by Cardinal Alessandro Farnese, scion of one of the great Italian aristocratic families, who became Pope Paul III. A man who wished the Catholic Church to reflect developments in learning, he chose to honour several leading reformers with cardinals' hats. Among them were Reginald Pole, later to become Mary Tudor's right-hand ecclesiastic, and John Fisher. Cardinals have traditionally always worn red because it is the colour of martyrdom; as the closest advisers to the pope, they are expected to be ready to shed their blood for Christ, the pope and the Church. For Fisher, that martyrdom came sooner rather than later. If Paul had thought such an honour might save Fisher's neck, he was wrong. Instead, it infuriated Henry VIII.

On 16 June 1535, Eustace Chapuys, diplomat of the Holy Roman Emperor Charles V, wrote to his boss from England, 'As soon as the king heard that the bishop of Rochester had been created a cardinal, he declared in anger several times that he would give him another hat and send the head afterwards to Rome for the cardinal's hat.'[12]

Fisher was tried in June by a court of seventeen, including Thomas Cromwell and Anne Boleyn's father, for treason. Given that Fisher himself had already made the connection between his own case and that of John the Baptist – beheaded for challenging the remarriage of another king, Herod – Henry's advisers decided not to risk having Fisher beheaded on John the Baptist's feast on 24 June. However, like many of today's PR teams, they found themselves creating more problems by fighting their corner. Their second choice of execution day was 22 June 1535, but that only served to provide another coincidence: it was the feast day of St Alban, England's first martyr. But they went ahead, beheading Fisher on Tower Hill.

The executions caused incredulity and outrage, not only in Rome but also across Catholic Europe, that the Defender of the Faith had not only defied the authority of the pope but had also killed those who stayed loyal to Rome. There were plenty of others whose executions would follow. As Tracy Borman comments, 'For the first time in England's history, its people were required not only to act as the King directed, but to believe as he did.'[13]

This was not just about a monarch falling out with the Church. It had happened before, most memorably when Henry II clashed with Thomas Becket, his Archbishop of Canterbury, a clash that led to Becket's assassination by four knights who believed they were following the King's orders. On that occasion, though, King Henry was penitent, and made his own pilgrimage to the place of Becket's death, which became one of the holiest sites in Christendom.

There was no penitence shown by this eighth Henry, but instead a firm belief in his own righteousness. The consequence was that he defined what being an English monarch was: an arbiter in matters religious as well as secular, dabbling in the stuff of people's souls. The control and the terrorism that went with it did not, however, lead to obeisance from all of society. Plenty were pragmatic enough to think that they should follow the King's lead. Others had been attracted to Protestantism for some time, and while Henry remained at heart a Catholic, except for allegiance to the pope, there was relief for those attracted to Protestant thinking and Lutheranism that change was on its way. They were gratified when Henry permitted the first translation of the Bible into English by William Tyndale. The Royal Injunctions Act of 1536 required all parish churches to acquire and display the newly authorised English translation of the Bible, while from 1543 onwards lessons during matins and evensong were to be read in English. This may reflect a personal enthusiasm of Henry's for the English vernacular – or his way of reminding people that the King was now in charge, and Latin, the language of the Roman Church, was no longer the language of religion.

But there was a rump of Catholics who were shocked at what had happened, and outraged too. More had declared that he died the good King's servant but God's first, and he and Fisher were honoured as martyrs by those loyal to Rome.

The loyal were to be traumatised again. In February 1536, eight months after Fisher's and More's executions, the 'Reformation Parliament' met to agree to new measures legalising iconoclasm. Images, relics and shrines were to be smashed and broken – including the shrine of Thomas Becket, which Henry VIII had come to loathe. This was but the beginning.

The monasteries of England were one of its riches: powerhouses of prayer, of art, but also of money. They were prosperous places with large amounts of land in their possession. Their monastic rules also meant that they were the providers of welfare and hospitality, but Thomas Cromwell's eye for detail and financial opportunism meant their days were numbered. Allegations, some no doubt true, of corrupt abbots living in luxury while those in the surrounding villages starved were used to justify their destruction. The Church's loss was Henry's gain: vast amounts of treasure, of land, even the lead from church roofs, were plundered and the profits handed over to the King's treasury.

The price to be paid for this act of state vandalism was rebellion. Many of Henry's subjects were outraged at the attacks on the monasteries, and there were uprisings across the Midlands and the north, including the march south in 1536 that came to be known as the Pilgrimage of Grace. Henry's brutal response was to put to death those who opposed him, from the aristocracy to the gentry, the clergy and peasants.

Yet the very thing that had caused this rupture with Rome and with the people had also been destroyed. That same year, Henry, ever desperate for a son, had rid himself of Anne Boleyn on the grounds of her adultery and treason. Like Catherine, she had provided the King with a daughter who thrived but no son who survived.

While Henry's marriages did not last, his reforms to the Church did, albeit some of them being revised over the centuries. There was no going back to the days when England was such a devout Catholic country that it was called [The Virgin] Mary's Dowry. The fortunes of the monarch, England and the Church were intricately entwined.

So it would continue through the next centuries, with the fortunes of the monarch and the nation bound up with the development of the Church of England, as well as antipathy – and sometimes attraction – towards Rome.

That ebb and flow of the relationship with Rome continued through the reigns of Henry's children, Edward, Mary and Elizabeth, made more complicated by relations with other European countries, not least Scotland and Spain. And within England itself, these monarchs represented different factions of the English people: those who, like Edward, embraced a new Protestantism; others, like Mary, who wished to stay loyal to the old religion; and the rest, like Elizabeth, who sought compromise and were more ready to be pragmatic.

When Henry died in 1547, succeeded by his son Edward by his third wife, Jane Seymour, the power of the monarch over the Church was consolidated even further, despite the new king being only nine years old. Henry, with his Act of Supremacy and Act of Succession, had ensured that the break with Rome was permanent, and that loyalty to England and the throne was marked by oath. Having a male heir, which was what Henry had wanted all along and had caused the rupture with the papacy, could have meant considering a path to return to the Romish fold. Instead, Henry used the severing of ties with Rome to develop a ferocious nationalism and triumphalism, a new Englishness and a new Church.

Ten years before his death, in 1537 Henry VIII instructed Hans Holbein to paint a mural to decorate the wall of his privy chamber at Whitehall Palace. The work is lost but a version of it remains in the Royal Collection. It showed Henry with Edward's mother, Jane Seymour, and his parents in the background. Its message effectively reversed Jesus' words in Scripture: 'I am going to the Father, because the Father is greater than I.'[14]

Henry had no such qualms, and instructed this inscription for the painting, about him and his father, Henry VII:

> Between them there was great competition and rivalry and [posterity] may well debate whether father or son should take the palm. Both were victorious. The father triumphed over his foes, quenched

> the fires of civil war and brought his people lasting peace. The son was born to a greater destiny. He it was who banished from the altars undeserving men and replaced them with men of worth. Presumptuous popes were forced to yield before him and when Henry VIII bore the sceptre true religion was established and, in his reign, God's teachings received their rightful reverence.[15]

A similar view of himself was taken in the English translation of the Bible that he authorised to be published, with an image showing a small Christ at the top and Henry dominating the page, enthroned as both monarch and Supreme Head of the Church, with the bishops and the Privy Council to his left and right, and the people below. But, as David Starkey has commented, this doing away with the pope, Henry asserting himself as head of the Church and introducing more biblically based theology meant that 'the genie of Protestantism was out of the bottle'.[16]

It wasn't what Henry had foreseen as a consequence – he was opposed to Lutheranism. What he really wanted was the old ways but without the pope to limit his own power. But his son embraced Protestantism with vehemence, no doubt encouraged by the adult Protestant radicals who surrounded the boy King, among them the Lord Protector – his uncle Edward Seymour – and the Archbishop of Canterbury, Thomas Cranmer.

Edward's was the first coronation to be enacted after the break with Rome, and it was also the crowning of a child, and so was contracted. Previous coronations had included a rite of election, but this was abandoned and instead Edward issued a proclamation, saying he had come to the throne 'invested and established in the crown imperial of this realm'.[17] A full text with the rubric of this coronation no longer exists, but surviving accounts of it describe a revised form of oath-taking, devised by Cranmer, with Edward placing his hands on the Gospels lying on the altar, calling on God and the holy evangelists to help him.

Cranmer's sermon included him telling the boy King, 'Your Majesty is God's Viceregent and Christ's Vicar within your own Dominion,' a confirmation of the King's absolute power, free from papal intervention.[18] Cranmer also compared Edward to Josiah, the boy-king of the Old Testament who rid his land of idols.[19] Edward, said Cranmer, would reward virtue and practise righteousness.

Just days later, on a visit to Westminster Abbey, Edward ordered that only two candles in future should be used during Communion and bells should no longer be rung at the moment of consecration. Their ringing was limited to just before and just after the service.[20]

Edward, tutored by Protestants, was encouraged to think not only that the pope was a 'true son of the Devil, a bad man, an Antichrist', as one of his essays put it, but also that England needed further ecclesiastical reform. Caution was thrown to the wind. More statues were smashed, relics destroyed and shrines demolished in a bid to erase Catholicism from the English record. Crucifixes were torn down from church walls and burnt. In their stead were Royal Coats of Arms. Cranmer replaced the Latin Mass with his own script, the 1549 Book of Common Prayer. The visual and the great spectacles of Catholicism – the stained-glass windows, the processions, and the pilgrimages that appealed to the senses and the emotions – gave way to the Word and an intellectualising of Christianity.

Cranmer's 1549 volume also established the tradition, which continues to this day, that a prayer be said for the sovereign every Sunday.

In 1552, Cranmer published his Second Book of Common prayer, which rejected the real presence of Christ in the Eucharist, and altars used for the Holy Sacrifice of the Mass were stripped from churches and replaced with plain Communion tables. It was the greatest assertion of Protestantism yet, trampling on those who had been horrified by the reform that Edward authorised. Rebellions of those who longed for the old ways – and no doubt fearing for their souls, given all they had been previously taught – were crushed by Edward's forces. This was not, though, a mere theological squabble. As the English monarchy was now at the head of the Church, rejection of the King's reforms was a treasonable act.

But even crushing the rebels did not end the conflict that threatened to rend England in two. As Edward grew sicker, the shadow of his Catholic sister Mary loomed large. The pair had clashed over religion continually, but especially during the family's Christmas festivities in 1550 when Edward had invited his two half-sisters, Mary and Elizabeth, to join him. Edward, aged thirteen, had upbraided his thirty-four-year-old sister Mary for attending Mass, which was then against the law. Mary could not countenance that a child would have spiritual authority over her, but more important for England than her diametrically opposed views to her brother was her political clout in Europe, and she knew how to flex this particular muscle.

It had happened before. On 9 June 1549, when Cranmer's prayer book was first introduced, she had arranged for Mass to be celebrated in her chapel in her home at Kenninghall, with all the rituals that Cranmer and Edward opposed, including the use of candles, incense and bells. Pressure was put on her to conform to the new laws. Soon after, Edward's secretary, Sir William Paget, visited the Holy Roman Emperor Charles V, and Mary's cousin, to discuss her possible marriage to the Infante Dom Luís of Portugal, Charles' brother-in-law. Charles told Paget, in no uncertain terms, that he was astonished at the pressure put on Mary regarding the practice of her religion, and if she agreed to reform, he would do everything to dissuade her. Charles demanded an assurance in writing that Mary 'should not be included in the regulations made by Parliament about religion or be kept in suspense in the matter'.[21]

Mary reached again for the strong arm of protection offered by Charles after the post-Christmas row with Edward in 1550. When the King summoned her back to court, accusing her of disobedience, she invoked Charles' aid, who sent his ambassador to court with a message of support for Mary that was also a threat. Edward recorded in his journal, 'The Emperor's ambassador came with a short message from his master, of war if I would not suffer his cousin, the princess, to use her mass. To this no answer was given at this time.'[22]

Edward and his advisers knew that Mary had supporters in England too; they had made a show of strength when she had arrived in London to see her brother: hundreds of them had followed her, each displaying banned rosary beads. To take on forces in Europe, the King and his advisers knew, would be unwise and costly. There were more conciliatory overtures too, to Mary herself, from her brother.

Then, by the winter of 1552–53, Edward's health had deteriorated. Those who worked for him knew that, if the end were in sight, it would not do to be at odds with the next heir to the throne. The alternative was to find another future monarch.

Edward's six-year reign had seen both the consolidation of England as a Protestant nation and the monarchy asserted as the ultimate Church authority. But just as the theology was being rewritten – the Real Presence was rejected – and the rituals bulldozed – church walls whitewashed, altars ripped away – with the Second Book of Common Prayer and the Forty-Two Articles published, it was under threat as never before. Edward, though dying, summoned enough energy to change the rules and rewrite the succession, ruling out both his sisters as illegitimate and instead naming Lady Jane Grey, great-granddaughter of Henry VII and daughter-in-law of Edward's chief minister, the Duke of Northumberland.

Lady Jane, said Edward, would support the new Protestant religion, and more than a hundred judges, nobles and other dignitaries countersigned his will. The boy-king's obsession with eradicating Catholicism was so fierce that it formed his dying words: 'O Lord God, save thy chosen people of England! O My Lord God, defend this realm from papistry and maintain thy true religion!'[23] He had fought like one of his forebears on crusade against the Infidel. If he had lived, the history of England and later Britain would have been very different, with Catholicism all but entirely eradicated. But the battle was not over, despite Edward's best efforts to thwart his Catholic sister and her European supporters.

Lady Jane had not been Edward's first choice – he considered women unfit to rule – but none of the Grey women, all considered possible Protestant monarchs, had male children, so Edward proposed Lady Jane and her male heirs. It was a sign of Edward's unfettered belief that he need not consult Parliament, nor the Church, about his plan. In the new dispensation, what counted was the monarch's God-given authority.

The Princess Mary, however, had other ideas about God, and believed that he would provide a miracle to bring her to the throne. What was also on her side was a belief of people in legality and legitimacy, seemingly greater than religious factionalism. When she tried to raise an army to support her cause and march on London, troops rallied to her side. Queen Jane lasted nine days.

Mary, however, was more wedded to factionalism than some of those who flocked to her cause in the name of justice might have assumed and the early days of her reign suggested.

Her coronation oath was to uphold England's law rather than uphold religious reforms. If she were to reverse the Protestant revolution of Edward and Cranmer, then she would need the support of Parliament, and it was not forthcoming.

Mary's coronation on 1 October 1553 was a first – the first that would involve anointing a woman to rule in her own right. It was notable for other reasons too: the Archbishop of Canterbury, Thomas Cranmer, was in the Tower of London for his part in the plot to put Jane Grey on the throne, and Mary was crowned instead by Stephen Gardiner, Bishop of Winchester.

Mary was anxious about the oath she would take, fearing it would involve her in condoning the new religion. No copy exists, but other records reveal that she wrote to her cousin, Cardinal Pole, asking for absolution for her and other Catholics who participated in the ceremony, and she received a new supply of oil for the anointing, uncontaminated by having been used for her brother's coronation. Witnesses wrote that she was crowned 'according to the rites of the old religion'.[24] Mary was described as kneeling throughout the Mass, with the King's sceptre in her right hand and the Queen's dove in the other. But when she left the Abbey she carried only the orb – that symbol of all the world under God, even its monarchs.[25]

If Mary was to restore Catholicism to England and thwart the ambitions of men like Cranmer to see Protestantism become its beating heart, she had to ensure that no other Protestant heir – be it her half-sister Elizabeth or any other member of the Reformed Religion, plucked from an offshoot of the Tudor tree – would succeed her. The sure way of doing that was to marry and produce her own brood of heirs.

Chief candidate for her hand in marriage was the son and heir of Charles V, Philip of Spain. Like Mary, Philip was a passionate Catholic, and his father was committed to stamping out Protestantism. The couple was married in Winchester Cathedral in July 1554, within a year of Mary acceding to the throne. Though thirty-seven, Mary reported that she had quickly become pregnant.

The prospect of a Catholic succession strengthened Mary's position, and Parliament voted to return the Church of England to be obedient to the pope. It also led to a revival of heresy laws so that those who rejected the Catholic religion could be condemned to death. By February 1555, burnings began. Although there had been signs of nostalgia for the old Catholic faith in England, there was also a xenophobic suspicion of things foreign and un-English – including the papacy and the Queen having a Spanish spouse. By the time she became pregnant, Mary had crushed a revolt led by Thomas Wyatt, had Jane Grey executed and imprisoned Princess Elizabeth in the Tower. But it was the burnings that most alienated the people. Some Protestants fled abroad, among them John Foxe.

*Foxe's Book of Martyrs* would become one of the most successful volumes of propaganda ever published: an account of Protestant martyrs, complete with gruesome images. It would earn the Queen the soubriquet Bloody Mary, by which she would always be remembered.

If Mary's pregnancy had produced a Catholic heir, the pendulum might have swung again, with England restored as a Catholic country. But it turned out to be a phantom, her hopes of a new dynasty dashed. Power ebbed from the Queen, and Philip left to deal with his Spanish interests. Mary's plans to suppress Protestantism continued, with her targeting of its followers. For one in particular, this led to a theological and philosophical problem.

Thomas Cranmer had helped to create the doctrine of royal supremacy – that the monarch was God's agent and therefore should be obeyed. So should he now obey the Queen? Cranmer had been first brought to trial in November 1553 and found guilty of treason and condemned to death. Mary, in her ambition to achieve full reunion with Rome, was determined that Pope Julius III's legate Cardinal Reginald Pole be appointed Archbishop of Canterbury, but he could not achieve that office unless Cranmer was legally removed. In 1555 Cranmer was tried again, this time for heresy, and although it took place in England the process was under papal jurisdiction. Cranmer denied every accusation of treachery, disobedience or heresy. However, he also issued several recantations of his Protestant belief and re-embraced papal supremacy and the impossibility of salvation outside the Catholic Church.

For Mary, her battle with Cranmer was personal, not just doctrinal. This was the man who had advised her father in his efforts to have his marriage to Mary's mother annulled. This was the man who had engineered to have her rendered illegitimate. This was Cranmer, right-hand man to her brother Edward, who had pursued her in her devotion to her Catholic faith. Cranmer's recantations did not save him, and he was sent to be burnt at the stake. He plunged the hand that had signed his recantation documents into the flames, recanting once more and this time embracing Protestantism.

The conflict between Cranmer and Mary had far-reaching consequences for the nation, the Church and the monarchy. Cranmer, from his earliest days of reform, had sought to write liturgies that were not mere translations from Latin but had their own distinct character. His Collects, with their particular use of language, helped to shape the newly formed Anglican Church. The place of the saints in the litanies was greatly reduced. Turning to Luther for inspiration, he shifted the Church towards a Protestant theology that had no space for human merit contributing to salvation. Instead, it was faith alone, not works, that led to salvation, and this was implicit in the prayer book.

Mary's attitude toward Cranmer and other churchmen, such as Nicholas Ridley and Hugh Latimer, as well as other Protestants, seemed merciless and was a gift to the propagandists determined to show that England should have no truck with Rome. In Mary's textbook of queenship, there was no place for compromise. It was her sister, Elizabeth, who would tread that path and attempt to find a middle way, enabling both Protestants and Catholics to be loyal subjects. The monarch as a unifying figurehead was vital to England's fortunes, and a role that not only Elizabeth I but also her successors would attempt. But starting with Elizabeth herself, they were to have very mixed fortunes, and were most often undone by religion.

Ordinary Catholics may well have had doubts from the very beginning of Elizabeth's reign about her apparent ambition to be Queen of all of England, given the events of January 1559. First, on the feast of the Epiphany – one of the greatest feasts of the Church – she sponsored the performance of a masque titled 'Papists', one of two performed by the Queen's Company at Whitehall, which ridiculed the Catholic hierarchy. The masque included more performers than was customary: in addition to four cardinals and six priests, performers played popes, monks, friars and vergers. For many, this masque confirmed Elizabeth's Protestant leanings. 'Papists' marked the third time in twenty-five years, according to W. R. Streitberger, that 'revels were used in the service of religious propaganda'.[26]

A week later came further reason for Catholics to be taken aback by the messages imparted by the new Queen. Ecclesiastical processions had once been part of English life. They had been banned by Edward VI, revived by Mary and were banned again by Elizabeth. The only ones that were permitted in the Elizabethan reign were secular ones, albeit with a religious connection: processing to the Chapel Royal in her palaces, attending the ceremonial of the Knights of the Garter on Garter Day. These ceremonials were to heighten the importance of monarchy – just as they have continued to do into the modern age. The English, later British, monarchy has found a way to entwine what is royal with what is religious in these processions.

One of the greatest ever – and one of the most effective – efforts at royal propaganda was Elizabeth I's vigil procession that took place on the eve of her Coronation Day in January 1559. The procession from the Tower of London, through the City of London and on to Whitehall Palace had included hundreds upon hundreds of officials, from clerks to judges, nobles, clerics and ambassadors, as well as dozens more on horseback, accompanying the Queen's litter. Within it she sat on eight cushions of yellow cloth of gold, surrounded by gold, silver and pink satin cloths, her canopy of purple cloth of gold held aloft by knights, while footmen in crimson velvet ran alongside.

Along the way, the Queen passed pageants signalling the Protestant and English path ahead. An arch revealed Henry VIII and Anne Boleyn (who had scarcely been mentioned in public since her execution twenty-three years before) at its summit, with Elizabeth, their daughter, enthroned and crowned. Another showed the seat of government with the Queen again enthroned, held up by the virtues of Pure Religion – as the Protestants regarded their reformed faith – which trod underfoot Superstition and Ignorance as the Protestants saw the characteristics of Roman Catholicism – as well as Love of Subject, Wisdom and Justice. Another pageant showed a decayed Commonwealth – her sister's – and Elizabeth's own prosperous one, guided by The Book of Truth – a copy of the New Testament. It was a further sign that this was a Protestant English realm, guided by the Bible, not the hand of the foreign pope.

The last pageant showed the Queen again, dressed in parliamentary robes, as the Old Testament's Deborah the Judge and restorer of the House of Israel – symbolising the Crown in Parliament at the heart of governance of England.[27] As Roy Strong suggests, 'This was post-Reformation Tudor Old Testament kingship returned in feminist guise . . . this could only refer to the coming Parliament, writs for which had been issued on December 5, which would pass the Act of Uniformity and return England to Protestantism.'[28]

Elizabeth's goal for her procession had been to win the hearts of the people. During her mother's procession twenty-six years earlier, the crowd had remained silent. For the new Queen, they roared their approval, won over by her showmanship and her approving response to them. The mutual fan club seemed assured. But the politics of the reign, not just the PR of one day, was going to be much more complicated, and religion was the stuff of these complications.

But before she dealt with them, Elizabeth had more messages to impart via her lavish coronation. She was escorted into Westminster Abbey, not by bishops, but by the Earls of Pembroke and Shrewsbury. All of the Catholic bishops of Queen Mary's time refused to perform the actual rite, bar one, and he refused to conform to the new Queen Elizabeth's demand that the host was not to be elevated during Mass. Eventually a dean of the Chapel Royal sang the Coronation Mass and omitted elevating the host. Elizabeth's oath included an addition likely to have been the work of her Secretary of State, William Cecil, that the sovereign would conduct her rule 'according to the laws of God and the true profession of the Gospel established in this Kingdom' – 'established' being a reference to being enforced through Parliament by statute.

There are few records left of the coronation, but in 1571, Queen Elizabeth commented to the French ambassador that she had been 'crowned and anointed according to the ceremonies of the Catholic Church . . . without however, attending Mass'. This suggests that she did not receive Communion, which would have been a signal as to the way the theological wind was blowing in England.[29]

Given that Mary's Parliament had made Catholicism once more the religion of England, undoing this and creating a new religious settlement was Elizabeth's first task. The issue was: what kind of settlement should there be? Elizabeth, though a learned Protestant, was no fanatic. Her chief adviser, William Cecil, was, like Elizabeth, a Protestant, who had conformed to Catholicism during Mary's reign. His view was that there should be no more Catholic monarchs and that England should be a Protestant country.

Cecil's influence ensured that the settlement agreed by the 1559 Parliament was more strongly Protestant, and more akin to Edward VI's Protestantism than Elizabeth might have wanted. The deal struck, secured by three votes in Parliament, included acceptance of Cranmer's Second Book of Common Prayer – a decision that pleased the Protestants who felt that the English Church had ended up midway between Catholicism and a watered-down Protestantism before Mary had tried to restore the Catholic Church for good.

Elizabeth, however, did secure a compromise through the Ornaments Rubric. As Supreme Governor of the Church of England she ruled that Catholic rituals, such as using the sign of the cross during the Sacrament of Baptism, and vestments, such as copes, should still be used. The Church of England was not heading in the same direction as other Protestant Churches, governed without bishops. Much of this was down to Elizabeth's personal religious preferences, although she tempered her inclinations faced with Cecil's persuasions: she was reluctant to think of the papacy as the Antichrist, she valued prayer more than preaching, and she loved liturgy, something that can be particularly seen in the music of her Chapel Royal and the composers of her age, such as Byrd.

As David Starkey says, 'Far from hurtling along the road of reform in the way that Edward and his supporters had envisioned, the Church of England was frozen in time. The result was a Church that was Protestant in doctrine, Catholic in appearance and which would, Elizabeth hoped, satisfy all but a handful of extremists on both sides.'[30]

Elizabeth's decision to call herself Supreme Governor, rather than Supreme Head, could arguably signify a certain humility – only Christ could be the head of the Church, and her title must therefore be a lesser one. It is also the title taken by all monarchs in this country since.

But with the title of Governor came the Oath of Supremacy, requiring anyone taking public or Church office to swear allegiance to the monarch as head of the Church and state. Anyone refusing to take the Oath could be charged with treason. An Act of Uniformity also made attendance at Church of England services compulsory. There were penalties for recusancy too. Elizabeth's tolerance through pragmatism only went so far.

In August that same year, just how much antipathy had developed towards the Catholic Church was apparent when the City of London celebrated St Bartholomew's Fair at Smithfield. The celebrations led to funeral pyres of all that Catholics held dear in their rituals – and it was no eruption of mob rule either. Rather, it was a stage-managed spectacle, with burnings at St Paul's Churchyard in Cheapside and other sites in the City that must have horrified Mass-goers. Into the flames went crucifixes, missals, vestments, altar cloths and anything else that suggested popery to the Protestants.[31]

There were grave dangers for Elizabeth in opposing Catholicism to the extent that she and her government did so, leading to growing frustrations among her population and increasing criticism abroad in Catholic countries and in Rome. Then there was the future: if she were to ensure the country would remain Protestant, she needed to marry and produce an heir – just as her sister Mary had sought to ensure a Catholic future but, being childless, had let in the Protestant Elizabeth. If she did not do so – and throughout her reign she ducked and dived when it came to marriage – she would likely be succeeded by a descendant of her father's sisters. And if that were to happen, it would please the Catholics, who continued to perceive her as a usurper, a bastard child of Henry and his bigamous marriage to Anne. It was unsettling for the country, which yearned for the stability that monarchs are supposed to bring.

The most likely successor to an unmarried, childless Elizabeth, and also the Catholic who most threatened her, was Mary, Queen of Scots, daughter of Mary of Guise and James V of Scotland, the son of Henry VIII's elder sister, Margaret Tudor. Mary had been married in 1558 to Francis, dauphin of France, who succeeded to the French throne a year later upon the death of his father, Henry II, in a jousting accident. But only eighteen months later, Francis died suddenly and she returned to her native Scotland.

The Catholic Queen was at odds with her largely Protestant kingdom. But her proximity to the north of England with its population of discontents, her renowned beauty and her links to the English throne – although Elizabeth's father, Henry, had cut his Scottish relatives out of the succession laid down in his will – made her an unsettling rival to Elizabeth.

The relationship between the two women was made complicated by their differences, not only over religion, but also over marriage. While Elizabeth showed reluctance and caution, even though it jeopardised the future stability of her kingdom, Mary damaged the fortunes of hers through her impulsiveness and continuing desire to be married. After she returned to Scotland she married, first, Lord Darnley, also descended from Margaret Tudor, and, after marrying in haste, she regretted it at leisure. In March 1566, Mary, then pregnant with the son who was to become James VI of Scotland, looked on in horror as her husband Darnley murdered her Italian secretary, David Rizzio. Almost a year later Darnley himself was found dead following an explosion at a house in Edinburgh, though it seems he had been suffocated rather than died in the explosion. Mary fled Edinburgh with the chief suspect in Darnley's death, the Earl of Boswell, whom she later married.

The Scottish lords who controlled the government raised an army, captured Mary, denounced her as a murderer and an adulterer, forced her to abdicate in favour of her son and kept her prisoner. In 1568, after more than a year imprisoned in Loch Leven, Mary tried to raise an army, was routed and then fled south, throwing herself upon her cousin's mercy.

Mary had become a huge problem for Elizabeth. If she were to help Mary regain her throne, she could pose a threat from Scotland. If she were to help her travel to France, she could raise an army to take over both Scotland and England. If Mary were to stay in England, she could become the focus of Catholic discontents, who would prefer her to Elizabeth as their monarch.

Elizabeth's opinion was swayed by the views of William Cecil, who told her, 'The Queen of Scots is, and always shall be, a dangerous person to your estate.'[32] Evidence shows, however, that Mary had wished to come to an accord with her cousin, suggesting that 'for we be both of one blood, of one country and in one island'.[33] After her return to Scotland in 1561, Mary had wanted Elizabeth to recognise her as her lawful successor should the English Queen not have her own child, and in return she would not push her own immediate dynastic claim to the throne. But Cecil advised Elizabeth against it, on the grounds of religion. As John Guy puts it, 'From 1559 onwards, Cecil had an almost messianic Protestant vision of a largely unified British Isles in which Scotland would become a satellite state of England, with Mary excluded from power. When debating the English succession, he put religion ahead of dynastic right, whereas Elizabeth took the opposite approach.'[34]

By 1569, Catholic frustrations were boiling over, and many of those opposed to Elizabeth's rule saw her cousin, the Catholic Mary, Queen of Scots, as an alternative monarch. Catholic nobles from the north, led by the Earl of Westmoreland and Thomas Percy, Earl of Northumberland, rose in rebellion against the Queen and sought to free Mary, who had been imprisoned by Elizabeth, and place her on the throne. After their defeat, Elizabeth exacted a furious revenge, having more than seven hundred rebels executed.

In Rome, Pope Pius V mistakenly believed that the uprising had been successful – which says little for the effectiveness of the papal spies based in England. His papal bull, *Regnans in Excelsis*, issued in 1570, declared that 'Elizabeth, the pretended Queen of England and the servant of crime', should be declared a heretic and excommunicated, and he released all her subjects from allegiance to her. Indeed, he went even further: Catholics who obeyed her orders would be excommunicated too.

This led to a 'tit for tat' threat to Catholics from the English state: in 1571 it became treasonable to question the Queen's position as head of the Church of England, and within thirteen years it had become a crime of treason for a priest abroad even to return to English soil. Harbouring a priest also became punishable by death.

This was an era of paranoia. Francis Walsingham, Elizabeth's spymaster, sought out plotters against the Queen's life. Certain Catholics did seek to remove her from the throne of England and replace her with her Scottish Catholic cousin, Mary, Queen of Scots. Then there was Spain – Catholic Spain – ruled over by Philip, widower of Elizabeth's sister Mary, who had ascended to the Spanish throne in 1556, two years before Elizabeth had taken hers. That nation was seen as a constant Catholic threat to the survival of England as a Protestant heartland.

Meanwhile, the Catholics of England itself, battered by the demands of the Vatican, hammered by the orders of Elizabeth and her advisers and sometimes suspected of treason by their Protestant fellow English, were in need of spiritual succour, just when it was increasingly difficult to secure it. For them, it was not so much the word of God that provided that nourishment as receiving the sacraments. For this to happen, they needed priests and the Mass. Catholic clerics were smuggled into England from seminaries in Spain, France and Rome. To be caught was certain death. It also meant being honoured by the Catholic Church as a martyr – and further proof to Catholics of the wickedness of the English Queen. England, ruled by a monarch who had presented herself as a pragmatist and compromiser, was in the midst of a religious war. Defending the faith had come to this.

Each year there seemed new plots involving the Scottish Queen and bids to free her and usurp Elizabeth. Mary was careful to distance herself from what men planned in her name until, in 1586, she fatefully mentioned the assassination of Elizabeth in letters between her and conspirators led by the Catholic gentleman, Anthony Babington. When Francis Walsingham saw her letter, he drew a hangman's noose upon it.

A noose, though, did not await Mary. Instead, in 1587, twenty years after she had first been imprisoned by Elizabeth, she mounted the scaffold at Fotheringhay Castle and, in her under-dress of martyrs' red, she was beheaded.

Executing Mary did not solve Elizabeth's personal insecurities, nor the anxieties of England regarding the Catholic threat. The Spanish were still waiting across the Bay of Biscay to trounce the Protestant realm. Both sides would claim God was on their side, but in 1588 it was the weather that proved the supportive act, blowing the Armada off course. Protestant England and its Protestant Queen triumphed. Together they had faced down Spain and emerged as a world power.

But the Queen was ageing and the Tudor era could not last. In 1601 she appeared before the final Parliament of her reign, saying, 'For myself, I was never so much enticed with the potent name of a king, or royal authority of a queen, as delighted that God hath made me his instrument to maintain his truth and glory and this kingdom from dishonour, damage, tyranny, and oppression.'[35]

The difficulty was that Elizabeth had not managed to keep her realm as peaceful as she suggested, because what was God's truth had been disputed throughout her reign. She might have been a less divisive monarch than her siblings had been, but peace had come at a devastating price for many of her subjects. And the Virgin Queen, once hailed as a great monarch, an English rival to the Virgin Mary and as worthy of adoration as her, was now a problem. She had not provided an heir.

Those in the Protestant camp had been thinking about the succession, even if the Queen had not, and approaches had been made north of the border to James VI, Stuart son of Mary, Queen of Scots. Whatever Henry VIII had declared in his will, they knew that James' claim to the throne was the strongest, and despite his mother's religion he was a Protestant. After thirty-five years as the Scottish King, he came south in 1603 to claim the English one, ruling as James I.

In Westminster Abbey Elizabeth I lies. Next to her is the Catholic Queen, Mary I. And also beside her is Mary, Queen of Scots, in a tomb ordered by her son. Protestant Gloriana could not escape Catholics in life. In death, they surround her. The House of Stuart would face similar tensions in its years of English monarchy.

The crowning of James VI of Scotland as James I of England brought the two kingdoms together for the first time. He was a product of the stern Scottish Reformation and had developed a strong aversion to Catholicism – a view that English Protestants might have thought would lead to the religious troubles of the past being finally settled. But the hundred years of Stuart monarchy, beginning with James I, were to be as turbulent as what had gone before, not least owing to the continuing conflict with Catholicism as well as the Stuart obsession with the divine right of kings.

This was thoroughly expressed by James in his two books *Basilikon* and *The Trew Law of Free Monarchies*, written between 1598 and 1599, just a few years before his accession to the English throne. *Basilikon* was written as a manual on kingship for his four-year-old son and heir, Henry, in which he declared, 'God made you a little God to sit on his throne, and rule over other men.' James, like Henry VIII, from whom he was descended, grounded his thinking about kingship in the stories of the Kings of the Old Testament. But he went even further than Henry, writing in *The Trew Law of Free Monarchies* that kings were unaccountable to human law. Instead, he wrote, 'Kings are called Gods; they are appointed by God and answerable only to God.' Therefore, if Kings are God's representatives on earth, then to act against the King is to act against God.

In Scotland, where the Kirk, created by the Scottish Reformation, held sway, along with the Scottish aristocracy, James had little chance of challenging its dominance and ensuring he was treated as a little god. But in England, which had already accepted that the monarch was supreme, answerable only to God, he had far more chance of being accepted as the almost-deity he believed himself to be.

James, like other philosopher advocates of the divine right of kings, such as John Wycliffe and Robert Filmer, believed that monarchy was divinely ordained, that hereditary right was inalienable, that that right, from birth, could never be forfeited and that obedience was required by God. There were, however, responsibilities that the King had to honour, according to James' theorising: it was not a role without obligation. In *The Trew Law of Free Monarchies* he had written that at his coronation, 'the King becomes a naturall Father to all his Lieges', and this entailed caring for their 'nourishing, education and vertuous government'.[36] In other words, the monarch would be akin to God the Father, in a patriarchal relationship with his people. Filmer, in his work *Patriarcha*, relating the divine right of kings to Adam in Genesis, argued that 'the first kings were fathers of families. It is unnatural for the people to govern or choose governors. Positive laws do not infringe the natural and fatherly power of kings.'[37]

James, however, did not see the coronation oath as a pledge to the people, but only to God, although it is between the King and his people, and he promised 'to profess the Religion presently professed within that countrie . . . And next to maintaine all the lowable and good Laws made by their predecessours'. Yet within his treatise, there was also a warning of the dangers of the divine right theory; the people, said James, have no right to overthrow the King if he violates his oath. Only God can do that. Therefore 'it is like unlawful . . . to displace him'.[38]

James' English coronation was like a pre-Reformation ritual but with blessing, censing and all references to saints deleted – although it took place on the feast day of his saintly namesake, the apostle James, on 25 July 1603. The Anglican clergy were vested, much like Roman Catholic bishops would be, while James himself was dressed as if a priest-king were being ordained, with a crimson velvet vestment, a surplice or cotta and a tunicle of a deacon embroidered with the arms of England.[39]

Though James was a firm Protestant, the fear of popery had not abated following his accession, not least because his own Queen, Anne of Denmark, was a Catholic convert and he had said that he would not persecute those Catholics who were quiet and obedient. But soon his officials drafted new legislation to push for further persecution, causing simmering resentments and leading to a series of failed plots to kidnap the King or remove him.

The most infamous of the plots was that of 5 November 1605, when Guy Fawkes and twelve fellow conspirators sought to blow up the Houses of Parliament on the day James was due to open it. Tipped off by letter that an explosion was likely to occur, James ordered that the vault of Parliament be searched at the last minute on the night of the fourth, hoping it would mean that the conspirators would be caught red-handed. And there was Guy Fawkes, surrounded by thirty-five barrels of gunpowder, a stash of firewood and a fuse in his pocket.

If he had succeeded, he would have wiped out the Royal Family and the parliamentarians of England. Instead, its consequence was to encourage the anti-Catholic mythology of England for generations. The Observance of the Fifth of November Act of 1606 led to special sermons, church bells being rung and bonfires being lit on 5 November every year until the Act was repealed in 1859. Even today, bonfires and fireworks are still used to celebrate Guy Fawkes, and in

East Sussex the bonfire societies of Lewes parade through the town, burning effigies of the pope.

James' view of religious differences was, however, not limited to countering terrorist plots, and he appeared to want to find a more peaceful way of dealing with them. According to Reformation historian Diarmaid MacCulloch, 'he had decades of experience in dealing with squabbling clergy' through his years as James VI of Scotland, and he sought to find ways of drawing people closer together.[40]

He tried to bring the national Churches of England, Scotland and Ireland together, including getting the Scottish Church to observe Christmas and Easter.

His efforts also resulted in the Hampton Court Conference on religion in 1604 – a notion that debate could solve the theological conflicts between Protestants, including the hardliners, and Catholics. A tradition of debate in Scotland led him to think this was a constructive way forward. If any of the low churchmen thought the conference would lead to a significant change, they were to be disappointed. James confirmed he was happy with the Elizabethan religious settlement: the Church of England would not become a kirk. But what he did agree to led to one of the most significant and finest works in the English language: a new translation of the Bible, known ever after as the King James Bible.

James might have been dogmatic regarding monarchy, but when it came to the translation of the Bible, he was much more open to debate, and brought together Puritan and High Church contributors, hoping that this would lead to the translation becoming an instrument of peace, founded on his divinely rooted authority. He looked for moderation, famously saying, 'I am for the medium in all things.'

Adam Nicolson, author of a book on the King James Bible marked to celebrate its four-hundredth anniversary, says that James wanted:

> to make royal power and divine glory into one indivisible garment which could be wrapped around the nation as a whole. Its grandeur of phrasing and the deep slow music of its rhythms – far more evident here than in any Bible the sixteenth century had produced – were conscious embodiments of regal glory. It is a book written

> for what James, the self-styled Rex Pacifus [king of peace] and his counsellors hoped might be an ideal world.[41]

It was also an era that saw the Bible asserted as ideal food for the soul of Britons, rather than the sacraments.

For James, as for all monarchs, one of the biggest issues confronting him was succession. James would have considered the matter settled with the birth of his heir, Prince Henry, in 1594, the boy he tutored in kingship with his manual extolling the divine right of kings. But in 1612 he suffered the terrible blow of Henry succumbing to typhoid fever. His heir therefore became his younger son, Charles, who until then had not been schooled in the ways of kingship. In November 1616, aged sixteen, Charles was invested as Prince of Wales. He became King and was crowned ten years later in February 1626.

There was already evidence of future difficulties at his coronation. Charles had been married by proxy on 1 May 1625 to the Catholic fifteen-year-old Princess Henrietta Maria of France, and they then met in person in Canterbury on 13 June. There was opposition to the marriage from members of the Commons who feared that Charles would lift restrictions on Catholic recusants and undermine the establishment of the Church of England. Although he pledged not to relax religious restrictions, he had promised the opposite in a treaty with his new brother-in-law, Louis XIII of France, upon marriage to Henrietta Maria. At the crowning, she refused to participate in a Protestant religious ceremony. Her Catholic worship was also tolerated as part of the marriage deal, while Puritans were also concerned by Charles' closeness to the High Church William Laud, whom he first appointed as Bishop of London and then as Archbishop of Canterbury.

Laud preached that no power but God could judge the King, so obedience therefore extended to obeying the King, reflecting the Stuarts' belief in the divine right of kings. This status also gave Charles, he believed, the right to govern according to his conscience. That included collecting taxes without parliamentary consent. For eleven years, after a breakdown in the relationship between Charles and MPs, he ruled without Parliament, ensuring growing resentment between the monarch and the political class. His autocratic approach and his failure to summon Parliament for ten years, from 1629 to 1640, led to the English Civil War.

The conflicts between Charles and the nation were as much religious as political. His appointment of High Anglicans Richard Montague and William Laud to the bishoprics of Chichester and London was a message, according to Simon Schama, that conveyed 'as loudly as possible that the king had no intention of conceding anything about his monopoly of wisdom and power in matters spiritual. Like his father, he thought of himself as God's "lieutenant on earth".'[42]

Charles saw himself as King as guardian of the nation – a position that required spiritual responsibility and his own austerity, self-denial and dedication. That dedication was not only to Christ but also to St George and the Order of the Garter, the ancient chivalric order dedicated to St George. His love of ceremony was satisfied by the Order but was also apparent in his desire for a particularly ceremonial form of Anglicanism. It was something that many felt was too close to the Roman Catholicism of his wife, Henrietta Maria.

It was in the country of his birth that the most violent rejection of Charles' commitment to the liturgy occurred. In July 1637, in St Giles' Cathedral in Edinburgh, the Dean and the Bishop of Edinburgh began reading from the new prayer book, authorised by the King. Footstools were thrown at them, and surplices torn from their backs. Rioters protested at the popish liturgy. While Charles may have been a Scot and a Stuart, he had left Scotland well behind him, and he had no idea of the sway of Calvinism over the land of his birth.

With civil war came the unravelling of the Stuart monarchy. For many it was also a struggle for the soul of the nation, a conflict between good and evil, between Puritanism and the followers of the Antichrist. Convinced that there would never be peace while the King lived, a rump of radical MPs, including Oliver Cromwell, put him on trial in 1649, charged with attempting to govern as an absolute monarch rather than with Parliament.

This must have been a mystifying accusation to Charles, given that he had been brought up to believe he had a special relationship with God, was anointed to rule and was a divine instrument, to be obeyed by his people. He saw his arrest and trial as illegal, but also believed that those ranged against him wanted to destroy the Church.

On 20 January 1649, Charles was brought to Westminster Hall and told that he was responsible for 'all the treasons, murders, ravages, burnings, spoils, desolations, damages and mischiefs to this nation'.[43] The trial itself was a great spectacle, with crowds cramming the space, and the wealthy watching in the galleries.

Asked to plead, he refused, and on insisting the trial was illegal, Charles explained:

> No earthly power can justly call me (who am your King) in question as a delinquent . . . this day's proceeding cannot be warranted by God's laws; for, on the contrary, the authority of obedience unto Kings is clearly warranted, and strictly commanded in both the Old and New Testament . . . for the law of this land, I am no less confident, that no learned lawyer will affirm that an impeachment can lie against the King, they all going in his name: and one of their maxims is, that the King can do no wrong . . . the higher House is totally excluded; and for the House of Commons, it is too well known that the major part of them are detained or deterred from sitting . . . the arms I took up were only to defend the fundamental laws of this kingdom against those who have supposed my power hath totally changed the ancient government.[44]

Charles I was brought to the scaffold through the Banqueting House, where he had commissioned Rubens to illustrate Stuart power by commemorating Charles' father, James I, as King Solomon. Now the ceiling was boarded up, that power was lost, and the concept of monarchy itself was subject on the scaffold to the will of the Roundhead revolutionaries. Charles was seen as a traitor. Blair Worden has described Charles in his recent account of the civil war: 'In his demeanour at the trial Charles achieved a kind of greatness. His dignified refusal to accept the legality of the court or to enter a plea made nonsense of the proceedings against him.'[45]

Eleven years after his death, when his son succeeded him as King Charles II, bringing to an end the short era when England was a republic, Parliament decreed that the anniversary of his death should be observed as a day of fasting and humiliation in every church in

England, and it was incorporated into the Book of Common Prayer two years later (although removed in 1928).

Charles was not always popular for his religious beliefs; the ecclesiastical policies of the 1630s that he and the Archbishop of Canterbury William Laud had supported – enforcing uniformity across Anglicanism and encouraging Catholic ritual – had contributed to the war that would engulf England, Scotland and Ireland. Charles had been devoted to the Church of England, founded less than a hundred years before he was crowned, and utterly resistant to the destruction of its episcopacy – something that, despite the Henrician break with Rome, represented a link back to the apostles and to Christ himself.

The King saw himself as perhaps greater than a king. His final words at the scaffold before his execution alluded to his sense that he was, indeed, a martyr: 'I go from a corruptible to an incorruptible crown; where no disturbance can be, no disturbance in the world.'[46] The following day, his head was reattached to his body and he was placed in a lead coffin. A week later his body was taken to Windsor and buried next to Henry VIII in the vault of St George's Chapel – two kings, side by side, whose reigns had been riven by religion.

The widespread cult of martyrdom that grew up around the executed King – his devotees included those who had dipped their handkerchiefs in his blood following his beheading, providing them with a precious relic – was encouraged by publication of a book of his supposed writings the day after his burial. *Eikon Basilike: The Portraiture of His Sacred Majesty in His Solitudes and Sufferings* was a collection of meditations and prayers with Charles on the cover, shown grasping a crown of thorns, his earthly crown discarded and his eyes on a heavenly crown. It indicated that he followed in Christ's suffering footsteps, and also in those of the Old Testament Kings, leading their people to prayer.

Regicide was too much for Charles' supporters, and even for the less enthusiastic royalists, and arguably it helped the royal cause for securing the restoration of Charles II.

The return of the House of Stuart after England's experimental republicanism also saw a revival of the old Church. Bishops, cathedrals and their deans and chapters had their lands restored that had been confiscated in 1660–62, without much protest from the landowners who had benefited. As Diarmaid MacCulloch puts it, 'It suggests a slow build-up of emotional reactions against the governments of the Interregnum, a reaction of revulsion which made the old Church seem like a good investment.'[47]

Yet the religious issues that had previously bedevilled the country, even though there were efforts to address them, came back to haunt it. Charles had won his throne back through his manifesto, The Declaration of Breda, and his promises on disputed titles to land, army pay arrears and war crimes soon passed into legislation. But his pledge on religion – to offer liberty to tender consciences or, in other words, to be tolerant of those who had rebelled against his father – did not. Whether that was owing to Charles or to his chief minister or Lord Chancellor, Edward Hyde, Earl of Clarendon, is open to debate, but the Clarendon Code, named after Hyde, ruled that the Church of England was the one true Church and that King Charles, its Supreme Governor, was owed obedience. Charles had little time for those who had opposed absolute royal power and won the Civil War; after all, they had killed his father.

Charles was more favourably inclined to Catholics, who shared the faith of his mother, the Dowager Queen Henrietta Maria, and he was also rumoured to be a Catholic convert himself.

The new King was crowned in April 1661, almost a year after his return from exile. But even before his coronation, ceremonies were conducted that highlighted the abiding belief among many of his subjects that the monarch had mystical powers, highlighting the link between kingship and divinity. The location for these ceremonies was a poignant choice: the Banqueting House, from which the new King's father had stepped out to his execution. It was there, every Friday from June 1660, that crowds flocked to see Charles, seated beneath a canopy, and to seek out his touch in the hope that this would cure those afflicted with disfiguring scrofula – known as the King's evil. He would eventually lay hands on more than 90,000 of his subjects during his reign.

Charles' coronation was a spectacular affair, with newly commissioned regalia after the previous ancient items had been broken up during the Republic. These included a new St Edward's Crown, which has been used ever since for coronations in this country, albeit with additions.

One of the most important documents on royalty and religion was prepared for Charles II prior to his coronation and full of advice about it. Written by William Cavendish, Duke of Newcastle, in 1659, it advised Charles, 'When you appear, to show yourself gloriously, to your people; like a God, for Holy Writ says, we have called you Gods.'

As with Elizabeth I's coronation, there was an extravagant procession prior to the crowning, which set off from the Tower of London and involved triumphal arches and pageants. The coronation itself was held on St George's Day, feast day of England's patron and that of the Order of the Garter, so beloved of Charles I and now restored.

In an era of Protestantism when the Word was so important, the sermon was of major importance at the coronation, and at Charles II's, George Morley, Bishop of Winchester, depicted the new King as a Christlike figure, whose impact was akin to a resurrection. Monarchy, said Bishop Morley, was 'recommended both by the Father and the Son as the best and only Form of Government for all Nations'.[48]

Although it had been an Anglican crowning, Charles II was still keen to be seen to be tolerant of other Christians, and eighteen months or so later he attempted once again, with a second Declaration of Breda, to dispense with the Clarendon Code for Protestants and Catholics who were modest in their church practices, and promised it would be abandoned altogether eventually. But the House of Commons would have none of it. Still scarred by battling Oliver Cromwell, they forced Charles to backtrack on his intentions. The King's efforts as a peacemaker and respecter of others' beliefs were thwarted by Parliament. There was only one version of faith they would have him defend.

For all these tensions over religions, the Restoration brought a renewed pleasure to life after the drudgery of the Roundhead years. The royal palaces were pleasure domes, filled with feasting and romantic dalliances. The closed-down theatres reopened, while the King also took great interest in scientific discovery, founding the Greenwich Royal Observatory. Charles was notorious for his mistresses, but he was also happily married, and his wife, like his mother, was Catholic.

Catherine of Braganza was not at first a popular Queen, with many of Charles' subjects preferring that he should marry a Protestant, and she was not crowned, because Roman Catholics were forbidden to participate in Anglican services. Despite her not producing an heir, and in spite of his licentiousness – fathering fourteen illegitimate children – the couple had no inclination to divorce. The Queen was also put under tremendous pressure as anti-Catholic feeling intensified – in 1673 the Test Act drove all Catholics out of public office – and in 1678 she stood accused by Titus Oates of intending to poison the King and therefore of high treason. The House of Commons ordered all Roman Catholics to be banned from the Palace of Whitehall and it was later decided that she should stand trial. Only the King's intervention saved her.

Catherine's devout faith impressed Charles – something that was expressed in letters to his sister. There is some evidence that he himself was interested in converting to Roman Catholicism in 1668 when his brother informed the King that he had done so, but lingering opposition to the Church of Rome remained in England and deterred him. But trouble was only stored up, not solved. With no legitimate heir, it was his brother James, now a committed Catholic, who inherited the throne in 1685. His was a troubled reign that would lead through its demise to a final and conclusive commitment to Anglicanism and an utter rejection of Roman Catholicism within the monarchy.

Opposition to James, the Catholic heir, had been formidable. Three Parliaments between 1679 and 1681 had a clear Commons majority to exclude him from the succession. Each time, Charles had dissolved Parliament, determined that James' hereditary right to rule should not be traduced by fears of the papacy (which, with a Catholic wife and mother and a certain flirtation himself with the religion, he did not share). Charles, who finally converted to Catholicism himself on his deathbed, thwarted all attempts to prevent his brother taking the throne, leaving the way clear for a test of the bond between monarchy and Anglicanism.

James II, as he was crowned on St George's Day in a glorious ceremony in Westminster Abbey, complete with compositions by Henry Purcell, must have thought he had ridden out the storm. He was a Roman Catholic who was head of the Church of England; the idea of the monarch's supremacy convinced the Protestant majority that they must indeed still obey the King, regardless of his own religious beliefs. But within just three years it would all unravel. There were already signs at his coronation that the religious divisions could not be covered over. As James was a Catholic, there was no Communion service.

James articulated his Catholicism in other ways too. Like Charles II, he regularly enacted the ritual of the King's evil, touching for scrofula, but he Catholicised it, with prayers in Latin, invoking the saints and the Virgin Mary and making a sign of the cross on the sufferer.

Within days of his crowning, James faced challenges to his kingship, with, first, supporters of a rival to the throne, Charles II's illegitimate Protestant son, the Duke of Monmouth, landing in Scotland, and then Monmouth himself landing in Dorset. He had arrived, he said, 'for the defence and vindication of the Protestant religion and of the laws, rights and privileges of England . . . and for delivering the Kingdom from the usurpation and tyranny of us by the name of James, Duke of York'.[49] Monmouth, routed by the King's forces at Sedgemoor, was executed in July 1685. But it did not end the alarm at James' Catholicism, fuelled by his decision to give army commands to Roman Catholics. When Parliament objected, he had it prorogued and it never met again during his reign.

James' desire for religious toleration in many ways undid him. In February 1687, he made a Declaration of Indulgence in Scotland, allowing Presbyterians to meet in their homes, Quakers to gather in a place they chose for worship, and laws against Catholics to be suspended. When this was received well, he attempted to do the same in England and Wales, by packing Parliament with his supporters. His efforts included abolishing the Test Act, which banned Catholics from high office, and he sought the pope's agreement to appoint four vicars apostolic as bishops in England – the first time the Roman Catholic hierarchs would have been based in the country since the time of Mary Tudor.

But, as had so often happened since Henry VIII's break with Rome, it was the succession that was the breaking point. After his first wife, Anne Hyde, had died in 1671, James had taken the devout Italian Roman Catholic Mary of Modena as his second in 1673. After a series of miscarriages, stillbirths and infant deaths, in 1688 Mary produced a son, James, who now became heir to the throne, superseding James' Protestant daughter, Mary, by his first wife, who had married the staunch Protestant William of Orange.

This newborn male heir created a prospect that delighted his father and horrified his Protestant enemies: a Catholic dynasty that would return England to the old faith and reverse the reforms of the past 130 years since Elizabeth I's settlement.

Rumours began to circulate that the Queen's child had been stillborn and this baby was an imposter, smuggled into the Queen's bed in a warming pan. At the same time, overtures were made to William to invade in the name of Protestantism and take the throne with his wife Mary. William's fleet landed at Brixham on 5 November – the anniversary of the failed Gunpowder Plot when Catholic insurgents had sought to blow the Protestant Parliament to smithereens.

James, despite having a larger army than William's, lost his nerve and fled to France to join his wife and son, eventually being given a palace by his cousin, Louis XIV of France. When Parliament convened in January 1689, it decreed that James had effectively abdicated and so declared that his daughter Mary would be Queen, ruling jointly with her husband King William. The victors, who had found a way to avert Catholicism casting its shadow over England's throne once more, were triumphant in what they called their Glorious Revolution.

Later that year, a Bill of Rights declared that, henceforward, no Roman Catholic could ascend the English throne and no English monarch could marry a Roman Catholic. History, being written by the victors, was unkind to James, who was frequently pictured as a Catholic fanatic who would have led England to disaster. But the evidence shows that he was keen to find a way to religious toleration. The English were not prepared for it.

William and Mary's Protestantism was their strongest card, and it was reinforced at their joint coronation. For the first time a Bible was carried in the procession in Westminster Abbey and their oaths included an unprecedented swearing to rule 'according to the true profession of the gospel and the Protestant reformed religion established by law'.

It was a definitive statement. Yet across the water, in continental Europe, James resided, as did his son James, a continuing thorn in the side of the Protestant Establishment. On James II's death in 1701, his son, now styling himself as James III but dubbed the Old Pretender in Britain, declared himself King of England, Scotland and Ireland.

Supported by successive popes, James III lived in various papal territories until Pope Clement XI offered him the Palazzo del Re in Rome. He and his successor, Pope Innocent XIII, supported James with money, enabling him to create a sumptuous Jacobite court in exile.

While Spain, the Papal States and Modena recognised James as King of Britain, they refused to recognise William III and Mary II, nor their successor Anne, who was also James II's daughter, as legitimate sovereigns. Anne's coronation went further in denouncing popery, with her having to declare that she rejected the doctrine of transubstantiation.

In England, as Anne grew close to death and yet another issue of succession concerned the country – the Queen had borne twelve children, but not one survived her – the government's thoughts turned to the surviving Stuart, James III, in exile, and offered him the throne, on condition that he renounce his Catholic faith and become a Protestant. His riposte was, 'I have chosen my course; therefore it is for others to change their sentiments.'[50]

James was the antithesis of the last Tudor, Elizabeth, and her sometime efforts at compromise. Instead, his devotion to his faith – or some might say his obstinacy – cost him and his son, Charles, the Young Pretender, dear. As Linda Colley says, 'The Stuart cause operated under an overwhelming handicap. Its representatives would not abandon the Catholicism that had cost their dynasty the throne in the first place. Steadfastly, admirably but in political terms, lethally, the Stuarts would not embrace Protestantism and this proved decisive.'[51]

A Catholic takeover of the throne was exactly what the British wished to avoid. Indeed, the Act of Settlement, passed thirteen years earlier in 1701, had confirmed that anyone who was Catholic or married to a Catholic was forever 'uncapable to inherit, possess or enjoy the crown and government of this realm' – a law that still stands today in terms of the monarch but was amended in terms of marriage in 2013 (see chapter five).[52]

The history of Britain, formed in 1707 by the Act of Union bringing together England, Scotland and Ireland, had been dominated by issues of succession as much as religion, but the country now believed that it was religion that mattered more than heredity. A hunt was on for a Protestant to inherit the throne. More than fifty individuals were passed over because of their Catholic faith, until the Protestant torchlight alighted upon the obscure Electress Sophia of Hanover. The Electress died two months before Queen Anne, so it was her son, George, Prince of Hanover, who emerged blinking into the light.

George was a minor aristocrat, a German, with little by way of charisma. How different were the Stuarts. James III and his son Charles, also known as Bonnie Prince Charlie or the Young Pretender, cut a dash as handsome, romantic figures. Visiting their court in Rome became a major stop on the Grand Tour for the wealthy. In Scotland, where the Act of Union with England was unpopular, these royals of Scottish descent had particular appeal. But James III's abortive attempt at reclaiming his throne in 1715, which led to him occupying Scone Palace but within weeks fleeing back to France, dented the Stuarts' popularity in Scotland.

It was the turn of James' son, Charles, the Young Pretender, to promote the Jacobite cause, and in 1745 he led an uprising of Highland clans who backed the Stuarts' claim to the throne. Beneath the musket fire of George II's army they were defeated at Culloden in 1746, and Charles fled, never to return. It was the end of Stuart hopes for the throne. When he died forty-two years later, he was buried with his father and brother, Cardinal Henry Benedict Stuart, in St Peter's Basilica and below the spot where the Stuarts' Royal Monument would later be erected. Years later, flowers would be laid on anniversaries by the British ambassador to the Holy See on behalf of Elizabeth II, descended from the Stuarts through her mother's line. In an age of greater religious toleration, the Stuart story had come full circle.

But as the Hanoverians monarchs took over, with their key asset being their Protestantism, there was a paradox at the heart of their succession.

Buffeted by religious tensions, the newly united nation of Great Britain had used Protestantism to shape its identity. It had required a bogeyman – the Roman Catholic Church – and many of its members, loyal to the religion that had endured for generations in these islands, were scapegoated, often losing their lives as the new Britain flexed its national muscles. Britannia was a Protestant.

In less than two hundred years the English monarch had switched from being a Defender of the Catholic faith, via an assertion of supremacy, attempts to control the people's religious beliefs and persecution of those who refused, to a Defender of the Protestant faith. But the efforts at total supremacy – through a fusion of divine right and royal power – were in turn thwarted, albeit by those who shared rejection of the pope's power. They did not want a home-grown pope either. Religious toleration was not a byword of this era. What mattered most was an assertion of first English and then British identity and nationhood. But it took first a Dutch King and then a German family to consolidate that identity – an identity that would soon be further characterised by its monarchs' attempts to become a symbol of domestic happiness – the ideal Christian family. And as the stability of the royal family helped steady the nation, so eventually fear of the great enemy, the papacy, faded. It is to these issues I will turn next.

# 3

# From turmoil to stability: the domestication of monarchy and religion

THE PAINTED HALL in Greenwich is one of the great masterpieces of the Baroque. Take a look around the Upper Hall's west side and there you will see Sir James Thornhill's accounts of the Protestant succession. In one, there is William of Orange landing at Brixham in Torbay in 1688, being welcomed by Britannia. And there too is that other great moment in Protestant triumph: the arrival of the new German Prince who would become George I of Britain, landing in Greenwich in 1714. He arrives in a horse-drawn Roman chariot, accompanied by St George, patron of England, who is on horseback and trampling a dragon, with Religion, Liberty, Truth and Justice in front, Eternity above and Fame preceding them, with her trumpet to announce the good news of the Protestant King. Nearby, Thornhill has painted a curtain drawn back to reveal the new King's family, many of them used to symbolise the various Virtues, accompanied by Justice and Time, while Peace and Plenty offer a cornucopia of delights.

Thornhill's composition must have delighted the King who appointed him History Painter the year of this masterpiece in grisaille, for he knighted him in 1720. It was certainly an effective piece of propaganda, and rather different from reality: George had indeed landed in Greenwich in 1714 to claim his throne, and after walking through the Royal Naval College he had spent the night at the Queen's House. But he was humbly dressed and a modest man, and though there were crowds to greet him, there was no scene of magnificent splendour. There was instead relief among parliamentarians that they had a Protestant King to succeed Anne, last of the Stuart monarchs.

But they also had a foreign King, for the second time in thirty years – and, one might fairly say, an even more foreign monarch. William of Orange had an English mother, he was married to an English heir to the throne and he spoke English. George had none of these things: his family was German, he brought German ministers with him, and he spoke German and only broken English. The nation of Britain, united just seven years earlier, was now in the hands of a man who knew nothing of it. It was an experiment that was highly risky.

How risky was also evident at George's coronation, when there were riots and talk of bringing back the Stuart Pretenders – riots that continued sporadically for the next five years. It was vital that the Hanoverians find a way to unite the newly formed nation – an aim that was reflected in the medal struck to mark George's coronation – depicting him crowned by Britannia – and in the oath put to him: 'And will you maintain and preserve inviolably the settlement of the Church of Scotland, and the Doctrine, Worship and Disciplined Government thereof as by Law established within the Kingdoms of England and Ireland, the Dominion of Wales, and Town of Berwick upon Tweed, and Territories thereunto belonging before the Union of the two Kingdoms?'[1]

The King was cast once more as Old Testament ruler and a saviour of the people, averting them from the horrors of popery. The Bishop of Oxford, William Talbot, viewed George as a new David, taking as his text Psalm 118 – This is the day the Lord hath made – said to have been written by David after his anointing as King of Israel. It was also a moment to remember what Britain had avoided, said Bishop Talbot, accession to the throne of 'one educated in the Maxims of French Tyranny and the Principles of Popish Superstition' – an allusion to the exiled would-be James III.[2]

The domestic stability that the Hanoverians would eventually come to typify was not evident upon George I's accession. He brought with him two of his mistresses, known owing to their size as the elephant and the maypole, but left behind his wife, Sophia Dorothea, whom he had locked up years earlier after discovering her infidelity. There was trouble elsewhere too: Jacobite risings erupted sporadically; some Anglicans feared for the Church, because George was a Lutheran. The new King did, however, make an effort, and attended Anglican services regularly, even though that meant enduring lengthy sermons in a language he barely understood. He attended the ritual of the Royal Maundy in person in 1715. But from 1716 onwards he began making prolonged visits back to Hanover, and spent a quarter of his reign away from Britain.

The House of Hanover was dominated by rivalries between fathers and sons that began with George I and his son, the Prince of Wales, who was to succeed him in 1727. Unlike George I, who made limited effort to demonstrate any interest in his new kingdom, his heir and his wife, Caroline, sought to cultivate Britain, and their popularity grew.

This was also the era when politicians started to grow in influence, although the Whigs, who had played a central role in the Glorious Revolution of 1688, emerged as a political faction that had opposed absolute monarchy. Their rivals, the Tories, feared that George I would be a mere puppet King in the Whigs' hands and that the Church of England would lose its status and privilege. Despite this affinity to the Anglican Church, they became embroiled in the Jacobite uprising of 1715, a movement to restore the Catholic Stuarts. But within a short time, as the rivalries between George I and the Prince of Wales grew, they shifted their loyalties to the next King, flocking, as did dissident Whigs, to the rival court he had set up to his father's at his home, Leicester House, in what is now London's Leicester Square.

For thirteen years, Britain's monarchy was muted, Germanic, lacking in spectacle and, indeed, often absent. George I died, appropriately, in his electorate of Hanover, having never truly become a British king, although the ready acceptance of his son and heir as the next monarch suggests that he had made enough of an impact to have the House of Hanover embraced as the rulers of the kingdom of Great Britain. There was no suggestion that the House of Stuart should be restored.

George II was determined to be different from his father, and nothing demonstrated that more than his coronation. He had previous experience of a British crowning, having been assigned a special place at his father's. Though parliamentary politics were becoming increasingly important in Britain, and the notion of an absolutist monarchy had been exiled along with the Stuarts, there was still a strong belief that the hand of God was at work in the land, and Providence had ensured the House of Hanover had secured the throne. It was a belief that inspired the sermon of John Potter, Bishop of Oxford, at George II's coronation, who told the congregation that the King was 'seated on God's throne and is King for the Lord his God'.[3]

The coronation of 1727 was a far more spectacular event than the previous one in 1714. There was a grand procession, and Queen Caroline's dress was so encrusted with jewels that a pulley was set up to lift her skirt so that she could kneel down during parts of the ceremony.[4] But it was the music that made George's coronation truly spectacular. In 1714, at his father's crowning, there had been just twenty-four singers, but for George II's there were around two hundred as well as musicians – the largest group ever gathered in England up until then. It did not go entirely to plan – some of the regular choristers' voices had broken so others had to be brought in, and a Grinling Gibbons altarpiece obstructed their view of one another.

Handel wrote sacred music only for special occasions. He had been a favourite of George I, writing the 'Water Music' for him, but George II wanted a special piece for his crowning and chose Handel to compose four anthems for his ceremony, including a new version of 'Zadok the Priest', the verses from the first book of Kings that were used frequently in English coronations. Not that there was a lack of such music: Henry Lawes, a composer and countertenor, had belonged to the Chapel Royal in the time of Charles I and after the Restoration returned to the revived choir there, composing a version of 'Zadok the Priest' for Charles II's coronation, which was sung again at James II's. But that was a piece of music associated with the Stuart monarchs; Handel was chosen to represent the Hanoverians.

Just as there had been trepidation as England sought its new monarch, so Handel ratcheted up the tension with his ceaseless arpeggios, until he released it with a glorious burst of sound, before the acclamation of the King. It has been used as the anthem at every coronation since, linking the British monarch to King Solomon.

Like his father, George II spent much of his time visiting his Hanover electorate, leaving his wife Caroline as regent – much to the fury of his heir, Prince Frederick – to drive the business of government. But after the Glorious Revolution, the role of the monarchy was limited in Britain.

The couple's long marriage was typical of people of their class of their time: the King took many mistresses and the Queen was expected to endure it, while her husband failed to practise any form of discretion, particularly alienating his daughters by his behaviour. Queen Caroline was a popular consort, admired for her Protestantism and her moral example. She was also admired for having turned down the hand in marriage of Archduke Charles of Austria in 1704, a year before she married George, as it would have required her conversion from Lutheranism to Catholicism. John Gay had written of her in *A Letter to A Lady*, in the year of her husband's succession:

The pomp of titles easy faith might shake,
She scorn'd an empire for religion's sake:
For this, on earth, the British crown is giv'n,
And an immortal crown decreed in heav'n.

There was, however, no problem with the succession, as there had been with previous monarchs: George and Caroline were a fecund pair with eight surviving children. But there was a problem with the Prince of Wales, much of it owing to the emerging pattern of eighteenth-century politics. Critics of the King flocked around Prince Frederick, who was already not close to his parents; his grandfather had kept him in Hanover while he was growing up, until he eventually arrived in London in 1727. Nor had they grown closer by the time Frederick married Augusta and had children. Queen Caroline died in 1738 and was mourned by her husband, who ensured that their coffins, alongside one another in Westminster Abbey, did not have sides, so that their bones, as they became dust, would mingle together. He joined her twenty-three years later.

The Queen had not lived long enough to see her first grandson, also named George, who was born a month after the Queen's death. Their bereavement brought the King and his heir no closer and they continued to fight about their differences through the medium of politics and their rival camps. But Frederick, unlike his father, had learned from his own experience of childhood, and he and Augusta created a happy home for their children.

But the domestic idyll came to an end suddenly in 1751 when Frederick died, aged forty-four. He complained of a cold, but probably suffered from pneumonia. His own heir, George, was just thirteen years old. The death of his father, and then the decision of George II to make Augusta his regent, meant that the remainder of young George's childhood was cloistered, in the care of his mother. The jollity and entertainments of his father's time ground to a halt, with Augusta focused on George and his younger brother Edward's lessons, provided by a variety of tutors, among them aristocrats and members of the clergy, chosen by George II. Augusta saw the world as wicked and threatening and considered it her place to protect her children from its temptations. The solution was to isolate them; as Janice Hadlow says: 'Beyond the inner circle of the family, everyone's behaviour, motives and desires were suspect: no one was really to be trusted. Exposed to temptation, even her own sons might not have the inner strength to resist it. The preservation of an untested virtue, secured by isolation and retirement, was thus the key foundation of their upbringing.'[5]

Young George was seriously unprepared for his destiny – inheriting the throne from his grandfather – until his mother, without consulting the King, hired John Stuart, third Earl of Bute, who had known Prince Frederick, to be the boy's tutor. By 1755 he had supplanted all other influences in the eighteen-year-old's life.

Bute, a Stuart Scot, was suspected by some of being an advocate of kingly absolutist rule. But Bute's thinking was not a throwback to the past, more an interpretation of the ideas of Henry, Viscount Bolingbroke's volume, *The Idea of a Patriot King*, first published in 1749 and popular with George's father Frederick. A king, according to Bute, should rise above the knockabout of eighteenth-century party politics and, rather than be linked to one faction or another, transcend them. The King should be impartial and stand for the national good.

Bute saw the virtue of the King as key to his power and the source of his authority. These virtues were the same as those expected of all people: they were about moral behaviour and moral standards. The place where those moral standards were best expressed was within the family, the building-block of society, and so family life was an essential prerequisite for the King as the exemplar for his subjects. 'Virtue, religion, joined to nobility of sentiment,' said Bute, 'will support a prince better and make a people happier than all the abilities of an Augustus with the heart of Tiberius.'[6]

George, shy, with low self-esteem and not particularly bright, flowered under Bute, who gave him confidence and a belief that if kingship involved becoming an example of moral rectitude, he could do it. But he had little regard for the world, sharing his mother's and Bute's pessimism about it, and viewing it with alarm and apprehension. 'This is I believe the wickedest age that ever was seen; an honest man must wish himself out of it; I begin to be sick of things I daily see; for ingratitude, avarice and ambition are the principles men act by.'[7]

If George were to become the godly exemplar of virtue that he and Bute believed a king should be, and that moral behaviour was best encouraged through the family, then one thing above all else was vital: that the heir to the throne should take a wife and that wife should also be capable of being a moral compass for the children, including the one who would succeed next to the throne. But destiny intervened, and before he found her, his grandfather, George II, died on 25 October 1760 at the age of seventy-seven.

The new King George III made finding a new Queen the utmost priority. It was not an easy task: she had to be a Protestant, therefore ruling out many of the royal houses of Europe, and she had to match George's ideals regarding a strong religious sense, the importance of the royal family as a flagship for virtue, a sense of duty and seriousness of intent. This was not royalty as bejewelled icons of glamour: being Queen was more of a vocation.

Baron Munchausen, the Hanoverian minister in London, was dispatched to find the ideal bride, and his choices were rejected, until Munchausen and the King alighted upon Princess Charlotte of Mecklenburg-Strelitz. She was just seventeen years old, from a rural duchy the size of Sussex. Charlotte was intelligent and well read, but unchallenged intellectually, and unquestioningly embraced her parents' Lutheran religion, and she had a strong sense of duty. They both agreed to the dynastic marriage and only met for the first time on their wedding day. A fortnight later they were crowned in a ceremony that took place nearly a year after the old King had died – an indication of the importance the new monarch placed on having a wife by his side.

The coronation had been revised since the time of the Tudors and Stuarts; there was no lengthy procession from the Tower of London, through the City, to Westminster Abbey, with pageants and tableaux the day before. But the spectacle nevertheless brought people out into the streets, which were crammed with pedestrians, coaches and carriages. The service itself lasted five hours and turned into an event of great jollity, with those attending consuming large amounts of food and drink to sustain them. The Chapter of Westminster Abbey allowed 'Rooms of Entertainment' to be built alongside the church, and advertised, 'Seats are to be let in Westminster Abbey, from the West Door to the Choir. Rooms are built for with drawing, and the best refreshments provided, and every convenience studied that can make it fit for the receptions of Ladies and Gentlemen.'[8]

William Hickey, a lawyer, recorded how he and his household could not hear a word of the crowning ceremony, some distance below them, so they decided the anointing – the most sacred part of the ceremony – was an opportune moment to eat their lunch, as did many others: 'As many thousands were out of the possibility of hearing a single syllable, they took that opportunity to eat their meal, when the general clattering of knives, forks, plates and glasses that ensued, produced a most ridiculous effect, and a universal bout of laughter followed.'[9]

For the King and Queen, it was a shambles. Chairs for them to sit on had been forgotten, as had been the canopy to hold over them, and delays were caused by having to improvise. The Sword of State was forgotten too, and the Lord Mayor of London had to lend his for use instead.

After the service ended, the new King and Queen and the congregation headed to Westminster Hall for a banquet. Spectators watched from the balcony, and, with nothing to eat themselves, sent down baskets and handkerchiefs to be filled with food and drink from the loaded tables below.

George and Charlotte, when they finally retired to St James's Palace, opted for a supper of bread, milk and gruel. It was a simple meal, befitting a couple who wished for a future where they would set an example, not of glamour and extravagance but of moral probity, seriousness and family devotion.

George's marriage was of inevitable importance to the nation, as the children of it would secure the succession of the House of Hanover, thereby providing stability for their subjects. George and his wife believed that the monarch's secure and stable domestic life would ensure that he ruled as a good king and would set an example to other Britons. They were also offering a version of marriage that was somewhat novel, especially in more aristocratic circles.

Marriage was almost always for life in the eighteenth century, when divorce was almost unheard of. The wealthy, however, were able to disregard its conventions much more easily than others. Large houses and more travel enabled them greater opportunities for extra-marital liaisons to which others turned a blind eye. Economics made it vital for others that they made the right match – not just in terms of spinsterhood being such an impossible state for women, as Jane Austen highlighted, but because there was no way out for the incompatible who lived lower down the financial pecking order.

The reality, though, for many, was that marriage was not always joyous but a miserable life sentence. Someone who sought to overturn any cynicism about it and instead offer an idealised version of marriage was the Rev. Wetenhall Wilkes, who wrote a bestselling pamphlet in 1714 that described marriage as a harmonious partnership in which husband and wife sacrificed their individual needs and desires to create a successful union. This was not about a passionate romance but something steady and dutiful. Wilkes' preoccupation was shared by other writers and moralists at this time and, indeed, by the royal couple, who strived to create what might be called a companion marriage. This was how they presented themselves to the court and to the world, and their large brood of children only added to the image of domestic bliss.

Monarchs of this era often had large numbers of children, but not necessarily by their wives. Their mistresses shared the burden. George III was different: his fifteen offspring were all by Charlotte. That she survived them all is remarkable; even for the wealthy, childbirth could pose an enormous risk to the health and even the life of a woman. But for Charlotte, childbirth was not a private, intimate occasion. Members of the Cabinet and the Archbishop of Canterbury had the right to be present, and when her first child, a boy, was born in 1762, it was only after the Archbishop had seen him and made a statement, declaring that he was truly the son of the Queen, that her physician was allowed to examine her.

George and Charlotte's ideas about family and moral values also shaped the way they raised their children, and they believed that instructing them in Christian beliefs about right and wrong was essential for their development. The King and Queen were committed Anglicans, well aware of the oath they had made at the coronation to uphold the faith, and they were keen churchgoers, with George often attending daily. Given they thought they should influence the public by virtue of their good example, it was to be expected that they would think they should do the same for their children. This would lead to the children in turn becoming moral leaders. The most important aim of his children's education, according to George, was 'the making of them Christians and useful members of society', while for Charlotte, Christian faith was a source of solace: 'I am certain that without religion, none can be happy,' she wrote, 'for it is the true and only support in every situation of life in prosperity, and it keeps us within bounds as it tells us that the hand who gives can also take from us, and in our adversity, it supports us in our distress.'[10]

While the early years of the King's reign were marked by this stability at home, there was turmoil elsewhere, with a series of Prime Ministers who bickered with the sovereign, and growing unrest in the American colonies. The settlers there complained of the King's usurping of their rights and liberties in their American Declaration of Independence and complained he had sought to enslave them. In fact, the King acted as a constitutional monarch, supporting his government, but was devastated when the British lost the eight-year-long American War of Independence and gave up its colonies.

Despite the loss of America and the political turbulence of his first decades, George was a popular king. The people admired his family values and they appreciated his charitable endeavours – he was the first monarch to engage in such works and, in doing so, helped to carve out a niche for the Royal Family that continues to this day. He gave away around £14,000 a year to charitable causes – the equivalent of £1 million today – and supported many philanthropic ventures, particularly London's hospitals. He was also passionate about art, helping to found the Royal Academy, and about science. Frank Prochaska, who defines the idea of a welfare monarchy as seen in the twentieth and twenty-first centuries, traces its origins to the philanthropy of George and Caroline.[11]

But for all their efforts at forging the ideal God-fearing, dutiful family, it did not last. The King's family troubles began with his siblings, whose rackety lives were in sharp contrast to George and Charlotte's. There was trouble from Edward, whose reckless antics led to his disgrace at court. Caroline, George's younger sister, who had married the King of Denmark, was arrested for adultery and her lover executed. Henry, George's third brother, was sued over his adulterous affair at court and then married a widow considered beneath his station. George, determined to avoid scandal in the future, pushed through the Royal Marriages Act of 1772, which prevented any member of the Royal Family under the age of twenty-five marrying without the monarch's approval.

Rather than be a solution, this merely stored up trouble for the future. It would be the perfect excuse for royal seducers to ensnare young women and then explain that they could not marry. Among them was George's heir, another George, known as Prinny. Chief among his interests were wine and women, and they led him into debt and embarrassing scrapes: one woman, the actress Perdita Robinson, was paid off by the King when she threatened to publish Prinny's love letters. But when it came to another of Prinny's affairs, the problem was further complicated: not only was the woman concerned of lower rank than the Prince; not only was he too young to wed without his father's permission, but he was also in love with a Roman Catholic.

Ever since the Act of Settlement, passed in the aftermath of the Glorious Revolution and during the reign of William III and Mary II, royal heirs were barred from marrying a Roman Catholic. King George was also well aware of the commitment British Kings made to uphold the Protestant religion and that he and the House of Hanover owed their role as British monarchs to their Protestantism. Having his son involved with a Roman Catholic would disbar the Prince of Wales from the throne – but it would also be a PR disaster for the King.

The Prince of Wales, however, was besotted by the twice-widowed, amply bosomed and somewhat older Maria Fitzherbert. He wrote her reams of letters, pursued her ardently, and threatened suicide. His reaction when told by the King to avert disaster was to court it: he married Maria in secret in December 1785, in a church wedding conducted by an impecunious priest who did so in exchange for his debts being paid.

Keen to be near her, he set about building his pleasure dome, the Brighton Pavilion, where they could see one another away from prying London eyes. The marriage foundered as Prinny returned to his old ways: drinking, womanising, and getting deeper and deeper into debt.

It finally came to an end when Prinny, up to his eyes in debt, was persuaded to wed Princess Caroline of Brunswick in 1794, as her dowry would pay his vast debts of £600,000 – around £70 million today. The marriage went ahead in April 1795 and the only child of the relationship, Princess Charlotte, was born the following year. Prinny, however, had not forsworn Maria Fitzherbert completely, and in a will made within days of the birth of his daughter, he left all his worldly property to the woman he called 'my wife, the wife of my heart and soul' – Maria Fitzherbert. Not only Mrs Fitzherbert but also Pope Pius VII said that they were legally married. In the Catholic Church of St John the Baptist in Brighton, which Mrs Fitzherbert endowed and where she is buried, is a marble relief depicting her with three wedding rings for her three legitimate marriages.[12]

For George III, though, the marriage of his son to Princess Caroline must have come as a relief, even though the couple were ill suited and the marriage broke down. He had plenty of other matters to deal with. George III, when faced with requests to emancipate Catholics, would make only limited overtures and only if there was something in it for the country as a whole, rather than as an attempt to offer Catholics justice. The Catholic Relief Act of 1778, which led to Catholics being relieved of certain historical penalties, was a pragmatic response to the need for more soldiers. As the country faced growing pressure to find infantry to fight the American War of Independence, it became apparent that one way of securing more of them was to lift the oath soldiers had to swear – an oath that Catholics were precluded from attesting. The Act also included some other measures to help Catholics: functioning as a Catholic priest and running a Catholic school were both no longer punishable by life imprisonment, and Catholics could buy land and inherit it, just as their Protestant neighbours could. There were to be prayers for the King at Catholic services held by priests abiding by the law, although the Act did not enforce freedom of worship.

But the country faced turmoil once more as opponents of Catholicism, including Lord George Gordon, stoked up antipathy. Lord Gordon accused the King of complicity in giving consent to this Catholic Relief Bill. It led to a wave of anti-Catholic demonstrations known as the Gordon Riots, where protest turned quickly into violent rioting, with Parliament invaded and Newgate Prison burned to the ground. The death toll was around a thousand. For a few days London was at the mercy of the mob.

The Gordon Riots revealed a suspicion of Catholics still bubbling just beneath the surface of British life. They were handy scapegoats for those filled with a sense of grievance. During Lord Gordon's trial, following his arrest for treason after the riots – a charge on which he was acquitted – one of his legal defenders said, 'I will not call up from the graves of martyrs all the precious blood that has been spilt in this land to save its established government and its reformed religion from the secret villainy and the open force of Papists.'[13]

Another Bill was passed by Parliament in 1791, continuing the relief that began with the 1778 Act: celebration of the Mass was made entirely legal and the Penal Laws were finally abolished. This easing of legal strictures may well have had an impact on the general population, but something else did far more profoundly. From across the English Channel came refugees from the Terror – Catholics, including priests and nuns, fleeing the French Revolution and the loathing of its leaders for the Church. Some of those who crossed to England were members of recusant families here, who had been in France for their Catholic education or had joined convents and seminaries there. Catholics and Britons now had something in common: fear of the guillotine, the tumbrils and the tricoteuses.

Among the refugees who landed in England were a group of nuns who landed at Shoreham in 1792 and found dozens of local people waiting to greet them on the beach. Prinny, who had built his Brighton Pavilion just along the coast, offered them help by way of money and the aid of his physician. At one point he met the nuns himself, and by his side was the Catholic widow he had secretly married – Maria Fitzherbert.[14] Bit by bit, Catholics were edging closer to acceptability in society and even to the throne. But the King himself would take more persuading. The sticking point was the sacred vow he had made at his crowning.

When another Bill was put forward in 1795 in favour of Catholic emancipation, the King made it clear that he was a defender of the faith – of the Protestant faith:

> A sense of religious as well as particular duty made me, from the moment I mounted the throne, consider the Oath that the wisdom of our forefathers had enjoined the Kings of this realm to take at their Coronation, and enforced by the obligation of instantly following it in the course of the ceremony with taking the Sacrament, as so binding a religious obligation on me to maintain the fundamental maxims on which our Constitution is placed, namely the Church of England being the established one, and that those who hold employments in the State must be members of it, and consequently obliged not only to take Oaths against Popery, but to receive the Holy Communion agreeable to the rites of the Church of England.[15]

By the time George was under pressure again to further liberate Catholics, he consulted the Lord Chief Justice Lord Kenyon and the Archbishop of Canterbury. They were unanimous that he could not repeal any laws discriminating against Catholics – the Act of Supremacy, the Test Acts, the Act of Settlement, the Act of Uniformity – without contravening his coronation oath. George III was to never change his stance, even when emancipation was due to follow the Act of Union with Ireland in 1801 – a stubbornness that was to cost William Pitt his premiership.

There had been simmering resentment among Catholics in Ireland for some time, and fears that it could lead to large-scale revolt and even a deal with the French, newly rid of their monarchy and now riven by revolution. Republican groups in Ireland were already seeking support from the French. Pitt's solution was to create a fully united Britain and Ireland, but that would require Catholic representation in Parliament in Westminster. The Act of Union gave George the title of King of the United Kingdom of Great Britain and Ireland, while an alternative might have been Emperor of the British Isles. George had been willing to consider emancipation for the Irish Catholics as Pitt's practical solution, but extending it to those in Britain was a step too far for him.

The levee at St James's Palace was a moment when politicians, diplomats and members of the military could be presented to and converse with the sovereign. It could be convivial; it could be concerning. On 28 January, for the government and for Catholics hoping for further reform, it was catastrophic. George III used the occasion to warn that anyone who even proposed Catholic emancipation would be his personal enemy. It would be a betrayal of his coronation oath. Pitt tried to persuade the King otherwise, but the King was having none of it; he feared the destruction of the England he had sworn to uphold, and Pitt quit in February 1801. Without the explicit support of the King, Catholic emancipation in Britain slid off the political agenda – for the time being.

While domestic politics tested George – and he was traumatised to lose his American colonies – the monarchy in Britain seemed safe. There appeared little chance of the British royals being led to the guillotine, as had happened to Louis XVI and Marie Antoinette of France in 1793, although the executions had certainly sent a shiver down the collective spine of the court. George, well aware of the threat the revolutionary French posed as they went to war with Britain, condemned them as savages who were determined 'to destroy the foundations of every civilized state'.[16] The eighteen-year-long war with the French was to cost Britain dear – in terms of both manpower and depletion of the treasury. George, though, was admired for his simplicity of lifestyle and his domestic set-up. Farmer George, as he was often dubbed, was dedicated to Britain, rather than Hanover, as his predecessor kings were, and was liked for it.

Yet there were serious troubles. This was the era when newspapers and journals grew in number and influence, and while caricaturists like George Cruikshank gently mocked Farmer George, there were also more vicious attacks on his foppish son, Prinny, and his extravagances. Coverage of the royals became a staple of the popular prints, and continues to be, with the monarchy having to both learn to live with it and adapt by developing its own PR machinery.

There was also the state of the King's health, both physical and mental, which led to his collapse, first in 1788 and again in 1810. The first was short and engendered great sympathy in the country. But the second, shortly after he appeared in public for the last time to mark the Golden Jubilee of his accession, was profound and devastating. The last decade of his life was spent as an invalid, and he eventually became deaf, blind, and unable to walk, and lived with dementia.

George's reign saw the emergence of the House of Commons as a greater force and the retreat of the monarchy from politics. In place of that influence, George created a different power, shaped by the connections of the Crown with the virtues he believed so important: nurturing of the family, duty, personal morality and charitable endeavour. It was a view of monarchy that is still in evidence today, as well as the need to proffer a public face: George would make visits around the country. The connection also grew between the monarch's life and church commemorations, with services held in the Church of England to mark his recovery from illness and his jubilees. *The Times* newspaper reported that there were services across the land to mark's George's fiftieth anniversary, not just in the Church of England but elsewhere too, 'among the various classes of Dissenters of all persuasions, we have heard of no exception to the general loyalty and piety of the day. The cathedral, the abbey, the parochial church, the meeting house of the dissenter, the chapel of the Methodist and the Catholic and the synagogue were alike opened.'[17]

*The Gentleman Magazine* and other journals published a gushing, celebratory Ode for the Royal Jubilee, by William Thomas Fitz-Gerald:

The fiftieth sun's autumnal ray,
Beholds the mildest Sov'reign sway,
A People, happy, great and free;
That People, with one common voice,
From Thames to Ganges' shores rejoice,
In Universal Jubilee!

Fitz-Gerald went on:

While half the world in shackles groan
Beneath a cruel Tyrant's throne;
Drench'd in an hundred people's blood!
Britons, with glowing bosoms, sing
May God preserve our PATRIOT KING![18]

Within a year of fireworks and feasting for George III's Golden Jubilee, his illness became so incapacitating that in February 1811, his son George, Prince of Wales, became regent. Kingship – or at least regency – seemed not to his taste and he soon sank into his usual dissolute ways. The once handsome Prinny was now an overweight forty-eight-year-old addict, hooked on drink, drugs (in his case laudanum) and large amounts of food. His official marriage to Caroline of Brunswick had been a disaster, but their one conjugal encounter on the night of their wedding had produced a daughter, Charlotte.

The young Princess was in direct line to the throne after her father and was a popular figure – a popularity that grew with her wedding to Prince Leopold of Saxe-Coburg-Saalfeld in May 1816. Within the year she gave birth to a son. But the child was stillborn and Charlotte herself died soon after, aged just twenty-one. There was an outpouring of grief, rarely seen, although replicated some 180 years later for the death of Diana, Princess of Wales – two beautiful young women, cut off in their prime. Princess Lieven, wife of the Russian ambassador, wrote of the reaction to the death of Charlotte:

It is impossible to find in the history of nations or families an event which had evoked such heartfelt mourning. One met in the streets

> people of every class in tears, the churches full at all hours, the shops shut for a fortnight (an eloquent testimony from a shop-owning community) and everyone, from the highest to the lowest, in a state of despair which it is impossible to describe.[19]

Diana, however, had already secured the succession with her two surviving sons. The death of Princess Charlotte and her child once more raised questions about who might inherit the throne in years to come: the Prince Regent, yes, but then who? His younger brother, William, and then all became uncertain.

As for Charlotte's mother, George wanted nothing to do with her – so much so, in fact, that when his father finally died in 1820 and he acceded to the throne, his first ambition was to secure a divorce from her by his government passing a Bill to dissolve the marriage. Rather than present evidence of the Queen's behaviour to the House of Lords, it sought to persuade the new King George IV that this would be a mistake. Eventually the Bill was dropped, but George was determined that his wife should not be crowned by his side, and on his coronation day he ordered security men, dressed as pages, to be on duty outside Westminster Abbey, ready to exclude unwanted guests – including the Queen.

Two people were on George's mind as he prepared for his coronation. One was Caroline, and thwarting her, and the other was Napoleon. The Corsican had made an extraordinary journey – from an island off the coast of southern France to becoming the country's most successful general. In 1804, he had declared himself Emperor of the French. He was crowned in Notre Dame Cathedral on 2 December, with Pope Pius VII in attendance, but Napoleon snatched the crown from him and crowned himself. The ceremony was full of pomp and set a new standard for grandiose statement.

By the time of George IV's coronation, Napoleon was yesterday's man: defeated at Waterloo by the British and their allies, loathed by those he had once conquered and in exile on St Helena. But for George, he had been an obsession. He had noted how Napoleon had rebuilt Paris into an imperial capital, and the Prince of Wales wished to do the same in London. He brought in John Nash to sweep away medieval warrens and in their place to build a theatrical stage set worthy of a Prince Regent and his processions: the crescents near Regent's Park, Regent Street and Pall Mall.

The obsession continued even after Napoleon's exile. The new George IV remembered what the French autocrat had achieved with his coronation and sought to give a similar message to the world – a message of power and influence. He even sent his tailor to Paris to produce a copy of Napoleon's coronation robe – except it was then to be bigger, grander and heavier. It took eight train bearers to carry it. He looked, wrote painter Robert Huish, as he arrived in his velvet, ruffles and feathers in Westminster Hall before the coronation in the Abbey, 'like some gorgeous bird of the east'.[20]

However much he was influenced by French ideas, George IV's coronation focused on Britain: his robes included motifs of the Scottish thistle, the English rose and the Irish shamrock. Standard bearers carried the flags of Ireland and Scotland as well as the Union flag and the Royal Standard, plus that of Hanover. The procession included Scottish and Irish peers as well as members of the Orders of the Thistle and the Shamrock, and members of both the English and Scottish episcopacy. The oath was altered from the previous ceremony's 'the people of this kingdom of Great Britain' to 'this united Kingdom of Great Britain and Ireland', and 'the Church of England' to 'the Church of England and Ireland'. Royal dukes and duchesses wore diamond coronets; others were dressed in velvet and ruffles as befitted a Tudorbethan spectacle ordered by the King.

The coronation was followed by fireworks in Hyde Park, with trees and the Serpentine illuminated. At one end of the water, over the cascade, there was an image of the King in a chariot drawn by white horses, and the temple opposite was surmounted by an imperial crown. There were other celebratory events across the country, while George also called for a festival booklet to record the day, but delays, including the artists producing their records of the day, meant that it was not published until three years later, and more deluxe editions were printed even later than that. Hand-coloured plates were decorated with gold. George wanted the whole event reported: journalists were accorded seats at the crowning.

Not that everything went to plan. Despite George's efforts in the preparation, including printed instructions for people involved with a list of their duties, the peerage left the Abbey before the King returned from St Edward's shrine, so that he walked past empty seats covered in litter. And despite the King's efforts to get rid of his wife, she turned up at Westminster Abbey for the coronation. After being refused entry at both the doors to the East Cloister and the West Cloister, she tried to get in via Westminster Hall but was thwarted again. The door was slammed in her face on the orders of the Lord Chamberlain. She tried a final time to enter through a door near Poets' Corner but was asked to leave. Within three weeks she was dead, some claiming she was poisoned. Fearing unrest, the police had her funeral cortège diverted so that it would avoid London and the grieving crowds en route to Harwich and a ship to take her back to her home state of Brunswick.

The treatment and death of Caroline, which had traumatised the nation, might have been disastrous for George IV at the start of his reign, but his charm offensive of a tour of his nations won them over, including the Scots, who had long been averse to the Hanoverians after the ousting of the Stuarts. But he failed to win over governments, given his lack of interest in work. The passion he had for the arts, including writers and artists, was in sharp contrast to his lack of interest in politics.

Nor did he have his father's religious sensibilities – except for one. Like George III, he was alarmed by Catholic emancipation, despite his sometime sympathy for the Catholic cause: in 1814 when the allies met in London to celebrate the defeat of France and the abdication of Napoleon, the Pope sent Cardinal Consalvi as a delegate – the first cardinal to set foot on English soil since the time of the Tudors – and the then Prince Regent's sympathetic ear and friendliness to the cardinal gave Catholics hope for their emancipation. But by the last years of his decade-long reign, George IV's view had hardened.

Matters came to a head in 1827 when the Duke of Wellington became Prime Minister. The hero of Waterloo – the man who had trounced Napoleon whose coronation had so inspired George IV – was a formidable opponent when it came to Catholic emancipation. The most English of heroes, the man who had saved the nation, was in fact Anglo-Irish, and became convinced that only the repeal of discriminatory laws could save England and Ireland from war.

The unfairness of the laws restricting Catholics was highlighted in 1828 when Daniel O'Connell was elected MP for Clare. He was the first Catholic to be returned in a parliamentary election since 1688, and it made an issue of the Oath of Supremacy by which parliamentarians had to swear that the monarch was the Supreme Governor of the Church of England. MPs also had to swear an anti-Catholic oath. During his election campaign, O'Connell read it out: 'That the sacrifice of the Mass and the invocation of the Blessed Virgin Mary and other saints, as now practised in the Church of Rome, are impious and idolatrous.' O'Connell told the crowd that he 'would rather be torn limb from limb than take it'.[21] O'Connell was duly elected. The enthusiasm with which his triumph was met – sixty thousand escorted him into Ennis, the County Clare market town, and even the Irish troops saluted him – after his victory was a sign to politicians such as Robert Peel, Home Secretary, that change might be needed. Catholic emancipation was the lesser of two evils, if the other were civil war in Ireland. Many years later, in his memoirs published after his death, Peel explained that his change of mind was because 'I was swayed by no fear except of public calamity'.[22]

Ireland and Britain were at a crossroads, and if Wellington and Peel were to take one path, they knew it would incur the displeasure of the King. By the autumn of 1828, George, well aware of what was afoot, was urging the dissolution of Parliament so that more Protestants in favour of the status quo could be voted in at a general election. Wellington rejected the idea, but he had other problems too. Not only was the King opposed to emancipation and the lay voices in favour of it, but so was the Church of England. Lengthy meetings between Wellington and the Archbishop of Canterbury failed to change the Anglican bishops' minds.

The conflict between the Prime Minister and the King went to the wire. The night before the Catholic Relief Bill was to be put to the House of Commons, Wellington, Peel and the Lord Chancellor, Lord Lyndhurst, spent six hours talking to the King about it. Drinking brandy throughout, George insisted it went against his sacred coronation oath. He even suggested he might abdicate. The three ministers said they would all resign if the King thwarted the Bill.

After the politicians left, the King dined and listened to his private secretary, Sir William Knighton, and other intimates. They persuaded him that summoning another government was a fantasy. The King wrote a note to the Duke: 'I have decided to yield my opinion to that which is considered by the Cabinet to be in the immediate interests of the country. Under the circumstances you have my consent to proceed as you propose with the measure . . . God knows what pain it costs me to write these words. G.R.'[23]

On 13 April, as he signed the Catholic Relief Act, he wrote that he had 'never before fixed his name, with pain or regret, to any act of the Legislature'.[24] The Act was not only a means of liberating the King's subjects – and there would be increasing numbers of Catholics among the British monarch's subjects around the globe as Britain's empire expanded – it was also highly significant as a sign that Britain had become a constitutional monarchy, and in a crisis between King and ministers, the monarch backed down, for the sake of stability, from the one thing he was supposed to stand for. Nevertheless, he still resented the Act: when the results of the vote for it were known, he remarked: 'Oh the Duke of Wellington is King of England, O'Connell is King of England and I suppose I am only considered Dean of Windsor.'[25]

There was a remarkable paradox in this landmark moment in the history of the British monarchy: it had broken away from Rome to limit the Church's power and snatch power for itself. Now its own power was limited as the monarchy had to accept that the liberties it had trampled all over – those of its Catholic subjects – should be restored. But this was a different world, with new allegiances being forged. A year after the Catholic Relief Act was passed, the Waterloo Chamber was completed in Windsor Castle. It was built to honour those who had come together to defeat Napoleon, and among those that George commissioned Thomas Lawrence to portray on its walls were Pope Pius VII and George's one-time friend, Secretary of State of the Papal States, Cardinal Ercole Consalvi. In the world of realpolitik, rather than ideals, one's enemy's enemy becomes one's friend – even for kings.

George IV, already suffering from considerable ill-health at the time of the Catholic Relief Bill, lasted just one more year before he died. After the death of Princess Charlotte, his brothers had been urged to secure the succession by marrying and having children. But first, before any nephew or niece might succeed George, it was the turn of his brother William IV to accede. William, at sixty-four, was the oldest heir to come to the throne, and his accession was caused not only by the death of Princess Charlotte but also by the death of Frederick, Duke of York, the brother between him and George, in 1827.

A former sailor and somewhat impecunious for a royal, William refused to move to Buckingham Palace and stayed in Clarence House. George IV may have had little spirituality, but he did take his coronation seriously, both in terms of demanding the most extravagant show possible and battling with Wellington over his sacred oath. William had even less time for religion. He viewed the coronation as a waste of time and money and suggested he merely take the oaths to the Protestant religion and have done with it. On a visit to Parliament for its dissolution, he grabbed the crown while in the robing room of the House of Lords, put it on his head and said to Lord Grey, the Prime Minister, 'The Coronation is over.'[26]

Horrified politicians urged him to go through with the real thing in Westminster Abbey, but it was an abbreviated version, nicknamed the Half-Crownation, and William allowed the sailor in him to come to the fore: he mocked the seriousness of the occasion during it. But later he admitted that there was a transcendent element to the coronation service that changed him, as he realised the enormity of what had befallen him: 'It was a great moment when I actually felt the crown descending upon me and touching my temples. I could not restrain a thrill, but not of joy . . . of awe, at the responsibilities Almighty God had been pleased to put upon me.'[27]

William IV's reign saw power slip further away from the monarch and constitutional monarchy gain an ever-greater foothold in Britain, with the Reform Act of 1832 becoming law as politicians sought to use their power, not the King's, to get legislation through the House. The future of the monarchy was to be seen in the work of his consort, Queen Adelaide, who focused on philanthropy and gave away much of her income to charitable causes. Adelaide, however, could not secure the future for her own line. Her two children died in infancy. William had many others, but all illegitimate, and so the heir was the daughter of his brother Edward, Duke of Kent, who had predeceased him in 1820.

It was on 20 June 1837 that William died. His niece Victoria had turned eighteen less than a month earlier, meaning she could reign in her own right, without a regent. Her long reign was to see the Royal

Family become a template for domestic rectitude – much as it had been in the time of George III – and to stand for particular moral and spiritual Christian values. It was also an era that saw the development of a fascination with death, its rituals and memorials, not seen before in a Protestant nation, and to place the monarchy and religious ceremonial at the heart of expressions of nationhood.

While a suspicion about Rome and an inherent belief in the Church of England as both an established Church and an innately superior one remained, the conflicts over Roman Catholicism would no longer dominate in the rest of the nineteenth century. Instead, what mattered was duty, self-sacrifice, service, dignity and charity – values many people still associate with monarchy today, and certainly did so with Elizabeth II. Churchgoing would be strongly associated with Victoria, much as it had been with George III and would be again with Elizabeth II. And in the public's mind, churchgoing would form a key part of royal ceremonial, whether regular events such as memorials for wars or thanksgiving for royal jubilees. It was an era when religion formed an absolutely essential part of the monarch's life, in terms of both her own personal faith and what she represented to the nation and how she communicated with it. In that sense, it was part of her soft power.

Victoria's reign began with prayer – an indication of her strong faith, imbued by her devout evangelical mother who brought her up after the early death of her father. She learnt the news of her accession when she was woken in the early hours by the Lord Chamberlain and Archbishop of Canterbury, whom she asked to pray for her.

For an eighteen-year-old like Victoria, the coronation ceremony must have seemed daunting. She was prepared for it by her Prime Minister, Lord Melbourne, who thought she might find so many high-ranking churchmen intimidating, so he entertained her with tales about them, such as saying that the Bishop of Durham was maladroit and never knew what was taking place. He also made light-hearted fun of the setting of the Abbey, especially St Edward's Chapel which he said was unlike any chapel he had seen, for its altar was covered with sandwiches and bottles of wine.[28]

Victoria's coronation was recorded in a series of paintings, including an official coronation portrait, soon to become a tradition. Like previous monarchs, she wore clothes akin to priestly vestments, including a supertunica. She also wore a colobium sindonis, a simple white linen shift that symbolises divesting oneself of all worldly vanity as one stands before God for anointing as sovereign.

The government agreed that this coronation should not be as grandiose as George IV's nor as parsimonious as William IV's, so they opted for a middle way, spending £79,000, compared to William's mere £30,000 and George's extravagant £240,000.

Liturgically, though, it followed William IV's, with anthems deleted and other parts of the text removed. Victorian ideas of delicacy were perhaps the reason for other changes: only Victoria's head and palms were anointed, not her breast, and nor did she pursue the centuries-old tradition of kissing the bishops after the benediction and before the enthronement. In the House of Lords, some peers complained that the procession of a young girl in public would expose her to the public gaze in an unacceptable way.

As always seems to happen with coronations, mistakes were made. When it came to putting the monarch's ring on her finger, the Archbishop of Canterbury botched it, pushing the ring down on the ring finger, hurting the Queen and making it almost impossible for her to later remove it. One peer rolled down the steps as he attempted to pay homage.

Some aspects of the ceremony were timeless: items of the regalia were used, including the two sceptres, one with a cross and one with a dove, and the orb. But the Crown of St Edward, used at the climax of the coronation ceremony for the actual moment of crowning, was thought too heavy for Victoria to wear. Instead, a special, lighter crown was made for her, using gems from the state crown of George I: the Black Prince's Ruby and St Edward's Sapphire, set into the cross and thought to be a jewel from either the ring or coronet of Edward the Confessor. Both are now in the Imperial State Crown, which has been worn since by British monarchs at the end of their coronation service, after Holy Communion, and is worn at the State Opening of Parliament.

As had become tradition, Handel's anthem, 'Zadok the Priest', was sung. Indeed, there was a great deal of Handel, including the 'Hallelujah Chorus', which was the only time it was used at a coronation. Just one new piece of music was played: the anthem 'This Is the Day the Lord Hath Made' by William Knyvett, composer to the Chapels Royal.

Victoria's coronation not only marked a new age but also reflected it. After the Reform Act of 1832 had given more power to Parliament and limited that of the monarch, it was decided that five hundred MPs should attend alongside the peerage. Then there was the public. The development of the railways made it much easier for people to travel to London for the coronation than ever before, and new road surfaces made the movement of traffic much smoother. There was a ready audience for a public spectacle and much more ease in providing it.

The processional route was designed to allow as many spectators as possible to view their sovereign. It followed a roughly circular route from the newly completed Buckingham Palace, past Hyde Park Corner and along Piccadilly, St James's Street, Pall Mall, Charing Cross and Whitehall, to Westminster Abbey: the journey took a whole hour. Victoria's procession included the Lifeguards, foreign ambassadors, two bands of the Household Brigade, carriages bearing members of the Royal Family and household, besides a hundred Yeomen of the Guard.

The Queen herself was in what is often called the coronation coach – the State Coach of George III, used for all coronations since. There was scaffolding for spectators all along the route. An estimated 400,000 people poured into central London for the event and were entertained by fireworks and a Hyde Park funfair. The monarch had been seen and the public entertained – both vital for a modern monarchy.[29]

Modern or not, every monarchy needs to consider the means to its continuation, and that usually means succession through the monarch's own children. Ruling alone is also a lonely burden, and few have done so in Britain – Elizabeth I because she avoided marriage, George IV because he had no wish to have his estranged wife as his consort, and Edward VIII for just a year until he refused to continue without Wallis, the wife of his choosing. Victoria, in her first years as Queen, depended on the counsel of Lord M, her Prime Minister Lord Melbourne, and at first she fretted, like Elizabeth I before her, that a husband would seek to curtail her power. But alone on the throne, she desired companionship. There was also the matter of children and the succession.

Chief matchmaker was Uncle Leopold, who had been married to Princess Charlotte, whose premature death after childbirth had in effect made way for Victoria to come to the throne. He was also the elder brother of Victoria's mother, Princess Victoria of Saxe-Coburg-Saalfeld. Leopold had been invited to become King of the newly independent Belgians in 1830 and he knew his way around the monarchies and grand families of Europe. Among them was the House of Saxe-Coburg and Gotha, to which he was himself connected, and Leopold was uncle to Prince Albert as well as to Victoria. A firm believer of using dynastic marriage ties to bind political allegiances, Leopold encouraged Victoria to consider Albert.

The pair had previously met when Victoria was seventeen but they met again in October 1839, two years after her accession, this time with marriage on everyone's mind. Within days they were engaged, and the wedding took place in the Chapel Royal at St James's Palace: royal weddings were then not public events. The marriage both reflected Victoria's superior position as Queen regnant and did not: she asked Albert to marry her, rather than the other way round, but when the Archbishop of Canterbury asked if he should omit the then standard promise of the wife to obey her husband, she declined, saying she was marrying as a woman, not a queen.

As a wife, Victoria deferred to her husband, reinforcing concepts of the conventional domestic power structure. But she came to defer to him in her role as monarch too, or at least to involve him to a considerable degree, whereas prior to their marriage she had placed restrictions on his future influence. She appointed him as her private secretary and, given the considerable amount of time she spent pregnant – the couple had nine children between 1840 and 1857 – she relied on him considerably for advice and, indeed, ideas. Ever since the death of Princess Charlotte following a difficult labour, royal mothers had been treated as invalids, and Victoria was often in low spirits after childbirth – today it would be called postnatal depression. This meant she leaned on Albert, not only as head of the family but also to help her with the business of monarchy. 'If only I could make him king!' she once said.[30]

To the public, Victoria and Albert and their brood offered a spectacle of domestic bliss, a message that this was Christianity writ large. To the newspaper editor W. T. Stead, writing at the time of her Diamond Jubilee, Victoria was 'the head and ideal exemplar of the family', which was 'the broadest and most catholic Church of all'.[31] Indeed, Victoria and Albert regarded the family and the home, rather than the Church, as the centre of religious faith, and it was their means of shaping a moral monarchy.

This is not to say that Victoria ignored her role regarding the institution of the Church. In the first meeting of her Privy Council on 10 June 1837, she had said it would be 'her increasing study to maintain the Reformed religion as by law established, securing at the same time to all the full enjoyment of religious liberty', and that she was also pledged to maintain the Church of Scotland.[32] But as the power of the monarchy had become limited following the reforms of the years prior to Victoria's accession, she found new ways to uphold that religion, and one, as W. T. Stead pointed out, was to be an exemplar of domestic virtue.

This particular virtue was given visual expression at key moments in the family's religious life. The christenings of her children were captured in paintings, and those of Vicky, her firstborn, and Albert Edward, her first son and heir, by Charles Leslie and George Hayter respectively show the newly acquired Lily Font, a transportable piece of ecclesiastical equipment. It was used for both, as it would be used frequently for future royal baptisms. All Christians might receive the same baptism, but it did not mean that royal babies would have to come into contact with a font used for hoi polloi.

The importance of royal baptism was emphasised in the change of venue for the heir to the throne. While Princess Vicky was baptised in Buckingham Palace's throne room, the young Albert Edward, Prince of Wales, was christened in St George's Chapel, Windsor, following the urging of the Bishop of London, who advised the then Prime Minister, Sir Robert Peel, of the wisdom of a public ceremonial.

The children's confirmations were also important, with photographer William Bambridge commissioned to take later posed photographs of them in his studio in their confirmation clothes

– white dresses for the girls. Victoria would later distribute copies of the images to friends and relatives, and paintings too would be commissioned. Royal religion was becoming more of a public spectacle – even the most personal of sacramental occasions.

Later in Victoria's reign, the weddings of her children would reinforce the role of the Queen and her family as exemplars, and also strengthen public interest and support in the monarchy. There was particular interest in the marriage of the Prince of Wales to Princess Alexandra in 1863, with huge crowds gathering when she arrived on board the yacht *Victoria and Albert* in Gravesend, Kent, in 1863. Churchmen preached on the wedding as a symbol of God's bond with his people. In 1893, when Victoria's grandson Prince George, Duke of York – later George V – married Princess May of Teck, one Anglican wrote, 'The Christian home, whether for Prince or Peasant, is the most sacred spot on earth.'[33]

Prince Albert not only helped Victoria create this domestic idyll, but also shaped her thinking on religion. Although Victoria was herself brought up in the Church of England, her parents had married in a Lutheran service, given her mother's German background – a background shared by Albert, who hailed from Saxe-Coburg, a stronghold of Protestantism. According to Michael Ledger-Lomas, a Victorian specialist, 'Marriage to Albert changed Victoria's Protestantism, making her conscious of a wider Protestant world beyond Britain's shores.'[34]

Victoria's thinking was not, however, as low church as this might suggest. She was influenced by Samuel Wilberforce – the clergyman son of the slavery abolitionist, William – who published an anthology of the work of Anglican divines who argued that grace acquired through the sacraments was vital to one's spiritual life; Victoria was a regular Communicant.

However, much as she was happy to demonstrate her family's faith through visual records of their devotional rites of passage, Victoria also liked her own sacramental life to be private. She was distressed by the prying attentions of the public. At one point, tourists started attending services at Crathie Church, near Balmoral, armed with opera glasses, so prayer services moved inside Balmoral. Services were also held in private at Windsor, with Prince Albert later commissioning private chapels at both Buckingham Palace and

Windsor, with the private chapel in the castle later used by Elizabeth II for receiving Holy Communion. Like her great-great-grandmother Victoria, there were certain moments that she felt should be kept private (see chapter five).

Balmoral, which Victoria and Albert bought in 1848, was much loved by the couple, and their annual holidays there took them to Crathie Church regularly too. Senior Anglican churchmen were affronted that the Queen attended the Presbyterian Church and that she would eventually receive Communion there. Her private secretary, Sir Henry Ponsonby, recorded that she did so despite objections from the Archbishop of Canterbury, the Dean of Westminster and the Dean of Windsor and that information about it was kept out of the Court Circular.[35] Victoria developed a great liking for Scottish preachers, and while she usually indicated that she liked sermons to be kept short and orthodox, there were Scots she was happy to listen to for forty-five minutes or more. Church of Scotland ministers provided her with a combination of 'liberal broad churchmanship and muscular Christianity'.[36]

At her accession, Victoria had pledged to maintain the Church of Scotland, but in the 1840s when evangelicals of the Kirk wanted legislation to take patronage rights away from the aristocracy and vest them in congregations, Victoria seemed surprised that she was not head of the Church of Scotland. She was also concerned that the Church of Scotland alienated aristocrats, who left it to become Episcopalians, and thus caused the Church of Scotland to be left to the working class. She saw the Church of Scotland as 'the real and true stronghold of Protestantism', and was alarmed when William Gladstone and his Liberal Party were re-elected in 1879, fearing he would disestablish the Church of Scotland. In 1874, the Church Patronage (Scotland) Act transferred control over the appointment of church ministers to congregations, which meant that Victoria was unable to pick the new minister of Crathie in 1897. The congregation voted against her candidate, even though she had funded a new church building at Crathie in 1893, the first one paid for by a monarch since the Reformation.[37]

In England, Victoria of course worshipped as an Anglican, but that Church was far from monochrome, riven by debate over liturgy and theology from the 1840s onwards, articulated in the Tracts for the Times, published from the early days of Victoria's reign. Known both as Tractarians and members of the Oxford Movement, the advocates for change argued that Anglicanism had lost devotional and liturgical customs and that they should be restored, bringing it closer to the Roman Catholic Church and the Church of England of earlier times. The Tractarians' idealisation of the celibate religious life, which resulted in the development of Anglican religious orders, was unpopular with other Anglicans, who argued that marriage and the home was the highest form of Christian vocation. Victoria, Albert and their children were highlighted by them as living the true Christian life.

Victoria was warned by several of her Prime Ministers – Melbourne, Peel and Lord John Russell – that the Tractarians would damage the Church of England and also cause wider tension, with their antipathy to dissenters. Her core conviction was that faith flourished best in established Churches. As monarch and Supreme Governor of the Church of England, she had the power to restrict the Tractarians' growth by working to deny them bishoprics, university chairs and crown livings. She was also concerned about extreme evangelicals, and told Benjamin Disraeli that appointing broad church bishops was essential to the Church of England: 'It is by such appointments alone that we can hope to strengthen the tottering fabric of the established church. The extreme evangelical school do the established church as much harm as the high church.'[38]

But thwarted by the Queen and by bishops who also declined to offer them popular livings, many Tractarians ended up working in the slums, where they proved both effective and influential, developing a critique of British society. In this sense, Victoria, in trying to stem their influence, helped them find other means of making an impact. The concern felt about the growing influence of Catholic liturgy was reflected in the Public Worship Regulation Act of 1874, which removed Catholic rituals from Anglican services; the Queen strongly supported it. The Act shocked many people for its interference in worship; many clergymen were investigated and five eventually imprisoned.

Victoria's concerns about the need to uphold the Protestant religion, which she had vowed to protect at her coronation, was evident in her own diaries, where she wrote of her anxiety at 'efforts at Romanizing forms and doctrines'.[39] She may well have been concerned, too, that Anglican 'Romanizing' was a Trojan horse, and would lead to converts to the Church of Rome. Certainly, the converts had increased following the Catholic Relief Act 1829. Then in 1850 came Pius IX's papal bull, which led to the restoration of the Roman Catholic hierarchy in England which had been extinguished at the time of Elizabeth I. As well as Anglican converts, there was a growing population of Irish immigrants bolstering the Roman Catholic Church in England.

Pius' move was seen in many British circles as papal aggression, with *Punch* magazine publishing a cartoon of him as Guy Fawkes – as if the gentle Pio Nono were a terrorist threatening the institutions of this nation. Lord Shaftesbury, the social reformer, politician, evangelical Anglican and firm opponent of the Oxford Movement, complained that Pope Pius was 'usurp[ing] the functions of our Royal Mistress'.[40]

Victoria's relations with Catholics were always complicated by the situation in Ireland, whose population was first suspicious of the British Queen and later hostile, over the Famine. She was concerned about the influence of Catholic priests, who contested the Union and approved of the non-denominational Queen's College in Belfast to foster the education of lay Catholics.

Victoria's last visit to Dublin came in 1900, after Irish Roman Catholics had boycotted her Diamond Jubilee. The primary intention of her visit was to thank soldiers who had served in the Second Boer War, but she also visited the Irish Institute of Mary of Loreto at Loreto Abbey. But she remained unpopular. The influential Irish republican Maud Gonne wrote a coruscating critique of Victoria, 'The Famine Queen', published in the *United Irishman* just prior to her visit, mocking her as a mother who had starved her children.[41]

On a personal level, though, Victoria had more time for Catholics. She met them abroad on holiday and was on good terms with the French Empress Eugénie, exiled in Britain with her husband, Napoleon III, after his overthrow. She visited the tombs Eugénie first built for her husband and son in Chislehurst, Kent, and their later mausoleum at the Benedictine monastery in Farnborough.

Victoria, as a religious woman herself, was a person of piety, yet she was no dour Christian. She was a Bible reader and a lover of hymns – she and Albert were particularly fond of 'Now Thank We All Our God' – and believed that the Sabbath should be honoured. It was not a day on which she did her paperwork. But the Victorian obsession with observance was not her way.

In 1855, Lord Grosvenor sought to introduce a Sunday Trading Bill to keep shops shut on Sundays. It led to a rally in Hyde Park with people protesting against the move, and caused Victoria and Karl Marx to become unlikely allies. Marx, then residing in England, argued that the ban on Sunday trading benefited the most prosperous businesses who were happy to see six-day-a-week trading, while the smaller shopkeepers would lose out if they could not open seven days a week, and poorer workers, paid on Saturday nights, would no longer be able to shop on Sundays. The clerics were in league with big business, he claimed. Victoria, no killjoy, also disapproved of the Bill, on the grounds that people should be able to enjoy innocent recreation on a Sunday. She wrote in her journal on 7 July 1855, 'Leave the poor people alone, who work all the week round and who require innocent recreation on a Sunday!'[42]

Within six years, though, any sense that Victoria was a woman with a sense of fun, sympathetic to those who might enjoy some innocent entertainment, was erased from the public mind. In 1861, what was arguably the most eventful moment of Victoria's reign occurred: the death of her beloved husband, Albert.

The Prince Consort had been by the Queen's side since almost the beginning of her reign. He had advised her, guided her, persuaded her to be less partisan in her dealings with Parliament, while also espousing causes such as scientific innovation, education reform and the abolition of slavery, and persuading the Queen to be interested too. He had influenced her social and religious outlook. Then, at the age of just forty-two, he became unwell. A physician diagnosed typhoid fever on 9 December; he died five days later at Windsor Castle. He had told his daughter Alice he was dying, but Victoria would not countenance it.

When Albert's final moment came, the Queen refused for some time to leave his body, until the royal physician Dr William Jenner said to her firmly, 'This is but the casket, you must look beyond' – an invitation to her to ponder paradise, rather than refuse to acknowledge that Albert was no more.[43]

At the time of Albert's death, women of the upper classes had their lives subsumed in those of their husbands, making their deaths all the more shattering blows. Often, they had a sense that their lives had ended too, and they looked to a reunion in the future, in another life. For many such women, faith was a consolation. But Victoria seemed inconsolable.

There had been earlier signs of the Queen's enthusiasm for death and for mourning. When her mother died in March 1861, she was heartbroken, despite their previous conflicted relationship, and left Albert to deal with much of her correspondence while she focused on grief. By that time she had been wearing mourning clothes for much of the previous ten years, owing to the deaths of other relatives and the Duke of Wellington. After Albert died, nine months later, she never returned to usual dress and wore black for the rest of her life. She created a shrine to Albert from the rooms where he had breathed his last. All his rooms in all their homes were kept as they had been when he died, with hot water brought in the morning and linen and towels changed daily.

Albert's sudden death at such a young age shocked the nation. Some learnt dramatically of his death when, the day after his demise on the Saturday night, his name was omitted when clergy read out prayers for the Royal Family at Sunday services. Crowds flocked to cathedrals for evensong that afternoon, instinctively seeking comfort in religion, but there were no prayers for the dead in these Anglican establishments.

There was also enormous sympathy for the Queen at the time of Albert's death, and clergy suggested that the Queen's grief was shared by the nation and the Empire. One clergyman, writing on the sovereign's bereavement said, 'It proves to us how much we ourselves are part of a mighty whole and how intimate our relationships to the throne . . . Her interests and ours are identical.'[44]

Published eulogies about Albert described him as a paragon of domestic virtue and a patron of the arts and science. The *Illustrated London News* offered a particularly Gothic description of the disaster that had beset the nation: 'Death stands within the walls of Windsor Palace [sic] – a Queen is widowed – Princes are orphans – and the Empire is shrouded in mourning! Every family in the land is smitten with awe and the sorrow which Death excites when he breaks into the domestic circle and snatches from it its chief pride and joy.'[45]

Later, a pamphlet of seventy sermons on the death of Albert was published, full of similarly obsequious and verbose lamentations.

The funeral at St George's Chapel, Windsor, was private, although government ministers and the Archbishop of Canterbury attended. There were no women, not even the Queen, who stayed at her Isle of Wight home, Osborne House: it was the convention of the time for women to not attend funerals and no exception was given, even for the monarch. Of Albert's nine children, just two were present: Bertie (the Prince of Wales, later Edward VII) and Arthur. The chapel was draped in black for the service while Albert lay in three coffins: the first of wood, lined with satin; then another, of lead and silver-gilt; and finally one of mahogany, covered with crimson velvet, and his crown, baton and hat. It was thought suitable not only for a royal Prince but also for someone who would not be in his final resting place for some time.[46]

He was temporarily interred at St George's Chapel, Windsor, and then a mausoleum was built for him at Frogmore, fashioned like a mausoleum in Coburg. Being in Windsor soon became preferable for the Queen to her other homes: there she could be close to Albert, and visitors to court there were expected to visit him. Frogmore, says Michael Ledger-Lomas, became 'a presence chamber, rather than a grave'.[47] Visiting clerics were asked to conduct services in the room in the castle where he had died, while Victoria commissioned countless busts and statues of him to be placed in her homes and presented as gifts to the family and members of the household.

At St George's Chapel, The Wolsey Chapel, to the east of the main church building, became the Albert Memorial Chapel, with Old Testament scenes reflecting his virtues. In the apse were scenes of Christ's Passion, and his monument showed him as a Christian knight, surrounded with figures representing truth, justice, charity and hope. Angels held shields with St Paul's verse upon them: 'I have fought the good fight.'[48]

At the mausoleum itself were four chapels for prayers for the dead, while Victoria was comforted by relics – she wore lockets containing Albert's hair. These were notions that Anglicanism had abandoned years before as too Roman, but Victoria sought solace in habits usually cultivated by grieving Roman Catholics.

Some twenty years before Albert had died, the fashion for spirit-rapping and mesmerism had arrived in Britain from America, and Albert and Victoria had expressed great interest in them. They certainly believed that a person's spirit survived after death, and there were rumours that Victoria had consulted spiritualists and mediums about reaching Albert. She had a strong sense of his continuing presence both in the homes they had shared and in his mausoleum. She often sat in front of a bust of him, and carried a miniature ivory bust of him in a case in her pocket. She would ask his images for approval and, when out driving in Scotland, would open a small brooch with a likeness of him to show him the view.

She was also devoted to 'In Memoriam' by her poet laureate, Alfred, Lord Tennyson, which comforted her with its articulation for a continuing connection with a beloved who has died.

Victoria's religion had always been dominated by feeling rather than doctrine, and the death of Albert prompted yet more spiritual emotion. She would regularly go to the Blue Room where he had died in Windsor Castle to pray, and on the first anniversary of his death had prayers from the burial service and readings on the resurrection from the Gospel of John recited in the same room. This became an annual ritual until the Queen herself died.

The years did not dilute Victoria's obsessive grief: in 1874 she commissioned Theodore Martin to write a five-volume biography of her husband which ended with *The Passion of the Prince Consort*, who had sacrificed his life for Britain and was 'a true follower of the Founder of the Christian faith, which he had striven by his life to illustrate'.

Though Albert was depicted as a man of faith, Victoria's all-consuming grief so dominated her life that it became like a religion in itself. Being a widow became a spiritual exercise and had an emotional potency, shared by some. But 'bolstering her spiritual credentials', as Michael Ledger-Lomas describes it, caused despair among her ministers in its consequences of removing Victoria from her duties as Queen. Churchmen were also critical, believing that Christians should have more hope.[49]

In 1867, she told a fellow widow, Lady Waterpark, that her original grief had given way 'to the constant black and constant cloud'.[50] She did rouse herself, however, to approve a plethora of monuments to Albert across Britain and the Empire, most notably the Albert Memorial in London. Opened by Victoria in 1872, it is akin to a canopy in the style of a ciborium that stands over the altar of a church. Where a monstrance with the Blessed Sacrament would be placed beneath the ciborium during Benediction, there is a statue of Albert. Indeed, critics of the Queen would suggest that her obsession with Albert and her sacralisation of things and places associated with him were akin to idolatry.

It was also deeply problematic. A monarch of necessity has to be engaged with the world, in terms of both dealing with government and diplomacy and leading the nation at times of trial and of celebration. But the Widow of Windsor, as Victoria became known, was not interested. It was a dangerous moment.

There had been another dangerous moment. In 1845, a million Irish people had died when potato blight caused terrible hunger. Despite Victoria donating funds to the British Relief Association and backing other fundraising efforts for the victims of the Great Famine, the life of luxury of the Queen and her large family was deeply resented by the Irish, and she became increasingly unpopular. Allegiance to the Crown had always been weakest in Ireland, of all the home territories ruled by British monarchs, and the Great Famine served to consolidate suspicion and resentment of it. But by the 1870s, resentment was also growing in mainland Britain. Partly inspired by another revolution in France and the deposing of Emperor Napoleon III, the republican movement grew in Britain, with more than fifty republican clubs founded across the nation. A major republican rally in Trafalgar Square saw radical MPs speak against her and others demand her removal. Her own government ministers were also exasperated. She refused to carry out her royal duties and refused to meet them in person.

But within two years Victoria, making the most of the worst, turned things around. In November 1871, the Prince of Wales contracted typhoid fever, the illness that had killed his father, and Victoria feared it would happen again. But he recovered, and a major service of thanksgiving was held at St Paul's Cathedral in February 1872. That, and an abortive attempt to threaten Victoria with a gun, two days later, by an Irish protester, only served to make Victoria popular once more.

The service at St Paul's was a reminder that major religious services, filled with ceremonial, are an asset to royalty, and remind the nation of the force of monarchy. Public spectacle, vested with meaning and full of celebration, helped to draw the country back to Victoria. When the Queen had been absent from the opening of Parliament in 1864, *The Times* had commented, 'It is impossible for a recluse to occupy the British throne without a gradual weakening of that authority which the sovereign has been accustomed to exert.'[51]

It had taken some persuading to get Victoria to agree to the thanksgiving service. She was someone who preferred privacy for her prayers, and at first she was not convinced the service at St Paul's was appropriate. But her Prime Minister at the time, William Gladstone, was convinced that religion and politics mixed, and that the monarchy was part of that mix. He stood his ground and the Queen conceded, but it was part of the reason for their relationship being strained. Nevertheless, Victoria agreed not only to the service, but also to a carriage procession through the streets of the City to St Paul's.

Being seen at events such as the St Paul's service, as well as the Golden and Diamond Jubilee services of 1887 and 1897, helped reassert the Queen's once fading authority. National thanksgiving services would emphasise the connections between Church, state and the people.

There had been such services previously, and even sometimes days of humiliation for disasters such as the Indian Mutiny of 1857 and the Cattle Plague of 1866. But the biggest service of thanksgiving in the earlier part of Victoria's reign was the one for the Crimean War in May 1856, a war that was enthusiastically supported by the British at its height but later became a symbol of mismanagement and tactical failures. As well as the service of thanksgiving, Victoria marked its end with a new honour, the Victoria Cross, awarded for valour, highlighting royal and Christian regard for extreme courage. Victoria also had a lasting admiration for the nursing of Florence Nightingale during the Crimean War, and was inspired by Nightingale's strong Christian beliefs, which the Queen shared.

In 1855, Victoria bestowed on the nurse a brooch, often called the Nightingale Jewel, as a mark of royal appreciation for her work. Made of enamel and set with diamond stars, a red cross and the royal insignia of VR, it bears the motto 'Blessed Are the Merciful' – well known to both Queen and nurse from the Beatitudes of the Gospel of Matthew chapter five. After the war was over, Nightingale was invited to Balmoral to give Victoria and Albert a first-hand account of her experience, and in May 1857 a Royal Warrant was given for a commission into the health of the army.

In 1868 Victoria carried out one of her only public acts during the years of her widowed seclusion when she opened St Thomas' Hospital to show her regard for Nightingale and her fellow nurses. This was further confirmed in 1887 when she asked that money donated by the public to mark her Golden Jubilee should be used to establish the Queen's Jubilee Nursing Institute, the world's first professional nursing institute.

By the time of the 1887 Golden Jubilee and 1897 Diamond Jubilee, the lives of the Victorians were very different from when their Queen had acceded to the throne. Communications had advanced: Victoria and her family were known to her subjects through the medium of photography; the telegraph enabled information to be disseminated more easily. They travelled more, by train and by ship, often to Europe but also further afield into the reaches of the British Empire. The thanksgiving service of the Golden Jubilee emphasised Victoria as the grandmother of Europe, through her children and grandchildren who had married into many of the royal houses of Europe. The Diamond Jubilee celebrated the Queen as mother of the Empire – an Empire seen as worthily Christianising the world. It also linked Anglicanism with Empire for generations to come.

However, there was also some acknowledgement that the Empire included people who were not Anglican and some of them were not Christian. Early in her reign and burgeoning Empire, Victoria had been keen to support the Christianisation of India, and by 1858 she had produced a proclamation that invoked the truth of Christianity, but also said that she disclaimed 'alike the Right and the Desire to impose our Convictions on any of our Subjects . . . all shall alike enjoy the equal and impartial protection of the Law'.[52]

Services were held in India to mark both the Golden and Diamond Jubilees, while at home Victoria grew increasingly interested in Islam through her servant Abdul Karim. There were other instances, though, that suggested that the bringing of Christianity to Empire was what Victoria most wanted, rather than being a prophet of diversity and religious tolerance. In 1852, Shazader Gouramma, the eleven-year-old daughter of the deposed Maharajah of Coorg was brought to court, and was christened, with Victoria acting as godmother and giving her a Bible. Fifteen years later it was the turn of Victor Albert, son of deposed Sikh ruler Duleep Singh, to be christened. She was also godmother to Sara Forbes Bonetta, a former slave of the King of Dahomey who gave her to naval captain Frederick Forbes as a gift for Queen Victoria. Sara arrived in Britain in 1850, forty-three years after the abolition of slavery, and lived as a free woman, later marrying and having three children, of whom one was named after the Queen, who was her godmother too.

While Victoria may have been kind to individuals she met from her colonies, she was nevertheless insistent of her status: that she ruled them and was head of an Empire. She may have shared beliefs in the Beatitudes with Florence Nightingale and the duties of good Christians, but she saw herself at the apex not only of British society but also had one-fifth of the globe's population as her subjects. When the German Empire was declared in 1871, it made her daughter Vicky an empress, as the wife of Emperor Frederick III. Victoria began to badger her government that she too should have the formal title of Empress, and the Bill to create her Empress was introduced in 1876.

Victoria died twenty-five years later, on 22 January at Osborne House, the home she had built with Albert, with her doctor on one side and her eldest grandson, Kaiser Wilhelm II, on the other. A crucifix was placed at the head of her bed. At nearly eighty-one years old, she was the oldest monarch Britain had had, and the longest reigning – her record of sixty-two years would only be broken by her great-great-granddaughter Elizabeth II. Her death was the end of an era – an era named after her – and a break with the age of her Hanoverian ancestors who had first come to claim Britain's throne 187 years earlier in 1714.

Her cortège and funeral was a narrative of the innovations wrought during her reign, from transport to colonisation. The coffin moved by boat from the Isle of Wight to Portsmouth, then by train to the London station named after her, by gun carriage to Paddington and then by train again to Windsor. Troops from the Indian and South African colonies accompanied her. For her daughters and her heir, the new King Edward VII, their mother's death required liturgy fitting for such a momentous occasion as the departure of such a long-reigning monarch. They wanted the Russian Orthodox Office of the Faithful Departed, but Randall Davidson, then Bishop of Winchester who had been at the dying Queen's bedside, blocked it, on the grounds that this would be intercessionary prayer for the dead. The twentieth century might have begun, but the Anglicans were not yet ready to be that ecumenical.

Instead, it was a standard Anglican funeral mixed with military moments and with one of the biggest gatherings ever held of European royalty, most of them related to the late Queen. As head of the army and daughter of a soldier, Victoria requested that there be a military procession and her coffin be brought to the funeral on a gun carriage. There was a simultaneous memorial service at St Paul's and others across the Empire.

Sometimes popular, sometimes disliked, Victoria died being loved, creating in death an emotional connection between herself and those she had ruled. Longevity had much to do with it: it was a psychological shock to people that the one stable thing they could rely on – the Queen – was gone. She was no longer present in their lives.

For Victoria, being a bulwark for her people matched how faith had been for her: that sturdy rock on which she could always rely. Yet her most sacred space had not been the churches and chapels of her Anglican estate: it had been the home. Religion had become domesticated. But her son Edward VII would be very different.

Edward had been raised in a household where religion played a highly significant part. The size of the family – he was one of nine – meant there were large numbers of religious ceremonies – baptisms, confirmations and later marriages – as well as the ceremonials of his mother's life. He was just twenty when his father died and, as befitted custom of the time, was chief mourner at Albert's funeral. His grief was evident in his letters, as it was when his sister Alice died exactly seventeen years after his father and four weeks after her four-year-old daughter May, both of diphtheria. 'The good are always taken and the bad remain,' he told his mother.[53]

Edward was not bad, but he had none of the high-minded seriousness that his parents would have wanted for him. Not that they helped: he was little prepared for kingship, the Queen refusing to let him share Cabinet papers, for example, although he did make visits abroad on her behalf during her widowed seclusion, and embarked upon public appearances – opening new buildings, for example – that are now viewed as the norm for royals, while he was Prince of Wales. But the affable, epicurean Prince spent most of his time enjoying a luxury lifestyle, biding his time before his accession.

When it came in 1901, he made it clear that he would not take the name Albert I as many expected, because the name would be forever associated with his father. Instead, his monarchical name would be his second name: Edward.

If a coronation offers an insight to a monarch's religious beliefs, then Edward VII had a strong faith. The ceremony – the first coronation for sixty-four years – had to be delayed because the new King was taken ill and required surgery. It had been carefully planned as a celebration of the Empire and of the Church of England. Victoria's Golden and Diamond Jubilees had awakened a taste for elaborate ceremonial, fusing royalty and religion, which was largely manufactured – and often considered by historians to be the invention of tradition – and Edward's coronation was expected to sate that appetite. These events could also be said to be a response to the extension of the franchise from 1867 onwards: people with a vote were that bit more engaged with civic society and what monarchy and the established Church did needed to involve them. And the growth of public transport made it much easier for people across Britain to travel to London to witness these grand events.

In June 1902, when the King became ill, instead of a coronation at Westminster Abbey, there was a service of intercession at St Paul's Cathedral, attended by many of the dignitaries that were in town for the Westminster Abbey ceremonial. Other events went ahead as planned. Edward, always a lover of a good party himself, insisted that parties, including A Coronation Dinner for the Poor of London, should not be shelved. Half a million Londoners were served a meal in eight hundred locations across the capital, with the King donating £30,000 himself to defray costs.

Edward also recognised that if the monarchy were to survive in the twentieth century, then it needed to connect more with people, from the working classes to the emerging middle class and the newly moneyed. One solution to this urgent issue was to associate royalty with philanthropy, and so he set up a committee to launch a Coronation Appeal for London's voluntary hospitals. He raised £600,000 for The King Edward's Hospital Fund for London.

The changes in society in the early years of the new century were also marked by the guests invited to Edward's coronation. As well as the usual members of the peerage, there were now chairmen of the newly created county councils, mayors of London boroughs, representatives of the medical and legal professions and representatives of non-Anglican churches. Huge numbers of representatives from around the Empire were originally invited, but when the coronation was delayed on account of Edward's illness, some went home and did not return for the later date. Instead, many of their countries were represented by their ambassadors, although thirty-one Indian Princes still attended, and various Prime Ministers of the Dominions. It was an entirely new spectacle – Victoria had only been declared Empress of India forty years after becoming Queen – and it was in many ways improbable: a Christian ceremony used to bring together people of a huge range of faiths from across the globe.

This religious endeavour was therefore of vital diplomatic and political significance to Britain and so needed to be managed well. Edward and the Privy Council therefore set in place a management structure which has continued since for the coronation: a Coronation Committee and a further Coronation Executive Committee, chaired by the Earl Marshal – always the Duke of Norfolk – with the Archbishop of

Canterbury and various government officials contributing as well to ensure that everything went smoothly. They did not manage to iron out every possibility for mishap, however: the peeresses' heels got caught in the thick pile of the carpet; the Archbishop of Canterbury, Frederick Temple, had such failing eyesight that the words of the service had to be printed on giant scrolls of paper – a sort of proto-teleprompter; he was so frail that he could not get up after kneeling to pay homage and the King had to lift him up; he put the crown on the King's head back to front.

The new King was keen to make connections with previous Edwards; the annexe, built next to the Abbey for the occasion, was adorned with statues of Edwards I to VI, and he was determined to wear St Edward's Crown. But his recuperation from illness meant it was too heavy and he had to wear the lighter Imperial State Crown instead. His wife – the long-suffering Alexandra, who endured his countless affairs – was crowned after him with a new crown containing the Koh-i-Noor diamond, one of the largest in the world. Above them in a gallery, where Edward's sisters sat, were the King's lady friends, among them Mrs Keppel, Jennie Churchill and Sarah Bernhardt – which a wit quipped was the King's loose box.[54]

The coronation was a liturgical celebration, adorned with mostly English music: coronation texts were given settings composed by Thomas Tallis, Orlando Gibbons and Henry Purcell, plus modern works by Arthur Sullivan, Charles Villiers Stanford and John Stainer. There was, of course, 'Zadok the Priest', and a setting of Psalm 122, 'I Was Glad', by Hubert Parry, which incorporated the traditional acclamation of *Vivat Rex* as the sovereign entered Westminster Abbey. It has been used at every coronation since.

While to modern minds the Anglican ceremony of 1902 seems a curious thing, given how many attended who were not Christian, it was barely an issue then. But the continuing hostility to Roman Catholics was, given the emerging tolerance towards that faith, striking. The reading of the declaration in which the monarch promises to uphold the Protestant religion, in violently anti-Catholic language, was moved from the coronation itself to be made instead before Parliament on the monarch's accession. With its repudiation of transubstantiation, it was still offensive to the King's Catholic subjects. Edward and the

Cabinet agreed, and a recasting of it rather than a rewriting was agreed, but this did not happen until the time of George V.

Edward himself was tolerant of Roman Catholicism, perhaps because his frequent travels in Europe, especially to France and Italy, had acquainted him with many Catholics. In 1905, King Alfonso XIII of Spain made a state visit to Britain, hosted by Edward VII at Buckingham Palace. There he met the King's niece, Princess Victoria Eugenie, daughter of his sister Beatrice and Prince Henry of Battenberg. Alfonso was looking for a wife and there was a mutual attraction between him and Princess Victoria Eugenie. Being a member of the British Royal Family, she was, however, a Protestant – an impediment to marrying into the Spanish Royal Family. Edward – no doubt with a pragmatic eye on diplomacy and further British interests abroad – encouraged the match and had no objection to Victoria Eugenie's conversion to Catholicism. The Lord Chancellor advised that it would not contravene the Royal Marriages Act of 1772 because the Princess was a Battenberg. Marrying out and into a Catholic family, therefore, proved to be OK, but having Catholic women marrying in – such as Princess Michael of Kent and Autumn Phillips in recent times – appears to be more tricky.

But was there more to Edward's interest in his niece's conversion than mere political pragmatism? He certainly seemed intrigued by Roman Catholicism himself. In 1903, Edward was due to visit Italy and, as part of a wider visit to Rome, he wished to meet Pope Leo XIII. The Cabinet thought it inappropriate as the King would be visiting Italy in his role of head of state, but at that time Britain did not recognise the pope as a head of state. The Cabinet also thought it inappropriate for the Supreme Governor of the Church of England to meet the pope when Britain was a Protestant nation. They recommended he not go. But leading Catholics, especially the Duke of Norfolk, thought this would be seen as a snub to the pope and therefore an insult to Edward's British Catholic subjects. After much debate, Edward eventually visited as a private individual, not as King or head of the Church.

Some time later, when he visited Maynooth, the Catholic seminary in Ireland, Edward wrote his name in the visitors' book with his own pen and told those with him that it was a pen that had once belonged to Pope Leo, who had given it 'to my friend Father Bernard Vaughan. He kindly sent it to me as a souvenir of His Holiness.'[55] Vaughan, a Jesuit, was the brother of Herbert Vaughan, the Cardinal Archbishop of Westminster from 1892 to 1903. A photograph of Edward VII with his friend, Fr Vaughan, is held in the archives of the British province of the Jesuits.

In 1910, during a visit to France, the King visited Lourdes, the pilgrimage town famous for St Bernadette's visions of the Virgin Mary and for many miraculous cures in its waters. There he was received by the Bishop of Lourdes and visited the Church of the Rosary and the Basilica.[56]

Edward's health was already in serious decline by the time he visited Lourdes, and at the time he was staying on in France to convalesce after collapsing. When he returned to Britain he was still not well, suffering from bronchitis, and on 6 May he suffered several heart attacks. It is well known that the ever-forgiving Queen Alexandra allowed her husband's mistress to visit as he lay dying, but was there another visitor to his bedside?

Speculation has grown that Fr Cyril Forster, chaplain to the Irish Guards, was summoned to the dying King's bedside. Edward's biographer, Jane Ridley, argued, 'Even if Fr Forster saw the King, this is not to say that Bertie underwent a dramatic deathbed conversion. Nor is there any reason to believe that he was given the sacraments or more than the blessing which any priest could give.'[57]

But in correspondence in the Catholic weekly, *The Tablet*, in 1978, following publication of a new biography of Edward VII, there was further evidence that the conversion had happened. Shane Leslie, in his review of the biography by Sir Philip Magnus, said that there was no doubt that Fr Forster was one of the dying King's last visitors, along with Mrs Keppel, and said Fr Forster was non-committal about whether he received the King. 'I wish I could tell you,' was his usual response. But if he definitely had not, why not say so?[58]

Veronica Salusbury, a former sacristan serving under Mgr Barton, a priest of St Peter and St Edward's Church, Palace Street, Westminster, threw more light on the matter in the letters pages of *The Tablet* in response to the review, when she recalled what Mgr Barton had told her. He had visited that same church in his teens with his mother not long after the death of Edward VII and was introduced to Fr Forster. Fr Forster had told them that he had been asked to urgently attend the King, 'that he had received the King into the Church and had conferred all last rites upon him, and that he thought all the policemen and staff who saw him hastening into the palace knew what he had come to do'.[59]

Edward VII, like Charles II, was a womanising, sociable king, full of human foibles that did nothing to lessen his popularity, especially after the gloom of his mother's widowed monarchy. And, like Charles II, it seems that at the end, the pull of Rome, with its last rites, absolution and hope of redemption proved attractive to King Edward. For both of them, conversion earlier in their reign would have been unacceptable, given the restrictions on a Catholic being the monarch, which continues to this day.

But from the earliest days of the Hanoverians to the time of Edward VII, the suspicion of Roman Catholicism had, bit by bit, lessened. On occasion, the impetus for change had come from the people and from politicians, and was resisted by monarchs who stubbornly adhered to their coronation oath. But their inability to block progress on this point symbolised the diluting of their power. Instead, they found new ways to express their Christian beliefs and what they stood for: from charitable endeavours to being exemplars of family stability. It was a form of virtuous kingship and queenship that would be continued into the twentieth century, although it would also lead to one of the greatest crises of that age too. And as Anglicanism eventually waned, the role of monarch would also come to shoulder a huge burden: to be not only an exemplar of that religion but also the means by which many people in Britain would encounter it. The issue was: how could the monarchy do that – to stand for something not shared by the majority yet make it still meaningful? Could the monarchy evolve and find a new way of defending the faith? It is that dilemma I will turn to next.

# 4

# God make good my vow: Elizabeth II, the forming of her faith and her coronation

CHRISTMAS 1952 WAS a sombre affair. There was some jollity, yes, with Frankie Howerd performing in *Dick Whittington* at the London Palladium, and West End theatregoers enjoying Agatha Christie's new play, *The Mousetrap*. Children were entertained by new TV shows that had started earlier that year, including *Bill and Ben* and *Sooty*. Their Christmas presents would have included Mary Norton's *The Borrowers* and C. S. Lewis' *The Voyage of the Dawn Treader*, both published earlier that year, while their parents might have enjoyed new publications such Evelyn Waugh's *Men at Arms*, H. E. Bates' *Love for Lydia* or, for a little lighter relief, Richard Gordon's *Doctor in the House*. Al Martino's 'Here in My Heart' topped the first-ever singles chart for twelve weeks. But sweets were still on the ration.

Earlier in December, the Great Smog had enveloped London for a week, causing four thousand people to lose their lives. Memories of two terrible disasters earlier in the year, the Harrow and Wealdstone rail crash and the Lynmouth flood disaster, were still raw. And in February, the British had lost their King: George VI, who had led them through six years of war, had died in his sleep.

That Christmas, his daughter Elizabeth, who succeeded him as monarch at just twenty-five years old, broke off from spending the festive season with her husband, two small children, her sister and widowed mother at 3.07 p.m. at Sandringham, where her father had died, to broadcast live to the nation. A fortnight earlier she had given permission for her coronation the following year to be televised – the first ever to be screened live for all the nation to watch. It was clearly something on her mind as she broadcast that day.

The Christmas radio message of the sovereign was a tradition started by her grandfather, George V, in 1932, and twenty years later his granddaughter made her radio address from the study at Sandringham house, using the same desk and chair as George V and George VI. It was a message that reflected the grief of her family, with its reference to her beloved father, and also highlighted themes that would be constants throughout her lengthy reign: the importance of family, the British connections across the globe as a force for good, duty, the importance of tradition balanced by optimism for the future. But it also included an appeal for people's support. This young mother, thrust on to the global stage and the throne long before she had expected it, was frank in her appeal for people's prayers as she faced the daunting prospect of being crowned sovereign:

> At my Coronation next June, I shall dedicate myself anew to your service. I shall do so in the presence of a great congregation, drawn from every part of the Commonwealth and Empire, while millions outside Westminster Abbey will hear the promises and the prayers being offered up within its walls, and see much of the ancient ceremony in which Kings and Queens before me have taken part through century upon century.
>
> You will be keeping it as a holiday; but I want to ask you all, whatever your religion may be, to pray for me on that day – to pray that God may give me wisdom and strength to carry out the solemn promises I shall be making, and that I may faithfully serve Him and you, all the days of my life.[1]

Those who knew Elizabeth II say that she was a shy person, and as private a person as it was possible to be during seventy years of being sovereign. She did not give interviews, nor wrote her autobiography – not even musings on life in the Highlands, as her great-great-grandmother Victoria did. Yet there was one subject on which she spoke openly on many occasions: her faith. Despite many of her comments on her religion being on the record through her Christmas messages, they often passed many commentators by. Look at any index of biographies of Queen Elizabeth and there is a section on her character and interests. There are references to her shyness, her modesty, her love of dogs and horses, and even her delight in jigsaws. Occasionally there is an index mention of her reticence. But on the subject for which she increasingly put reticence to one side – her faith – there is barely a mention in such biographical volumes. But as one who knew more than most about her faith put it to me in the last years of her life:

> There is a kind of scaffolding about her life, much of it due to routine that is followed. That scaffolding is the Christian year. The way she would see it is that she has been called by God to care for her people and the primary thing is to be obedient to that call. Her Christian faith is something that is taken for granted. It is in her DNA, as it was with her mother.[2]

For Elizabeth II, religious faith was both a personal matter and a public one: it was the place where her private life and her role of sovereign merged. The British Royal Family today serves many roles: as a welfare monarchy, providing patronage and leadership of many charitable organisations; as a source of soft power for the United Kingdom, especially representing it abroad and in encounters with representatives of other nations when they visit the United Kingdom; as the leaders of public ceremonial; and as supporters of and leaders of the armed services. All these, to some degree, can involve public expressions of religious belief – Remembrance Sunday would be a prime example. The public religious figure is, of course, particularly evident in the sovereign's role as Supreme Governor of the Church of England. But the British monarch is also someone who leads through personal example, as a spiritual leader. And it was here that Elizabeth II's personal faith played its part as much as her public persona. It became increasingly evident in her final decades, through her increasingly overtly religious Christmas messages, which changed in tone at the time of the Millennium.

In the late 1990s, John Major's Conservative government began planning an event akin to the Festival of Britain – the postwar celebration of the nation that took place in 1951 – to mark the start of the third millennium. But it was Tony Blair's New Labour administration, first elected in 1997, that greatly expanded the size and scope of the proposed Millennium Dome, which opened on 31 December 1999. The Dome's exhibits focused on several themes: what we do, where we live and who we are, with the third including a section on faith.

On New Year's Eve, Elizabeth II attended the grand opening, looking rather uncomfortable as Tony Blair pumped her arm while she and her husband sang 'Auld Lang Syne' with the Prime Minister and his wife. A year later, on Christmas Day 2000, she made it clear that faith being a subset of a topic in the Dome was not enough. Her focus in that year's Christmas broadcast was clearly on what 2000 really marked:

> But as this year draws to a close I would like to reflect more directly and more personally on what lies behind all the celebrations of these past twelve months.
>
> Christmas is the traditional, if not the actual, birthday of a man who was destined to change the course of our history. And today we are celebrating the fact that Jesus Christ was born two thousand years ago; this is the true Millennium anniversary.

And she went on:

> To many of us our beliefs are of fundamental importance. For me the teachings of Christ and my own personal accountability before God provide a framework in which I try to lead my life. I, like so many of you, have drawn great comfort in difficult times from Christ's words and example.[3]

While the content might have been explicitly Christian and remarkably personal, it was nevertheless constant, for this public expression of belief began before she was even crowned Queen.

In 1947, the then Princess Elizabeth made an official tour of South Africa with her parents, and on 21 April, her twenty-first birthday, she spoke in a radio broadcast from Cape Town of dedicating her life to the service of the Commonwealth:

> If we all go forward together with an unwavering faith, a high courage, and a quiet heart, we shall be able to make of this ancient commonwealth, which we all love so dearly, an even grander thing – more free, more prosperous, more happy and a more powerful influence for good in the world – than it has been in the greatest days of our forefathers . . .
>
> I declare before you all that my whole life whether it be long or short shall be devoted to your service and the service of our great imperial family to which we all belong.
>
> But I shall not have strength to carry out this resolution alone unless you join in it with me, as I now invite you to do: I know that your support will be unfailingly given. God help me to make good my vow, and God bless all of you who are willing to share in it.[4]

The speech conveyed learning, a sense of history, a commitment to service and religious faith, and it came from the pen of Dermot Morrah. Biographers of the Queen long assumed that it was written by Sir Alan 'Tommy' Lascelles, King George VI's private secretary, but Morrah was revealed as the author by his grandson, the columnist Tom Utley. Morrah was a gifted writer and intellectual who had been, in his time, a fellow of All Souls, a leader writer for *The Times* and a speechwriter for George VI. After serving the King and Queen during the war years, they asked him to take on the crucial task of writing the words that would set the tone for their daughter's future.[5] The prose with its sacred promise may well be explained by Morrah's own Roman Catholic faith. Indeed, the Queen's biographer, Ben Pimlott, who mistakenly thought Lascelles had written it, described it as 'a nun-like promise'.[6]

The faith expressed in that speech was matched by a clear sense that the young Princess Elizabeth recognised her future life of duty, as head of state and of a religious institution. Her understanding of this role came early. Since her birth she had been in direct line to the throne, through her grandfather George V, whose heir was her uncle David, the Prince of Wales, who had no children, and her father, the Duke of York. In 1937, for her eleventh birthday, crowds gathered outside Windsor Castle to greet her, just two weeks before her parents' coronation, following the abdication of Uncle David, as Edward VIII.

The abdication had traumatised the Royal Family, immersed in a life of duty as articulated by George V.

When his eldest son, David, the Prince of Wales, acceded to the throne after his father's death in 1936, there were signs of the problems to come. He was already involved in a relationship with the American divorcee, Wallis Simpson, and even before his accession rumours abounded in circles close to the court that he wanted to move out of the line of succession and retire into private life with Mrs Simpson.[7]

As Prince of Wales, Edward VIII had seen himself – and been perceived by many others – as a moderniser and entirely different from his father, George V, who was steeped in tradition. There were early signs that he thought he could continue in the same radical vein on succeeding to the throne. This was evident in his attitude to Cosmo Lang, the Archbishop of Canterbury, for whom he had little time and with whom he was most definitely not on the same wavelength. According to a story related by the Prime Minister, Stanley Baldwin, the King damned the episcopacy and 'shooed the Archbishop of Canterbury out of the house'.[8] He was probably aware that Lang disapproved of his relationship with the divorced and remarried Mrs Simpson.

This lack of understanding between the two boded ill for the crisis that was soon to emerge as the new King insisted on marriage to Mrs Simpson, despite the Church of England's belief in the indissolubility of marriage and its opposition to divorce.

Signs emerged that marriage was an issue as early as mid-February 1936, just a month after Edward VIII acceded to the throne, when Lord Wigram, who remained in post as the monarch's principal private secretary, consulted the Lord Chancellor about the marriage laws of a sovereign 'so that I could have a ready answer if HM suddenly said he was going to marry Mrs S'. At that stage, Wigram thought the new King, told he would have to abdicate, would put an end to his marriage plans because he 'likes this King business too much'.[9]

Wigram was to be proved wrong. As rumours grew in political circles and abroad – while the British public knew nothing of what was afoot – the idea emerged that the King might have a morganatic marriage with Mrs Simpson. This would have meant that Edward would remain King but his wife would not be Queen Consort. The King suggested to Baldwin that Mrs Simpson might be made a Duchess without having a royal title, but Baldwin indicated that British public opinion would not tolerate it. Nor did the Cabinet or the Dominions, including Canada and Australia.

While the King thought that it was possible for a monarch to have a clear dividing line between his personal life and his public one – a public one that would involve his consecration before God – the Church of England thought otherwise, and in 1936 it was confident that the British people took the same view.

Lang confided to his diary that he agonised over whether he could administer the coronation oath in conscience, given the circumstances, and that he wished to persuade the King to reconsider his intention regarding Mrs Simpson, but the King refused to see him.[10] The King himself later blamed Lang for his influence over others, with his views of Christian marriage and the duties of a monarch, and described Lang's 'shadowy, hovering presence' during the abdication crisis.[11]

While the Archbishop of Canterbury intimated to Number 10 that he was receiving sackfuls of letters from concerned individuals about the King and his behaviour, it was a lesser bishop, that of Bradford, who spoke most publicly and articulated what kingship meant in 1936.

Dr Alfred Blunt made his comments at a Bradford diocesan conference on 1 December, which in those days was thought important enough for a reporter to have been despatched to it by the local paper, the *Bradford Telegraph and Argus*.

The reporter, Ronald Harker, not only wrote up the story for the *Argus*, but also sent it to the Press Association. Bishop Blunt had spoken of the forthcoming coronation and commented on the role of both the King at the coronation and the nation and the dedication of both to God:

> On this occasion the King holds an avowedly representative position. His personal views and opinions are his own, and as an

> individual he has the right of us all to be the keeper of his own private conscience. But in his public capacity at his Coronation, he stands for the English people's idea of kingship. It has for long centuries been, and I hope still is, an essential part of that idea that the King needs the grace of God for his office. In the Coronation ceremony the nation definitely acknowledges that need. Whatever it may mean, much or little, to the individual who is crowned, to the people as a whole it means their dedication of the English monarchy to the care of God, in whose rule and governance are the hearts of kings.
>
> Thus, in the second place, not only as important as but far more important than the King's personal feelings are to his Coronation, is the feeling with which we – the people of England – view it. Our part of the ceremony is to fill it with reality, by the sincerity of our belief in the power of God to over-rule for good our national history, and by the sincerity with which we commend the King and nation to his Providence.
>
> Are we going to be merely spectators or listeners-in as at any other interesting function, with a sort of passive curiosity? Or are we in some sense going to consecrate ourselves to the service of God and the welfare of mankind?

If Harker wondered where this was leading, Bishop Blunt then made it plain with his pointed remark about the King and the direction in which he was going:

> First, on the faith, prayer, and self-dedication of the King himself; and on that it would be improper for me to say anything except to commend him to God's grace, which he will so abundantly need, as we all need it – for the King is a man like ourselves – if he is to do his duty faithfully. We hope that he is aware of his need. Some of us wish that he gave more positive signs of such awareness.[12]

Until that moment, Baldwin and the King had found the press to be pliant, not reporting on the unease in political, ecclesiastical and court circles about the immediate future, the looming coronation and the place of Mrs Simpson in the King's life. But Blunt's comments were the starting gun for the national press to comment on the situation. As the early days of December wore on, the signs were that, while some people supported the King's desire to marry Wallis Simpson, her second divorce from Ernest Simpson was disapproved of, and seen as a step too far for a prospective queen consort. On 10 December, Edward VIII signed his abdication papers and broadcast to the nation, famously declaring, 'I have found it impossible to carry the heavy burden of responsibility and to discharge my duty as King as I would wish to do, without the help and support of the woman I love.'[13]

Two days later, Archbishop Lang decided to broadcast to the nation as well, via the BBC, in which he set out a clear distinction – as had Edward VIII – between private happiness and public duty. For Edward, sacrificing private happiness on the altar of royal duty was not something he was prepared to do. For Lang, it was a given that he should: 'From God he received a high and sacred trust. Yet by his own will he has . . . surrendered the trust.' The King's motive had been 'a craving for private happiness' that he had sought 'in a manner inconsistent with the Christian principles of marriage'.[14]

Baldwin, Lord Reith, Director-General of the BBC, and Queen Mary all wrote to congratulate Lang, but members of the public and Winston Churchill wrote to him to complain of his uncharitable view of the former King.

This idea of duty coming first and the significance of making a commitment to the people, before God, was a concept embraced by Edward's brother, the Duke of York, and his wife, and as King and Queen Consort they imparted it to their elder daughter and heir, Elizabeth. Throughout her life, Elizabeth was to make that duty her vocation, but as the twentieth century wore on, it was to become an issue again through the choices made by her children and her grandchildren, most evident in their marriage complexities.

This commitment Elizabeth inherited from her grandfather and her parents was powerfully expressed by her father George VI in his coronation broadcast, describing his own role as akin to that of a priest: 'The highest of distinctions is the service of others and to the Ministry of Kingship I have in your hearing dedicated myself . . . in words of the deepest solemnity.'[15]

As a child, Elizabeth was prepared for her destiny by her grandmother, Queen Mary, who provided her with Queen Victoria's account of her own coronation, a coloured panorama of George IV's coronation procession, and visits to royal sites such as Hampton Court Palace and the Tower of London. This, says historian Matthew Dennison, ensured she and her sister Margaret understood their 'royal past to which they themselves were linked by consanguinity and tradition'. In other words, the royal sisters were being prepared for lives of duty while also recognising their own specialness in terms of their position.[16]

Countering this notion, however, were the views of George VI and Queen Elizabeth regarding their daughter, which made a clear distinction between role and person. According to Dermot Morrah, who wrote her vow speech, in an illustrated book published to mark Princess Elizabeth's twenty-first birthday:

> The King and Queen have never encouraged her to regard herself as anything but an ordinary person, and as such she sees herself still. It is her position, not her personality, that she knows to be exceptional; and she fully understands that by showing the capacity of an ordinary woman to play an extraordinary part in the national life, she best discharges the high task of royalty.[17]

The commentaries of George VI and Elizabeth II on their roles – found in their Christmas messages and other statements at landmark moments such as jubilees and major national occasions – articulate this special role while countering it with an acknowledgement that they are answerable to another power. For both of them, this is God and also the people. The Crown might mean power and status; in the United Kingdom it also means service.

For both George VI and his daughter, being crowned sovereign was a symbolic moment of transcendence, transforming them through anointing, much as a priest is transformed through his anointing during ordination. It was a profound experience of sensing that God had given them a particular role to play while also trusting in him. Those who knew Elizabeth II commented that her faith was not one shaped by philosophy or theological study. 'It is a simple faith. She isn't one for reading. She knows her prayer book,' said one to me in 2021 who observed her religious worship for many years. The Lord's Prayer, which she recited every day, was central to her faith.

Her father shared it. In 1938, when he was in London while his wife, accompanied by their daughters, launched a ship in Glasgow, he sent a message at a time when the country realised that Europe was edging closer to conflict: 'The people of this country . . . be of good cheer in spite of the dark clouds hanging over them and indeed the whole world . . . we cannot foretell the future but in preparing for it, we show our trust in a divine providence and in ourselves.'[18]

Trust in God was also evident in George VI's choice of words at the start of war. In 1939, during his Christmas broadcast – the first since Britain had declared war on Germany in September – he quoted a prayer: 'I said to the man who stood at the Gate of the Year, "Give me a light that I may tread safely into the unknown." And he replied: "Go out into the darkness and put your hand into the Hand of God. That shall be better to you than light, and safer than a known way." '

It was a prayer that his daughter went on to quote in her foreword to a special booklet to mark her ninetieth birthday, produced by the Bible Society.

For George VI's wife, Queen Elizabeth, religious faith was a practical thing. She had 'a marked preference for Christian kindness and voluntary service over the corporate and the abstract'.[19]

Queen Elizabeth was also a staunch supporter of the idea that the monarchy should articulate its commitment to Christianity through its public pronouncements. The BBC's Lord Reith recorded that they sat next to one another at dinner in Buckingham Palace in 1940 and that she 'agreed emphatically with me that the Christian ethic should be the basis of the post-war policy' and thought the King ought to make a pronouncement about it. 'He believes it, you know,' she added.[20] Indeed, the King had said in his 1939 Christmas broadcast that the war was fought 'for the cause of Christian civilization'.[21]

Queen Elizabeth's religious beliefs also played an influential role in the life of her family through her lingering antipathy to divorce, which led to her opposition to the marriage plans of Edward VIII, and later to her daughter Margaret's desire to marry the divorced Captain Peter Townsend. Her grandson Prince Charles' decision to marry the divorced Camilla Parker-Bowles in 2005 was said by many commentators to have come about only after his grandmother had died; she had passed away three years earlier.

By the 1990s, Queen Elizabeth's trenchant view of divorce was a minority one, but in the 1930s she shared it with the Royal Family and the Church of England's hierarchy. It was a view that led Edward VIII to step down as monarch in order to marry the twice-divorced Wallis Simpson – with the direct consequence that Princess Elizabeth was heir to the throne – bar the sudden addition of a brother to her family.

It was an outcome that would have delighted her grandfather, George V, who had said: 'Pray to God my eldest son will never marry and that nothing will come between Bertie and Lilibet [Princess Elizabeth's family pet name] and the throne.'[22]

The young Princess was profoundly influenced by her grandfather and his faith. It was simple, Bible-based belief, with George V reading a chapter of Scripture every night until the end of his life. While George V listened closely to the sermons of visiting clergy at Windsor and Sandringham, he preferred them not to be lengthy. His private secretary, Sir Arthur Bigge, the first Baron Stamfordham, warned clerics, 'Preach for about 14 minutes. If you preach for less, the King may say you are too lazy to prepare a sermon; if you preach for more than 14 minutes, the King may say that the man did not know when to stop.'[23] It was an attitude mirrored by that of Elizabeth II and the Duke of Edinburgh years later, who also preferred what was frequently termed by wits as 'short church', rather than high or low.

It was George V who had reintroduced one tradition to the Royal Family and invented another that were to become staples of Elizabeth II's years: the distribution of Maundy money and the monarch's Christmas message. The first on Maundy Thursday reinforced a message that the monarch was, like all Christians, mandated to follow in Christ's footsteps with concern for the poor, the sick and the lame, and to distribute alms. The second emphasised the role of the monarch as much more than the head of the Church of England, but as a spiritual leader – in effect, a preacher at the most important time of the year. And Christmas also stressed a certain solidarity and commonality too: that the monarch, like the rest of Britain, marked an event that was essentially about the family. As other families through the land gathered together, often around their Christmas trees, so did the House of Windsor.

While Elizabeth II followed in these two traditions in her grandfather's and father's footsteps, her personal faith, the circumstances of her reign and its longevity saw her mark more of these occasions and attend more church services than most – yet, paradoxically, it occurred in an era when religious belief declined, as did the membership of the Church of which she was Supreme Governor.

As the historian David Cannadine noted in a recent history of Westminster Abbey, the Queen 'attended Abbey services more frequently and assiduously than any previous monarch'. He says, 'It is tempting to regard this close personal relationship between the Abbey and the monarchy as having been the natural and permanent state of affairs since the time of Edward the Confessor but it is in fact a recent, twentieth century development.'[24]

It was in Westminster Abbey that the Queen was to participate in the three most important religious ceremonies of her life – her parents' coronation, her marriage and her own crowning. There was a sense of completion when the Abbey was also chosen for her funeral, sixty-nine years after her coronation.

The coronation of George VI and Queen Elizabeth took place on 12 May 1937, just five months after the King's accession. When a monarch dies, there is usually a suitable period of mourning before the next coronation. But given the trauma of the abdication and the instability it created, there was a much shorter interval on this occasion. Plans had been put in place for Edward's enthronement, who, when he showed little interest in the arrangements, had been replaced in meetings by the then Duke of York, so on his accession, he was well prepared. The coronation went ahead on the day that had been earmarked for Edward VIII.

The country, the government and the Church of England must have breathed a sigh of relief that at last there was to be an anointed King, pledged to serve his country and God. The editor of the left-leaning *The New Statesman*, Kingsley Martin, described the nation's mood as, 'George didn't ask to get there. He's only doing his duty, and it's up to us to show we appreciate it.' There was as much relief as there was rejoicing.[25]

Some saw the coronation as a vital propaganda exercise, showing that Britain could do these things better than any European nation – Kingsley Martin thought it had upstaged Goebbels. Another commentator suggested that George VI's coronation was 'a pageant more splendid than any dictators can put on: beating Rome and Nuremberg hollow at their own bewildering best and with no obverse of compulsion or horror'.[26]

For the Establishment, it was also, like the coronations of Edward VII and George V, an articulation of Britain's status – the nation that led an Empire. Indian Princes and, for the first time, native African royalty attended, while the Prime Ministers of each Dominion took part in the procession to Westminster Abbey, also for the first time. In the Abbey, the new King promised to maintain the Protestant Reformed Religion in Britain, but in the Dominions he pledged to uphold the Gospel of whichever Communion they adhered to.[27]

At the time, it was considered a way of enforcing the monarch's kingship of each country; today, it suggests a possible way forward for Charles III's coronation in a country where the Church of England is in decline and has friendly ecumenical relations with many other denominations.

In 1937, though, for an eleven-year-old little girl it was a profound moment, watching as her parents were crowned. As Princess Elizabeth looked down, she saw, as Heiress Presumptive (not Heir Apparent; if a brother were yet to be born, she would no longer inherit the throne), what her destiny was most likely to be. As she turned to comment to her grandmother, Mary, also a crowned queen, she would have been reminded again of the duties, obligations and privileges of the role that would one day be hers. 'I thought it all very, very wonderful and I expect the Abbey did too,' she wrote in an account of the coronation she later gave to her parents. 'The arches and beams at the top were covered with a sort of haze of wonder as Papa was crowned, at least I thought so.'[28]

Instruction of the Heiress Presumptive about her future role and the history of the British monarchy and constitution not only fell upon the shoulders of her parents and her grandmother but also involved the Vice-Provost of Eton College, Henry Marten, who taught her history. He later recalled that he taught her that the only other institution that matched the British monarchy in antiquity was the papacy, and that it had survived because of its ability to adapt.[29]

It was not just the monarchy that had to learn to adapt to survive but soon also the entire country as it went to war with Germany in 1939. For Princess Elizabeth and her sister, the war mostly involved living at Windsor Castle, away from the London bombing, and being part of a propaganda initiative, with photographs of them and their parents highlighting that they were enduring rationing and other limitations just like the rest of Britain. The King and Queen, since they were the Duke and Duchess of York, had regularly promoted themselves and their two daughters as an idealised family, and continued to do so during the war: a stable, Christian family unit. It was something that would probably not have happened if Edward VIII had remained King, married to Wallis Simpson. The couple married in their forties, probably too late to become parents.

As the King's radio broadcasts made clear, he, like the wartime Prime Minister Winston Churchill, saw the war as a moral crusade, against the might of fascist Germany. The Princess was also recruited to do her bit through the medium of radio, with a broadcast on the BBC in 1940 targeted at children displaced through war. With her sister Margaret at her side, she said, 'We know from experience what it means to be away from those we love most of all.' Jock Colville, private secretary to Churchill and later to the Princess, thought it sentimental, but 'her voice was most impressive and if the Monarchy survives, Queen Elizabeth II should be a most successful radio Queen'.[30]

Elizabeth II, of course, became not only a radio Queen, but also a TV Queen, and eventually a YouTube Queen. The House of Windsor, with one eye firmly on tradition, also kept an eye on innovation and technology, making use of it to impart messages about its role and its creed. During the war years, other messages about Elizabeth's commitment to the nation were imparted: at the age of eighteen she became a counsellor of state and was considered old enough to succeed her father without a regent; she began solo engagements, and in 1945 she joined the Auxiliary Territorial Service as a driver. But for the Heiress Presumptive, there was one pressing need above all: to be married and continue the royal line.

Her marriage to Prince Philip of Greece was the second of the great occasions of her life at Westminster Abbey, and her second great religious moment at the nation's church. The couple, both descended from Queen Victoria, had known one another for more than a decade when they wed in 1947. A nomadic lifestyle combined with royal connections had been Prince Philip's lot, until he eventually settled in Britain, serving in the Royal Navy with distinction during the war (see chapter six for further details of Prince Philip's life and beliefs).

In April 1947 Princess Elizabeth reached her actual majority, despite the roles given to her at eighteen, and she marked it with her famous vow speech, akin to a marital promise. But it was not to preclude her from a further vow – to Prince Philip.

Marriage of a royal, and most definitely of an heir to the throne, is not just a private matter, and it required the King and other members of the Privy Council, including the Prime Minister and the Archbishop of Canterbury, to approve it under the terms of the Royal Marriages Act 1772. This they did in August, with the wedding ceremony planned for November 1947.

This was the first major postwar celebration and a chance for the monarchy to consolidate its position and reinforce the idea that royal marriages were major national, religious events. One of the skills of the House of Windsor has been the way in which it adapts to such a degree that it invents what many think must be tradition. While their predecessors had for some time used marriage and the family to market their image as not so much set apart from but mirroring their subjects, their actual weddings had been modest and essentially intimate events. Elizabeth's parents had married in Westminster Abbey, but this was a departure from tradition. Now, after the years of austerity and war, the Abbey was chosen again. This royal church wedding would become a state occasion expressing faith, celebrating love and the pre-eminence still of the Church of England, and would be in stark contrast to the 1930s when the heir to the throne failed to make a suitable match that would propagate the House of Windsor for years to come.

The royal wedding of 1947 highlighted the way in which the personal and the constitutional always collide in issues surrounding the hatching, matching and despatching of the monarch and his or her family. Clement Attlee's Labour government, elected by a landslide in 1945, was conscious of the state of the economy just as the Royals requested financial assistance for the wedding of the Heiress Presumptive. The loan from North America used for postwar reconstruction was running out; there was a fuel crisis affecting factories during a big freeze, and a feeling that a big state occasion neither could be afforded nor would be popular.

There were also concerns that the Royal Family should set an example and buy British, with attention focused on the Princess' wedding dress. Reassuring word reached Number 10 that the silk, even if coming from Chinese silkworms, was being woven in Scotland and Kent. The dress designer, Norman Hartnell, made his views known to the Labour government: 'Our worms are Chinese worms, from nationalist China, of course!'[31] Meanwhile the anti-royal Chancellor, Hugh Dalton, aware that many left-wing MPs would not take kindly to expense, haggled with Buckingham Palace over increases to the Civil List that were being asked for following Princess Elizabeth's wedding. The row was solved when Dalton's Budget was leaked, just days before the wedding. He then resigned, with the arguments over the funds for the newly married couple settled by Dalton's successor, Stafford Cripps.

Any worries that the royal wedding would not be welcomed by a hard-up nation came to nothing, and Britain enjoyed a week of partying. Few seemed to resent that the wedding dress cost £1,200 and three hundred clothing coupons.

The wedding, while less a state occasion than a coronation, provided a moment for Britain to show itself to the world as still a major power, and its royalty to be heads and shoulders above other royal houses. Thanks to Queen Victoria and Prince Albert, most of European royalty was related to Elizabeth and Philip, and they turned out in moth-eaten furs for the Abbey ceremony. 'It was a tremendous meeting-place,' Princess Margaret recalled to the historian Ben Pimlott. 'People who had been starving in little garrets all over Europe reappeared.'[32] Not everyone related to the royal couple did leave their attics, though: it was too soon after the war for Prince Philip's three sisters, all married to Germans, to be welcomed, and they stayed away.

Prince Philip's 'foreignness' was something that concerned the Establishment in more ways than one, and two months before his wedding this member of the Greek Orthodox Church was received into the Church of England by the Archbishop of Canterbury.[33]

The wedding ceremony itself also provided the Windsors with an opportunity to simultaneously communicate two entirely different messages: that they are both 'other' and 'entirely the same' as the rest of the nation. Here was a bride clothed in a sublime dress few could afford, embroidered with garlands of stars, made of crystals and pearls, travelling to her wedding in the Irish State Coach and walking up the aisle on the arm of the King, to a service of pomp and pageantry. But as the Archbishop of York, Cyril Garbett, said in his sermon, the marriage service 'was in all essentials exactly the same as it would have been for any cottager who might be married this afternoon in some small country church in a remote village in the Dales'.[34]

The next great moment in the Queen's life in the Abbey would be, however, essentially about her otherness: the coronation of 1953. And yet this otherness was to be transmitted right into living rooms across the nation, a broadcast which was first thought to be unacceptable, as if it might let daylight in upon magic. At first, the Prime Minister, Winston Churchill, the Cabinet, the Queen and her advisers, including her husband Prince Philip, who was chairing the Coronation Joint Executive set up to help the traditional coronation organiser, the Earl Marshal, rejected the notion that it should be broadcast. The clergy of Westminster Abbey and the Archbishop of Canterbury also vetoed the idea, fearful of TV cameras detracting from the dignity of the religious service.[35]

It took lobbying by the BBC and newspapers, as well as letters of complaint from the public about the lack of a broadcast, to reverse the decision – a decision that state papers, released under the thirty-year rule, show was eventually made by the Queen herself. Even when the broadcast went ahead, though, there were restrictions about what could be seen and what should be hidden. This sacred ritual, in part, remained too sacred to be screened.

The ritual was ancient and yet not writ in stone. Parts of it, as had happened on previous occasions, were moved so that the order was different. The Church of England, mindful of its responsibilities and also of the opportunities such an event gave it to remind people of its connections to the Crown and its denominational primacy as the established Church, had a committee set up by the Archbishop of Canterbury, Geoffrey Fisher, to prepare for it. Its members included people who had witnessed previous coronations of the twentieth century, as well as E. C. Ratcliff, professor of divinity, and Norman Sykes, Dixie professor of ecclesiastical history, both at Cambridge, and Dr Alan Don, Dean of Westminster.

As always with liturgy, the concern was not so much with what seemed appealing or attractive but to build, symbol upon symbol, a narrative of meaning. Those involved in 1953's planning sought to make the ceremony more coherent, moving the regalia procession to the start of the service. The Bible's presentation to Queen Elizabeth was also moved, ensuring that the Word preceded the Eucharistic, sacramental service. The emphasis on the coronation's sacramental nature was highlighted by arrangements made to prepare the young Queen for it: Geoffrey Fisher wrote her a personal book of prayers, which she kept for the rest of her life, and sometimes showed to guests at Windsor Castle.[36]

The service was in part a constitutional exercise, with Elizabeth II promising in her oath to uphold the laws of the nation. It was a confirmation of the Church of England's settlement, with her promise to maintain the Protestant Reformed Religion; it was also an idealised vision of Britain, according to a series of sermons given by Archbishop Fisher in the run-up to the coronation. In them he suggested that the Queen's role was to uphold 'the pillars of a true society', based on domestic fidelity and united homes.[37]

But above all, the ceremony was about Christianity, its beliefs, its focus on the divine, on the importance of sacrifice, and a certain moral sensibility as well.

It began, as far as the liturgists were concerned, not with the entrance of the Queen, but with The Preparation, early in the morning, when the items essential for anointing were laid on the altar: the ampulla, filled with oil, and the spoon for the oil. Altars are always places of sacrifice, and these items placed there indicated that this young woman was about to participate in a ceremony akin to a priestly ordination, and to commit – or sacrifice – her life to come to the role of Queen. The symbolism of sacrifice is also reflected in a Communion service, remembering Christ's commitment unto death of himself for the world, and at the start of the coronation service, the Chalice and Paten, to be used for the Eucharist, were also placed on the altar, together with the regalia for the coronation.

After Queen Elizabeth had processed into the Abbey, and prayed at her chair in the Sacrarium, she turned to show herself to the people. Anne Glenconner, one of her maids of honour that day, recalled, 'the Queen curtsied to all four sides of the Abbey, a beautiful gesture and a rare one (though she does bow twice to the peers at the State Opening of Parliament)' – an observation that indicates how the coronation was used to show that the highest in the land was also there to serve.[38]

While she did this, the Archbishop of Canterbury, cried out:

Sirs, I here present unto you  
Queen ELIZABETH,  
your undoubted Queen:  
Wherefore all you who are come this day  
to do your homage and service,  
Are you willing to do the same?

In response, the congregation acclaimed her: 'God save Queen Elizabeth!' and trumpets sounded. It was a moment, according to Edward Shils and Michael Young's analysis in *The Sociological Review* of 1953, when Fisher was 'asking the assembly to reaffirm their allegiance to [The Queen] not so much as an individual as the incumbent of an office of authority charged with moral responsibility'.[39]

The monarch's role takes several forms – secular and religious, but also ecclesiastical in that he or she is Supreme Governor of the

Church of England – and it is noticeable that of the three, it was Elizabeth's role in the Church of England that dominated the oaths that she took that day. Two were about ensuring good government, justice and the law, tempered with mercy. One was a promise about the Gospel. But three were about the Church – maintaining the Protestant Reformed Religion to the utmost of her power; maintaining and preserving 'inviolably the settlement of the Church of England, and the doctrine, worship, discipline, and government thereof, as by law established in England', and finally, preserving 'unto the Bishops and Clergy of England, and to the Churches there committed to their charge, all such rights and privileges, as by law do or shall appertain to them or any of them'. She answered, 'All this I promise to do.'

According to Shils and Young, she was acknowledging 'the superiority of the transcendent moral standards and their divine source, and therewith the sacred character of moral standards of British society'.[40] But if it was British, it was most certainly, in 1953, still Anglican, according to the rite of the coronation.

This connection between the nature of Britain and a Christian ethos was also evident when the Moderator of the Church of Scotland – chosen as the one moment of ecumenism in an otherwise staunchly Anglican ceremony – handed the Queen the Bible on which she took her oath and said, 'Here is Wisdom. This is the Royal Law.'[41]

In the early 1950s, sociologists were more concerned with poverty and deprivation, but Shils and Young were intrigued by a ceremony at once so alien from ordinary people's lives yet so attractive to them. They saw the coronation, from their sociological perspective, as an act of national communion, something that confirmed a collectivity in the face of modern anomie and egotism, and an expression of shared moral values, of solidarity, even if few would express it in that way. Shils and Young began their analysis with the memorable line, 'the heart has its reasons which the mind does not suspect'[42] – a paraphrasing of seventeenth-century French philosopher Blaise Pascal and later used as the title of the memoir of Wallis Simpson, the woman who nearly upended the monarchy, but which this ceremony confirmed was no longer rocking on its foundations.

A television audience, like the thousands in Westminster Abbey, watched one individual become so much more than that – a representative of the nation, of the relationship between Church and state, of the Crown, of the link with the divine.

The encounter with the divine – the anointing – was the most sacred and most private of moments in the whole coronation. It was, in the words of Shils and Young, the moment when the Queen 'is presented as a frail creature who has now to be brought into contact with the divine, and thus transformed into a Queen, who will be something more than the human being who has received the previous instruction'.[43] Divested of her coronation robes and all her adornments, she wore a simple white shift, hidden from view beneath a canopy held by Knights of the Garter. The Archbishop anointed her on her head, hands and breast, with the holy oil from the ampulla left on the altar that morning. It was like a priestly ordination, set within a Communion service, with Handel's 'Zadok the Priest' sung and its words, from 1 Kings, mentioned again at the anointing. That a young woman, dressed plainly in white, should be the subject of such a ceremony only served to reinforce its power and sense of sacrifice.

Once the anointing was over, the Queen was dressed in the colobium sindonis – effectively an alb with white lace and the supertunica, on this occasion made of silk ornamented with red roses, green shamrocks and purple thistles. These were essentially garments based on a priest's vestments and a symbol of the monarchy's links to priesthood. Later, she was also clothed in a royal stole and robe of cloth of gold, with the Archbishop saying, 'the Lord clothe you with the role of righteousness and with the garments of salvation',[44] another suggestion of priesthood given these items resembled the stole and cope of a priest.

Then came the moment when that item so familiar from every coronation portrait of a British monarch, the orb, was placed in her right hand. A gold sphere, it is studded with diamonds, surmounted by a large cross also marked with diamonds. It serves for every monarch and, on this occasion, the congregation in the Abbey and the people watching on TV at home saw that even royalty is a subject, a subject of the one on the cross, and, as the coronation service put it 'the whole world is subject to the Power and Empire of Christ'.[45]

No Christian service involving vows, whether marriage or ordination or indeed a coronation, would be complete without a ring, and on the finger of the Queen's right hand was placed one, set with a sapphire and a ruby cross of St George. Although known as the wedding ring of England and associated with St Edward the Confessor, its placement was another moment for the Archbishop to remind Elizabeth of her religious as well as queenly role:

> You are this day
> consecrated to be our Head and Prince,
> so may you continue steadfastly
> as the Defender of Christ's Religion;
> that being rich in faith
> and blessed in all good works,
> you may reign with him who is the King of Kings.[46]

Then came the sceptres and baculus, thought to represent the rod and staff of Psalm 23, one with a cross standing for power and justice and the other with a dove representing equity and mercy.

All these moments, step by step, had signified the Queen as being a vehicle for the great virtues of Christianity, as one who served under God, and was a link in her own particular way between God and the people. But for most people, the climax of any coronation is the crowning. Yet this key moment only took place at this very late stage in the ceremony. This is the moment that today is looked at again and again on YouTube – the very essence of spectacle, the climax of the drama.

The one who earlier had been the epitome of sacrifice, divested of all her grandeur, in a white shift for her anointing, was now bound up with all the formality and grandeur of her role, standing not so much for something aligned to God, but now for earthly power: bejewelled, hailed, acclaimed. Wearing St Edward's Crown, and lifted into her throne by bishops and peers, she was surrounded by those come to pay homage: bishops, her husband, her ducal cousins, the peers of the realm.

For the sociologist Grace Davie, this was 'a ceremony that brought together the Church of England, the monarchy and the nation in an impressive act of sacralisation witnessed by a television audience numbered in millions'.[47]

It certainly brought the nation together that day for a celebration and a time of levity after the war years and the immediate grey postwar ones. The Festival of Britain was supposed to do that but, according to Churchill, this was far greater. That levity was everywhere, from the Queen's own, 'Ready, girls,' to her maids of honour[48] to her struggle not to laugh at the Bishop of Winchester's eyebrows during the coronation, and the countless street parties of a nation tired of rationing. But could this newly crowned monarch keep the nation together in the years to come, not only with levity, but also with a sense of purpose and, above all, with ideals, Christian ideals?

# 5
# The framework of her life: Elizabeth II's quiet faith and some quiet revolutions

After what might be termed a 'honeymoon period' in the very early years of her reign, Elizabeth II came in for trenchant criticism by the end of the 1950s, as did the spiritual nature of her role that had been at the centre of the coronation. Within seven years of her accession, the writer John Grigg, newly ennobled as the second Lord Altrincham, wrote an article, later collected in a volume of writing on the monarchy, in which he lambasted the Queen for her speaking voice, poor education and lack of knowledge of people other than the aristocracy. The problem, he said, was that 'the Coronation had emphasised the priestly aspect of her office and in the ensuing period she had continued to appear more sacerdotal than secular'.[1]

Grigg also went on to predict:

> Those who care for the Monarchy as an institution should look beyond the hideous coloured photographs of a glamorous young woman in sparkling attire to the more testing realities of twenty years hence. The Monarchy will not survive, let alone thrive, unless its leading figures exert themselves to the full and with all the imagination they and their advisers can command . . .
>
> When she has lost the bloom of youth the Queen's reputation will depend, far more than it does now, upon her personality. It will not then be enough for her to go through the motions; she will have to say things which people can remember, and do things on her own initiative which will make people sit up and take notice.[2]

In many ways, Altrincham was right: Elizabeth II's reign and her reputation were influenced by two aspects of her life: what she did, in terms of embodying values that express something of the nation's values, and what she said.

Much of what she did in expressing values was bound up with family and with religion. And while Queen Elizabeth never granted an interview, she spoke about her most personal beliefs – her religious ones – constantly throughout her seventy-year reign. She was expected to stay above politics, as head of state. She did not stay above faith: where she stood was abundantly clear.

Since the reign of George III, the British Royal Family has represented a familial ideal, which, given the past misdemeanours of its monarchs, has been a remarkable turnaround. The large families of George III and Victoria were idealised and both monarchs saw the importance of the family in terms of connecting to the common experience of their subjects. Some monarchs' lives were more questionable: both Edward VII and Edward VIII had a series of mistresses. Between them came George V, a model of husbandly duty, while George VI and his wife created a model of familial rectitude, known to the King as 'Us Four', and to the public as first the Yorks and then the Royal Family, celebrated through photo features in newspapers and women's magazines. This continued into the early years of Elizabeth II's reign, as her children grew in number, consolidating her family in the Establishment eye as a symbol of domestic stability at a time when marriage break-up was starting to grow. This view was articulated by the Archbishop of Canterbury, Michael Ramsey, in 1964 when he officiated at the christening of the Queen and Prince Philip's youngest child, Edward, in Buckingham Palace. 'There was around the throne,' he said, 'a Christian family united, happy and setting to all an example of what the words "home and family" truly meant.'[3]

In 1969 there was some concern among some of Queen Elizabeth's advisers that she and her family were considered dull, with little known about their lives. Her then private secretary, William Heseltine, and Lord Mountbatten's son-in-law, the film-maker Lord Brabourne, approached Prince Philip with an idea that a fly-on-the-wall documentary might be made about them. The Queen took some persuading, but her husband's enthusiasm for the project helped convince her of its merits. The result was a sort of family next door meets pomp and circumstance. Scenes of the family having a barbecue together at Balmoral or chatting over the lunch table were interspersed with day-by-day footage of the Queen's year, from formal presentations of diplomats to tours and meetings with the Prime Minister, Harold Wilson.

The film was ecstatically received, with the politician Julian Critchley commentating that it was 'devoted to the proposition that the Queen is a human being', while Prince Philip went much further, suggesting that the documentary countered the very kind of otherness of the monarch that the deeply religious service of the coronation had tried to communicate: 'I think it is quite wrong that there should be a sense of remoteness or majesty. If people see, whoever it happens to be, whatever head of state, as individuals, as people, I think it makes it much easier for them to accept the system or to feel part of the system.'[4]

If the film was made to convey that this was a model family, then it was a successful exercise, but in letting the door be opened ajar, it did encourage others to think they might push it even further to let yet more light in on the private family within, albeit one with a very public role. The path from *Royal Family* to the later intrusions of the paparazzi is one that can be easily mapped, and despite their eventual opening of the doors to other film-makers, for documentaries such as *Elizabeth R*, *Royal Family* was eventually banned, and considered a mistake.

It was also impossible to consider that the Royal Family was as ideal an exemplar of Christian familial virtue as the film made out, when in years to come it was beset once more by marital discord and divorce – an aspect of life that was always difficult for a family whose members included the Supreme Governor of the Church of England.

Yet the most painful issue involving divorce had happened some sixteen years before *Royal Family* was conceived, and it directly concerned the Church's teaching on marriage.

In the early 1950s, divorce was still frowned upon, although after the Second World War, when many people had made hasty marriages, it was becoming far less rare. One person who had had such a wartime wedding was Group Captain Peter Townsend, a good-looking, intelligent RAF officer who had joined the Royal Household, first as equerry to George VI and, after his death, to his widow, Queen Elizabeth the Queen Mother. In 1951 his wife Rosemary left him, and he gained a divorce as well as custody of his two sons. It was two years later, just before the coronation, that a love affair between Townsend and her twenty-two-year-old sister Margaret became known to the young Queen. The couple, with an age gap of twenty-five years, a lifetime of experience and differing classes between them, informed her themselves.

This was an early test of the complicated set of roles that Elizabeth II had to play: to respond to a member of her family who wished to be married to the man she loved, to consider the issue as the monarch, and how the matter would play with the British people, and to tackle the matter as the Supreme Governor of the Church of England. And then there was the Royal Marriages Act of 1772.

The Act, introduced by George III to contain his unruly sons from making unsuitable marriages, was still on the statute books, restricting what anybody in the royal line of succession could do regarding marriage. Margaret was in the direct line of succession after her nephew Charles and niece Anne, and it meant she had to be given the permission of both her sister the monarch and Parliament to be legally married. She could go ahead without their consent once she reached the age of twenty-five if she gave the Privy Council twelve months' notice, but there was a heavy price to pay: if she opted for that choice, she would have to surrender all her royal rights and the financial benefits of the Civil List.

Twelve months is also what Queen Elizabeth asked of the couple, which might have been her way of offering them some hope while removing her from the equation as the villain, banning the marriage. But it could also be seen as only drawing out the situation and therefore making it more painful.

There was opposition, too, from the Queen's private secretary, Tommy Lascelles, who had been Edward VIII's assistant private secretary at the time of the abdication – a drama that still resonated with the Royal Family and its courtiers. Lascelles, according to

Townsend, made his views known when they met: 'You must be mad or bad,' he said.[5]

Lascelles alerted the government through Jock Colville, Churchill's secretary. The message came back that the Cabinet was unanimous that the Prime Minister should advise the Queen against the marriage. Despite seeming opposition from all quarters, it was Lascelles' influence that Princess Margaret most blamed for the thwarting of her desire to marry, perhaps because she realised the force of his opposition, given it was tied up with his experience of the abdication, a shadow that hung over the Royal Family. She was later quoted as saying, 'I shall curse him to the grave.' She also never spoke to him again.[6]

Townsend, already having heard the Queen's admonition that the couple should wait a year, found himself posted as air attaché to the British Embassy in Brussels for two years. The press, which had reported on the affair between the couple after Margaret had been spotted tenderly picking lint off Townsend's jacket at the coronation, sympathised with Margaret as some latter-day princess trapped in a tower. But nothing changed during that time when Townsend was in exile, and the pair wrote to one another daily. It was surely impossible for the Supreme Governor of the Church of England to advise her sister to marry a divorced man, albeit the innocent party in a divorce, thereby condoning Margaret going against canon law.

When Margaret reached her twenty-fifth birthday on 21 August 1955, press speculation had reached fever pitch over the possibility of her marrying Group Captain Townsend, as this was the moment when she could go ahead without the Queen's permission. 'Come on Margaret!' said the *Daily Mirror*, urging her to make up her mind, while another headline in mid-October said in frustration, 'No Ring Yet!'

At the start of that month, the new Prime Minister, Anthony Eden, had visited Queen Elizabeth at Balmoral, and although he himself was a divorcee, the government did not think it could support the Princess retaining her royal status if the marriage were to go ahead. It did, however, consider drawing up a Bill of Renunciation so that Princess Margaret and any children of the marriage would be removed from the line of succession.

The odds, however, remained stacked against Margaret and Townsend. In these early days of the 1950s, certain values – faith, duty, sacrifice – still had a profound hold on society, or at least, the Establishment. On 21 October, Elizabeth II, surrounded by the Royal Family, the Prime Minister and members of the Cabinet, unveiled a statue of her father. George VI, she said, 'had shirked no task, however difficult', and 'never faltered in his duty to his peoples'.[7] Five days later, on 26 October, *The Times* showed itself to be the Establishment paper, par excellence, with its leader focusing on the role that the monarchy plays by being a model family, and in the Queen, society saw itself ideally reflected. Princess Margaret played her role in this as part of that ideal family. The leader had been written by the editor, Sir William Haley. 'If one of the Family's members become a cause for division, then the salt has lost its savour,' it declaimed. 'The Princess will be entering into a union which vast numbers of her sister's people, all sincerely anxious for her lifelong happiness, cannot in conscience regard as a marriage.'[8] It was damning, but it illustrated the burden of office, and one that was shared by the monarch's own family.

Haley was not the only Establishment figure to expect the Princess to sacrifice personal happiness for the sake of the Church, its teaching and her sister's position. Before the Princess made her decision publicly known, she went to see the Archbishop of Canterbury, Geoffrey Fisher, a churchman known for his views opposing divorce and remarriage. Princess Margaret's own account of this encounter, told to the Countess of Longford, was that after they had greeted one another, Dr Fisher put on his glasses and hauled a large reference book from his shelves. 'Put it back,' said Princess Margaret. 'I have come to give you information, not to ask for it.' She then told him that she had decided not to marry Peter Townsend. Dr Fisher then said with a beaming smile, 'What a wonderful person the Holy Spirit is!'[9]

On 31 October, Princess Margaret issued a statement:

> I would like it to be known that I have decided not to marry Group Captain Peter Townsend. I have been aware that subject to my renouncing my rights of succession, it might have been

> possible for me to contract a civil marriage. But, mindful of the Church's teaching that Christian marriage is indissoluble, and conscious of my duty to the Commonwealth, I have resolved to put these considerations before any others.

For those who had hoped for a New Elizabethan age, this did not indicate the wondrous work of the Holy Spirit, but the distressing drama of a young woman forced to toe the constitutional and religious line, as if it were still 1936 and the time of the abdication. Others wondered if the Princess also had a more pragmatic reason for backing out of any idea of marriage: Peter Townsend, with his RAF pension and limited earnings, could hardly have helped Margaret live in the manner to which she had grown accustomed within the privileged bosom of the Royal Family, should she have chosen to renounce her rights of succession in order to marry him. But two years later, Dr Fisher told the writer and biographer, James Pope-Hennessy, that Princess Margaret was theologically literate and indicated that she was inspired by her faith. She was 'a thoroughly good churchwoman', he said, and 'really understands doctrine'.[10]

Princess Margaret was known to continue her devotion to churchgoing: the churchwoman would, from time to time, attend services in Westminster Abbey, sitting high up in a private balcony which could be reached via the deanery, but unseen by the rest of the congregation. For Queen Elizabeth and the Church of England, the marriage of someone so senior in the line of succession to a divorcee had been avoided, but the damage had been done, and not only to Princess Margaret personally. It was an unsettling time, when both monarch and the established Church had seemed out of kilter with much of popular opinion, and would continue to be so.

The shade of the abdication played its part, but so did the idea that the Royal Family, with its head playing such a significant role in the established Church, should set an example. But bit by bit, failed marriage by failed marriage, divorce edged closer to the Royal Family. The government played its part in attempting to distance the Queen from these traumas; when her cousin, Lord Harewood, and seventeenth in line to the throne, was separated from his wife, it was announced in 1967 that 'the Cabinet has advised the Queen to give her consent'.[11]

It was a tricky moment. Should the Royal Family move with the times or should it be seen as a beacon of tradition and adherence to the teaching of the Church of England? The Queen found a get-out clause by appealing to Prime Minister Harold Wilson's government to be a sounding board. In this situation, the Cabinet found a way through the Royal Marriages Act maze – Harewood wanted to not only divorce but also to remarry, and so needed the Queen's permission – so it gave Queen Elizabeth advice that the remarriage should go ahead, advice that she was bound to take. In that way, the titular head of the Church of England could retain her support for its traditional opposition to divorce while enabling her cousin to secure his future happiness. But it only put off a problem which was going to keep coming up in the Queen's own family.

Nine years later, Princess Margaret herself was divorced, after her 1960 marriage to Antony Armstrong-Jones failed. The Queen's sister was never to marry again, but in 1992, her divorced daughter Anne did so.

Princess Anne had married Captain Mark Phillips, a fellow equestrian, in 1973, in a service in Westminster Abbey watched by a hundred million around the globe. But, despite their common interests in sport and horses, the marriage failed, and in 1989 they announced their decision to separate. The statement published about the state of the Phillipses' marriage said that there was no intention to divorce. But by then there had been a press furore over the theft of letters to the Princess from the Queen's equerry, Commander Timothy Laurence. Three years later, in April 1992, Buckingham Palace announced that the Princess and Mark Phillips were divorcing.

But could the Supreme Governor's daughter marry for the second time in the Church of England, which still frowned on divorce? The solution for Princess Anne was to cross the border over to Scotland and marry, eight months after her divorce, for the second time, swapping Westminster Abbey for Crathie Kirk, where the Royal Family worship when they are staying at Balmoral. This fitted in with Church of Scotland advice that, 'In all cases, a minister will wish to interview a couple before agreeing to marry them, so that he or she is satisfied that a religious ceremony is appropriate. It is helpful if the couple have a reason for approaching a particular parish minister – family, knowledge of the place, etc.'[12] Clearly, the Princess's connections to Balmoral and Crathie fitted the bill.

The ceremony was dubbed as private and was certainly small compared to the grandeur of other royal weddings, including Anne's previous one: just thirty guests attended. But it also proved to be a deft solution to the issue of the divorcee Anne remarrying in church. The Church of Scotland is a national Church, but not a state Church, so the Queen worships within it as an individual. There is no issue there of her or her family having to be models of conformity, although she did take an oath at her coronation to maintain its government and is represented at its annual meetings by a Lord High Commissioner. But the key issue that offered a lifeline for Anne was the Church of Scotland's view of marriage and divorce at the time. While the Church of England perceived a marriage as a sacrament that could not be undone, the Church of Scotland saw it as an ordinance of religion, thus making remarriage of a divorcee permissible in some circumstances.

That a pragmatic solution was found to Princess Anne's marital problems must have been a crumb of comfort for the Queen. The year 1992 was the one she famously called her annus horribilis during a speech on 24 November at the Guildhall to mark her Ruby Jubilee as Queen. Its horribilis quotient was upped by not only Anne's divorce but also by the separation of the Queen's second son, Prince Andrew, from his wife, the Duchess of York, in March that year, as well as publication of Andrew Morton's *Diana: Her True Story*, revealing the marital discord between the Princess of Wales and her husband, the heir to the throne. The year only got worse after the speech: three days before Anne's second wedding and a fortnight after the Guildhall comments, it was announced that Charles and Diana were to separate.

The lives of the younger royals had become a permanent soapy distraction for the British as well as people in America, Australia and European nations. Even as a general election campaign got underway in 1992, with Premier Margaret Thatcher facing Labour's Neil

Kinnock, the tabloids were full of stories of the antics of Fergie, the Duchess of York, and the lives of Charles and Di. At a time when Buckingham Palace had hoped attention would be focused on the fortieth anniversary of the accession of the Queen, the attention of many journalists was on the private lives of her children.

Much of the coverage was speculative for some time, until publication of Morton's *Diana: Her True Story* and its serialisation in *The Sunday Times*. Morton had checked his evidence and authenticated quotations. There was a hint that this book was Diana's own story in that the Princess declined to reject publicly that she knew of the content in advance. Later, after her death in a Paris car crash in 1997, her active involvement in providing Morton with tapes of accounts of her life was revealed.

Morton's biography was a new form of royal reporting, a venture that made emoting an art form. It pleased people's voyeuristic inclinations, providing them with what seemed to be a bird's eye view of the intimate travails and griefs of a mismatched couple. But it was not just about Charles and Diana and how the fairy tale had unravelled. It also threw a light on the Windsor family, whose idealisation still formed a major part of their impact on the nation. The British watched them gather together at Sandringham for Christmas, Easter at Windsor, Balmoral in the summer, at the Cenotaph every November, as regular as the seasons. While church attendance fell away, the Windsors turned out en masse for the big occasions. But Morton's book told a story of dysfunction, coldness and lack of empathy.

While the prurient relished the details of the Yorks' failing marriage, as they had Princess Anne's, it was the Prince of Wales' marriage that had dynastic issues, given that his immediate family was the one in which another heir to the throne was being raised. But it also raised issues regarding the indissolubility of marriage. As had happened with the marriage of Princess Anne, the immediate response was to tell the public – in this case via a Prime Minister's statement in the House of Commons – that there was no question of a divorce. They divorced four years later, but only after further excruciating episodes in the wars of the Waleses, as the tabloid press dubbed them, with revelations via headline-grabbing TV interviews of Charles' feelings for

Camilla Parker-Bowles and Diana's distress at the breakdown of their marriage.

The issue of whether the Prince of Wales might remarry as a divorcee could well have become a controversy (although his eventual marriage to the divorced Mrs Parker-Bowles did become one, as is examined in chapter eight), but for the death of Diana, Princess of Wales, a year after her divorce, in Paris.

Diana's death did, though, show the Windsors' capacity for flexibility in the funeral service organised for her in Westminster Abbey. Although its starting point was Tay Bridge – the code-named plan for the funeral of the Queen Mother – Diana's obsequies were rather like many others allowed nowadays in the Church of England. The rudiments of the Anglican service were there, but added to it was pop music, a procession by her charities and a deeply moving piece by John Tavener, combining words from the Greek Orthodox funeral service with quotations from *Hamlet*: 'life is but a dream'.

Quite how much the Queen was consulted is arguable, but the funeral was of deep significance in that it exposed how much Britain had changed since she had acceded to the throne: it was a more emotional nation that used religion to express itself while reshaping traditional liturgy in its own image. New ritual became evident during the days leading up to Diana's funeral: the cellophane meadow of flowers that surrounded her home, Kensington Palace, and the flowers strewn before her hearse as it wended its way through crowded streets to her resting place at her Spencer family seat of Althorp. This suggested, according to the author and critic, Peter Ackroyd, interviewed a year later, hints of another England, a pre-Reformation Catholic sensibility buried for hundreds of years glimpsed in this appetite for spectacle and ritual that surfaced at such a dramatic moment. 'If you think about it,' he said, 'England was Catholic for 1,500 years and Protestant for just 500, so where does the balance lie?'[13]

Diana's funeral, was not, however, a one-off. There is a long list of religious services indicating that as Supreme Governor of the Church of England, Queen Elizabeth II was not resistant to change but willing to embrace it from time to time. Just two months after the Princess of Wales' funeral, the Queen and the Duke of Edinburgh returned to Westminster Abbey for a special service to mark their golden wedding anniversary and the Queen requested that interfaith representatives be present. Invitations were sent to the Chief Rabbi and the Director of the Muslim College.

Most notable among the church services that reflected this changing approach and personal interest in interfaith were the Commonwealth Day Services, held each year at Westminster Abbey. Commonwealth Day itself is a reinvention in post-colonial times of Empire Day, created at the start of the twentieth century to encourage a sense of collective identity and imperial responsibility among young citizens. The name was changed to Commonwealth Day in 1958, and in 1963 and 1964 Commonwealth Day services were held for the first time in Westminster Abbey.

When the leaders of Commonwealth countries asked in 1965 for the service to be a multi-faith occasion, reflecting the other faiths of their nations, the Dean, Eric Abbott, was unwilling to experiment, and the service was transferred to the secular space of the City of London Guildhall. The Church of England Church Assembly, predecessor of General Synod, had also expressed its unease about a Christian space being used for an interfaith gathering. But the Abbey, as a royal peculiar, was not under ecclesiastical jurisdiction, and the Dean answers to the monarch. Elizabeth II, well aware of this and frustrated by the Guildhall event, asked Abbott to let the service be restored to the Abbey. He agreed, on the condition that it was called an observance rather than a service. It was a moment when the Queen led and the Anglican primacy followed.

Indeed, it could be argued that she led the way even earlier on interfaith, with her 1952 Christmas broadcast when she asked people in Britain, her Commonwealth and the last outposts of the British Empire to remember her at the forthcoming coronation, and 'whatever your religion may be, to pray for me on that day'.

The Commonwealth Day event at the Abbey has since been a firm fixture in its calendar, and interfaith gatherings at other churches have also grown in importance. But it is the Abbey's Commonwealth Service that is the most significant and indeed vivid expression of Anglican commitment to such dialogue. In March 2001, the historian Roy Strong, who had been appointed high bailiff of the Abbey, described seeing 'a group of Zulus singing and dancing their way round the abbey. They really used the space and, at the very end, returned to burst out of the West Door to give the public something to think about.'[14]

Queen Elizabeth's personal interest in dialogue was also evident in her 2002 address to both Houses of Parliament, given to mark the Golden Jubilee of her accession, when she commented that 'the consolidation of our richly multicultural and multifaith society, a major development since 1952, is being achieved remarkably peacefully and with much goodwill'.[15] Four years later, in 2006, the service of thanksgiving to mark her eightieth birthday held in St Paul's Cathedral included a procession with world faith representatives and prayers delivered by High Commissioners from Pakistan, Nigeria, Papua New Guinea and Barbados.

That same year, Dr John Hall was appointed Dean of Westminster and for the next thirteen years was closely involved in the Commonwealth Day Services held there. Over the years, prayers from other traditions were included in the services, 'and the Queen was actively happy about that', he recalled, but at the same time it also became a more outwardly liturgical, Anglican service. 'At one time we had just cassocks, but then we introduced copes,' he said.[16] There were to be no half-measures with this encounter between the established Church and other faiths, in other words. It was the equivalent of getting out the best china for the guests coming to tea.

Elizabeth II used visual spectacle and liturgy, then, to express her interest in interfaith dialogue on many occasions. But her most articulate, theological expression of this interest came in 2012 at a reception at Lambeth Palace to mark her Diamond Jubilee. It was the first event of her jubilee year, and those who gathered there must have thought, as it began, that it would be much like any other event that year: the Queen and her husband made small talk with the guests. But what she had to say, before representatives of various Christian denominations and the Bahá'í, Buddhist, Hindu, Jain, Jewish, Muslim, Sikh and Zoroastrian faiths, rewrote what the Church of England existed for.

Historically, the Church of England's role was to provide the English with a Christian Church, one that was separate from Rome and had at its core the Bible, the sacraments ordained by Jesus and a way of life and worship set out in the Book of Common Prayer. But that day, its Supreme Governor declared, 'Its role is not to defend Anglicanism to the exclusion of other religions. Instead, the Church has a duty to protect the free practice of all faiths in this country.'

And she went on: 'gently and assuredly, the Church of England has created an environment for other faith communities and indeed people of no faith to live freely. Woven into the fabric of this country, the Church has helped to build a better society – more and more in active co-operation for the common good with those of other faiths.'[17]

The speech had been some time in the making, according to Lord (Rowan) Williams, who was Archbishop of Canterbury at the time. It had gone to and fro between Buckingham Palace and Lambeth Palace, he recalled, while the original idea 'mysteriously emerged between the two palaces, as these things do'.[18]

The speech was part of a rethinking, he believes, of what the monarchy is about.

> [Elizabeth II] always thought of her role as a vocation, and at that time the Royal Family's standing was shifting. It was becoming more of a convening, unifying role, and about keeping the community together. So the ideas in this speech chimed deeply with her thoughts about her role.[19]

While others may have found challenges in the way in which Britain had changed in the latter half of the twentieth century and the early years of the twenty-first, Lord Williams believes that the Queen's familiarity with the different cultures and religions of the Commonwealth meant she was more at ease with these changes than others were. 'The experience with the Commonwealth helped her not to panic about diversity,' he said.[20]

Yet her speech was not just about her observations; it was in effect the Supreme Governor of the Church of England rethinking the Anglican settlement and the function of the established Church changing so that it does not close the door on anybody.

At the time, in 2012, few people outside the Church recognised the significance of what the Queen was saying, and there was limited coverage in the general media. But within Anglicanism, her nod to both religious liberty, protected by the Church of England, and her abiding commitment to Christianity as the faith, while respecting other traditions, was noted. It was a quiet revolution.

In an address before her speech, the then Dr Williams caused laughter when he said the Queen had shown that being religious was 'not eccentric or abnormal'.

Referring to her, he said:

> Thus you have been able to show so effectively that being religious is not eccentric or abnormal in terms of the kind of society we claim to be.
>
> On the contrary, if we take seriously the way our constitution works, the United Kingdom is a society where we might expect people to grasp the importance of symbols and traditions, not as a sign of mere conservatism or nostalgia but as a sign of what holds us together, what commits us to each other.[21]

It is this idea that was at the heart of her Christmas messages, particularly in the latter years of her reign. Television viewing figures indicated that the broadcast (also transmitted by radio) was the must-see for Christmas TV viewers, even more important than the *Strictly Special* or *Call the Midwife*. At 3 p.m. on Christmas Day, whether tucking into a mince pie or just before serving a late turkey lunch, the nation would take a collective break and head for the sofa to listen to the Queen. And as that nation became increasingly diverse and increasingly secular, Queen Elizabeth managed to retain her popularity and yet head in the opposite direction, with messages that were increasingly overtly Christian in content. As one who knew her and her faith well, put it, 'What you need to remember is that the Queen's commitment to her Christian faith is more important to her than her commitment to the Church of England. She is not sectarian.'[22]

Others, such as religious and royal commentators, argued that the Queen's Christmas message was always the big religious moment of the season – bigger even than going to church, given the relatively small numbers who would attend a service.

The Queen's Christmas speech was a high point of the festive season not only for those listening but also for the monarch and her royal household, where it was known as the QXB (the Queen's Christmas broadcast). For them it was a highlight of the year because it was her most personal commentary. The government was not involved at all. It was up to the Queen and her advisers to decide on the message's content, and from the turn of the century, the broadcasts followed a particular trajectory, highlighting her own personal faith.

Since that first live radio broadcast from Sandringham house on Christmas Day 1952, when the new Queen, recently bereaved by the death of her father, somewhat tentatively engaged with her subjects by modestly asking for their prayers at her forthcoming coronation, the Christmas broadcasts underwent significant changes. The speech was first televised in 1957, and they were prerecorded from 1960. They could also in later years be downloaded as podcasts and were available on the Royal Family's Facebook and YouTube channels.

The broadcasts often included footage of trips abroad, particularly of visits to Commonwealth nations, which also broadcast the Christmas message. And while the early broadcasts were more overtly religious, they became more and more of an account of the Queen's year, her trips abroad, family milestones such as weddings and christenings and comments about contemporary events. In 1966, for example, she spoke of the progress of women, and in 1972 she commented on Britain joining the European Community in language that would make any Remainer proud.

During this middle period of her reign, there were few explicit remarks about what her own faith and Christ meant to her, but rather more general festive sentiments. She said in 1963, 'Much has been achieved but there is still much to do and on this day of reunions and festivities in the glow of Christmas, let us remember the many undernourished people, young and old, scattered throughout the world,'[23] and in 1970, she remarked, 'That, very simply, is the message of Christmas – learning to be concerned about one another; to treat your neighbour as you would like him to treat you; and to care about the future of all life on earth.'[24]

The changing point was the year 2000, which began with the Queen at midnight on 31 December 1999 singing 'Auld Lang Syne' in the Millennium Dome with Prime Minister Tony Blair, his wife Cherie and New Labour ministers. The monarch looked somewhat uncomfortable at the enforced jollity as the clock struck midnight and a new century began. Twelve months later, the Queen decided to be explicit about what she thought the Millennium was all about – and it wasn't a Cool Britannia knees-up. As described in chapter four, she told the nation what she thought was the true Millennium anniversary. She spoke frankly about her own faith: 'For me the teachings of Christ and my own personal accountability before God provide a framework in which I try to lead my life. I, like so many of you, have drawn great comfort in difficult times from Christ's words and example.'[25]

Some royal watchers believe it was the then Archbishop of Canterbury, George Carey, who encouraged the Queen's explicit message in 2000, while others say the Duke of Edinburgh suggested she speak more openly about her Christian beliefs. Ian Bradley, an academic expert on the royals and religion and the author of *God Save the Queen: The Spiritual Heart of the Monarchy*, has said that the Queen was persuaded to continue in this vein after Christmas 2000 because she had twenty-five times more letters than usual in response to that particular Christmas broadcast than any other.

While journalists, theologians and churchmen noted the Queen's willingness to speak frankly to the nation about faith, it was not her only outlet to express her beliefs. She made five-yearly visits to the Church of England's General Synod throughout its fifty-one-year history, quoting St Paul and other parts of Scripture, until 2021 when ill-health meant Prince Edward read her address. But the audience there was more 'niche'; the viewers and listeners for the Christmas message were inevitably a much broader group.[26]

The former Dean of Westminster, Dr John Hall, noted before her death the frankness with which she spoke in the twenty-first century at Christmas to an audience whose numbers included people quite untutored in Christianity: 'The Queen is usually a somewhat reticent and shy person, so I've been very struck by her decision to speak up about her faith. We saw in the year 2000 how strongly she spoke and how personally, and that was a watershed. That approach seems to have continued.'[27]

Dr Hall said that the Queen's faith focused on human interaction with God, and 'you can see her father George VI's influence on her faith, still shining through what she says'.[28]

The theologian and former Archbishop of Canterbury, Lord (Rowan) Williams, said that the Queen adapted her messages according to the times and so felt a religious input at Christmas was down to her, when fewer people went to church. 'In 1956, say, there would have been a lot more religious scaffolding around. The Queen must be aware of this shift, so in her message, she puts up some of the scaffolding poles herself,' he said, commenting before she died. 'She's not aggressively evangelical but she doesn't mince words either.'[29]

The veteran royal reporter and columnist, Richard Kay, who has been covering the beat for many decades for the *Daily Mail*, agreed that the most significant religious moment at Christmas for a large part of the nation was the Queen's Christmas message:

> The Queen's faith is central to her life, and while a lot of people nowadays don't go to church, even at Christmas, they do listen to the Queen, and they hear what she has to say about her faith.
>
> It's still a hugely important part of Christmas, and viewers are looking for something else, something different from politics at this time of year.[30]

For royal correspondents like Kay, the Queen's Christmas message was always a key news story over the festive season.

Royal watchers would also take note of Queen Elizabeth's surroundings to divine other messages too, such as the way that family photos were arranged. For Christmas 2018, the photos included the newly married Prince Harry and Meghan Markle, but for Christmas 2019, there were photos indicating the line of succession: ones of George VI, the Prince of Wales and the Duchess of Cornwall, the Cambridges and their children – but no Harry, Meghan and their new baby, Archie.

During 2020's broadcast the Queen was filmed with just a photograph of her husband, Prince Philip, beside her. The couple had to isolate at Windsor together because of the Covid-19 lockdown, rather than spend the holiday with their extended family at Sandringham as was their tradition. The Queen commented on other people's isolation, assuring them of her prayers and offered, despite the mourning of many for those who had died, a message of Christian hope.

In December 2021, what turned out to be her last Christmas message was broadcast eight months after her own mourning for Prince Philip, who had died in April, and it was a deeply personal tribute to the husband she called 'my beloved Philip'. There was also an acknowledgement of the next generations taking over from her and the Duke of Edinburgh, with her reference to 'passing the baton', perhaps sensing that her own life was soon to draw to a close. This hope of continuity was evident, but there was no sense of hope of heaven or praying for the dead: the Protestant Queen had clearly not absorbed any Roman Catholic notions of intercessionary prayer. But, as had become the norm in recent years, there was a final overtly expressed reference to her own beliefs: 'It is this simplicity of the Christmas story that makes it so universally appealing, simple happenings that formed the starting point of the life of Jesus – a man whose teachings have been handed down from generation to generation, and have been the bedrock of my faith.'[31]

The message, with its Christian content, was heard, of course, by many people who did not share her faith. Jonathan Romain, a reform rabbi, says that Jewish people and those of many faiths and none would listen attentively 'because she is our Queen, as much as anybody else's. It is still a powerful message because she is a unifying force.'[32]

While the royal Christmas commentary became a mix of observation on the year and an intimate advocacy of the Queen's own faith, Romain perceived it as a subtle vehicle for powerful messages: 'She can hold a mirror up to society in a way that others can't. In 2000, she talked a lot about Christianity but she mentioned other faiths too. It caused a tremor; people noticed and appreciated it.'

On that occasion the Queen observed, 'Of course religion can be divisive, but the Bible, the Koran and the sacred texts of the Jews and Hindus, Buddhists and Sikhs, are all sources of divine inspiration and practical guidance passed down through the generations.'[33]

'It was an important acknowledgement that the country had changed,' said Romain, 'and that sort of recognition registers on the Richter scale.'[34]

In 2004, Queen Elizabeth returned at Christmas to the issue of diversity when she said, 'Religion and culture are much in the news these days, usually as sources of difference and conflict, rather than for bringing people together. But the irony is that every religion has something to say about tolerance and respecting others.'

Again, there was an acknowledgment of the changing nature of Britain when she continued, 'Most of us have learned to acknowledge and respect the ways of other cultures and religions, but what matters even more is the way in which those from different backgrounds behave towards each other in everyday life.'[35]

The nature of her messages and their Christian content was noted beyond Britain as well. Some years ago, one Vatican official told me that the Queen and her leadership were highly regarded in Rome, saying that in the Vatican, she was seen as 'the last Christian monarch'.[36]

It was the Queen's engagement with the Roman Catholic Church, said one who knew her and her faith well, that was 'arguably one of the most significant religious developments of her reign'.[37] For generations, relations between the British monarchy and the papacy were neuralgic, following the break with Rome initiated by Henry VIII and consolidated by his daughter Elizabeth I. While there were monarchs who dabbled with Roman Catholicism – Charles II converted on his deathbed, James II was a Catholic but was deposed, George IV signed into statute the Catholic Emancipation Act 1829, Edward VII pragmatically permitted his niece to convert to Catholicism for the sake of a dynastic marriage and was also rumoured to have undergone a deathbed conversion to Rome – the British throne has remained staunchly Protestant. The sovereign vows to uphold that faith, they continue to be Supreme Governor of the Church of England and they cannot be Roman Catholic themselves. Yet they continue to hold on to the title first bestowed on an English monarch, Henry VIII, by Pope Leo X in 1521: *Fidei Defensor* – Defender of the Faith. When Pope Paul II revoked it after Henry's momentous rejection of Rome, the English Parliament conferred it on Henry and all his successors.

The Vatican has a long collective memory. Its archive includes items stolen by its spies, including love letters between Henry VIII and Anne Boleyn, the woman Henry was prepared to put before his fidelity to not only his wife, Catherine of Aragon, but also to the Church. It has canonised plenty of Catholics, martyred by Henry and his daughter, the first Elizabeth, including forty such saints, raised to the altars in the reign of the second Elizabeth. But if relations grew stronger between the United Kingdom and Rome, much of that was down to the regard in which Elizabeth II was held, not least because of her personal faith and also the seriousness with which she approached her commitment over the years. As Nigel Baker, a former UK ambassador to the Holy See, put it to me while serving in Rome, 'While people in Rome are aware of her role as Supreme Governor of the Church of England, it is her sacral role that matters: they are well aware of the vows she took at the coronation.'[38]

As with all diplomacy, personal encounters matter in the recent history of the British and the papacy, and longevity played its part in this diplomatic success story. As the longest-reigning monarch in Europe, Elizabeth II encountered more popes than any other royal head of state: Pius XII in 1951, when she was still Princess Elizabeth; John XXIII in 1961; John Paul II in 1980, 1982 (during his pastoral visit to Britain) and 2000; Benedict XVI in 2010 (during his state visit to the UK) and Francis in 2014.

While the regard in which she was held was owing to religion, her encounters with popes were constitutional: she acted in her capacity as head of state. Nevertheless, they did show that the Holy See and Britain, with its Protestant established Church, had moved on. Significant barriers were broken down. As Lord (Rowan) Williams, former Archbishop of Canterbury, put it to me some years ago:

> The fact of her breaking the duck – she has done that by meeting so many popes. It is a way of saying that whatever was the case in 1535, there is no longer rivalry between the crown and the papacy. Doing what she has done – head of state meeting head of state – shows that we really have moved on from the sixteenth century.[39]

It happened bit by bit over a long reign: another instance of a quiet religious revolution.

The encounters between Elizabeth II and the successors of St Peter were very public events and a crucial aspect of diplomacy and governance. This was evident in the addresses given when the Queen and successive popes met, using the occasions to reinforce ties between the UK and the Holy See, and to identify common ground. John Paul II, for example, used his address to the Queen when she visited the Vatican in 1980 to speak about Britain's ideals of freedom and democracy, growing connections between the Catholic Church and the Church of England, and also to warn of the importance of spiritual values being vital if peace and development were to thrive.[40]

The reasons for Britain's relationship with Rome were highlighted clearly in the speeches of both the Queen and Pope Benedict XVI as he began his visit to Britain at Holyroodhouse in Edinburgh in September 2010. Queen Elizabeth emphasised the role of the Holy See in peace and development issues and in addressing common problems such as poverty and climate change. She also made it clear that Rome had played its part in Northern Ireland: 'In this country, we deeply appreciate the involvement of the Holy See in the dramatic improvement in the situation in Northern Ireland,'[41] a sentiment which might not have been uttered thirty years earlier during tensions over interventions by John Paul II.[42]

The importance of religion in national life and the risks it can pose to stability was also referred to by the Queen:

> Religion has always been a crucial element in national identity and historical self-consciousness. This has made the relationship between the different faiths a fundamental factor in the necessary cooperation within and between nation states. It is, therefore, vital to encourage a greater mutual, and respectful understanding. We know from experience that through committed dialogue, old suspicions can be transcended and a greater mutual trust established.[43]

These encounters between sovereign and pope have always been conducted with the sanction of the British government of the day, and in twenty-first-century Britain they have gone ahead with barely a murmur of controversy.

But in 1980, just days after the Queen's visit to Rome and during the planning for the visit of John Paul to Britain, a warning note was sounded by Enoch Powell about the consequences of the papal visit to Britain for the monarchy. Powell, a noted expert on the unwritten British constitution, argued that because the source of authority in the national Church was the same as the source of secular authority – namely, the Crown in Parliament – the visit of the Pope had immense consequences. 'It is constitutionally and logically unthinkable for England to contain both the Queen and the pope,' he said:

> Before that could happen, the essential character of the one or the other would have to be surrendered. If the Queen is on earth 'the Supreme Governor of the Church in England' then His Holiness is not in this realm 'Christ's vicar on earth'. Either the Pope's authority is not universal or the Church of England is not the Catholic and Apostolic Church in this land. The assertion that His Holiness personifies and the assertion that Her Majesty personifies are irreconcilable.

Powell did not take issue with the Queen visiting Rome but with the Pope's presence on English soil, seeing it as a threat to her position in the country where she was sovereign. And that in turn, he argued, jeopardised Britain, for royal supremacy is a living reality on which the Church of England and the British nation depend.[44]

Powell's thesis is worth considering because it highlights how inextricably woven together Church, state and monarch have been in the United Kingdom, and underlying it, for centuries, was a deep suspicion of Rome. Article 37 of the Thirty-Nine Articles of 1562, outlining the doctrine of the Church of England, states the royal role in the Church of England and makes it clear: 'The Bishop of Rome hath no jurisdiction in this Realm of England.'[45]

But by 1980, the strength of that argument was waning. Cabinet papers for 25 May 1982, discussing the visit of John Paul II, confirmed the view of Mrs Thatcher's government: 'The Queen would receive the Pope as a fellow head of state.'[46]

The mutual suspicion that Britain and Rome once shared gave way during Elizabeth II's reign to a mutual regard, with the odd hint here and there on both sides of an historic tension. In the last thirty years of her reign Queen Elizabeth played a key role in developing warmer relations, not least because of her personal faith and her occasional commentaries in speeches on the matter. Five years after Pope Benedict's visit to Britain, the Queen spoke at the opening of General Synod, where Fr Raniero Cantalamessa, the preacher to the Papal Household, was also due to speak, and she commented that 'St. Paul reminds us that all Christians, as ambassadors for Christ, are entrusted with the ministry of reconciliation'.[47]

Rome's regard was evident in the letter sent to her by Benedict XVI, two years after his state visit, on the occasion of her Diamond Jubilee in 2012, in which he praised her dedication to duty 'and a commitment to maintaining the principles of freedom, justice and democracy, in keeping with a noble vision of the role of a Christian monarch'.[48] It was also apparent in the comment made by Pope Francis two days after his election in 2013 when he spoke to Cardinal Cormac Murphy-O'Connor in the Hall of Benedictions where all the cardinals had come to greet the new Pope. Murphy-O'Connor revealed, 'Just as I was leaving he said, "Don't forget: give the Queen my warmest greetings."' The Cardinal promptly rang the Queen's secretary from the English College where he was staying to pass on the message.[49] Within six months, the Queen, accompanied by the Duke of Edinburgh, flew to Rome for a meeting with the Italian President, followed by a visit to the Vatican, where they spent an hour with Pope Francis. There were no formal speeches or statements, just an exchange of gifts and private conversation, plus a brief photocall. But the visit, within less than a year of Francis' election and just a week after he met US President Barack Obama at the Vatican, confirmed the importance given to Elizabeth II by the Roman Catholic Church.

Continuity, longevity and Christian faith held in common rather than a focus on the divisions between Church and Crown characterised contact between the Queen and the holders of Roman Catholic office. This was as true in Britain as it was in Rome. A personal regard and even fondness emerged in the Queen's dealings with some heads of the Roman Catholic Church in England and Wales, with her calling first Basil Hume and later Cormac Murphy-O'Connor 'my cardinal'.

This respect was most apparent when she appointed Cardinal Hume to the Order of Merit in 1999, an honour in her personal gift, weeks before he died. One reason for it may have been that the Queen felt he had dealt sensitively and discreetly with the marriage of her cousin Prince Michael of Kent to a Catholic divorcee, Marie-Christine von Reibnitz, and the Duchess of Kent's conversion to Catholicism. While the Cardinal and the Queen met infrequently, there was reciprocated warmth. As Hume's biographer, Anthony Howard put it, 'In a sense, no doubt, the presence of the one tended to reassure the other; in a changing world in which the politicians and officials change and move on all the time, a Cardinal Archbishop of 20 years standing becomes almost as much a symbol of continuity as the Crown itself.'[50]

The Order of Merit was offered after Basil Hume had announced that he was terminally ill with cancer, but there is no evidence to suggest the illness was the cause of Queen Elizabeth's offer of the honour.[51] But by the time Hume received it he was in hospital, and he made the trip from there to Buckingham Palace. He spent half an hour with Queen Elizabeth, later telling his confessor that they had talked about 'death, suffering, the after-life – that sort of thing', although in his acceptance letter he had focused on more worldly but vital matters – the relationship between the Crown and Roman Catholics. 'I am happy too,' he wrote, 'to think that this honour will strengthen the ties between your Catholic subjects and Your Majesty.'[52]

The Queen also acknowledged Cardinal Cormac Murphy-O'Connor's contribution to public life when he retired as Archbishop of Westminster in 2009 by accepting an invitation for her and Prince Philip to lunch at Archbishop's House. Murphy-O'Connor had the canny idea of placing next to her an Irish nun from his household who knew nearly as much about horseracing as the monarch; the conversation never faltered, said one witness.

Yet, for all this warmth, there was hesitation about the monarch who vowed to uphold the Protestant religion attending Catholic services. Fourteen years before that lunch, in 1995, Elizabeth II did break convention when she became the first monarch in four hundred years to attend a Catholic liturgy when she went to Westminster Cathedral for vespers to mark the church's centenary in 1995. The choice of vespers was thought to have been taken with regard to certain people's sensitivities about Romish practices, and no attendance of Queen Elizabeth at a Catholic Mass in Britain was recorded during her seventy years on the throne. However, in 1993 she very discreetly put aside tradition to honour a friend: she made a little-noticed trip to Brussels to attend the Requiem Mass for King Baudouin of the Belgians, sitting amid other European royals during the obsequies. There was no question of the Queen receiving Holy Communion at a Catholic Mass; that was still a step too far.[53]

Meanwhile, the Queen's family ties to Catholicism became stronger over the years, with some of them even treading the path to Rome themselves. Fourteen years after Prince Michael of Kent married a Catholic, his sister-in-law, the Duchess of Kent, became the first modern-day Royal convert to the Catholic Church in 1994, when she was received by Cardinal Basil Hume, after the Queen had sanctioned the conversion. The Duchess's son, the Earl of St Andrews, married the Catholic academic Sylvana Tomaselli, while her other son, Lord Nicholas Windsor, was also received into the Catholic Church. But Lord Nicholas Windsor was a very different convert and the Queen herself noted the distinction regarding Lord Nicholas' choice; when Benedict XVI visited Holyroodhouse, she asked that Lord Nicholas be introduced to the Pope because he was a Catholic who was also a 'blood Royal'.[54]

There is another, little-known family link between the late Queen and her family and the Roman Catholic Church. Through her mother she had Stuart blood, thus linking her to the Old Pretender, the son of deposed James II, and sometimes called James III. After a life in exile he died in Rome, where Pope Clement XIII gave him a state funeral. His tomb, and that of his son, Henry Benedict, Duke of York, who later became a Cardinal, was designed by Canova and can still be seen in St Peter's Basilica. In the 1940s, the then Queen Elizabeth, later the Queen Mother, paid for the restoration of the tomb, and in January 2016 her daughter approved a wreath to be placed on the tomb to mark the 250th anniversary of the Old Pretender's death.

While the improving relationship between Rome and Britain owed much to the role Elizabeth II played during her reign, it is ironic that it was in personal matters involving the sovereign that discrimination against Catholics lingered for far longer than in other areas of life.

Succession to the British throne is still determined not only by legitimacy and descent but also by religion. Under the Act of Settlement of 1701, brought in to secure the English and Irish thrones, succession is restricted to the descendants of Electress Sophia of Hanover, and only to her Protestant descendants in communion with the Church of England. Sophia's line was the most junior of the House of Stuart, but the Act's purpose was to exclude all Roman Catholics, and all other lines were Roman Catholic. The Act effectively bars anyone who becomes a Roman Catholic, or who marries one, from the line of succession, with the words: '[E]very Person [who] shall professe the Popish Religion or marry a Papist should be excluded [. . .] to inherit [. . .] the Crown [. . .] of this Realm [. . .].'[55]

Two Royal marriages in recent times highlighted very different responses to the restrictions. When Prince Michael of Kent, grandson of George V, married the Catholic Marie-Christine von Reibnitz, he thereby forfeited his place in the line of succession. Thirty years later, in 2008, Peter Phillips, son of the Princess Royal and grandson of the Queen, married Autumn Kelly, a Canadian raised in the French-speaking, largely Catholic province of Quebec. That she was a Roman Catholic herself jeopardised Phillips' place in the line of succession. But on this occasion, the Royal Family member did not renounce his right for love. Miss Kelly chose to renounce her religion and became a member of the Church of England before her marriage.[56] Earlier that year, the former Conservative Cabinet minister John Gummer, who had himself converted to Catholicism fifteen years earlier, had tried to overturn the restrictive legislation regarding Catholics marrying into the Royal Family. On this occasion he complained, 'It is unacceptable that the part of the Christian Church that has more adherents than any other should be discriminated against in this way.'[57]

John Gummer's intervention was unusual, for many Catholics declined to speak openly about the issue, perhaps having a historic sense that it was important not to seem to be disloyal to the Crown, and that it was wiser to keep heads down. Charles Moore was one such Catholic to maintain support for the Act of Settlement. During his editorship of the *Daily Telegraph* between 1995 and 2003, the paper consistently opposed repeal of the Act, on the grounds that it would pave the way for a split between the monarch and the Church of England and would lead to disestablishment. But other supporters of the status quo hinted in their arguments at the age-old suspicion of Catholics and their divided loyalties, as if being loyal to the pope would jeopardise loyalty to the United Kingdom and the Crown. This was exactly what made many Catholics fret about speaking out. In a *Spectator* article in 2003, Adrian Hilton warned that it would be 'intolerable to have, as the sovereign of a Protestant and free country, one who owes any allegiance to the head of any other state'.[58]

But reform was coming. Two years after Peter and Autumn Phillips married, Prime Minister Gordon Brown announced that he was committed to addressing what he called an 'anomaly' that bans Catholics from marrying into the Royal Family. The route to reform involved unlikely allies to this Catholic cause: Brown, son of a Presbyterian minister, agreed it was an injustice, speaking out ahead of a debate on a Private Members' Bill promoted by Evan Harris, a Liberal Democrat MP who was usually a stern secular opponent of many of the Catholic Church's positions on issues such as assisted dying. Brown's position was diametrically opposite to that of Tony Blair – married to a Catholic and a regular Mass attender while in office who converted once he left Number 10 – who had declined to overturn the law.[59]

The Coalition government, elected in 2010, shared Brown's enthusiasm for change. Under the terms of the Perth Agreement of 2011, it was announced that the rules about primogeniture and about marrying Catholics were being changed. The statement said that all sixteen Commonwealth countries of which the Queen was head had agreed to change the law, and it made it clear that the situation was iniquitous:

> All countries wish to see change in two areas. First, they wish to end the system of male preference primogeniture under which a younger son can displace an elder daughter in the line of succession. Second, they wish to remove the legal provision that anyone who marries a Roman Catholic shall be ineligible to succeed to the Crown. There are no other restrictions in the rules about the religion of the spouse of a person in the line of succession and the Prime Ministers felt that this unique barrier could no longer be justified. The Prime Ministers have agreed that they will each work within their respective administrations to bring forward the necessary measures to enable all the realms to give effect to these changes simultaneously.[60]

While the Perth Agreement, which came into law as the Succession to the Crown Act 2013, restored members of the Royal Family to the line of succession who had been forcibly moved on marriage, such as Prince Michael of Kent, it did not change the requirement under the Act of Settlement that the monarch must be a Protestant. Given that the British sovereign is also in law the head of the Church of England, this seems an intractable problem, unless that role is abolished (see chapter ten for more on this matter).

In secular Britain, this issue is the stuff of counting angels on a pinhead to many people, and if it matters it is only in the context of the spirit of the age, much characterised by an abiding concern with inequality. Is it really fair to block a Catholic from being sovereign, some may ask? Yet, for all the concerns in our era with equality, the monarchy, a prime example of elitism, seems not to bother the majority. Republicanism is a minority interest – or at least it was during the reign of Elizabeth II, barring a moment in 1997, in the days following the death of Diana, Princess of Wales, when sympathy for the House of Windsor and the Queen seemed to ebb away. The baying mob of the tabloid press thought she should lower the flag on her palace and fly from Balmoral to London to be with her grieving people. 'Show us you care, Ma'am', bellowed *The Sun*, and, as if summoned, Elizabeth II did return to the capital and walked among her people outside Buckingham Palace.

The Queen was not someone who emoted in public and there were no tears shed for Diana. But in a live broadcast to the nation in which she paid tribute to Diana, she spoke, she said, 'as your Queen and as a grandmother'. In the late twentieth and early twenty-first centuries, there were more references like this – the beloved Philip remark during her Christmas broadcast in 2021 – her first and last as a widow – was one such. But Queen Elizabeth clearly did not think that in her position as the figurehead of the country anyone would benefit from her public weeping.

This was particularly apparent in 1966 when she visited the Welsh village of Aberfan, following the collapse of a mining spoil tip which fell upon the school, killing 116 children and twenty-eight adults. As happened often with Elizabeth II, there was some hesitancy about visiting in the wake of trauma – she hesitated before coming to London following Diana's death – even though her advisers suggested she should hasten to Wales. But the Queen stalled, with the notion somehow entering the ether that she did so because she thought her presence might get in the way of rescue operations. Others considered it the moment for a spontaneous gesture, but Elizabeth II did not do spontaneous.

The visit to Aberfan was a key example of a time when the Queen's public role was intertwined with her personal standing. In 1997, it was the Queen herself who made use of her personal role – as a grandmother – when reflecting on the death of Diana. In 1966, it was the press that made the connection, reporting that because she herself was a mother (her youngest, Edward, was only two at the time), she was 'linked by a common bond of understanding with the [village's] bereaved mothers'.[61]

Elizabeth II did not have her own mother's or Princess Diana's talent for easy connection with others whose lives were different from hers, and this kind of visit was for her an ordeal. Some suggested that she wiped away a tear and looked dark-eyed, but there was also a stiffness, and she returned to Aberfan on four subsequent occasions – a sign, some said, that she felt her judgement on that occasion was flawed. In terms of ancient ideas of monarchy, Aberfan was a place she should indeed have visited: this could have been a moment when the anointed sovereign could bring healing, and some press reports suggested a certain catharsis. In later years there would be other visits by the Queen and her family to the bedsides of those caught up in disasters, including terrorist attacks. In secular, twenty-first-century Britain, such visits were approved of, not so much for that mystical idea of healing but for a sense of royals representing the solidarity of the nation to the afflicted.

While concern for those who are vulnerable is seen as both a desirable and an acceptable expression of compassion by the sovereign and other members of the Royal Family, the general view is that they must simultaneously retain political impartiality. Edward VIII strayed close to the line during his months of kingship when he visited South Wales in November 1936, less than a month before his abdication, and was shocked by the numbers of unemployed. As he visited the derelict Dowlais steel works he commented, 'These works brought all these people here. Something should be done to get them at work again,' a phrase often misquoted as, 'something must be done'. Edward VIII believed it acceptable to intervene in state affairs, and on this occasion the impartial monarch came perilously close to passing judgement on Stanley Baldwin's Conservative government, even if his intention was to express compassion for his subjects.

On one occasion, Elizabeth II's similar concern for the vulnerable – that suitable characteristic of royalty in a democracy – saw her balancing on the trapeze wire of impartiality with some danger. Again, it was at the time of a Conservative premier. On 20 July 1986, *The Sunday Times* published an explosive story indicating that the Queen was dismayed by some of Margaret Thatcher's policies.

The paper intimated that the Queen's own advisers had briefed its journalists about her alarm regarding the Premier's approach to the Commonwealth, which was precious to the Queen with its affairs making up a substantial part of her workload. In contrast, Mrs Thatcher had little time for it, doubting it brought much by way of economic benefit to Britain. So Queen Elizabeth's dismay was indeed plausible; the story was published just days before the opening of the Commonwealth Games in Edinburgh, when thirty-two black nations boycotted the event in protest at Thatcher's resistance to sanctions against South Africa's apartheid regime. Queen Elizabeth's later warm relations with Nelson Mandela, when he became

President of South Africa, four years after his release from twenty-seven years in prison and soon after abandonment of the apartheid regime, indicated that Thatcher's policy found no friend in the monarch. Her warm tribute to Archbishop Desmond Tutu, on his death in December 2021, also highlighted her regard for those involved in the struggle against apartheid.

But in 1986, *The Sunday Times*' story went further, indicating that the Queen was also concerned that the Thatcher government was uncaring in its approach to Britain. By 1986, unemployment had been more than three million for three years; the previous year, Thatcher had clashed with the Church of England over *Faith in the City: A Call for Action by Church and Nation*, a report in which the Archbishop of Canterbury's Commission on Urban Priority Areas had concluded that much of the blame for the nation's growing spiritual and material poverty was owing to government policies.[62]

The official response from Buckingham Palace to *The Sunday Times*' story was to express astonishment. The Queen's press secretary, Michael Shea, believed to be the 'sources close to the Queen' of the story, denied making the comments in any way that was similar to the views expressed in the story. Months later, Shea quit, with many still thinking he had played a role in the saga.

The episode was another instance of the monarch entering dangerous waters when thoughts, expressed either publicly or privately but leaked, can be viewed as political commentary. But this incident could also be seen as an insight into different interpretations of Christianity. The Queen, like her bishops, saw a moral imperative for those with more to engage with those with less, whether material or spiritual. They took their thinking from Matthew 25:35–40: 'I was hungry and you gave me food, I was thirsty and you gave me something to drink,' the Gospel always used at the monarch's Maundy services. Mrs Thatcher, a committed Methodist cum Anglican, interpreted the call of Christian teaching in a rather different way. Two years after *The Sunday Times*' claims that the Queen thought Thatcher divisive, the Prime Minister spoke to the Church of Scotland's General Assembly, arguing that enterprise and effort were the bedrock of the Christian ethos: 'We are told we must work and use our talents to create wealth. "If a man will not work he shall not eat" wrote Paul to the Thessalonians. Indeed, abundance rather than poverty has a legitimacy which derives from the very nature of Creation.'

This particular speech is often thought of as Thatcher's Good Samaritan speech, but the Samaritan was not mentioned on this occasion. On two previous occasions, in 1968 and again on television in 1980, she said, 'No one would remember the good Samaritan if he'd only had good intentions; he had money as well.'[63]

To the bishops, the Good Samaritan parable was more about the universality of human fellowship, and the point was as much about those who passed by on the other side as it was about the man who stopped. Elizabeth II's articulation of Christianity over the years indicated that she shared this approach too.

Another instance of the Queen and the episcopacy sharing theological thinking and being in diametric opposition to Margaret Thatcher had come a few years earlier, after the United Kingdom's victory in the Falklands War. Following the end of the ten-week war and the retaking of the Falkland Islands by UK troops following their illegal invasion by Argentina, it was decided that there would be a thanksgiving service in July 1982. The Dean of St Paul's, Alan Webster, was a well-known pacifist, whose choice of hymns and readings were challenged at every turn by the government. However, it had not been thought necessary to probe what the Archbishop of Canterbury, Robert Runcie, who was a former Scots Guards officer, might say in his sermon. 'War,' Runcie told the congregation, which included the Prime Minister and the Queen, 'is a sign of human failure.'

After paying tribute to the courage and endurance of those who served in the South Atlantic, Runcie went on to criticise the nations that continued to perfect weapons of mass destruction and failed to halt the international arms trade, and then had a go at the jingoism apparent in Britain at the time: 'War springs from the love and loyalty which should be offered to God being applied to some God substitute, one of the most dangerous being nationalism.' Then, in reconciliatory mood, at the service of thanksgiving that the government had insisted upon, he urged, 'In our prayers we shall quite rightly remember those who are bereaved in our own country and the relations of the young Argentinian soldiers who were killed. Common sorrow could do something to re-unite those who were engaged in this struggle.'

The Prime Minister was furious, with her cheerleaders at *The Sun* saying that she was outraged at the 'wet' sermon, while her husband, Denis, told those drinking on the House of Commons terrace later that day that 'the boss was livid'.[64]

The Queen, however, was not. Though not known about at the time, some fourteen years later Runcie shared with his biographer a letter he had received from the Queen's private secretary following the service: 'The Queen has asked me to thank you most warmly for preaching the sermon at St Paul's yesterday for the Falkland Islands service. It must have been a daunting task for you and Her Majesty was full of admiration for the way in which you met this formidable challenge.'[65]

The message was deft. There was no direct criticism of the Prime Minister's 'Rejoice, rejoice at that news' approach to the British trouncing of the Argentinians, but Queen Elizabeth clearly put her support behind the reconciling Archbishop.

Reconciliation was clearly part of Elizabeth II's remit during her seventy-year reign, from troubles in South Africa to acknowledgement of the past in Ireland. She served as sovereign at a time of turmoil for her Commonwealth and the United Kingdom, coming to the throne in the twilight of Empire, and stood for both tradition and efforts to come to terms with change. For her there was one constant, inspiring her to be in turn a constant for the country, and that was her faith. She spoke openly of it, yet it was also something that was very private. She chose not to be seen receiving Holy Communion, for example. The canopy that sheltered her receiving the Eucharist at her coronation was replaced by closed doors. She used to receive it just twice a year and very much held a low church approach to Holy Communion, which may well surprise other more frequent communicants in the Roman Catholic Church and the Church of England. But one who knew her well said, 'It signifies the Queen's deep respect for the Eucharist and its specialness. It means a lot.'

She would usually receive Holy Communion in the privacy of her chapel within Windsor Castle – the one where the 1992 Windsor

Castle fire began and where her husband lay at rest the night before his funeral.

Prince Philip's funeral, in the midst of the Covid-19 pandemic, was a much smaller and simpler affair than it might have been in normal times. The lasting image from his obsequies was of his widow – small, in black, masked and sitting alone in St George's Chapel, a woman bereaved after seventy-three years of marriage. The power of the image came from the way in which the Queen at that moment was everyman – or at least everywoman. In her mourning she embodied the grief of all those who had been bereaved during the pandemic. It was the monarch in solidarity with her subjects, understanding their plight in experiencing it too, just as she had in enduring lockdown with her husband, unable to see the rest of their family.

It was also more than that. As a ninety-five-year-old widow, Elizabeth II was seen not as grand, or at the pinnacle of society, or as someone who bestrode the national and even global stage. But the image of her was extraordinarily powerful, in that it embodied vulnerability. And this was the paradox at the heart of Elizabeth II's monarchy and her reign, longer than any other British sovereign's. For most people, the monarch is a symbol of power; the words of the national anthem wish him or her to be 'victorious', 'happy and glorious'. But at the heart of her coronation service was the ceremony of anointing, when, divested of all the rich robes and jewels, she wore but a simple shift to be anointed and to commit herself to a life of service. As the philosopher priest Giles Fraser pointed out, that moment was about vulnerability, in placing oneself in the service of God and other people.

Fraser linked it to the theological idea of kenosis, meaning self-emptying, articulated in St Paul's letter to the Philippians about Christ: 'he emptied himself, taking the form of a slave'.[66] 'What is being described here is a process by which the ego is set aside for the fullness of God's love to enter into a human life,' wrote Fraser. 'The less of me, the more of You. In this way vulnerability is regarded as the defining feature of precisely the sort of holiness that was there in that moment of the Queen's anointing.' As Fraser argued, an old Queen and a tired Queen 'is the perfect sacrificial embodiment of what a monarch should be', or, at least, what a Christian leader should be.[67]

Later in 2021, the Queen was forced to cancel engagements, including one of the most important in her calendar, the Remembrance Sunday ceremony at the Cenotaph, owing to ill-health. Once more, it highlighted her vulnerability, and on BBC Radio 4's 'Thought for the Day' slot, I compared her frailty to that of Pope John Paul II, who struggled to continue as pontiff in his later years when beset by illness.

'The paradox is that for some leaders, vulnerability can be strikingly powerful,' I said. 'It runs counter to the all too common notion that a leader must actively shape their image, and so take on a particular persona. But leaders, honest about their frailty, have a notable authenticity. The personal story becomes greater than themselves.'[68]

To one who knew her and her faith well, the entire *raison d'être* of the Queen's reign was about trying to focus attention on something greater than the individual: 'The power of the monarchy is that the sovereign is pointing to something beyond themselves. It is beyond politics. It is something more important. Much of it is about religion. And so I believe that a purely secular monarchy would be impossible to sustain; you need that faith. In that sense there is a priestly nature about monarchy.'[69]

When I broadcast my 'Thought for the Day' on the importance of vulnerability in leaders, it did not specifically mention the Queen's ill-health, on instruction from the BBC. At the time, there was little information about what was wrong, and Buckingham Palace had only confirmed that she had spent a night in hospital when it had been leaked by *The Sun* newspaper. It was as though it was not quite polite to mention the Queen's advancing years, or that the nation was not yet ready to accept that the Platinum Queen could not reign for ever. The passing of the Mother, or indeed Grandmother, of the Nation was too profound a blow to contemplate.

But behind the scenes, for some years, plans had been put in place for the funeral of Queen Elizabeth and the transition of her son, Charles III, through his accession, proclamation and coronation. The discussions included a conversation between the Queen and her heir, the then Prince of Wales, about the hymns that might be sung at her funeral. The Queen's choice included 'The Day Thou Gavest' with its lines:

The day thou gavest, Lord, is ended,
The darkness falls at Thy behest
To Thee our morning hymns ascended
Thy praise shall sanctify our rest.

Later, it includes the words:

So be it, Lord; Thy throne shall never,
Like earth's proud empires, pass away.

While the Queen expressed great fondness for the hymn, and believed it highly appropriate, the Prince was said to have been horrified by its selection: it was sung regularly during his loathed schooldays at Gordonstoun.[70] The clash over hymns can be said to symbolise a Prince who shared his mother's faith yet interprets it and his role very differently from hers. In the following pages, that will be my concern. But before that I will turn my attention to the man who profoundly shaped the Queen's reign and influenced her faith, and also brought enormous influence to bear on King Charles III, his son: Prince Philip, Duke of Edinburgh.

# 6

# Her strength and stay: the influence of Prince Philip

GLAMOUR, CEREMONIAL, MASSES of eligible people – the whole atmosphere of a wedding begets romance and quite possibly other weddings. Another event with even more glamour, ceremonial and party atmosphere is a coronation.

In 1902, two people met at the crowning of Edward VII, fell in love and later married. If they had never met as part of the sprawling family network of royalty created by Victoria and Albert, then the Royal Family that we have been familiar with for the last seventy years would never have existed.

The pair that met through Edward's crowning were Prince Andrew of Greece and Princess Alice of Battenberg. Andrew, then twenty, and sometimes known as Andrea, was the son of King George I of Greece, who had been invited to become King of the Hellenes, although he was a Dane and the son of King Christian IX of Denmark. It was his father's sister Alexandra who was also being crowned that day as Queen Consort of Edward VII.

Princess Alice was there in her capacity as great-niece of the new British King; her grandmother Alice, after whom she had been named, was Edward VII's sister, both of them the offspring of Victoria and Albert. Tragedy had befallen Queen Victoria's daughter Alice, in 1878, when her family had caught diphtheria. It killed both Alice and her daughter May. It was left to the older Princess Alice's daughter, Victoria – named after her grandmother, the Queen – to raise her siblings, including her sister Alix. In 1884 she married Prince Louis of Battenberg and a year later they had their first child, Alice – the young woman of seventeen who caught Prince Andrew's eye at that 1902 coronation. In fact, the two had met previously when the royalty of Europe had first gathered for Edward's coronation in June 1902, only for it to be cancelled at the last minute when the King fell ill with appendicitis. They returned in August, shared a carriage to Westminster Abbey for the coronation and, after countless letters and some snobbish family commentaries – that she was a Battenberg, the daughter of an illegitimate father and he was the fourth son of a newly baked king – they became engaged.

Nevertheless, their wedding in October 1903 in Darmstadt was a spectacular affair and, like the coronation the previous summer, attracted plenty of royalty, including Queen Alexandra, Andrew's aunt, and Tsar Nicholas II, son of Andrew's aunt Dagmar, and husband of Alix, aunt of Alice, who had been raised by her sister and Alice's mother, Victoria. The wedding required two religious ceremonies, one Protestant and one Orthodox, as befitted the Greek Prince and which must have pleased Andrew's Russian Orthodox cousin Nicholas. The couple, who lived in the royal palace in Athens, eventually had five children: four girls, and one boy, Philip, born in 1921.

Beset by family upheavals and the political turbulence of early twentieth-century Europe, Philip was to eventually return to Westminster Abbey, where his parents had encountered one another, for first, his wedding to Princess Elizabeth, and then another coronation, that of his young wife, when she became Elizabeth II.

For Elizabeth II, her Christian faith was her strength and stay – the same term she used to describe the steadfast loyalty of her husband on the occasion of their Golden Wedding Anniversary. Elizabeth's faith was a comfort and was consistent: Anglican, steady, fixed. For Philip, faith was in many ways an adventure – a spiritual expedition that matched his equally eventful life and was profoundly influenced by his family's religious history.

Even before Philip was born, his parents endured dramas owing to the tensions in Europe at the time. Disgruntlement regarding the royal family of Greece led to Andrew and his brothers not being able to serve in the army as planned, until the First Balkan War against Turkey in 1912, when they successfully fought the Turks, and the royals' popularity revived. In the meantime, Alice, inspired by her aunt Elizabeth (also known as Ella) – another of her mother Victoria's sisters, who had married another Romanov and had become a nurse – set up a series of hospitals for wounded Greek soldiers during the First Balkan War. Alice was akin to Florence Nightingale, in the thick of war, tending to the horribly wounded and organising care by setting up field hospitals. 'God! What things we saw. Shattered arms and legs and heads, such awful sights,' she wrote, 'and then to have to bandage those dreadful things for three days and three nights. The corridor full of blood and cast-off bandages knee high.'[1] She was awarded the Royal Red Cross, a decoration given for exceptional services in military nursing, by George V in 1913.

The outbreak of the First World War brought yet more upheaval to the family. For Princess Alice, it was particularly difficult because she had been born German, but her father, Prince Louis of Battenberg, was serving as Britain's First Sea Lord, although he was effectively forced out because of his German connections, and also changed his name to Mountbatten. He later became known as the Marquess of Milford Haven. In Athens, capital of a country that was neutral, the people faced bombardment from the Allied fleet, and Alice helped run soup kitchens.

Eventually the royal family, including Andrew, Alice and their children, was forced into exile, while their relatives in Russia, Nicholas and Alexandra (also known in the family as Alix), were overthrown by the Bolsheviks. George V, who had succeeded his father Edward VII in 1910, at first offered the Romanovs sanctuary in Britain, but he withdrew it, for fear of angering the new rulers of Russia. Left to their fate, the Romanovs – including Alice's two aunts Empress Alexandra and Grand Duchess Elizabeth – were executed. The terrible deaths of the family were to shake the entire network of royal cousins across Europe, but would particularly have an impact on Alice, and influence how she would later live her life.

The Greek royal family, meanwhile, returned from exile, with Andrew once more serving in the army. By the early summer of 1921, Alice was staying at Mon Repos, a villa in Corfu that Andrew had inherited from his father. It was there that Alice gave birth to her fifth child and only son, Philip, in a place that was the epitome of southern Europe – looking over the Ionian Sea and towards Albania and Greece, with eucalyptus trees and cypresses nodding in the breeze – so different from the cold and cloudy country to the west that he would eventually make his home for most of his life.

Philip first travelled to that country – to Britain – when he was three months old, when Alice visited for the funeral of her father and his grandfather, the renamed Louis Mountbatten, Marquess of Milford Haven. The following year Alice returned again, with Philip and her daughters, for the wedding of her brother, another Louis, or 'Dickie' Mountbatten, to Edwina Ashley. It was another reminder of how close Philip's family were to their relatives, the British Royal Family: George V was a guest, and his son, the Prince of Wales and future Edward VIII, was best man.

By the time Alice and the children returned to Corfu to rejoin Andrew, the Greeks had been routed by the Turks and the Greek monarchy was in trouble again.

A revolutionary committee led by Colonels Nikolaos Plastiras and Stylianos Gonatas seized power and forced the King into exile. Prince Andrew, who had served as an army commander, was arrested, as were several politicians and army generals, who were shot. The Prince, however, was banished from his own country, escaping a worse fate after an intervention on behalf of George V; this time, he came to the aid of his European relations. Andrew, Alice and their children were rescued and taken on board a British ship, HMS *Calypso*, sailing to Italy.

The family eventually settled in a Paris suburb, although Alice's anxiety, exacerbated by the trauma of having to leave Greece, meant that the children were regularly shipped off to relatives. She eventually suffered a serious nervous breakdown, while some have since suggested that she suffered from bipolar disorder.[2]

In 1928, Philip's mother converted to the Greek Orthodox faith. The family's home in St Cloud was in a neighbourhood with clusters of Greek and Russian émigrés, many of whom felt a powerful connection to their exiled homes through their religion. Her husband and all her children, including Philip, had also been baptised into the Greek Orthodox Church.

Alice was also greatly inspired by her aunt, Grand Duchess Elizabeth

Feodorovna of Russia, the sister of her mother Victoria and of Empress Alexandra of Russia, who had converted to Russian Orthodoxy on marriage. It was at her wedding to Sergei that his nephew, the then Tsarevich Nicholas, first met Elizabeth and Victoria's sister, Alexandra – another example of royal dating and matchmaking through their grand ceremonials. She was later instrumental in persuading Alexandra to convert too, without which she could not marry Nicholas.

In 1905, Elizabeth's husband, Sergei, who was Governor of Moscow, was assassinated by a socialist revolutionary, an act which Elizabeth believed was divine retribution for her husband's decision to expel 20,000 Jews from the city. Elizabeth, always intensely religious, spent the days before her husband's funeral in prayer and visited his assassin, urging him to seek forgiveness, which could save him from execution. He refused to do so.[3]

Elizabeth's life changed profoundly after her husband's death. In 1909 she sold off her jewellery and possessions and with the money opened the Convent of Saints Martha and Mary, becoming the abbess. The convent helped wounded soldiers and the poor of Moscow, and a hospital, a pharmacy and an orphanage were opened in its grounds. But less than a decade later, Elizabeth's vision of a religious institution committed to the poor was destroyed by Lenin, who had her arrested. In May 1918 she was taken with several other royal prisoners to an abandoned iron mine where they were flung sixty-six feet into a pit, into which were tossed grenades. Lenin is said to have welcomed Elizabeth's death by saying, 'Virtue with the crown on it is a greater enemy to the world revolution than 100 tyrant tsars.'[4]

Elizabeth would indeed receive a crown – the martyr's crown – eventually hailed by the Orthodox Church as a saint. Her remains were first discovered with those of the others in the pit by the White Army in May 1918. Knowing the Red Army was on its way, they took the remains east and buried them in the Russian Orthodox mission's cemetery in Peking. Then, in 1921, Elizabeth's body was moved again, this time to the Orthodox Church of Mary Magdalene, on the Mount of Olives in Jerusalem, which she and her husband had helped found. She was canonised by the Russian Orthodox Church Outside Russia in 1981, and by the Moscow Patriarchate in

1992. Her sister Alexandra and her husband Tsar Nicholas, murdered with their children two months later, were also canonised in 1981 and then later by the Patriarchate in 2000.

Then, nearly eighty years later, her great-nephew Philip, grandson of her sister Victoria, became involved in a remarkable memorial to Elizabeth. In 1996, a major restoration of Westminster Abbey was being completed. An appeal committee chaired by Philip – who had been known as the Duke of Edinburgh since his marriage in 1948 to the then Princess Elizabeth – had raised £37 million for the refurbishment and restoration of the medieval church. While the restoration was complete, part of the church was not, for niches above the Great West Door were empty. While the then surveyor of the fabric thought that statues of monarchs would be most suitable to fill the vacant space, given the church had been used for coronations, the Abbey's canon theologian Anthony Harvey thought otherwise. As the twentieth century drew to a close, he was very conscious of its terrible place in history as an era of violence and martyrdom. He suggested that the niches should be used to honour those who had died because of their Christian faith, just as the Abbey's patron, St Peter, had. The idea won support from the Abbey and Prince Philip's committee and the martyrs won the day.

The martyrs chosen included those killed because their own families objected to their conversion to Christianity, and several killed by despotic regimes: among them was Elizabeth. When the Queen and Prince Philip attended in 1998 to unveil that statue, there was his great-aunt, honoured in the country her great-nephew had made his own.

Elizabeth's Orthodox faith profoundly influenced her sister Alice, and in turn Orthodoxy, the Christian denomination into which he was born and baptised, was to intrigue Philip, even though he became an Anglican when he married Elizabeth, heir to the British throne and future Supreme Governor of the Church of England. But his interest in the Orthodox Church would never leave him.

Back in 1928, when Philip was seven, his mother's new-found devout Orthodox faith coincided with extreme behaviour, including claims of visions of Christ, and she was hospitalised at several sanatoria. Within two years, family life effectively came to an end for

Philip. The family home in France was shut up, his father drifted aimlessly around Europe, and within eighteen months his sisters would all be married. He was sent to stay with various relatives, and then from the age of nine until sixteen, his mother's elder brother, George, the second Marquess of Milford Haven, took him in and acted as his guardian, while he would also spend time with his grandmother Princess Victoria at Kensington Palace.

He only saw his mother a handful of times in the next two years, and then from 1932 until spring 1937, there was no contact with her at all. He did, however, continue to have contact with his sisters during holidays and, in 1933, having been educated for some time at prep school in England, he was sent to Germany to be educated at a school based in a wing of the home of his sister Theodora. His sisters had all married Germans, and this was the era when Hitler was becoming increasingly powerful. Rather than Hitler, though, the German who was to have the greatest impact on Philip's life was Kurt Hahn, the head of Salem, the school he attended.

By 1933, Hahn had become a vocal critic of Hitler following the violent death of a communist supporter at the hands of Nazi stormtroopers. Hahn had written a letter to all old boys of his school, saying that they had to break with the school or Hitler. He wrote, 'Salem cannot remain neutral. Germany is at stake, her Christian civilization, her reputation, her military honour.'[5]

After this denunciation and because of his part-Jewish heritage, Hahn was at risk. He fled to Britain, just as Philip was starting his schooling at Salem. His time there was short-lived, and in September 1934 his family agreed to send him to Hahn's new educational enterprise, Gordonstoun, in Morayshire.

Hahn brought with him his focus on health, fitness, fresh air and discipline. His critics doubted that his methods would work in Britain, saying they were incompatible with liberal educational ideals, but he also had supporters who believed he would help develop dynamic individuals. Among his backers was William Temple, the Archbishop of York, who would later chair Gordonstoun's board of governors and be appointed Archbishop of Canterbury in 1942. It was a system of education that suited Philip, though, and he excelled at much of what the school offered, from sports to learning seamanship.

The break-up of his parents' marriage, his mother's psychiatric troubles and the end of family life were all profound traumas for a child to endure, but during Philip's adolescence there were more to come. In 1937, when he was sixteen, his sister Cecile, her husband and two sons were killed in a plane crash as they flew from Germany to London for a family wedding. Then a year later, his uncle and guardian, George Milford Haven, died of cancer. It led to George's brother, Louis 'Dickie' Mountbatten, a rising star of the Royal Navy, becoming far more of an influence in Philip's life, and encouraging his own interest in a naval career.

By the time Britain declared war on Germany in September 1939, Philip was a navel cadet at the naval college in Dartmouth, Devon, where he had famously entertained thirteen-year-old Princess Elizabeth and her sister when they had visited with their parents two months earlier. But at the time of the actual declaration of war, Philip was reunited with his recovered mother who had decided to take a flat in Athens and wanted to introduce her son to Greece. Philip's situation was becoming more complicated. His sisters were all married to Germans and living in the country now at war with Britain, which he had made his home. Family deaths and changes meant he was also now closer to the Greek throne than before; he was still Prince Philip of Greece. His uncle, George II, asked him to go back to England to finish his naval training, which he agreed to do.

His mother, meanwhile, stayed in Athens for the duration of the war, while most of the Greek family lived it out in South Africa. She worked for the Red Cross, helping organise soup kitchens, shelters for orphans and nursing care, all vital aid for the Athenians when the Germans occupied the city. The German forces assumed she was pro-German, as Prince Christoph of Hesse, married to her daughter Sophie, was in the SS, but Alice was utterly opposed to its creed. When the majority of Jews living in Athens were deported to concentration camps, Alice hid one Jewish woman and her two children who had appealed to her for help.

While Philip had returned to Britain to continue his naval training and career, the future was not clear-cut for someone who was not a British citizen when the war had put naturalisation applications on hold. But his Uncle Dickie had pulled strings so that he was able to serve on several ships, seeing battle in the Mediterranean. Then, in 1941, he spent some shore leave in Athens and saw his mother, learning of her social and nursing work with people in the city.

Alice's only fellow member of the Greek royal family to stay in Athens during the German occupation was Philip's aunt, Princess Nicholas, who, in conversation with the diarist and MP, Chips Channon, confided that there was a certain *tendresse* between Prince Philip of Greece and Princess Elizabeth. 'He is to be our Prince Consort,' Chips told his diary, 'and that is why he is serving in the Navy.'

Philip's naval career continued until the end of the Second World War and beyond, and saw him mentioned in despatches and promoted. Throughout his service he and Princess Elizabeth exchanged letters and he spent several of his shore leaves at Windsor with the Royal Family, including Christmas 1943; they were, after all, his relatives. It was about this time that Philip told his cousin George II of Greece of his interest in the Princess. The Greek King then wrote to George VI and his wife to ask whether they might consider Philip as husband for their daughter.[6]

Feelings within the Royal Family and among their courtiers were mixed about Philip; some thought him rough and ill-educated, others charming and knowledgeable. There was also the strange matter of the Royal Family's regular preoccupation with foreignness, even though its own roots were hardly thoroughbred English. Philip of Greece, with his Danish antecedents, was viewed as an outsider, despite the fact that George VI and his daughters were descended from the Dutch King William, Hanoverian Victoria, the German Albert, the Danish Queen Alexandra and the half-German Queen Mary of Teck.

As Philip and Elizabeth's love affair became serious, there was, however, another issue that made marriage between the pair more complicated: all his sisters had married Germans and some of their husbands had been involved with Nazism. Indeed, Sophie, married to Prince Christoph of Hesse, who served in the SS, was close to some Nazi leaders herself; one of her friends married Hermann Goering. Courtiers who did not like Dickie Mountbatten were those who did not like Philip either. According to one of them, 'It was all bound up in a single word: German.'[7]

Philip's religion, of course – Greek Orthodox – was also a reminder of his otherness – an issue that would have to be addressed should he marry into the Royal Family, although, unlike Roman Catholicism, it was not a full bar to marriage under the 1701 Act of Settlement.

The first change to Philip's situation came in March 1947 when he became a naturalised British citizen, forsaking his Greek nationality, becoming a commoner and relinquishing his right of succession to the Greek throne. Formerly known as Philip of Greece, Philip could have taken his paternal dynastic name and become Philip Schleswig-Holstein-Sonderburg-Glücksburg. But just two years on from the war, and with the anxieties about Philip's family links to Nazism and the Nuremberg trials fresh in the memory, he took instead his uncle's anglicised surname of Mountbatten.

Philip's naturalisation was made official while Elizabeth and her family were on tour in South Africa – a tour that the King had asked to go ahead before the couple became engaged. They returned in May, and two months later it was announced that Philip, aged twenty-six, and Elizabeth, aged twenty-one, were engaged.

The wedding took place on 20 November 1947, and as part of his preparation, Philip was received into the Church of England, officially forsaking his Greek Orthodoxy, in a private service conducted by the Archbishop of Canterbury, Geoffrey Fisher. There was little sign of his Greek roots at the wedding, nor his German connections. His father had died three years earlier, living with his mistress in the Hotel Metropole in Monte Carlo. His mother Alice was the only member of his immediate family in the congregation at Westminster Abbey, and she sat alongside her mother, Princess Victoria, her sister Louise, married to Crown Prince Gustav Adolf of Sweden, her brother Dickie and other Battenbergs, now Mountbattens.

Other royals from Europe, who had endured the upheavals of war and were related to Philip, were also guests: his cousin Alexandra, married to the former King of Yugoslavia; Queen Frederika of Greece; his cousin King Michael of Romania. Others from Norway and Denmark were related to both bride and groom.

Life as the husband of the heir to the British throne brought Philip frustrations and contentments. He found court life, and especially courtiers, trying. Increasing public duties meant he had to limit his work for the Admiralty. But he had a home of his own for the first time since he was ten years old when the couple moved into Clarence House, and he had a happy marriage, with children arriving soon: Prince Charles was born in October 1948, eleven months after the wedding. Philip was to enjoy further time at sea in the first years of their marriage, including on the destroyer HMS *Chequers*, while having a home base with the Queen in Malta, and then on the frigate HMS *Magpie*. By July 1951 they left Malta for good.

As George VI's health declined, the couple embarked on more and more public duties. Prince Philip went on indefinite leave from the Navy, never to return. He had signed up to a marriage and a life that mixed exceptional privilege with duty and sacrifice. This combination, well known to monarchs, would be highlighted within two years at the next coronation: the crowning of his wife as Elizabeth II in June 1953.

Although George VI had been ill for some while, his death was not expected when it happened. When his daughter and Philip married, the King was just fifty-one, and he came from a line of monarchs who had lived long lives: George V died at seventy; Edward VII at sixty-eight; Queen Victoria at eighty-one; William IV at seventy-one; George IV at sixty-eight; George III at eighty-one. So Prince Philip may well have thought that he would have a fifteen- to twenty-year career ahead of him, rising in naval ranks. Instead, after less than five years of marriage, and at just thirty-one years old, he would become the Queen's consort.

There was no job description; he would have to make it up himself. There were, of course, comparisons with Prince Albert, Queen Victoria's consort, who found ways to make his own mark. But Albert's time at the side of Victoria lasted just twenty-one years. Prince Philip was to be by the side of his wife as Queen for sixty-nine years. And as he formed his distinctive role, his personal interests – in sports, in young people, in matters maritime, in science and in religion – were to have a marked impact on the life of the Queen and on the monarchy.

So would his capacity to organise, and in 1952, at the suggestion of his mother-in-law and the new Queen's private secretary, Sir Alan 'Tommy' Lascelles, he was appointed by Prime Minister Winston Churchill as chairman of the Coronation Commission. Both the Queen Mother and Sir Alan agreed that Philip was in need of a role; according to Lascelles, the Prince was 'insupportable when idle'.[8]

The Coronation Commission, which included Churchill and the Archbishop of Canterbury, Geoffrey Fisher, was to help organise the ceremony. Its first decision was that the coronation should wait a year because Westminster Abbey was undergoing restoration and there was an economic crisis going on.

Another crisis soon developed – that of the issue of the name that the Royal Family would use. Philip had been made Duke of Edinburgh upon his marriage to Princess Elizabeth, and while she became known for a time as Duchess of Edinburgh, as heir to the throne she belonged to the House of Windsor. Prior to that, the Royal House had been named House of Saxe-Coburg and Gotha, when Edward VII succeeded his mother Victoria of the House of Hanover, taking the House's name from his father, Prince Albert of Saxe-Coburg and Gotha. But in 1917 the name was changed during the reign of George V, because of anti-German sentiment during the First World War, to the very English-sounding House of Windsor.

The rumpus over the Royal House's name began when George V's widow, Queen Mary, heard of a dinner party held days after her son George VI's death during which Philip's uncle Dickie Mountbatten raised a triumphant glass to toast the new House of Mountbatten. Outraged, the old Queen alerted Jock Colville, Winston Churchill's secretary, who in turn alerted Churchill. The Prime Minister, who was not a fan of Mountbatten, took the matter to Cabinet and secured its wholehearted support for no changes being made to the Royal House.

A surname may seem to be an intimate matter for a family, but in these circumstances it was not. The Queen agreed with Churchill – as she was obliged to do – that the House of Windsor would remain the House of Windsor, and a proclamation was issued on 4 April, nearly two months after her accession, to say that her descendants would keep the House of Windsor name. Her husband was, however, annoyed, complaining, 'I am the only man in the country not allowed to give his name to his children.' It was a situation that left the Queen caught in both a constitutional quagmire and a family one. While Philip was put out, her mother and grandmother were adamant the name should stay the same. Queen Mary went so far as to complain, 'What the devil does that damned fool Edinburgh think that the family name has got to do with him?'[9]

Philip may have thought that the name change would be perfectly acceptable, given that Elizabeth's great-grandfather, Edward VII, had changed the House's name to his own father's. But Philip's name was, of course, not really Mountbatten anyway: that was an anglicised version of Battenberg, which was also his mother's surname. If Philip's children were not to be named after him, he was following in the footsteps of his own father, whose name Philip himself had abandoned.

It was a clear sign of Philip's submissive role as consort – one that would be highlighted during the coronation ceremony, which used ecclesiastical language to describe his status. On 2 June 1953, he travelled in the State Coach to Westminster Abbey with his wife, but walked behind her down the long aisle, whereas a female consort to a new monarch would walk alongside and would also be crowned. He was the first to pay obeisance after her crowning: 'I, Philip, Duke of Edinburgh, do become your liege man of life and limb and of earthly worship, and faith and truth I will bear unto you, to live and die against all manner of folks. So help me God.' Philip, who had been kneeling with his hands between hers, then rose to his feet, touched her St Edward's Crown and kissed her cheek.

The coronation was a combination of church liturgy, with amendments made to suit 1953, and some government input via the Coronation Commission, chaired by Philip. That the seating plans and the timings, together with the plans for the ceremony being broadcast, went smoothly, was down to Philip's organisational abilities and those of the Earl Marshal, a historic position always held by the Duke of Norfolk, who was responsible for bringing all the strands – religious, ceremonial, public events – together and who worked with Philip as his Commission deputy. This particular Duke, Bernard Fitzalan-Howard, was a stickler for timing but less particular about guests. He told Philip's private secretary, Mike Parker, that Elizabeth would be crowned at '12.34, give or take a few seconds', and said to a peer, worried he might not be invited on account of his divorce, 'Good God, man, this is a coronation, not Royal Ascot.'[10]

While in the Britain of the 1950s, divorce might preclude you from the Royal Enclosure at Ascot – and Princess Margaret was soon to find out how problematic divorce could still be in some circumstances (as explained in chapter five) – other problems had dissipated in the previous five years. In 1947, when Philip and Elizabeth had married, the proximity of the Second World War meant courtiers had kept his German relatives off the guest list. Now, in 1953, with Philip in charge of the arrangements, it was deemed acceptable to have them at the Abbey. His surviving sisters Theodora, Margarita and Sophie, together with their German husbands, all attended, seated in the royal box behind the Queen Mother and Prince Charles. Also with them was their mother, Princess Alice, dressed in her grey nun's habit, which she had taken to wearing since she had founded her religious order of Martha and Mary, inspired by her aunt's foundation in Moscow, and which she had based on the Greek island of Tinos.

Princess Alice continued to run her foundation until a far-right group of colonels overthrew the government to take over Greece in 1967. By then frail and increasingly deaf – she had been plagued by hearing problems all her life – she accepted her son and daughter-in-law's invitation to live permanently with them. It was a return to the bosom of the British Royal Family: Alice had been born in Windsor Castle, then home to her grandmother, Queen Victoria, and she lived in Buckingham Palace, where she created a private chapel, until her death two years later.

She had expressed a wish to be buried on the Mount of Olives in Jerusalem, and in 1988, after eight years of negotiation, her remains were moved from Windsor to the Orthodox Convent of Mary Magdalene there. Prince Philip made a pilgrimage to her grave, where he spoke of her charitable work as a natural extension of and response to her Christian faith. She was buried alongside her aunt Elizabeth, the Russian Orthodox nun and martyr who had so inspired her.

Although he talked little about her, Philip was almost certainly moved and affected by his mother's deep religious conviction and its practical expression in philanthropic projects. While a man with a reputation for action and energy, Prince Philip was also someone who sought the comfort of religion and was fascinated by it. Religion, for him, was not to be kept in a box and taken out on Sundays for a service. Nor was it an intellectual pursuit, although he read voraciously about it with great interest. It was a source and inspiration for action.[11]

The clearest expression of his interest in religion was his founding of St George's House, part of the College of St George, which includes St George's Chapel, Windsor, where prayers have been said for the nation, three times a day, since the fourteenth century, and where countless royal christenings, weddings and funerals have taken place. Prince Philip got involved because he was asked to take on the reorganisation of the College in 1962 after the Rt Rev. Robin Woods was appointed Dean of Windsor. As Philip later recalled, it was his organisational abilities that came first, rather than his spiritual aptitude: 'I was dragged into religious things by being invited to become involved in the reorganization of St George's, Windsor. Theological dialogue was forced on me. I never had any great difficulty in being an ordinary Christian.'[12]

Woods had been asked to become Dean of Windsor after the Queen had heard him preach. Both she and the Duke always liked short sermons, to the point, and they were familiar enough with Scripture to spot someone who had something worthwhile to say. Woods and the Prince got on well and together raised funds to set up a conference centre, St George's House, alongside the Chapel. It provides a space where people of influence can explore ideas and arguments in quiet and confidential surroundings, staying overnight, enjoying meals together and joining in the Chapel daily office if they choose. Prince Philip and Robin Woods were keen that the Chapel's prayer life and theological purpose would give the house its impetus. Apart from offering space for secular discussions, it also provides clergy with a week's stay to 'reboot' and engage in discourse.

Being within the precincts of the castle afforded privacy but also a certain glamour, and an invitation to a St George's House consultation, as they are still called, was always welcome.

Philip endorsed the enterprise by speaking at the first St George's House gathering on 'The Role of the Church in Society Today'. He initiated talks there on interfaith long before it became fashionable, as well as on religion and the environment – a combination of subjects that would become one of the abiding passions of his life.

A sense of how Philip believed that Christianity and, indeed, other religions could contribute to contemporary society is evident in a speech he gave in 1969 when he was invited to give an address to the General Assembly of the Church of Scotland. It was called 'The Challenge of Change', and he argued that religions, especially Christianity, had to rethink the way their leaders communicated their message:

> If they are to retain their influence their message needs to be preached to present-day man in his present-day environment. We often hear of the church being rejected, but I don't believe that the Christian message is being rejected. I rather suspect that the messengers are still struggling to find the best way to convey the message so that it holds the attention of a much larger proportion of the younger generation and so that its meaning shines out like a beacon in the gloom of the doubt and confusion of the modern world.
>
> Arnold Toynbee is an agnostic but he had this to say in a recent article on Christianity's chance to triumph over technology: 'The historic religions have now reappeared above our horizon in a spirit of mutual charity, and this change of heart has removed the age-old stumbling block. It has opened the way for these religions to perform the spiritual services for a human being which they have always had it in their power to perform if only they had not stultified themselves, as they have persistently in the past, by exhibitions of spitefulness and intolerance that have justly brought them into discredit. Their service is one that they alone can provide, and it is a service of superlative value.'[13]

St George's House also provided an in-house space for the rows that beset the Church of England to be aired. On one memorable occasion, the arch-critic of the market, David Jenkins, Bishop of Durham, and John Gummer, Conservative Party chairman and later Cabinet minister, were part of a gathering there at the height of the rumpus between the Church of England and the Tory government, which was exacerbated by the Church of England's *Faith in the City* report on the plight of urban Britain.

Another Dean of Windsor with whom Prince Philip got on particularly well was Michael Mann, who served at St George's Chapel from 1976 to 1989. Mann was a former soldier who served during the Second World War and later in Colonial Service in Nigeria before becoming a member of the clergy. The two worked together over the protracted negotiations regarding the reburial of Princess Alice in Jerusalem. But they also developed a rapport over their interests in science and religion.

In 1982, Prince Philip sent Mann a copy of astronomer Fred Hoyle's lecture 'Evolution from Space', in which he challenged some of Darwin's theory of evolution. Hoyle argued for the possibility that life on earth might have derived from elsewhere and Prince Philip believed there was a compatibility between the scientific theory of evolution and the Scriptural account of Creation. This led to a lively correspondence between them on religion and science, and their letters, showing how an inquiring mind was responded to by a sympathetic theologian, were later published as *A Windsor Correspondence*.[14]

It was in 1988, in a talk given at St George's Chapel and later broadcast as part of an Advent service on BBC Radio 4, that Prince Philip most publicly expressed his profound faith, love of Creation and interest in science:

> Advent reminds Christians that there is the hope of spiritual re-birth at Christmas; it should also remind us that humanity is part of the natural order and it is our responsibility to give all life on earth that same chance of renewal and re-birth . . . God did not make us masters of His Creation, He expects us to be its guardians.[15]

As mentioned, it was also at Windsor, at St George's House, that Prince Philip's interest in interfaith dialogue first became evident, long before the topic was fashionable. While Philip led the Christian contingent, Muslim participants had Prince Hassan of Jordan at the helm, while Evelyn de Rothschild was also involved, along with other representatives of Judaism. The meetings struggled to find much in common via theological theory, but there was more agreement on practical applications of theology. This led to the creation of a code of business ethics.

Jonathan Romain, a Reform rabbi who has worked with St George's House, has pointed out how ahead of the game Prince Philip was: 'We talk now of interfaith as a commonplace but forty years ago it wasn't. Prince Philip was someone who first endorsed it. He also gave out a clear message that people who worship in a synagogue, mosque or gurdwara are as much a part of British society as those who worship in church.'[16]

One businessman with whom Philip had much in common was Sir John Templeton, the billionaire who was also fascinated by the links between science and religion. For twenty years, Philip made the presentation of the annual Templeton Prize at Buckingham Palace, an award for progress in religion that honoured spiritual leaders as well as scientists, including astronomer Sir Martin Rees and geneticist Francis Collins.

St George's House also hosted sessions on religion and science, attended by leaders in their field and sometimes journalists, although under Chatham House rules. Andrew Brown, a journalist who was himself a reporter on both religion and science and technology, recalled:

> I remember Sir John Polkinghorne, who died last month, lecturing on chaos theory and its implication for God's freedom to act in the world; the gentle Arthur Peacocke; and the brilliant Oxford philosopher John Lucas talking on human freedom and artificial intelligence – all this in the early 1990s, long before these ideas had emerged into public consciousness. And Philip would sometimes appear and listen quietly.
>
> After one of these meetings, it was suggested that he would like to write an article for *The Independent*'s god slot, which I then edited. Overriding the paper's anti-monarchist stance, I commissioned it, but

> did demand quite a lot of editing – which, to his great credit, was done without fuss.[17]

The emergence of Prince Philip's conviction that faith was key to the future of the planet came from his interest in wildlife. In 1985, the Prince, who at the time was International President of the World Wildlife Fund, met Martin Palmer, who had written extensively on how religions view the natural world. The following year was the twenty-fifth anniversary of the World Wildlife Fund, and as its international president, Prince Philip invited leaders of Buddhism, Christianity, Hinduism, Islam and Judaism to Assisi, birthplace of St Francis of Assisi, patron saint of ecology, to discuss with conservationists and environmentalists how they could work together and how humanity could live harmoniously within nature. This led to the Assisi Declarations, theological statements showing the spiritual links between religion and nature and leading to a growth in engagement between religion and the conservation movement. Prince Philip and Martin Palmer consolidated this work in 1995, when, with representatives of these religions, plus Bahá'ís, Daoists, Jains and Sikhs, Prince Philip founded the Alliance of Religions and Conservation (ARC) to explore this issue further.

The launch event of the ARC that year caused some traditionalist eyebrows to be raised. At Philip's suggestion it was held in Windsor and included people of different religions using St George's Chapel, with Daoist monks chanting by the porch and Hindu dancers performing near the altar.

Palmer became Philip's principal adviser on religion and the environment for thirty-six years and spent many hours in conversation with him about the issue. While others perceived Prince Philip to be on occasion abrupt, difficult and self-opinionated, Palmer saw another side to him:

> There was a humility there. He wanted people to learn from one another and that good things might emerge from conversation.
>
> He thought that [people in the environmental world] were not touching hearts and mind and the only things that ever touched hearts and mind and changed people are the arts and religion.

> At the heart of his faith was that God was authoritative and God had created the world. He totally believed in evolution as well; that was no problem for him. Our responsibility is to do what God wants and what God wants is for us to care for this planet.

Care, to Prince Philip, Palmer explained, 'was not the master model but the servant model and comes from Orthodoxy. We are here simply yet gloriously to be God's channel of blessing for creation . . . and to be able to help it express its cry for help and joy and delight at being part of something so generous.'[18]

Prince Philip's concerns were evident in his 1988 Advent sermon:

> We should reflect that, unlike many other species, we ought to know that we have the choice of doing good or untold damage to our planet. We know that our successors will inherit the earth, yet the physical systems of the planet and all the life that they support are being seriously damaged as a direct consequence of the continuing growth of the human population and human activities, and the increasing human exploitation of natural resources. If people with knowledge and in positions of influence, power or authority are not very careful, their decisions could, in this generation, achieve the ultimate idiocy by starting a process of decline that could make life very difficult for future generations and ultimately condemn our own species itself to extinction.[19]

He developed his views in a second book he co-wrote with Michael Mann. *Survival or Extinction: A Christian Attitude to the Environment* included material from a series of consultations that he had convened at St George's House, Windsor, on Christian attitudes to nature. It expressed his conviction that 'the urgent need to face up to what we humans are doing to the earth must lie heavily on the Christian conscience'.[20]

On another occasion he made his point about the vulnerability of Creation by saying, 'If you knock down Westminster Abbey you can rebuild it but once a dodo has gone, that's it.'[21]

The ARC later issued a declaration that the faiths had signed up to, which included a promise that maintaining and sustaining environmental life systems is a religious responsibility and that nature should be treated with respect and compassion. The organisation continues to hold gatherings and encourages religions to be advocates for God's creation and also to find practical ways of helping the environment, including those places going under the waves as global warming causes rising seas. Among the most badly affected are islands in the Pacific. The people of one of them, Tanna, otherwise known as Vanuatu, long venerated Philip as a god.

The people of Tanna believed that the ancestral god, Kalkaben, lived within the island's volcano, Mount Yasur, and that one of his sons had taken the body of a man and headed off to marry a powerful woman abroad but would eventually return. There was interest in Prince Philip, who seemed to the islanders to have been of no fixed abode until he married Elizabeth, when the Queen was crowned in 1953. Then, in 1974, the royal couple, on board the Royal Yacht *Britannia*, visited the nearby New Hebrides and anchored at the island of Aneityum. Several chiefs in canoes sailed out from nearby Tanna to see Philip. Later, one of them said that when they saw Philip standing on deck in his white naval uniform, 'I knew then that he was the true messiah.'[22]

Although English and French missionaries had attempted to convert the islanders to Christianity in the nineteenth and twentieth centuries, the native religion somehow survived, until, in 1974, the people found they had a living deity. After Prince Philip learned of the islanders' beliefs, Buckingham Palace consulted an anthropologist to help them understand the culture, and a British delegation visited the island, providing them with a signed photo of Prince Philip. They in return sent him a traditional pig-killing stick.

Author Anna Della Subin, who took up the story, recalled:

> In consultation with anthropologists and palace advisers, and after much debate as to the proper way to hold the stick, Philip staged a photo-shoot of himself on the lawn of Buckingham Palace, wielding the weapon, and dressed in a sharp charcoal suit. The graven image was dispatched to Tanna, and over the years the correspondence would continue, with letters and photographs passing between the god and his worshippers, though it was

deemed unadvisable by the palace for Philip to return to the area in the flesh.[23]

The islanders must have been thrilled, even stunned, to have contact with Philip, and the Palace may well have thought it possible that if he were to visit the island, the islanders might not let him leave, thereby causing an awkward diplomatic incident. Meanwhile, even Philip's mild intervention did not go down well with the French, who had an agreement with the British to jointly run the island as part of the New Hebrides, but both countries were withdrawing from the islands at the time in the face of calls for independence. The French perceived Philip's response to the islanders as part of an attempt by the British to try to maintain influence in the region.

On another occasion, Philip did intervene in the affairs of Vanuatu, although the consequence was probably not what he expected. After the island gained independence in July 1980 and the villagers of Yaohnanen were told they had to pay taxes, their chiefs wrote to the Prince to appeal. He replied to say that they should pay up, but the letter on Palace headed notepaper proved immensely powerful. When tax collectors came to the village, his followers waved it at them as proof that they were exempt. Philip, said Della Subin, had become 'a vessel for a message not quite his own'.[24]

In 2021, when news reached the island that Prince Philip had died, there were a hundred days of mourning, centred on Yaohnanen, which they believe is where he was born. Chiefs began a discussion as to who will succeed him. Some say that Prince Charles was anointed to the task when he visited Vanuatu in 2018.

As to the idea that Philip is a vessel for a message not quite his own, this is not a notion that can be readily applied to Prince Philip's other engagements with religion. He embraced certain religious beliefs with the same enthusiasm that he showed for, first, polo, and later carriage riding, throwing himself into them. This was clearly the case with his interest in the links between religion and environment, which for almost forty years was one of his most abiding passions.

As he grew older, he was also more drawn to the form of Christianity into which he was baptised – Orthodoxy – and which he had had to give up upon his marriage to the future Supreme Governor of the Church of England. At Easter services in the Church of England, he would talk about the real Easter, noting that the Greek Orthodox would mark it later in the calendar.[25] He also began visiting Mount Athos, one of Greek Orthodoxy's most sacred places.

His developing interest in the Orthodox Church coincided with his passion for the environment and what religions could do to help preserve Creation, and there was a strong link between Orthodoxy and the environment, with the Ecumenical Patriarch and Archbishop of Constantinople, Bartholomew I, speaking about its importance from the 1990s onwards. He, Prince Philip and Martin Palmer met together at many events, and the Patriarch visited Buckingham Palace when he was in Britain.

In 1991, Philip spoke at an Orthodox conference on ecology in Crete, saying, 'The Orthodox Church has always known that every form of religious expression, worship, prayer, festival, preaching, monastic life or mysticism – can provide the inspiration to a practical response to the ecological crisis.'[26]

Philip's interest in nature made him particularly critical of the Roman Catholic Church regarding its position on artificial birth control, which he blamed for over-population, although the irony of a man who was the father of four privileged children who swallowed up far more of the world's resources than a poor African family of eight, berating those with large families, was not lost on Roman Catholics.

The Roman Catholic Archbishop of Westminster, Cardinal Cormac Murphy-O'Connor, who got on well with the Prince and was happy to sit next to him at meals at Sandringham when others preferred not to, finding Philip's abruptness difficult, recalled that he was often regaled by Philip voicing antipathy to Rome on contraception. He described one occasion when he was asked to preach at the morning service at St Mary's Church, near Sandringham, with the Queen and Prince Philip listening, sitting in the choir. Over the years many Anglican bishops spent weekends at Sandringham where they would be asked to preach at the Sunday service, many of them dreading it because of the Duke of Edinburgh's lengthy interrogation of them about their preaching during the rest of the weekend. 'The

Prince was thoughtful enough to make a few comments over lunch,' the Cardinal said, with that degree of tact and twinkly wit for which he was known. 'So I knew he at least hadn't nodded off to sleep. He could rarely resist making a few digs at Church teaching.'[27]

Philip himself met many popes when he accompanied his wife to the Vatican, and in 2010, at the start of the papal state visit to Britain, he represented the Queen when Pope Benedict XVI landed at Edinburgh Airport. It was a rare honour for the Queen to send her husband to meet her guest, and was perceived as a sign of the couple's high regard for Pope Benedict. They later met Pope Francis in Rome, soon after his election, who shared Prince Philip's interest in the environment and climate change and in 2013 published an encyclical, *Laudato Si'*, on the topic. 'His attitude to the Catholic Church was: "why are you so late to the game with *Laudato Si'*", said Palmer. 'But he was so frustrated with the Church of England which has still yet to get any significant environment movement going.'[28]

Over the years the Queen and Prince Philip met countless clerics at official church occasions and on Sundays when they attended morning service. Neither of them liked lengthy sermons, and various Deans of Windsor and clergy at Balmoral and Sandringham were advised to keep them short. Although a conventional Anglican in many ways, the Prince was not keen on authority, and many sermon-givers found him argumentative as well as knowledgeable.

Both the Queen and her husband found great solace in their faith, and to them it seemed utterly normal for Princes William and Harry to accompany them to Crathie Church in Balmoral the morning after their mother Diana, Princess of Wales, was killed in a car crash in 1997. They were shocked when this gesture was decried as unfeeling in the tense days before Diana's funeral.

For his own funeral, Prince Philip long planned for it to be held at St George's Chapel, Windsor, the church with which he had been long associated not only through worship but also through his innovative ventures. It is also the resting place of his father-in-law, whose premature death so profoundly changed Philip's own life.

At one time, there might have been a call for the funeral of a monarch's consort who had lived so long and made such a significant contribution to public life to be moved to the larger Westminster

Abbey. But Covid-19 and lockdown rules in place when Philip died on 9 April 2021, with funeral attendance limited to thirty people, put paid to any large ceremony, and so he got his wish for the service to be held at St George's, on 17 April.

From the liturgy to the lack of sermon and eulogy and to the specially adapted Land Rover which carried his coffin from the nearby Windsor Castle to the Chapel, the service had all been overseen by the Prince himself. The congregation was limited to family members, led by his widow, the Queen, his four children and their spouses, and his eight grandchildren and most of their partners. There were also three German relatives from his mother's side of his family: Donatus, Prince and Landgrave of Hesse, a cousin; Prince Philipp of Hohenlohe-Langenburg, another cousin and grandson of Margarita, Philip's oldest sister; and Bernhard, Hereditary Prince of Baden, cousin and grandson of Philip's second sister, Theodora. As the years had gone by, the difficulties over Philip's German family had clearly dissipated.

While the Prince's appetite for interfaith was not so evident, it was an Anglican service with ecumenical flourishes. Four voices intoned nine lines from the Kontakion – the Orthodox Church's prayers for the dead and set to the Kiev melody, arranged by Sir Walter Parratt. The last time that there had been an attempt to include Orthodox prayers for the dead in a royal funeral in St George's Chapel – that of Queen Victoria – they had been blocked by the then Archbishop of Canterbury (see chapter three). This time, there was no such objection. Instead, they were a link not only to the Orthodox faith into which the Prince had been baptised but also to his Orthodox family, the Romanovs, and his former daughter-in-law, Diana, Princess of Wales.

The haunting words, 'where sorrow and pain are no more . . . And we are mortal, formed of the earth', would have been familiar to his parents, Princess Alice and Prince Andrew, to his great-aunt, the canonised Duchess Elizabeth, and to the murdered last Tsar of Russia and the Romanov royal family, also related to Prince Philip. As the last lines – 'weeping o'er the grave, we make our song' – echoed through St George's Chapel, they were a reminder of another funeral, that of Diana. Then, they formed part of Sir John Tavener's 'Song for Athene', sung as Diana's coffin left Westminster Abbey.

There were also the words, so familiar to Roman Catholics, from the last rites, as the coffin was lowered into the royal vault: 'Go forth upon thy journey from this world, O Christian soul.'

Another unusual choice of the Duke was the first reading from the Old Testament book of Ecclesiasticus, not usually picked for obsequies, and officially recognised by the Roman Catholic and Orthodox Churches but viewed as apochryphal by Protestant ones. But its celebration of God's creation fitted with Prince Philip's concerns about the environment and his belief that humanity should serve God through their stewardship of the earth. This was also evident in the choice of Psalm 104, sung during the service, set to music by William Lovelady and which had first been sung to mark Philip's seventy-fifth birthday:

My soul give praise unto the Lord of heaven,
In majesty and honour clothed;
The earth he made will not be moved;
The seas he made to be its robe. Give praise.

That idea of service was also apparent in three other key prayers during the service read by the Dean of Windsor, Bishop David Conner, who is also Register of the Order of the Garter. The Order, whose patron is St George, is the most ancient and prestigious of the chivalric orders in England, and its spiritual home is St George's Chapel. Bishop Conner prayed for the Duke, 'who has left us a fair pattern of valiant and true knighthood'.

As a Garter Knight, Prince Philip had his helmet, his crest and sword and stall plate in St George's Chapel. By tradition, all of these 'achievements' are given back on death to the sovereign, bar the stall plate. The Queen, then, received the insignia of her valiant knight; the stall plate will remain in the Chapel.

The Queen sat alone at her husband's funeral owing to Covid-19 regulations, a poignant reminder of all the many times he had accompanied her to church over the years, whether for Sunday service, for christenings, weddings and funerals of their relatives, or for the grand occasions of state. They shared a faith and no doubt both found consolation in it.

But his approach – not stymied by the formality of being Supreme Governor of the established Church – was one of exploration, myriad influences and even experiment. It gave him a spiritual freedom that his wife did not and even could not have.

Just over a year after Philip's funeral and the haunting moment when his widow, Elizabeth II, sat alone in St George's Chapel, their family returned there for, first, the Queen's committal, and then, entirely privately, for the burial of the couple together in the George VI Memorial Chapel, together with her parents, George VI and Queen Elizabeth. The death of Elizabeth II came at the end of a seventy-year reign and, like her coronation and her time as monarch, her funeral was an expression of her personal faith. It also highlighted the way in which Elizabeth II, throughout her life, but particularly through her involvement in religion, had been a symbol of tradition and stability, yet managed to simultaneously stand for change and a certain innovation, even if she was not the experimenter her husband was able to be. It is to this remarkable time – the eleven days in September 2022 when Britain and the Commonwealth marked the death of the Platinum Queen, paid tribute to her, was in mourning and also witnessed the accession of Elizabeth and Philip's son, Charles III – that I will now turn, and to the transition from one era to the next.

# 7

# Demise: the end of the Elizabethan age

THE DEATH OF Elizabeth II was expected – and yet unexpected. Millions had realised she was in decline, her public appearances increasingly sporadic, affected by last-minute cancellations owing to what her household called mobility problems. After years of robust health, she had started to look frail in her ninety-sixth, Platinum Jubilee year. But she had also seemed like Tennyson's Brook: 'For men may come and men may go, but I go on forever.'[1] And then, suddenly, news began to filter out on the late morning of Thursday 8 September that perhaps the Queen was not, after all, immortal.

Her death came in the midst of political drama. She had originally been due to leave Balmoral to receive her outgoing Prime Minister in London and ask his successor to form a government. But the mobility problems that had beset her for some months meant that she didn't leave Balmoral, and on Tuesday 6 September, first Boris Johnson and then Liz Truss visited her in Scotland.

The final photograph of her was taken that day, showing her standing beside a roaring fire in Balmoral, somewhat stooped, holding a stick. There was a bruise on her hand, of the kind caused by a canula, but other than that the Queen looked well, though frail and decidedly thin. The following day, a Privy Council meeting she was due to attend virtually was cancelled, after doctors advised her to rest.

As rumours swept London newsrooms on that Thursday morning of the Queen's ill-health, and there was an unprecedented admission by her doctors that there was cause for concern, television and radio newsreaders worked on the hoof to bring viewers and listeners up to date with what was happening – except they didn't really know. At the BBC, health correspondent Hugh Pym was drafted in to talk about what was wrong, but he had little idea, nor been given information to offer. Neither had Nicholas Witchell, its royal correspondent. Reporters had some idea but nothing official to say. It was clearly deemed unacceptable to say the Queen was dying, although behind the scenes, journalists realised that she was.[2]

The closest that Witchell got to unofficially confirming the Queen's death was when he commented on a photograph of the Earl and Countess of Wessex, the Duke of York and Prince William arriving at Balmoral just after 5 p.m. Sophie Wessex, he pointed out, looked stricken.

By the time the group arrived, the Queen was dead. At her deathbed had been her son and daughter, the Prince of Wales and the Princess Royal. Her doctor of thirty years, Dr Douglas James Allan Glass, who was Apothecary to the Queen's Household at Balmoral, was also in attendance. The death certificate recorded that the Queen died at 3.10 p.m. on 8 September 2022.[3] It was, according to the language of constitutional experts, the demise of the sovereign.

News of the Queen's death caused speculation, from jocular commentary that dealing with Johnson and Truss in quick succession had caused her to lose the will to live, to her having known her days were numbered and that she had chosen to die in Balmoral, her favourite home. But staff at another of her favourite places, Windsor Castle, had been bidden goodbye by the Queen when she left for Scotland and they say she fully expected to see them again in the autumn.[4] She had indeed been ill – although her death certificate, released three weeks after her death, said that she had died of old age. However, it is understood that she was suffering from bone cancer, which caused her pain and the mobility problems frequently mentioned in 2022 when she had to pull out of engagements, including some of those usually considered unmissable: Commonwealth Day, the Cenotaph on Remembrance Sunday, Ascot, the Maundy Thursday service.

But the end came suddenly. I am told that she unexpectedly collapsed, and the Princess Royal was called to her side.[5] There was no suggestion of her being taken to hospital and instead her death was in her own bed, with her family at her side – a death many would prefer to have. As a low church Anglican, there was no suggestion of the last rites being given, but those close to her have said that she was ready to meet her maker. The Rt Rev. Dr Iain Greenshields, the Moderator of the Church of Scotland, had been staying with the Queen at Balmoral the previous weekend and had preached at Crathie Church. According to royal biographer Gyles Brandreth, the Queen knew her remaining time was limited, and Dr Greenshields said of his final conversation with her, 'Her faith was everything to her. She told me she had no regrets.'[6]

The death of Elizabeth II was, like her life, conducted in private, but also on the public stage, and constantly surrounded by ceremonial. Just her immediate family accompanied her in her last hours, and then eleven days later they again were alone with her when she was laid to rest beside her parents, George VI and Queen Elizabeth, and her husband, Prince Philip, in the George VI Chapel, in St George's Chapel, Windsor. Her daughter, the Princess Royal, accompanied her mother's coffin throughout its journeys through Scotland to Edinburgh and onward to London for her funeral. There were just a few hours for private grief on the day she died – from 3.10 p.m., the moment of her death, until the official announcement released to the world at 6.30 p.m. Even as a monarch dies, though, public duty hovers by the bedside. Her eldest son, Charles, Prince of Wales, who was with her, became King at that moment.

At Buckingham Palace, footmen solemnly posted the statement of Elizabeth II's death and the succession at the gates. On the BBC, news presenter Huw Edwards, dressed in black, intoned the words slowly and carefully, later saying, 'I felt I was announcing the end of something very special . . . It was the end of an era in British history, the end of a presence that has been with many people throughout their entire lives.'[7]

On LBC radio, Andrew Marr, his politics evident by his column for the left-leaning *New Statesman*, was presenting his news show. As he read the official announcement, he broke down and wept. The next morning, Allison Pearson, the right-wing Brexit-loving columnist for *The Telegraph*, wrote, 'It is unbearably sad. A loss almost too great to process . . . How are we supposed to manage without her? Who are we without her? She had always been there; a still point in a tumultuous world.'[8] The regard in which the Queen was held, across the political spectrum and across the globe, became quickly evident, with tributes from world leaders, the Prime Ministers of her seventy-year reign and the public. British newspapers, much like their counterparts in the Royal Household, government and the Church of England, had been planning this moment for years, with supplements at the ready.

As soon as the Queen had died, ceremonial took over as the response to the Queen's death, to provide shape and form to the national mourning, but also to ensure that there was continuity. Britain is never without a monarch, its head of state. The twenty-five-word statement from Buckingham Palace made the immediate accession plain in simple language that was full of drama, profundity and history:

> The Queen died peacefully at Balmoral this afternoon.
>
> The King and The Queen Consort will remain at Balmoral this evening and will return to London tomorrow.[9]

The King. It was a phrase that had not been heard in Britain for seventy years. To hear it for the first time that day was to realise that something momentous but seamless had happened – the crown had passed from one head of state to the next.

The ceremonial surrounding the death of the Queen and the Accession of the King meshed Church and state, monarchy and belief. From the moment Elizabeth II left Balmoral for the last time to the end of the committal service at St George's Chapel, and throughout the time she lay in state in Westminster Hall and during her funeral at Westminster Abbey, resting on her coffin were the signs of her office. There was the Imperial State Crown, used in part of the coronation service and always at State Openings of Parliament; the sceptre, denoting authority, but under God, with its fabulous Cullinan diamond topped by a cross; and the orb, the jewelled sphere, also with a cross, symbol of how the world, and even its kings and queens, is the dominion of Christ.

While the rest of her immediate family stayed at Balmoral, the King and the Queen Consort flew back to London, where the couple took an impromptu walkabout outside Buckingham Palace. Inside, Charles III filmed an address to the nation, broadcast at 6 p.m., with words that combined an emotional tribute to his mother and a pledge to serve the nation himself. In the ten-minute speech, the King spoke of his 'darling Mama' who had been an inspiration to her family.

> Queen Elizabeth's was a life well lived: a promise with destiny kept and she is mourned most deeply in her passing. That promise of lifelong service I renew to you all today.[10]

From the moment the news emerged of her death until after the funeral and committal, crowds gathered outside royal palaces. *The Guardian*, the most republican of the national papers, reported that 'Britain mourns'. 'No hysteria, just quiet respect as crowds gather in remembrance' – an acknowledgement that the death of a loved monarch after seventy years of duty was not the moment to question the value of the institution of monarchy. The day after her death, on Friday 9 September, it despatched its chief reporter, Daniel Boffey, to report from outside Buckingham Palace, long associated with Elizabeth II and her balcony appearances, audiences with Prime Ministers and state visits, but abandoned as her home during Covid in favour of Windsor. There he found crowds participating in what he called 'their pilgrimage' and noted that the crowd at the Victoria Memorial was 'refreshed by ever more people as the day went on, from every walk of life, of every age and ethnicity'.[11]

In Parliament, the Prime Minister of just two days (and only a few more to come), Liz Truss, told the House of Commons, 'On the death of [the Queen's] father, King George VI, Winston Churchill said the news had stilled the clatter and traffic of 20th century life in many lands. Now, 70 years later, in the tumult of the 21st century, life has paused again.'[12]

Elizabeth II had always made her Christian commitment known, and in the ceremonial following her death, it was apparent. The lying-in-state, funeral and committal had been planned for years through Operation London Bridge, while simultaneously, Operation Spring Tide was drawn up to plan for the new King's accession.

Planning meant that not only might the various events go smoothly but also that rituals were used to reinforce the monarchy's standing, to provide a vehicle for public mourning and to encourage a belief that people were part of history, through unchanging tradition. In fact, the genius of the British monarchy has been to reinvent itself constantly. Yes, there is tradition, but so too is there change, as the eleven days of mourning for Elizabeth II proved.

Something else too was going on with this ritual, in a country of increasing secularity. It became a means of people connecting with one another, with something possibly greater than themselves, in a ceremony that was full of religious symbolism. The columnist Janice Turner hinted at something numinous in *The Times*:

> We've been reminded that beneath the shiny edifice of modern society, where in our pockets are devices streaming all the world's knowledge, there is still hunger for the unknowable . . . Britain hasn't 'lost the plot'. Rather, many of us are connecting with a deeper human impulse that transcends all societies and eras: a yearning for the mysterious and sublime.

And she went on, 'If the royal family has a sacred role, it is to connect us with our ancient selves . . . we are an old country.'[13]

As the Queen's last journey began on Sunday 11 September, when her cortège made its way from Royal Deeside, through country lanes and main roads to Edinburgh, there were rituals both ancient and modern. On roadsides, people stood to attention, but occasionally flowers were thrown and silence was sometimes broken by applause. The hearse wended its way along the Scottish capital's Royal Mile to Holyroodhouse, where the coffin lay in state, draped with the Royal Standard of Scotland.

Elsewhere across the nation, in different city squares and on town hall steps, Elizabeth II 'of beloved memory' was remembered and her son Charles was proclaimed to be her successor, by Almighty God. At Anglican church services, the new Supreme Governor of the Church of England was prayed for. Quentin Letts, released from his usual duties as *The Times'* parliamentary sketch-writer, reported, 'In our own little hamlet of How Caple, Herefordshire, matins drew a large attendance, soberly suited, as the Prayer Book's liturgy about "our most gracious Sovereign Lord, King Charles", was heard for the first time. The organist struck up God Save The King. Stabbed by a sudden sadness, your sketch-writer wobbled.'[14]

The following afternoon, the coffin was driven along the Royal Mile once more, this time to St Giles' Cathedral, the High Kirk of the Church of Scotland, where the public could come to pay tribute. That evening there was also a service of thanksgiving, the first of three planned for the capitals of the devolved nations.

They had always formed part of Operation London Bridge, the plan for the Queen's death, but nevertheless were surprising – innovations that had never happened before. It was clearly a way of ensuring that Scotland, Wales and Northern Ireland played their part in mourning the monarch, and that London was not the only focus.

Nothing for the death of the monarch was left to chance. The heavy oak casket, in which Elizabeth II travelled from Balmoral to Edinburgh and on to London and Windsor, and in which she was laid to rest, had been made more than thirty years earlier.[15] It was of English oak, now hard to acquire, and lined with lead, given that the Queen was not to be buried in the earth. This made it extremely heavy, requiring eight military bearers to carry it through Westminster Abbey and up the steps of St George's Chapel. Perhaps most importantly of all, it had been built with fitments on the coffin lid to allow the instruments of state – the Imperial State Crown, the sceptre and the orb – to be clipped into place and not fall off. Such a drama once took place, when the Maltese cross fell off the crown into the gutter as the cortège of George V made its way into New Palace Yard from the vigil in Westminster Hall. Harold Nicolson recorded in his diary that this was 'a most terrible omen' – a prescient remark, given the new king, Edward VIII, abdicated less than a year later.

The three services in Edinburgh, Cardiff and Belfast, all attended by the new King and Queen Consort, were also a means of involving different Christian denominations and other faiths. Previous farewells to British monarchs had been Anglican affairs. Some clerics, though, raised their eyebrows. One, close to the Queen, was concerned that these services should not be proto-funerals, and also felt it was not appropriate to have services of thanksgiving amid the mourning and before the funeral.[16] But, as with the death of Diana, Princess of Wales, the response was a mix of tradition and invention, thought appropriate to current mores.

In Edinburgh, there were nods to Scottish culture, with the singing of Psalm 118 – 'I shall not die, but live' – in Scots Gaelic. The Gospel was read by the Most Rev. Mark Strange, Primus of the Scottish Episcopal Church – the Scottish Anglicans – while the homily, which is more of an attempt at spiritual edification than doctrinal instruction, as a sermon is, was given by Dr Greenshields, who had been the Queen's guest during her last weekend at Balmoral. But it was the lesson reader that showed how much more ecumenical Christianity has become in recent time: St Paul's Letter to the Romans was read by the Most Rev. Leo Cushley, the Roman Catholic Archbishop of St Andrews and Edinburgh. The quiet, gentle burr of Archbishop Cushley, once a Vatican official who helped draft speeches for Pope Benedict XVI during his state visit to Britain in 2010, when the Pope was greeted by the Queen at Holyroodhouse, might sound reassuringly establishment. But in a country once scarred by sectarianism, having a Catholic hierarch read the lesson in the High Kirk at a thanksgiving service for a Protestant Queen was a modern, progressive touch.[17]

The following day, a similar effort at ecumenical tolerance was made in a nation even more scarred by sectarianism than Scotland, when the King and Queen Consort attended a service at Belfast Cathedral. This time, the concerns about thanksgiving pre-empting funerals and mourning had been more heeded by the Northern Irish than in Scotland, and the Church of Ireland Cathedral hosted a Service of Reflection for the Life of the Queen. This time, the two Archbishops of Armagh both attended: Eamon Martin, the ecclesiastical head of the Roman Catholic Church of all Ireland, and the other, Francis McDowell, the ecclesiastical head of the Church of Ireland. The first reading was given by Alex Maskey, Speaker of the Northern Ireland Assembly who was the first Sinn Fein Lord Mayor of Belfast, a one-time ally of Gerry Adams and a survivor of an attack by loyalist paramilitaries. He and the rest of the congregation, which included the Irish Taoiseach, Micheál Martin, and Irish President, Michael D. Higgins, listened as the Presbyterian Moderator and the

President of the Methodist Conference offered prayers of thanks for the life of the Queen and asked God to comfort the new King in his sorrow.

The service ended as all the Church leaders gave this mixed community of Catholics and Protestants, Irish and British, the Celtic blessing: 'Deep peace of the running wave to you.'[18] A country once riven by sectarian hatred remembered the woman who had once been as much a symbol of colonial power to one side as she was of rightful authority to the other. Perhaps that day, though, the ecumenical service was more imbued with the emotions felt in 2011 when the Queen had given a speech at Dublin Castle, during her state visit to Ireland. Then she had amazed the room with a few words of Irish before commenting:

> It is impossible to ignore the weight of history . . . To all those who have suffered as a consequence of our troubled past I extend my sincere thoughts and deep sympathy. With the benefit of historical hindsight we can all see things which we would wish had been done differently or not at all . . .
>
> The lessons from the peace process are clear: whatever life throws at us, our individual responses will be all the stronger for working together and sharing the load.[19]

In Wales, three days later on 16 September, the helicopter of the King and Queen landed in Cardiff for a service of prayer and reflection at the Church in Wales' Llandaff Cathedral. This was a far more adventurous service even than the one in Northern Ireland. While much attention was focused on it being bilingual, with some readings and hymns in Welsh, the prayers were strongly interfaith, with some given by Kate McColgan, chair of the Interfaith Council for Wales, John Minkes of the South Wales Jewish Representative Council, and Dr Abdul-Azim Ahmed, Secretary General of the Muslim Council of Wales. They called upon the Lord of healing and wholeness, the Lord of hope and truth, and the Lord of the call to serve – words full of meaning for all the Abrahamic faiths and others. Dr Ahmed included *rabbana*, a word often found in the Koran, meaning 'Lord', as he said, 'Rabbana, grant us peace.'[20]

Not everyone was impressed. When the Muslim Council of Wales tweeted footage of Dr Ahmed reading in the cathedral, some fellow Muslims accused him of 'boot-licking behaviour' – evidence of the high-wire act that being royal and seeking to embrace different parts of the nation can be. The efforts to engage with the leaders of different Christian denominations and other faiths continued after the services, where various representatives, not just those who had spoken at them, were introduced to the King and Queen Consort.

While the new monarch and his wife travelled across the devolved nations, the queues in London were growing for Queen Elizabeth's lying-in-state. There was antipathy about that, too, with negative comments suggesting that the Queen's appeal had been narrow and that only a particular faction of society would turn out: white, elderly and possibly linked to the military. The soft left political commentator Steve Richards said on Twitter, 'I wonder how many of the millions queueing up for around 24 hours to see the Queen's coffin can't be bothered to vote in UK/local elections, the outcome of which have a direct impact on their lives.'[21]

After I riposted that those who queue might be the kind of people who engage with what's going on in the world, another Tweeter suggested they would engage, because they were elderly Tory voters. So I set out to find out about the queue myself.

The queue in London, of course, was not the only one. There had been people lining the streets across Scotland and in Edinburgh as the Queen's hearse passed by. There were even queues of people paying their respects in the dark and the pouring rain on Tuesday 13 September as the Queen's coffin was driven along the A40 from RAF Northolt, after a flight from Edinburgh, and then through London to rest at Buckingham Palace, before the vigil began at Westminster Hall the next day. Some reports suggested that lighting the hearse, enabling people to see the coffin, draped in the Royal Standard, had been at the Queen's own suggestion while planning the lying-in-state.

From Wednesday 14 September to the early morning of Monday 19 September, when Westminster Hall closed before the coffin was moved to Westminster Abbey for the funeral, people queued in their thousands, sometimes for as long as twelve hours or more, to file past the Queen's coffin.

Westminster Hall was kept open day and night to allow as many people as possible to pay their tribute, some by saluting, bowing or making a sign of the cross. The BBC kept a twenty-four-hour webcam going, which became a must-view that week.

Arriving at 6 a.m., I joined the queue – thanks to the government queue tracker showing us where its tail could be found – at Blackfriars Bridge. There were marshals saying good morning, first aid volunteers on hand and police officers with little to do, as people walked slowly, talking to the people they found themselves alongside.

And what a mixed, multicultural, multifaith group of people the British are, going by the crowd I joined. There were old soldiers in their regimental berets, young men in their Jewish yarmulkes, women in hijabs, people I met from Cambridge, others from the Midlands, and plenty who had taken the first Tube trains of the day from the London suburbs.

A retired GP from Buckinghamshire spoke to a shop assistant from Sydenham; a parliamentary intern chatted to a PR executive from west London. These were not profound conversations about deeply held beliefs or philosophical debates about the meaning of monarchy, but people making connections between their own experiences and the previous week. Mostly, they seemed to reconnect with people they loved and had lost through their loss of the Queen, remembering their own parents and grandparents – the people of the Queen's own generation – as well as people who had died in recent times because of Covid. The link was made with what had gone before as well. One woman recalled how her own mother went to the lying-in-state of the Queen's father, George VI, in 1952, so she felt it was right to attend that of Elizabeth II. Others wanted to be part of an occasion that would become part of history, or to honour the only monarch they had ever known.

The former England football captain, David Beckham, was one of those who queued patiently to pay his respects and spoke of his desire to be part of a communal experience: 'To be honest, it's what we all envisioned. We all want to be there together, we all want to experience something where we celebrate the amazing life of our Queen. Something like this today is meant to be shared together.'[22]

After Brexit, Covid lockdown disputes and economic crises, the country for once seemed a United Kingdom.

We went from that chatter of the outside world into the spectacle of royalty inside Westminster Hall: the Queen's coffin surrounded by Beefeaters and the Household Cavalry who never moved an inch. The coffin was draped in the Royal Standard and adorned by the Imperial State Crown. But even more extraordinary a sight was the sceptre and orb atop the coffin – the first time since Elizabeth II held them during her 1953 coronation that they had been back in her presence. The orb was topped with a cross, as was the Imperial State Crown too. Another cross was at the foot of the coffin: this was most definitely a Christian monarch's lying-in-state.

But above all, it was not the grandeur that was so startling. It was the full enveloping silence as people processed past the coffin. The fleeting moment each person had before the coffin felt much more than a mere glance. This was a time of contemplation, rather like a pilgrimage. Then the pilgrims of all faiths and none headed back out into London, and the bustle, rush and noise swallowed them up.

By Monday 19 September, the day of the funeral, the world's media had focused its camera lenses on Britain for eleven days, ever since the death of Elizabeth II. Those lenses had taken in Balmoral and Edinburgh, Cardiff and Belfast. They had shown crowds outside Buckingham Palace, people arriving at St Paul's Cathedral the day after the Queen died for a service of reflection, and others outside Windsor Castle, where they were visited by the Duke and Duchess of Cambridge and the Duke and Duchess of Sussex. The Duke of Cambridge, newly appointed Prince of Wales upon his father's accession to the throne, had joined Charles III for an impromptu walkabout to greet those in the queue for Westminster Hall. As had happened in Scotland, Wales and Northern Ireland when the King greeted the crowds, the mood was a mix of mourning for the old Queen and welcome for her successor. 'God Save The King' was called out and occasionally sung tentatively by a nation that had not heard it for seventy years – a sign that Britain could cope with change despite the dread often expressed about a time without the Queen.

When 19 September dawned, Westminster Abbey, where Elizabeth II had been married in 1947 and crowned in 1953, became the focus of attention. Sixty-nine years on from her coronation, she returned once more to the Abbey, for a funeral service meticulously planned for years. According to the former Archbishop of York, John Sentamu, the Queen had not wanted a long, boring funeral. While packed with readings, music and processions, it was organised to last just an hour. It was, said Archbishop Sentamu, talking on the eve of the funeral with Laura Kuenssberg on BBC One, 'the prayer book service, the words which were an inspiration to Shakespeare . . . a funeral service that is glorious in its setting'.[23]

So great was the interest at home and abroad – an estimated 37 million in Britain alone and 11 million in the United States, plus more elsewhere[24] – that the columnist and former newspaper editor, Charles Moore, suggested, 'The framers of this funeral, who included the new King . . . will not have been unaware that they were organising what must surely have been the most watched Christian service in the whole of human history.'[25]

It was a military and religious spectacle, full of pomp and pageantry, from the moment when the coffin was moved from Westminster Hall to the Abbey by 142 Royal Navy ratings who heaved the State Gun Carriage carrying the coffin. The two-and-a-half-ton carriage was previously used for the funerals of Victoria, Edward VII, George V and George VI.

The years of planning were evident in the music especially composed for the service and commissioned by Westminster Abbey from two of Britain's leading composers, Sir James MacMillan and Judith Weir, Master of the Queen's Music. Both put to music parts of Scripture: Romans chapter 8 for MacMillan – 'Who shall separate us from the love of Christ' – and Psalm 42 – 'Like as the hart desireth the water-brooks: so longeth my soul after thee, O God' – for Weir.

This first state funeral to be held at the Abbey since George II's in 1760 was, at heart, an Anglican service, with aspects that could be found in any funeral in a Church of England country parish: prayers, including the Lord's Prayer, a sermon, a blessing and the commendation.

The Archbishop of Canterbury, Justin Welby, focused on the Christian idea of service in his sermon, centring attention on how the Queen had served the people of Britain and the Commonwealth, but above all her service had been dedicated to God:

> In 1953 the Queen began her Coronation with silent prayer, just there at the High Altar. Her allegiance to God was given before any person gave allegiance to her. Her service to so many people in this nation, the Commonwealth and the world, had its foundation in her following Christ – God himself – who said that he 'came not to be served but to serve and to give his life as a ransom for many'.

And he went on – quite possibly with a message to the politicians in the congregation – 'People of loving service are rare in any walk of life. Leaders of loving service are still rarer. But in all cases those who serve will be loved and remembered when those who cling to power and privileges are long forgotten.'

There was also a reminder that whether rich or poor, commoner or queen, the end brings a certain equality: 'We will all face the merciful judgement of God.'[26]

The hymns were those that the Queen was particularly fond of, just as anyone might pick the ones that meant the most to them for their funeral service. Hers turned out to be 'The Day Thou Gavest, Lord, Is Ended', 'The Lord's My Shepherd', set to Crimond, a nod both to Scotland and to her marriage to the Duke of Edinburgh, as it was sung at their wedding in the Abbey, and 'Love Divine, All Loves Excelling'.

The readings were popular ones too, listed in the 1662 Book of Common Prayer for the Church of England's Order for the Burial of the Dead. The first was St Paul's first Letter to the Corinthians, chapter 15, with its affirmation of the Christian belief in resurrection, and how Christ destroyed death by rising from the dead. The second lesson was from the Gospel of St John, chapter 14, a highly popular reading for Christian funerals with its message of hope that where Christ goes, back to his Father in heaven after his ministry on earth, there will be a place for all his followers. It also confirms that Christ is the way to God and that he is God: 'I am the way, and the truth, and the life.'

The prayers reflected Elizabeth II's years of service to country and Commonwealth while they also reflected that she was a Christian soul, with hope of the resurrection. This was evident in the prayers that topped and tailed the service: the Sentences, sung to music by William Croft and Henry Purcell, first composed for the funeral of Queen Mary II in 1695, and a prayer said as part of the commendation – 'Go forth, O Christian soul, from this world' – a version of which had been said at the funeral of Prince Philip, Duke of Edinburgh.

Once, reciting such words would have caused raised eyebrows. It is based on an ancient Catholic prayer, the Proficiscere, which formed part of Elgar's *The Dream of Gerontius*, and is often said as part of the last rites, prayers for the dying.

That was just one of the innovations of the funeral. Plenty of the liturgy was identified as Anglican and traditional. But there were touches here and there that were far more ecumenical, and nods to interfaith dialogue as well.

No funeral of a British monarch had ever previously included leaders of other faiths and Christian denominations. The interfaith representatives were among the first to process into Westminster Abbey at the start of the funeral. There were Jews, Muslims, Hindus, Sikhs, Buddhists, Jains, Zoroastrians and a Bahá'í representative.

Next came Christian leaders from Wales, Scotland and Northern Ireland, including Roman Catholics and Presbyterians, while from England there were also Pentecostalists, Copts and the Greek Orthodox. Some of them read prayers, including the Rev. Helen Cameron, Moderator of the Free Churches Group, Cardinal Vincent Nichols, Roman Catholic Archbishop of Westminster, and the Rt Rev. Dr Iain Greenshields, Moderator of the General Assembly of the Church of Scotland who had been with the Queen at Balmoral during her last weekend.

Scotland's special place in the Queen's affection and its being where she spent her final days was affectingly remembered in the final touch of the funeral, specially requested by her son, the new King. The Queen's Piper, Paul Burns, played a lament, and the sound of 'Sleep Dearie Sleep' filled the Abbey's nave as the Queen's coffin and procession left for the last time.

There was no mistaking this was a funeral of grandeur: the bell tolling to mark each year of the Queen's life, the processions, the choirs of Westminster Abbey and the Chapel Royal, St James's Palace, the trumpeters of the Household Cavalry. There were so many heads of state and political leaders from around the globe that they gathered at the Royal Hospital, Chelsea, for tea and were then driven to the Abbey by coach – apart from US President Joe Biden, whose security detail insisted on him still using 'The Beast', the armoured presidential limousine.

The reign of Elizabeth II was bookended by television. Hers was the first coronation to be televised, leading to a surge in TV sales in 1953. Her funeral became the television event of 2022: Hannah Furness, reporting for *The Daily Telegraph*, wrote that 'the National Grid reported a two-gigawatt power drop – the equivalent of 200 million lightbulbs being turned off – as people paused everyday life to turn off their Hoovers and kettles to concentrate on their television'.[27]

Amid this ceremonial, though, was also a grieving family, its members filling most of the south transept of the Abbey, the eyes of the world upon them, observing body language for signs of how grief had papered over the cracks – or not – between the disgraced Andrew, Duke of York – no longer a working royal because of his connections with the paedophile Jeffrey Epstein – and his siblings; and between the Duke and Duchess of Sussex, no longer working royals; and William, the new Prince of Wales; and the new King. A sign of that personal loss was evident in the single wreath upon the coffin. Chosen by the King himself, it contained roses, hydrangea, sedum and uxorious myrtle, from the same bush which had produced the sprig for the Queen's own wedding bouquet in 1947. It was topped by a handwritten message: 'In loving and devoted memory. Charles R' – the R denoting the Latin, *rex*, for 'king'.

Emerging into the sunshine from Westminster Abbey after the service, the Queen's funeral procession set off to walk the 1.7 miles to the Wellington Arch. There were some three thousand members of the armed forces, led by the Canadian Mounties and with other troops from across the Commonwealth. The royal men and the Princess Royal came on foot, while other women and the Queen's grandchildren, Prince George and Princess Charlotte, travelled by car.

As they passed Buckingham Palace, all the staff lined the railings to acknowledge their late sovereign, and then, as the procession wound its way to the Wellington Arch at Hyde Park Corner, the crowds were eighty deep. Practicality took over: while the Queen's cortège wound its way along the A4, through the suburbs, to Windsor, allowing yet more to see the Queen along the journey to her final resting place, members of her family zipped along the faster M4, to await her arrival along the Long Walk that led up to Windsor Castle and St George's Chapel. Flowers were strewn by the crowds along the A-road as the hearse passed by, and at Windsor, flowers left throughout the previous week by the public had been tied into tiny posies dotting the grass. The Queen's groom, Terry Pendry, and her last Fell Pony, Emma, that she had ridden in Windsor Great Park, nodded as her coffin passed, while her last two pet corgis awaited her outside the chapel.

Although the committal was televised and involved prime ministers and governors general of the Queen's Realms, it was a more intimate occasion than the Westminster Abbey service. Also there, alongside her family, were members of her Household who had served her for many years. While the Bidding, like that at the Abbey, set out why the service was taking place and reflected the Christian hope of eternal life, it was also much more personal, about the relationship between the Queen and her family. The Dean of Windsor, the Rt Rev. David Conner, spoke of someone 'whose uncomplicated yet profound Christian Faith bore so much fruit'. And, rather as a village rector might say at any funeral, he went on to refer to her 'kindness, concern and reassuring care for her family and friends and neighbours'.[28] Some weeks later, another special service was held in the chapel to allow the Queen's special friends - her ladies in waiting - to remember her.

There were other intimate touches: the motet, 'Bring us, O Lord God, at Our Last Awakening', written by John Donne, put to music by Sir William Henry Harris, who had taught the piano to the Queen and her sister; and then there was the Russian Kontakion of the Departed. These are prayers for the dead from the Orthodox Church set to the Kiev Melody, arranged by Sir Walter Parratt. The very same piece was sung at the funeral of Prince Philip in April 2021, thought to have been chosen because of his links to Greek Orthodoxy through his mother, and the British monarchy's links to the murdered last Czar and his family – they were cousins. Some lines from the Kontakion were also used in John Tavener's 'Song for Athene', used at Princess Diana's funeral in 1997.

The prayers were read by three clergy from the Queen's homes – the Rector of Sandringham; the Minister of Crathie Church, Balmoral;

and the Rector of All Saints Chapel in Windsor Great Park. One of the prayers – 'O Lord, support us all the day long of this troublous life' – was written by John Henry Newman, the Anglican cleric who had scandalised Victorian society by converting to Roman Catholicism, and had been made a saint during the Queen's reign in 2019.

Then, as a last act, before the cameras left and the curtain came down on this public ceremony, the regalia that had been placed on her coffin ten days earlier and had remained with it throughout were finally removed. The Dean of Windsor placed them with great tenderness on the high altar. It was as if to say that, finally, Elizabeth Alexandra Mary Windsor was no longer Elizabeth II, a queen, but a Christian soul like any other mentioned in the hymns and readings. The burden of office was gone.

Later, when night had fallen, and just her family was present, the Queen's coffin was brought up from the vault, where it had lain after the committal, together with that of her husband, Prince Philip, and the pair were laid to rest in the George VI Chapel with her parents.

Elizabeth II had been, the historian Simon Schama wrote, 'to us and to much of the world, quintessential Britain; not all of it, of course, but more than the head of state – the heart of the matter, the personification of a common, idealised identity. The sustaining myth of the monarchy is that while kings and queens are mortal, the institution is not – the Queen is dead, long live the King.'[29]

That idea is evident in the choir of St George's Chapel, just yards from where the committal service took place, and close by Elizabeth II's grave. There stands the sovereign's stall in the choir. The other stalls, used by members of the Order of the Garter, commemorate deceased members of the Order. But there are no memorial plaques on the sovereign's stall, because there is always a sovereign.

Yet, as Simon Schama wrote just a day after her death, 'at this particular moment of mourning for this particular sovereign, the magnitude of the loss overwhelms the truism of continuity'.[30]

The pomp and circumstance surrounding the Queen's death was as much about that continuity as about mourning her passing. That was the challenge for the nation and for those who run it. Above all, it was a challenge for the longest-serving Prince of Wales – the new King Charles III.

# 8

# Defender of Faith: Charles' spiritual pilgrimage

THE 1960s WERE a decade when the British Royal Family might have come unstuck. Miniskirts, The Beatles and The Rolling Stones, Woodstock, Carnaby Street, Vietnam protests – the world was turned upside down, while the fusty, dusty royals seemed stuck in their ways. But some advisers thought Elizabeth II and her family, not least her eldest son and heir, should, if not get with it, at least meet the cultural upheaval halfway. Two episodes indicated this more than any others, and both involved a starring role for the young Prince. They both occurred in 1969; one involved cameras trailing him as part of a fly-on-the-wall documentary about his family, and the other involved a crown made in part with a ping-pong ball.

In 1969, Charles was a university student. Lengthy discussions had led to him attending Trinity College, Cambridge, where he studied archaeology and anthropology for the first part of the Tripos, and later switched to history. Then, in the middle of his Cambridge studies, he was dispatched to University College, Aberystwyth, to learn Welsh in preparation for his investiture as Prince of Wales. Since the time of Edward I, who was asked by the Welsh for their own Prince and presented them in 1301 with his son, later Edward II, who had been born in Caernarfon Castle in 1284, the eldest son and heir apparent of the monarch has been called the Prince of Wales. Modern-day investitures began in 1911 with a ceremony at Caernarfon Castle involving the future Edward VIII, at the instigation of the Welsh politician, David Lloyd George.

Preparations for Charles' ceremony were altogether different. There was a sense that this event had to be modern and have a contemporary feel about it, and part of that preparation included a focus on how Charles and his whole family might be presented to the public through the medium of television. William Heseltine, the Queen's Australian private secretary, conceived the idea of a fly-on-the-wall documentary with the help of the television producer John Brabourne, son-in-law of Lord Mountbatten, while the actual documentary was put together under the control of a committee chaired by Prince Philip and produced by the BBC producer Richard Cawston. It combined footage of Queen Elizabeth and her family engaged in formal occasions, including hosting US President Richard Nixon on a state visit to Britain, and the informal behind-the-scenes moments of a supposedly ordinary family, chatting over breakfast, barbecuing at Balmoral, fishing and playing music. It was hardly earth-shattering – this was a family that seemed more of the fifties than the psychedelic sixties – but the very fact the cameras were there was revolutionary. First broadcast on BBC1 on 21 June 1969 and a week later on 29 June on ITV, it garnered an audience of thirty million – more than half the nation.

Then, a week after the second showing, the family appeared at one of the biggest ceremonial occasions since the 1953 coronation: the investiture of Charles as Prince of Wales. He had been named Prince of Wales when he was ten years old, but this was the formal moment when he would pledge himself to follow the ancient motto of Princes of Wales – the German *Ich Dien*, or I Serve.

The investiture in Caernarfon Castle was the brainchild of his uncle, the Earl of Snowdon, husband of Princess Margaret, who came up with a ceremony that vastly reduced military involvement from the 1911 occasion and excluded all mention of the subjugation of the Welsh by the English Edward I 687 years earlier. There was pageantry, men decked out in red velvet and ermine and an ancient-sounding vow from Prince Charles to his mother, using the exact words his father had recited at the coronation in 1953: 'I do become your liege man of life and limb and of earthly worship, and faith and truth I will bear unto you, to live and die against all manner of folks.'

Alongside this invention of tradition was modern innovation, an enthusiasm of both Lord Snowdon and the Prime Minister of the time, Harold Wilson. This 1960s event involved a great deal of perspex, used to create a canopy to keep the rain off the royal party, Prince Charles giving his speech in Welsh to please an increasingly nationalistic nation, the Queen wearing a yellow silk mock-Tudor hat, made up of a pearl crown and silk panels, and Charles' coronet, designed for the event, which had an orb in the centre of it which was a ping-pong ball coated in gold.

But the coronet was more than that. In an investiture that had but a token nod to religion, with a handful of prayers, and hints at medieval grandeur, there was an intriguing symbolism going on with Charles' coronet. The designer Louis Osman had included in it just one arch rather than the traditional two arches or four half-arches of British monarchs' crowns, to show that the Prince of Wales is inferior to the monarch but outranks the other royal princes and dukes. The monde, or orb, had, like the coronation orb, a cross placed upon it, denoting the world ruled by Jesus Christ, but Osman added another detail: on the base were seven diamonds to denote the seven deadly sins – pride, greed, lust, envy, gluttony, wrath and sloth – and the seven gifts of the Holy Spirit – wisdom, understanding, counsel, fortitude, knowledge, piety and fear of the Lord. One of those, wisdom, was to become a particular preoccupation of the Prince in later years. By including these symbols, Osman created a coronet of that acknowledged the capacity of humanity, including princes, for goodness and temptation.

From a young age, what Charles had shown capacity for was a curiosity about the world and particularly about religion. He shared his father's desire for knowledge, including a willingness to learn about religions that were alien to his own experience, as well as his mother's liking for tradition and stability. Steeped in the Church of England, he was not a *tabula rasa*, yet he seemed to have far more interest in that which was uncommon to him than many of his peers who experienced a similarly privileged upbringing.

Over the years, King Charles' interest in religion has been called eclectic. Those of a more disparaging character see it otherwise: one commentator who has come across him in Church circles said, 'There's nothing coherent about his theology. His Anglicanism is The Book of Common Prayer, the King James Bible, and he likes little churches. It's nostalgia and beauty. Then he'll whizz off to a Sikh temple.'[1]

Whether coherent or not, what comes across from the King is a genuine curiosity and, above all, a desire for religion to offer something transcendent: a numinous experience that hints at another world, at beauty and – one of his favourite terms – harmony. There is a sense that humankind has almost lost touch with something vital for a thriving life. As he put it in 'A Time to Heal', an essay written in 2002:

> Deep down in the recesses of your heart, is there not a faint memory of distant harmony that rustles like a breeze through the leaves? Call it a forgotten instinct; call it, perhaps, if you want to be exceptionally daring, a sense of the sacred, call it an awareness at a greater depth than the mere intellect.[2]

His father's flourishing at Gordonstoun led Charles' parents to opt for the faraway Scottish school rather than Eton, just up the road from Windsor Castle, or other conventional English public schools. But Charles' time there did not replicate the way his father had thrived at Gordonstoun. He wrote once of the atmosphere of the school which dismayed him:

> There's hardly any religion . . . and you should see where we have to have church. It's a sort of hall which is used for films and assemblies and plays, sometimes for football or gymnastics if the weather is too foul for going outside during break. And then one is expected to worship in there. It's hopeless, there's no atmosphere of the mysterious that a church gives one.[3]

It was a seriousness about faith and a desire for mystery that few adolescent boys experience, and this intensity was noticed by those who engaged with the young Prince as he prepared for his Anglican confirmation the same year that the remarks about the ghastly hall were written. The clergy who instructed him were Gordonstoun's own chaplain, Philip Crosfield, an Anglican rather than a member of the Church of Scotland, and Robin Woods, the Dean of Windsor, who went on to found St George's House with the Duke of Edinburgh.[4] This was a time when postwar change, and even turmoil, was being felt within Christianity. In Rome, the Second Vatican Council was meeting; in the Church of England, Trevor Huddleston had written *Naught For Your Comfort*, championing the rights of non-whites and denouncing apartheid in South Africa, while John Robinson had rocked the Church in this country with *Honest to God*, his challenge to convention. In the nine years since the Prince's mother had taken her oath to uphold the Church of England, the old certainties were under fire.

Within two years, Robin Woods' influence was felt once more when the prospect of Charles attending university was discussed. Neither of his parents had been an undergraduate, and in 1965 the Queen organised a dinner party to discuss her eldest son's educational future. Those around the table were the Prime Minister Harold Wilson, the Archbishop of Canterbury Michael Ramsey, the Chief of the Defence Staff Lord Mountbatten – the Royal Family's Uncle Dickie – as well as the chairman of the Committee of Vice-Chancellors Sir Charles Wilson, and Robin Woods.

Edward VII had attended three universities, while Edward VIII had gone to Oxford, and his brother, later George VI, had attended Cambridge. There was debate as to whether Charles should enter the armed forces first – Mountbatten was firmly in favour – while Harold Wilson spoke up for Oxford, his own university and where he had also been an academic. It took nine months for a decision to be made, with Woods, a Cambridge man, thought to have been particularly key to Charles' parents' conviction that it was the best option. Woods, then dispatched by the Queen to sound out several colleges as options for her son, returned convinced his own was the best choice: Trinity. Charles, who seems to have been more or less told he was going to Trinity, Cambridge, put his foot down over choice of subject and got his way: the first part of the Tripos would be in archaeology.

It was at Trinity that Charles came within the orbit of another Anglican clergyman, the Rev. Harry Williams, in his capacity as chaplain. Williams had developed a reputation for unorthodox thinking on theology, imbibing Freud and Jung, and then exploring his ideas with others through sometimes mesmerising sermons and lectures. Williams and the Prince had hit it off when Charles had first visited Trinity prior to joining the college, and during his undergraduate years he regularly attended the chaplain's dinners. Williams, from an Anglo-Catholic tradition, became increasingly interested in the development of the self and argued that to say 'I believe' is to say 'I am'.

Both Crosfield at Gordonstoun and Williams at Cambridge spotted the Prince's diligence and intensity. But Crosfield found the young teenager to be disinclined to challenge the tenets of the Christian faith it would one day be his to defend, while by the time he was at Cambridge, under the influence of Williams and others whom he would hear lecturing at Great St Mary's, Cambridge, on Sunday evenings, invited by its vicar Hugh Montefiore, he was encouraged to explore further.

Williams left Trinity in 1969 to become a member of the Community of the Resurrection at Mirfield. At his memorial service at Trinity College thirty-seven years later, in May 2006, the Rt Rev. Richard Chartres, the former Bishop of London, gave an insight into how impressionable young men, like Charles and himself, who were exploring theological ideas, had been so influenced by Williams:

> Harry's preaching and writing was disturbing because there was so little fig leaf about it. He described the wasteland and the fantasy pavilions we build, with such clarity and candour that it was impossible to keep them at a safe objective distance. He realised that it is impossible to convey spiritual electricity by public readings from the wiring diagram but there was life in the blood shed in the solitary wrestling before climbing into this pulpit.[5]

Chartres was one of the few Trinity students with whom Charles found rapport. Over the years the priest, who was quickly recognised as one of the more intellectual clerics, with appointments as chaplain to Robert Runcie, Archbishop of Canterbury, as Professor of Divinity at Gresham College, as Bishop of Stepney and finally as Bishop of London, was considered to be one of the Anglican clerics whom Charles found most sympathetic. Chartres, in turn, has watched his fellow Cambridge undergraduate maintain not just an interest in but a passion for religion.

'The strength of faith in our monarchs in the last two hundred years has not been great,' Chartres told me. 'And then came Elizabeth II, who was a person of extraordinary faith but not one to speculate about divinity.

'Charles is very, very different. He is enthralled by religion. It has partly come from his father, who had a great interest, but it's a mystery why religious belief is so real for the King.'[6]

Charles' regard for Chartres was evident when he asked him to confirm his elder son Prince William, breaking a tradition that heirs to the throne are confirmed by the Archbishop of Canterbury. At the time, in early 1997, it was deemed a snub to the then holder of that office, George Carey, and an indication that Charles preferred the high churchmanship of Chartres to the evangelical Carey.[7] This regard was further confirmed when Charles attended a private dinner to mark Chartres' retirement after twenty-two years as Bishop of London, hosted by Justin Welby, the Archbishop of Canterbury.[8]

As well as Philip Crosfield, Harry Williams and Richard Chartres, Charles was influenced by Mervyn Stockwood.

The King first came across Stockwood while a pupil at Gordonstoun, when the then Bishop of Southwark came to speak. Left-leaning, voluble, hard-drinking and engaging, Stockwood was a maverick in the Church of England. He also had a deep interest in parapsychology, to which he introduced Charles. The bishop kept a series of case studies of people who had communicated with others in the afterlife, including a woman who made contact with dead composers, and which he passed to the young Prince. Stockwood went further, challenging conventional ideas about the miracles of Jesus, arguing that they indicated his oneness with nature and his openness to the capabilities of the mind.

At Cambridge, the Prince listened as Harry Williams also expounded on parapsychology and introduced the young student to the works of Carl Jung. Charles and the priest held one another in mutual high regard, Williams going so far as to say years later that Charles when young 'had the makings of a saint', owing to his 'grace, humility and the desire to help other people'. Williams also noted,

'He had an interest in the deeper things of life, in the source of life, an openness of mind, a readiness to evaluate ideas.'[9]

The King's early interest in alternative forms of religion, but with a link to Anglicanism, had also been piqued during a stay in Papua New Guinea, made during his time at school at Timbertop, Australia, where he spent two terms in 1966, before returning to Gordonstoun. The Anglican mission in Papua New Guinea was influenced by ideas of inculturation, which were first in vogue in Christian circles in the 1960s: the idea that a mission should meet people where they are at, rather than fully impose Western ideas of Christianity. So the congregation in the cathedral in Dogura, near the eastern tip of Papua, would sit cross-legged on the floor for services, rather than sit in pews. And while the congregation received Holy Communion, some of its members also participated in faith-healing, inspired by their indigenous religion. In a book, written about her son's education with the approval of Queen Elizabeth, it was reported that Charles later indicated that encountering this transcendent form of religious experience was life-changing – 'the most formative part of his spiritual development'.[10]

Like many people, Charles' passions are often inspired by those whom he likes, and his interest in religions was down to both those he admired and a particular aesthetic. His interest in Islam, for example, drew much from Islamic art, to which he was introduced by the art dealer Oliver Hoare, long before Hoare became known for his relationship with Charles' first wife, Diana, Princess of Wales. In more recent times, Charles encouraged the preservation and development of traditional buildings and crafts in Muslim countries through funding the charity Turquoise Mountain, which in 2020 raised and spent around £8.5 million.

Later in life, when he seemed to be somewhat estranged from the Church of England, the Prince's links with Anglicanism were in part kept going through his friendship with Billa Harrod. Lady Harrod, an architectural conservationist, shared a passion for churches with her friend John Betjeman and co-authored the *Shell Guide to Norfolk*. She campaigned to save the many churches of that county that were in such a poor state of repair that they were in danger of demolition. She revived Charles' interest in the Church, with excursions from Sandringham to visit the hidden gems of the flat Norfolk countryside.

This connection with Christianity through aesthetics is also evident in his delight in the two key texts of Anglicanism, the Book of Common Prayer and the King James Bible, taking swipes at those who have the temerity to offer prayer and Scripture in a more modern vernacular style. In April 1997 he spoke at a reception for the Prayer Book Society about what he termed 'the genius of Cranmer's Prayer Book', which 'lies in the conveyance of that sense of the sacred through the power and majesty of the language . . . We commend "the beauty of holiness", yet we forget the holiness of beauty.

'If we encourage the use of mean, trite, ordinary language, we encourage a mean, trite and ordinary view of the world we inhabit.'[11]

In 2011, to mark the four-hundredth anniversary of the King James Bible, the then Prince of Wales wrote the foreword to a new edition in which he explained why he loved this particular version of Scripture:

> Few can argue against the dignity, power and cadence of the Authorized Version. The translators aimed for nothing less than theological and literary excellence. They could certainly never be accused of banality! When we want to convey something that goes beyond the ordinary, we need language that does the same – transcending our everyday speech. If the Word of God can seem a bit over our heads, perhaps it is supposed to be. Elevated is what God is; it is part of His very nature.[12]

Music has also played a part, with the King expressing a particular fondness for composers of church music such as Howells and Parry. He became patron of the charity Music in Country Churches at its founding in 1989.

One of the most influential friends Charles had was the former soldier, writer and explorer Laurens van der Post. Originally from South Africa, van der Post joined the British Army during the Second World War and later served on the staff of Lord Mountbatten – and he also knew Queen Elizabeth the Queen Mother. Like Harry Williams, van der Post was an apostle of Carl Jung, and believed in

Jung's theory of the collective subconscious – the idea that human beings can be bound together across barriers.

He gained an enormous following through his best-selling *The Lost World of the Kalahari*, in which he claimed to have lived a long time among the Bushmen, who were, he said, primitive, instinctual and childlike, and connected with nature, while those in the West had mostly lost this deep link with the natural world. By 1975, he had developed a friendship with the Prince, and began to advise him on spiritual matters. That same year, he proposed that the Prince should accompany him to revisit the Kalahari, with BBC cameras to record the trip: the Foreign Office, alarmed at the prospect of what the public would make of it, at a time when there were troubles in nearby Botswana, put an end to the plan. In the end the pair took a trip to the Aberdare mountains of Kenya.

Charles, then aged twenty-seven, and idealistic but not altogether sure of himself, was flattered by the older man's attentions and seduced by his prose. Van der Post took it upon himself to write a script for the future of the monarchy and to analyse Charles' dreams. At one point he told the Prince of Wales that he could transform the monarchy into 'a dynamic and as yet unimagined role to suit the future shape of a fundamentally reappraised and renewed modern society', which would involve 'a prolonged fight for all that is good and creative in the human imagination'. This battle would require restoring people's reverence for life and love of nature – a notion that chimed with Charles' own thinking.[13]

It was during the trip to the Aberdare mountains that van der Post first persuaded Charles to record his dreams and pass them to him to interpret according to Jungian notions. These included the idea that dreams bring to the surface archaic knowledge that a person carried within them, the power of the collective unconscious – what humanity inherits from other eras and culture, and the Wise Old Man, an archetype representing insights that can be found within us. According to Jonathan Dimbleby, who was authorised to write Charles' biography and had access to confidential writings, van der Post managed to convince Charles that in his case the Wise Old Man, or guru, was represented by the Old Man of Lothnagar, the mythic figure that Charles had created to entertain his young brothers as living in the hills around Balmoral. Van der Post went further, trying to persuade Charles to withdraw from public life for some time in order to contemplate his inner soul, but a sense of duty prevailed, and Charles declined to take up the idea.[14]

Some years later, after van der Post's death, another disciple of his, J. D. F. Jones, wrote a biography of the man, with the agreement of his daughter. But Jones, after researching the South African's life, wrote a book outlining van der Post's exaggerations and fantasies, from his time with the Kalahari Bushmen to accounts he gave about his family background, as well as his exploitative relationships with women. The book was denounced by some of van der Post's disciples while highly praised by critics for its thorough research. It led one person who has encountered the King on various occasions to suggest that he had been influenced by a man who could only be described as 'an old fraud'.[15]

Jones also argued convincingly that van der Post's personal hatred of Nelson Mandela persuaded another of his devotees, Margaret Thatcher, to oppose sanctions against the South African government, thus prolonging apartheid. Jones also wrote that van der Post had gone beyond his dreams analysis of Charles and had introduced him to his second wife, Ingaret, a Jungian analyst, with whom he underwent psychoanalysis, and then with another analyst, van der Post's friend, Alan McGlashan. According to Jones' account, this man also treated Princess Diana during the couple's troubled marriage.[16] Seeing someone so much in van der Post's camp seems surprising, given that Diana voiced her irritation on several occasions that Charles brought a pile of van der Post's books with him to read on their honeymoon trip on the Royal Yacht *Britannia*.

The wedding of Charles and Diana in 1981 had been a moment of celebration for the nation and was typical of the occasions when Church, state and monarchy come together in an expression of national unity. Just as had happened at the time of Queen Elizabeth's own wedding, her coronation and her Silver Jubilee four years earlier, the wedding of the heir to the throne also saw a synchronicity between the Establishment asserting itself and the public wanting a reason for a party, complete with Union Flag bunting, windows of shops and houses adorned with posters of the couple and a boom in sales of mugs, commemorative coins and tea towels.

While retailers and souvenir manufacturers had been gearing up for the wedding, Charles and Diana had spent some time preparing with the then Archbishop of Canterbury, Robert Runcie, who was to marry them in St Paul's Cathedral. At the time, Charles' Trinity College friend, Richard Chartres, was Runcie's chaplain, and he too was present at the meeting about the wedding.

Runcie later recalled that Chartres, whom he described as observant, but who as a friend may well have relied on more than canny perception, told him that the Prince 'was seriously depressed' – not a mental state normally associated with those engaged to be married. Runcie also recalled that they thought it an arranged marriage. Given that Charles was by then nudging thirty-three; that as Prince of Wales he was expected to marry and produce the next royal generation; that the woman he might have married then, Camilla Shand, had married Andrew Parker-Bowles instead; that Diana came from an aristocratic family and, unlike most young women then was a virgin and therefore unsullied with a 'past', the marriage may well have seemed a pragmatic solution rather than a love match.

Runcie remembered from this early encounter that 'my view was they're a nice young couple, and she'll grow into it', and that they were serious about the marriage: 'they weren't casual about their preparation . . . I remember that we had a private Communion service together, and Charles encouraged her a lot when she looked a little anxious and wan about it.'[17]

Runcie's sermon at the wedding, given what we all now know about the ill-starred marriage, seems the absolute antithesis of apposite: 'Here is the stuff of which fairy tales are made.' In fact, Runcie went on to suggest that this marriage would be unlike the fairy tale because it wasn't an ending so much as a beginning. For Charles and Diana, it proved to be not much of a beginning either: they hardly knew one another, had little in common, and the age gap of twelve years between them when she was just twenty was enormous. Yet Runcie's recollections of the couple indicated a concern, if rather patronising, on Charles' part for Diana and a willingness to learn on hers.

Charles viewed Diana as untutored and Runcie recollected that when the marriage began to unravel he suggested the Archbishop might help by seeing Diana because the Prince thought 'religion hasn't much stuck with her'. The couple had a lunch together with Runcie, and then the Archbishop saw Diana on his own for what he said 'amounted to two or three not very successful confirmation talks. That's what [Charles] thought she needed: a bit of instruction. What I quickly saw she needed was some encouragement and some "Are you all right, girl?".'[18]

Runcie spotted not only Diana's need for validation but also her qualities, describing her as 'very tender, very unformed' with 'a sort of shrewdness, always very observant', who saw herself as not up to Charles when it came to spirituality and intelligence. Runcie, however, put her straight, telling her:

> Don't worry about all this religious vocabulary to start with. You may have more spiritual insight than your cerebrally inclined husband. The trouble is that you believe that to be religious you have to be capable of handling ideas, religious ideas. But that's not necessarily true at all. The inarticulate is just as valuable in the eyes of God as the articulate, maybe even more so.[19]

Runcie found, as did many of his Anglican confrères, that the Prince was a mass of religious contradictions and seemed not to be strongly linked to the Church of England. At the time of his marriage, Runcie noted – as did Diana on the honeymoon – 'he was deeply into the Laurens van der Post spirituality'.[20]

His encounters with the Prince of Wales also made him note his hidden acts of kindness to people in need, and support of worthwhile but unglamorous causes, as well as those contradictions: 'He's on about the grandeur of our cathedrals and the epic language of the Prayer Book, but he wants to be exploring Hinduism with people in inner cities. He hunts regularly, but is a great man about the environment. So that the public don't really know where they are.'[21]

The contradictions mattered to Runcie, but even more did the Prince's apparent lukewarm attitude to the Church of England. 'When it came to his concern to do something about the state of the country, I don't think he took the Church of England very seriously,' he said, speaking to his biographer in the mid-nineties. 'It would quite help if he loved the Church of England a bit more.'[22]

Much of Charles' difficult relationship with the Church was tied up with his private life. It was his misfortune to be the first Prince of Wales after his great-uncle Edward, whose abdication derived from his desire to marry the twice-married Wallis Simpson. There was an unspoken desire from that time for a Prince of Wales to avoid marital complications. It was also his misfortune to be the heir to the throne at a time when much of the popular media treated the monarchy as a branch of celebrity, with all the attendant prurient curiosity and desire to simplify stories about the royals' private lives into Manichean tales of heroes and villains. It was not helped, though, by the Prince and Princess of Wales being tempted to participate in the media frenzy by their own camps tipping off journalists.

The moment that first caused particular strain between Charles and the Church of England came in December 1993 when George Austin, the Archdeacon of York, said that the Prince of Wales should not succeed to the throne, or at least not become Supreme Governor of the Church of England, because he had committed adultery with Camilla Parker-Bowles.

Austin had long dabbled in journalism, beginning with the *Church Times* in 1959, and became a go-to figure in the Church when journalists and editors wanted a cleric to knock contemporary mores and the Church of England's succumbing to them. It was he who invented the pejorative term 'the liberal agenda'. By December 1993, public and media deliberations about the marriage of the Prince and Princess of Wales were at their height, fuelled by the publication in June 1992 of Andrew Morton's biography, *Diana: Her True Story*. Philosophers will spend hours arguing about the meaning of truth, and the volume was far from being a study in epistemology, but an account told from the perspective of the Princess. Indeed, the extent to which her opinions shaped the book became known after her death in 1997, when it was revealed that Morton had been covertly supplied with tapes of her talking about her life and in particular her marriage.

The book led to constant speculation and debate about the couple, who then separated in December, six months after its publication. A year later, Diana, who had continued with public engagements, announced that she would be stepping back from public life and limiting the charities she would work with. It caused another stirring of the debate over the Prince and Princess, with considerable support offered to her, particularly by newspaper columnists.

Then came a story in *The Sun*, claiming that the Archbishop of Canterbury had told Church leaders Charles would have to consider his future position as Defender of the Faith. The story got short shrift from Lambeth Palace, but BBC Radio 4's *Today* programme looked around for someone from the Church to come on air and comment. It alighted upon the enemy of 'the liberal agenda'. Austin didn't hold back, telling listeners, 'Charles made solemn vows before God about his marriage, and it seems – if the rumours are true about Camilla – that he began to break them almost immediately.' Given that these vows were broken, Austin argued, 'How can he then go into Westminster Abbey and take the coronation vows?'[23]

This led to yet more speculation but also outrage at the way a man of the cloth was dabbling in the stuff of other people's souls, as Press Complaints Commission chair Lord McGregor had so memorably put it at the beginning of that year, when commenting about media coverage of the royal marriage. The Archbishop of Canterbury, George Carey, gave Austin a hefty verbal slap on the wrist, accusing him of practising 'megaphone theology'.[24] Around the same time, however, a *Sunday Times* poll of members of the Church of England's General Synod showed 47 per cent of them thought the Prince of Wales could not become leader of their Church – that is, Supreme Governor of the Church of England – if he had committed adultery.[25] A few months later, Charles did admit to a certain extent that he had broken his marriage vows when he was asked by Jonathan Dimbleby, in an interview linked to his biography, whether he had been 'faithful and honourable' to his wife. 'Yes,' said Charles, before pausing and then adding, 'until [the marriage] became irretrievably broken down, us both having tried.'[26]

But the damage to the relationship between future Supreme Governor and the established Church over the criticism of various clerics was done. Several people I have spoken to have suggested that, for some years, Charles was reluctant to attend Anglican services, other than formal ceremonial occasions when his absence would have been cause for yet further speculation.

Particular friendships kept Charles connected to the Church. As well as Richard Chartres, Charles developed a strong friendship with Bishop Peter Ball, but that connection was to cause him deep embarrassment years later. Charles first took note of Peter Ball through his preaching during the 1980s, when Ball served as Bishop of Lewes, and then from 1993 he invited him to give him Holy Communion at his home from time to time; in 1992 Ball had been appointed Bishop of Gloucester – effectively Charles' diocesan bishop through his home at Highgrove.

Only a year later Ball had to resign from his position as bishop after admitting to an act of gross indecency and being given a police caution. The Crown Prosecution Service decided not to go ahead with a prosecution after dozens of people, including those in positions of influence, urged them not to. George Carey, the Archbishop of Canterbury, allowed him to continue to officiate, and he was found a home in Somerset, owned by Charles' Duchy of Cornwall.

Some years later, after witnesses came forward, Ball was put on trial, and in 2015 was found guilty of indecent assault and misconduct in a public office. The extent of the friendship between the disgraced bishop and the Prince came to light in evidence submitted in a letter from the Prince of Wales to the Independent Inquiry into Child Sexual Abuse in 2018. He told the inquiry that he had been deceived and misled by Ball and had not had contact with him since 2015.

Two interesting matters arose from Charles' six-page letter to the inquiry. One was that he pointed out, 'As context, it seems important to say that in the 1980s and 1990s there was a presumption that people such as bishops could be taken at their word and, as a result of the high office they held, were worthy of trust and confidence . . . At the time there was a presumption on my part of good faith.' They were the words of someone who has on more than one occasion been taken in by people others consider far less trustworthy than the Prince does – Laurens van der Post and staff who have embroiled him in scandal come to mind. It suggests a certain naivety on his part. Indeed, Ball pulled the wool over his eyes to the extent that the Prince wrote to Ball in 1995 to sympathise with him over the 'monstrous wrongs' done to him.[27] The Independent Inquiry into Child Sexual Abuse pulled no punches in its 2019 assessment of the Prince's involvement with Ball, saying that his actions 'were misguided' and could have been interpreted as expressions of support for Ball, which, 'given the Prince of Wales' future role within the Church of England, had the potential to influence the actions of the Church'.[28]

The other significant matter was Charles' admission that he would receive Holy Communion at his home in the 1990s, well before he built a sanctuary, or tiny chapel, in the Highgrove grounds. It suggests someone who, despite his noticed frustrations with the Church of England, still found spiritual consolation in its sacraments.

Around this same time, Charles indicated his determination to be crowned, when the time came, and it was clear that he was thinking seriously about what the role involves and what possible reforms might be needed. As well as talking about his failed marriage to Jonathan Dimbleby in the 1994 television documentary linked to his biography, he spoke about his awareness that Britain had become a very different nation since the last coronation in 1953, with a diverse population of different ethnic minorities and religions. He acknowledged the difficulties of a modern monarch vowing to uphold the Protestant faith as if Britain is a monochrome society: 'The Catholic subjects of the sovereign are equally as important as the Anglican ones, as the Protestant ones,' he said. 'I think that the Islamic subjects or the Hindu subjects or the Zoroastrian subjects of the sovereign are of equal and vital importance.'

He then went on to explain how the title of Defender of the Faith – the ancient nomenclature used by all monarchs since Henry VIII – might be reinterpreted for such a diverse society:

> I personally would rather see it as Defender of Faith, not the Faith, because it (Defender of the Faith) means just one particular interpretation of the Faith, which I think is something that causes a deal of a problem. It has done for hundreds of years. People have fought each other to the death over these things, which seems to me a peculiar waste of people's energy, when we're all equally aiming for the same ultimate goal, I think. So I would much rather it was seen as defending faith itself which is so often under threat in our day where, you know, the whole concept of faith itself or

> anything beyond this existence, beyond life itself is considered almost old-fashioned and irrelevant.

He then expanded on his theme further, that being Defender of Faith would mean being 'Defender of the Divine in existence, the pattern of the divine which is, I think, in all of us but which, because we are human beings, can be expressed in so many ways'.[29]

The remarks of the King at that time were among the most significant he ever made on religion, both in terms of the established Church and on his thinking about other faiths and the importance of dialogue between them. But his standing, as heir to the throne and therefore to the role he would inherit – Supreme Governor of the Church of England – and the title he would use on becoming sovereign – was the focus of most of the attention he attracted about his comments.

The tone was set by the leaking of the Prince's comments to *The Sunday Times*, which said that 'Charles plans to break royal link with church' in its front page headline, while its news story claimed that the Prince of Wales thought 'the church should be disestablished'.

There was confusion in *The Sunday Times* story but also in the way that Jonathan Dimbleby wrote about the matter in his biography. In none of his remarks to Dimbleby did Charles mention disestablishment, and neither did he mention the role of Supreme Governor. The title of Defender of the Faith and the role of Supreme Governor do not mean the same thing, nor are they interchangeable. The title of Defender of the Faith, because it has been used by monarchs for so long who also swear a coronation oath to uphold the Church of England, has assumed to be linked to the Supreme Governor role by many people. But the Defender of the Faith title originated in Henry VIII being approved of for being, in common parlance, a champion or advocate of particular beliefs, not overseeing the existence of a particular religious institution. That is what the Supreme Governor role is for. Jonathan Dimbleby, too, was somewhat inaccurate in claiming in his biography that in his remarks about Defender of the Faith, Charles 'expressed strong sentiments about the relationship of the sovereign to the Church of England'.[30]

He had not: the Prince had said nothing about that constitutional relationship and was focusing instead on a role for the monarchy in an increasingly diverse, multifaith society.

Dimbleby, though, certainly added fuel to the fire and, given that the flames were being fanned so soon after Charles' disgruntlement over Austin, it was an uncomfortable time for the relationship between the then Prince of Wales and the Church, with both the Archbishop of Canterbury and the Archbishop of York feeling the need to try to smooth things over. George Carey claimed to BBC Radio that what the Prince had intended to say was that he wanted to be Defender of the Christian Faith, while, after consulting the Prince's office, John Habgood told the Church of England's General Synod in July 1994 that the Prince's comments should not be seen as being in favour of disestablishment, nor of changes to the country's constitutional arrangements.[31] However, the controversy lingered, with the Evangelical Alliance demanding in 2006 in its 'Faith and Nation' report that evangelicals should 'resist the current heir to the throne's suggested re-titling of himself as "Defender of Faith", on the grounds that such a change may too readily be interpreted as an endorsement of syncretism'.[32]

This seemed a particularly harsh judgement, for King Charles appears not to have at any time suggested that he favours an amalgamation of different religions. What he appears to have consistently expressed is his profound interest in many faiths, his sense that they share their origins in a universal yearning for meaning and for the divine, and that in the contemporary world, sorely affected by conflict as well as experiencing greater proximity of people of different religions, interfaith dialogue is not only desirable but necessary. But for hardliners, interfaith dialogue is the slippery slope to syncretism.

Charles' idealism about interfaith dialogue was evident in comments he made to Dimbleby during the interview that were later cut from the broadcast, but the journalist repeated in his biography:

> I feel, you know, that certainly the great Middle Eastern religions – Judaism, Islam, Christianity, all stemming from the same geographical area – all have a great deal in common . . . But I also

> think there are aspects of Hinduism and Buddhism, again further east, which are attached by very profound threads to Islam, Christianity and Judaism. And when you begin to look at what these religions are saying you find that so much of the wisdom that is represented within these religions coincides.[33]

The importance of wisdom has been one of the overarching themes of Prince Charles' interventions over the years when speaking about faith, or indeed about contemporary society. Another is harmony – a lack of harmony in modern architecture, a lack of harmony in humanity's relationship with nature, a lack of harmony in people's relations with one another. The special place that harmony holds in his thinking is evident in the publication of a two-volume set of his speeches and articles by the University of Wales. The volume highlights Charles' chief interests – the natural world, medicine, architecture, education and religion – but it is noticeable that the first section is devoted to harmony, and the editor of the collection is David Cadman, a professor of harmony who has become an influential member of the Prince's camp.[34]

Cadman is 'harmony adviser' to the Prince's Foundation and is also a fellow of the Temenos Academy – which had as its patron, HRH Charles, The Prince of Wales. It describes itself as an educational charity that provides 'education in philosophy and the arts in the light of the sacred traditions of East and West'.[35] Its offerings include a diploma in Perennial Philosophy which 'runs like a golden thread through history and offers each generation contact with the values that nourish all civilisations' – the kind of phrasing often found in the King's own statements. Indeed, his own message to the Temenos Academy said:

> I admire the courage and conviction of all those who are prepared to challenge the deadening effects of the 'industrialisation' of life itself, a process which carries no sensitivity to the qualities which go to sustain a truly civilised and harmonious society. I pray that the wise and compassionate work for which Temenos stands will prevail. I myself will do all I can to help, preserve and encourage it.[36]

The Prince's involvement with Temenos grew out of the inspiration he drew from the poet Kathleen Raine, to whom he was introduced by Laurens van der Post, and who founded the Academy. Raine, a Roman Catholic convert, was also enamoured of Eastern spiritual traditions and of Plato, about whom she wrote scholarly studies.[37] Raine saw powerful connections between different religious and philosophical thinkers and perceived that not only they but also she and Charles were involved in what she called the Great Battle to combat the forces of scientific rationalism. It is telling that, in his address at her memorial after she died in 2003, he chose to quote Raine telling him that:

> the general climate of our culture is to see these spiritual values at best as an 'optional extra' to the real values of the orthodoxy of materialism, as taught by Dawkins, Hawking, the Postmodernists and other people who at present control the media, the press and the universities in this spiritually and imaginatively illiterate Western civilisation, that treats the living world – animals and plants itself – as pieces of mindless mechanism, while at the same time imputing thought and mind to their machines.[38]

This was Charles aligning himself not so much with those who fought the enemies of progress, but with those who fought the enemies of tradition or even mysticism or eternity. Previous monarchs, such as George III with his endorsement by Royal Charter of the Royal Institution, put themselves on the side of engineers, physicists and chemists. Charles seemed to prefer to be on the side of the angels and other ethereal figures.

A sense of Raine's stalwart support of Charles – cynics might describe it as her massaging his ego – also emerges in his memorial address:

> I remember her saying to me that it had been her 'unlooked for privilege to carry the lamp of vision for a few years in this country' and then – I shall never forget it because it moved me so deeply – she went on to say that 'being here for you is part of that task' . . . she had never given the subject of the position I happen to occupy

> any thought until I came into her life and her thought was not 'how wonderful to be royal' but 'that poor young man, he has the most difficult task in England'.[39]

The King's own interest in harmony and Plato mirrors not only Raine's but also that of his doomed predecessor, Charles I, who was devoted to the Platonist ideal of harmony, focusing on the good as it benefits society and the individual human soul. The then Prince of Wales' interest in his namesake was evident in his support for the Royal Academy's 2018 exhibition of works once owned by Charles I, which was believed to have smoothed the path for getting works loaned.[40]

Eighteen years before that show, the dawn of the twenty-first century was marked by large numbers of people with an almighty hangover, after seeing in the New Year on 31 December 1999. Those who did manage a more normal start to the day would have heard the Prince of Wales' contribution to BBC Radio Four's *Today* programme in its 'Thought for the Day' slot. The dawn of a new millennium, he said, 'should not be the excuse for a bonfire of the past, but a chance to discover the profound wisdom of those who made the difficult journey through this life before us; those who, like our Lord Jesus Christ, taught that this life is but one passing phase of our existence and that the reality lies within each one of us'.

There were also barbed remarks about science not having all the answers, references to Plato, Einstein and Dante, a desire for hope and a belief in the importance of harmony. Traditional Anglicans will have noted with some relief that the Prince's *raison d'être* for his 'Thought for the Day' was that the Millennium marked two thousand years since the birth of Christ – the importance of which his mother would also comment on in her Christmas Day 2000 broadcast twelve months later.[41] But there was also talk of 'the immensity of the mystery and the Divinity of ourselves and our world', which may have left some scratching their heads.[42]

The then Prince's view of the importance of wisdom, harmony and also the sacred was given another outing that same year when the BBC changed its usual format for the Reith Lectures. Rather than have one notable thinker give a series of talks, it asked five different contributors for Millennium Year to lecture on sustainable development and then gather for a final conversation with the Prince at his home, Highgrove House. Charles used the occasion to once more expound on the importance of harmony in nature and the dangers of science and what he described as 'almost impenetrable layers of scientific rationalism'. And he went on:

> I believe that if we are to achieve genuinely sustainable development we will first have to rediscover, or re-acknowledge a sense of the sacred in our dealings with the natural world, and with each other. If literally nothing is held sacred anymore – because it is considered synonymous with superstition or in some other way 'irrational' – what is there to prevent us treating our entire world as some 'great laboratory of life' with potentially disastrous long term consequences?
>
> . . . Only by rediscovering the essential unity and order of the living and spiritual world – as in the case of organic agriculture or integrated medicine or in the way we build – and by bridging the destructive chasm between cynical secularism and the timelessness of traditional religion, will we avoid the disintegration of our overall environment.[43]

The Prince had begun Millennium Year with a retreat at Mount Athos in Greece, one of the most sacred places in Greek Orthodoxy, the form of Christianity for which he holds a special affection. His regard for it was obvious when he was speaking about that most Anglican of religious books, Thomas Cranmer's Book of Common Prayer, and spoke plaintively of the need to hold on to a sense of the sacred and to religious tradition.

'The Orthodox Church,' he said, 'has never lost, abandoned or diminished the sacred beauty and symbolism of its liturgy. The great, overwhelming sadness for me – and I am sure for you too – is that we seem to have forgotten that for solemn occasions we need exceptional and solemn language: something which transcends our everyday speech.'[44]

This offers an insight into how Orthodoxy came to charm an Anglican king. Orthodox ceremonies are an aesthetic feast for every sense and combine the spiritual, the emotional and the physical. Its services are steeped in tradition and held in heavily decorated, shadowy interiors, illuminated by candlelight. There, devotees prostrate themselves and tenderly kiss their icons amid the heavy scent of incense.

While Charles' interest in Orthodoxy is particularly keen, the link between the Orthodox version of Christianity and the British Royal Family stretches back to Queen Victoria's power as a royal marriage broker. Her granddaughter Elizabeth married Grand Duke Sergei Alexandrovich of Russia and, after he died, she devoted her life to founding a religious institution to serve the poor. But she was later killed by the Bolsheviks, like her youngest sister Alexandra, Empress of Russia. The two sisters had converted on marriage to the Russian Orthodox Church, which later made them saints, along with Alexandra's husband, Czar Nicholas, another relative of the British Royal Family through his mother Dagmar, sister of George V's mother, Queen Alexandra. Grand Duchess Elizabeth's niece, Alice, whose mother Victoria was another granddaughter of Queen Victoria, converted to Orthodoxy some years after her marriage to Prince Andrew of Greece. The couple's children, including Charles' father, Prince Philip, were all baptised Orthodox.[45]

The then Prince of Wales used official visits in 2016 and 2020 to Israel and Palestine to pay his respects at the graves of both Grand Duchess Elizabeth and Princess Alice in the Russian Orthodox Church of St Mary Magdalene on the Mount of Olives. He laid flowers on both, lit candles and on his 2016 visit sang the troparion – a chanted hymn – dedicated to Mary Magdalene.

That prayerful devotion, using the Orthodox liturgy, would once have been frowned upon by the Church of England, which until recent times was suspicious of Orthodoxy, but now enjoys greater ecumenical warmth with the Eastern Churches. The number of Orthodox in Britain has also grown considerably in recent decades. More than a million belong to Orthodox Churches in Britain, and although it is the Greek and Russian Orthodox that have the greatest numbers across the globe, Romanian Orthodox make up the largest numbers here through migration in recent years. Their faith is something the King knows well – he first visited Transylvania, now part of central Romania, thirty years ago and visits almost every spring, staying in the house he bought there in the village of Zalanpatak, in the foothills of the Carpathian mountains.

The combination of countryside, unspoiled by modern farming methods, the medieval buildings and the Orthodox faith of the people are the twitch upon the thread for him. When he visited in the spring of 2022 he was reported as saying, 'There is a sense of age-old continuity here. A virtuous circle where man and nature are in balance.'[46]

Like other Christians, the most sacred book for the Orthodox is the Bible, but almost equally precious is the Philokalia, a collection of ancient manuscripts by revered sages. It is this text that matters most to the King. His friend, the former Bishop of London, Lord (Richard) Chartres said, 'He has a really deep feeling for it.'[47]

According to Father Dragos Herescu, of Cambridge University's Institute for Orthodox Christian Studies, 'People who read the Philokalia want to take a step further in enhancing their knowledge of the theology of the Orthodox Church. It helps understand Scripture and for us, Scripture and Tradition go together. They are two sides of the same coin.'[48]

One of the foremost translators of the Philokalia into English was Philip Sherrard, who profoundly influenced the King with his conviction that the ecological crisis was evidence of a deeper spiritual crisis, and that it was Orthodox tradition that could save the fragmented secular world.

If the Orthodox Church has led the Christian field in its concern for the environment, then it is mostly down to the man nicknamed the Green Patriarch – Ecumenical Patriarch Bartholomew of Constantinople, considered the leader of the Orthodox Churches, and greatly admired by the King's father, the Duke of Edinburgh (see chapter six). In October 2022, the Patriarch and the King met at Buckingham Palace during Bartholomew's visit to Britain to mark the centenary of the Orthodox Church by first appointing an archbishop here.

Charles' admiration for and devotion to Orthodoxy is evident at his Gloucestershire country house, Highgrove, the home that the Duchy of Cornwall acquired for him in 1980. There he developed a garden where he could put to practical use his interest in organic gardening and pursue his belief that humanity can thrive best when in harmony with nature.

The twenty-five-acre garden requires a staff of twelve to maintain it, with its wildflower meadow, stumpery and organic vegetable plots. In 1998, after a visit to Mount Athos, the Prince decided to build a sacred space of his own to commemorate the Millennium. As his mother so memorably pointed out on Christmas Day 2000, the Millennium marked the two-thousandth anniversary of Christ's birth. The then Prince commissioned the architect Charles Morris to design the space, apparently convinced that Morris was his kind of person because, said Morris, 'he had seen the stitching along the soles' of his shoes' – a sign that Morris understood the value of something well made and therefore worth preserving.[49]

The result was The Sanctuary, a building that connected ancient Greek thinking, Greek Orthodoxy, a love of nature and some Anglican tradition. The basic shape is cruciform, a reminder of Christ's cross, while the inscription above the door is from the Collect for Evensong from the Book of Common Prayer: 'Lighten our darkness, we beseech thee, O Lord.' Made from local stone, timber, clay and tiles, there is a fireplace, no electricity, and stained-glass windows depicting Highgrove's flowers, while the altar is of rock cut into three layers. Morris recalled that Charles told him that if you look closely enough and for long enough, 'you can see the Holy Dove'.[50] Charles also chose Byzantine icons made by a Mount Athos hermit for his Sanctuary and asked Richard Chartres to consecrate it. It is one of his most private spaces where only a few trusted intimates are invited.

Geoffrey Lean, the award-winning environment writer, who has spent time at Highgrove talking to the King about green issues, says that it is religion, especially Orthodoxy, that has had the most profound impact on his thinking about ecology and green issues. Like his father before him, he came to realise that the Greek Orthodox Church had developed a theology of creation which led to keen concern about the plight of the planet – something that Charles' Reith Lecture had also highlighted.

'He looks at these issues through a spiritual lens,' said Lean. 'His attitude to genetically modified crops – he's opposed to them because he thinks it's wrong to mess about with God's creation.'[51]

This fascination for Greek Orthodoxy is matched by interest in other Christian denominations, as well as Judaism and Islam. Just as his grandmother, Princess Alice, has been an influence on the King regarding his interest in Orthodoxy, she also inspired him with her work helping Jews hiding from the Nazis in wartime Athens – work which led to her being honoured by the state of Israel as 'righteous among the Gentiles'. The King has regularly marked notable anniversaries regarding the Holocaust; in 2013 he hosted a reception for the seventy-fifth anniversary of the Kindertransport, and in 2015 he attended the Holocaust Memorial Day commemorations of the seventieth anniversary of the liberation of Auschwitz-Birkenau, saying, 'The Holocaust is an unparalleled human tragedy and an act of evil unique in human history and it is for these reasons that we must always remember it and honour its Jewish victims and the Nazis' other victims.'[52] A year later he became the patron of the Holocaust Memorial Day Trust, succeeding his mother.

Within a few years of becoming involved with the Trust, he brought together his concerns about religious hatred, his particular interest in the Holocaust and his influence as a royal patron of the arts to commission portraits of seven Holocaust survivors. The portraits were displayed in an exhibition in The Queen's Gallery and are retained in the Royal Collection. A BBC documentary about the commission highlighted the traumas experienced by the seven portrayed, who were all children in Nazi camps and survived to make new lives in Britain. At the time of the portraits first being exhibited, Charles said:

> As the number of Holocaust survivors sadly, but inevitably, declines, my abiding hope is that this special collection will act as a further guiding light for our society, reminding us not only of history's darkest days, but of humanity's interconnectedness as we strive to create a better world for our children, grandchildren and generations as yet unborn; one where hope is victorious over despair and love triumphs over hate.[53]

As often happens with Charles and his enthusiasm for particular issues and causes, his interest in Judaism has been influenced by personal encounter. He met Jonathan Sacks on several occasions after he became Chief Rabbi in 1991 and admired his writings. But according to Zaki Cooper, a former adviser to Sacks, it was a long conversation during a flight to Israel for the funeral of Yitzhak Rabin, the assassinated Prime Minister of Israel, that caused the pair to really bond. When Sacks died in 2020, the then Prince of Wales recorded a speech for a tribute to mark the end of thirty days mourning for the former Chief Rabbi in which he called him 'a light unto this nation', and spoke of Sacks' 'moral conviction, which, in a confused and confusing world, was all too rare'.[54]

Cooper, who also worked at one time as part of the Buckingham Palace team, was able to observe the impact of the King's interest in Judaism and in Jewish people. Charles' appreciation of Sacks is matched by an appreciation of the King by the Jewish community, he said: 'The King's engagement with Jewish people and his concern about anti-Semitism makes a huge impact on our community.'

Cooper has noted Charles' interest in other faiths too: 'He isn't ticking boxes. It goes deeper than that. He feels a kinship and a comfort with other communities.'[55]

In 2021, the then Prince of Wales received the Bridge Award from the Council for Christians and Jews for his efforts to build bridges and understanding between communities. During his acceptance speech he referred to the work in conflict resolution that he had seen during visits to the Holy Land and the need for continuing dialogue between different faiths – including Islam. As happens often with Charles talking about religion and the sacred, his speech was peppered with references to harmony. It was this focus on harmony that first excited his interest in Islam.[56]

His first major address on Islam was given prior to official visits to Saudi Arabia, Kuwait and the United Arab Emirates in October 1993, but long before that he had developed a keen interest in Eastern religions and was particularly taken with Islamic art and architecture and their focus on harmony. That interest had led him to be a patron of the Oxford Centre for Islamic Studies, for whom he made the speech, at the Sheldonian Theatre, Oxford.

The speech's sentiments were typical of a particular kind of upper-crust Englishman, such as T. E. Lawrence, whose views of the East are tinged with a romantic view of the Orient. Christianity had lost, Charles said, what he thought was at the heart of Islam – 'a metaphysical and unified view of ourselves and the world around us'.

The speech went down well with people in the Arab world and those who hoped for dialogue, as he suggested, 'I believe wholeheartedly that the links between these two worlds matter more today than ever before, because the degree of misunderstanding between the Islamic and Western worlds remains dangerously high, and because the need for the two to live and work together in our increasingly interdependent world has never been greater.'[57]

And he pointed out:

> That which binds our two worlds together is so much more powerful than that which divides us. Muslims, Christians – and Jews – are all 'peoples of the Book'. Islam and Christianity share a common monotheistic vision: a belief in one divine God, in the transience of our earthly life, in our accountability for our actions, and in the assurance of life to come. We share many key values in common: respect for knowledge, for justice, compassion towards the poor and underprivileged, the importance of family life, respect for parents.[58]

It was also a speech by someone who was fully aware of the growing importance to the Royal Family of Muslims in Britain and abroad; the Prince pointed out that many millions of them lived in Commonwealth countries, and there were five hundred mosques in Britain at the time of the speech.

Some had grave doubts. Feminists noted that he made no reference to the oppression of women in some Muslim countries, not least Saudi Arabia, where he was heading, and instead focused on women who wore the veil as a personal statement of Muslim identity.

Others felt that the speech, made less than a year after the first bombing of the World Trade Center in New York by Islamist extremists, seemed tough on Christianity while saying little about Islamic fundamentalism other than to warn of the dangers of using 'that emotive label'.[59]

The idea that Islam is a standard-bearer for particular values was revisited in 1996 when Charles spoke at a Foreign Office conference in Wilton Park when he urged that Islamic thinking would benefit British schools. After praising the religion's integrated, spiritual view of the world, he went on, 'We could begin by having more Muslim teachers in British schools, or by encouraging exchanges of teachers. Everywhere in the world people want to learn English. But in the West, in turn, we need to be taught by Islamic teachers how to learn with our hearts, as well as our heads.'[60]

It seemed that Charles developed a tendency to compare the best of Islam with the worst of the Christian world, and this inherent bias would ensure that Islam came out on top.

Naturally enough, his views have gone down particularly well in the Middle East, where Charles has travelled extensively. The British Foreign Office has taken a pragmatic view, recognising that Charles' apparent fondness for Islam can open doors that will benefit British political, diplomatic and business interests. In 2021, when he and his wife Camilla travelled to Egypt and Cairo for meetings about inter-faith dialogue with the Grand Imam of al-Azhar and on climate change – it came just after COP26, the UN climate change gathering in Glasgow and as Egypt took over the presidency of the next one, COP27 – diplomats commented on Charles' soft power. The BBC's royal correspondent, Jonny Dymond, explained that a royal overseas tour might not have meant a lot to the British public, but abroad he could have tremendous clout, influencing people on the importance of religious toleration and of better stewardship of the environment. In doing so through his speeches and comments to guests at receptions, the Prince would have had input from the British Foreign Office as well as his own team.

The impact, a diplomat told Dymond, was 'massive', and his role 'hugely important'. Such trips involved not only the royal presence but also opportunities for the Foreign Office to build networks, get people listening and put forward ideas.[61]

This soft power has also paid charitable dividends: in May 1997, Prince Bandar bin Sultan of Saudi Arabia announced a donation by King Fahd of $33 million to Oxford University towards the building for the Centre for Islamic Studies at Oxford, a gift designed 'to establish Islamic studies at the heart of the British education system'.[62]

Charles' own charitable body, The Prince's Foundation, also secured financial support from two prominent Muslim businessmen: Mohammed Abdul Latif Jameel, whose business interests include a Saudi hotel and who was given an honorary knighthood by the Queen for his philanthropy, and Mahfouz Marei Mubarak bin Mahfouz, a Saudi billionaire. His involvement in The Prince's Foundation is now being examined by the police as part of an investigation into an alleged cash-for-honours scandal.[63]

In 2017, Charles made another speech at the Centre for Islamic Studies, this time to mark the inauguration of its new building. Once more, he returned to his theme of the need for dialogue between religions: 'We need to rediscover and explore what unites rather than what divides us. And that involves a recognition that we have all learned from each other and should continue to do so. No one culture contains the complete truth. We are all seekers. And our search is – or should be – a collective human enterprise.'[64]

But there was not the same paean of praise for Islam that there had been when he had spoken in Oxford twenty-three years earlier, describing how Islam had held on to values that Christianity had lost. The bulk of his speech was taken up with praise of the Centre's new building and the importance of harmony in architecture – another constant topic which had inspired projects such as his model village of Poundbury, in Dorset, and caused him to vilify contemporary British architects for their monstrous carbuncles. What had changed?

The world certainly had. In 2001 came the second of the attacks on the World Trade Center, and a growing realisation across the world of the threats by Islamist terrorists. Some of those attacks had led to deaths on British soil, notably the 7/7 bombings in London in 2005.

The Prince of Wales, like many Christian clerics, was concerned that in condemning Islamist terrorism, there was a tendency for politicians to focus on Muslims to such an extent that innocent, devout practitioners of that faith were scapegoated too. Within two weeks of the 9/11 attacks on the World Trade Center, he hosted an event in London for Muslim leaders where he was said to have expressed his concern to them that the language coming from America was too confrontational. Those at the meeting at St James's Palace included Sir Iqbal Sacranie, Secretary General of the Muslim Council of Great Britain, and Khalid Mahmood, the Labour MP for Birmingham Perry Bar, who later said, 'His criticism of America was a general one of the Americans not having the appreciation we have for Islam and its culture.' The Prince, who, like his mother, is expected to be politically impartial, was said not to have criticised the American interventions in Afghanistan and Iraq and to be sympathetic to Americans who were traumatised by the attacks on their own soil that led to three thousand of them losing their lives. But the meeting confirmed his conviction that dialogue – interfaith dialogue – is a way forward.

In November 2005, he and his wife Camilla went on an eight-day trip to the United States where he met President George W. Bush and was believed to have shared his view that Islam should not be condemned. The visit also included the Prince's attendance at a seminar on religion and its role in the community, hosted by Georgetown University, the elite Jesuit foundation in Washington DC, where he met representatives of Christian, Muslim and Jewish groups at the Center for Muslim-Christian Understanding.[65]

The following spring, Charles and Camilla travelled to the other side of the world, to Saudi Arabia, where he is fêted and admired for his sympathy for Islam. On this occasion, though, the Prince conducted something of a trapeze act, balancing his view that the West does not understand Islam with a critique of some of its more rigid followers, who stick so closely to its sacred texts that they do not hold with contemporary interpretation. In other words, the man who is now the Supreme Governor of the Church of England – a role the English monarch takes on because of the Reformation in the Christian religion his forebears initiated – was urging something of a Reformation in Islam. He made his appeal at the theologically conservative Imam Muhammad bin Saud Islamic University, whose 24,000 male-only student population provides the country with its preachers, judges and religious police. His appeal focused on his favourite topic of wisdom: 'We need to recover the depth, the subtlety, the generosity of imagination, the respect for wisdom that so marked Islam in its great ages.'

But then he went on to suggest, 'What was so distinctive of the great ages of faith surely was that they understood, that as well as sacred texts, there is the art of interpretation of sacred texts – between the meaning of God's word for all time and its meaning for this time.'[66]

By 2015, he was voicing concern about the radicalisation of young people, saying that the extent to which this was happening was alarming and one of the 'greatest worries'. When he was asked about radicalisation, he said:

> Well, of course, this is one of the greatest worries, I think, and the extent to which this is happening is the alarming part.
>
> And particularly in a country like ours where you know the values we hold dear.
>
> You think that the people who have come here, [are] born here, go to school here, would imbibe those values and outlooks.
>
> The frightening part is that people can be so radicalised either through contact with somebody else or through the internet, and the extraordinary amount of crazy stuff which is on the internet.[67]

He also spoke of his endeavours through The Prince's Trust to help young people find constructive paths to channel their enthusiasm, energy, aggression and desire to take risks.

Then, in May 2017, the horrific consequences of radicalisation were writ large when an Islamist extremist suicide bomber detonated a bomb full of shrapnel at Manchester Arena, killing twenty-three people and injuring a thousand more as crowds of young people left an Ariana Grande concert. It took place almost a week after Charles' Oxford speech urging a renewed focus on what unites us rather than divides us. People had become more sensitive to the championing of Islam, and there was a sense that there had to be more tact in how it was expressed, while at the same time dialogue was essential. Some have suggested to me that the government thought the Prince of Wales should pipe down regarding Islam and that his desire for dialogue might be interpreted by some as partiality.

But something else was happening too. As the Middle East endured increasing turmoil, often as dictators were overthrown and anarchy prevailed, the victims were often the Christian minorities of these lands. Charities who worked to help them complained that the British government was slow to recognise the suffering that some of the oldest Christian communities were facing: their homes, churches and schools were razed to the ground; many of them were killed while others fled.

But Prince Charles noticed. The Middle East was not a Muslim monopoly. It was where Christians had lived since their faith had been founded. The harmony of which he spoke so often as vital was being lost – and the Christian communities were the victims, caught up in a maelstrom caused by religious extremism and international politics and aggression.

There were quiet, private meetings behind the scenes between the Prince and charity officials and, later, with refugees themselves, with some invited to meet him at his Scottish home in Birkhall. Substantial donations were made to help charities working in the field. Then came public gatherings to draw attention to the plight of those affected. In December 2013, after visiting the Coptic Orthodox Centre in Stevenage and the Syriac Orthodox Cathedral in Acton, west London, he hosted a reception at Clarence House for faith leaders, including those from Eastern Christian churches, and acknowledged how Christians were being increasingly targeted by Islamist militants.

A year later, in December 2014, Charles was back in Acton, visiting the Iraqi Chaldean Catholic Community at the church it uses there, to hear first-hand what many of those attending had suffered. They included people who had been driven from their homes after coming under attack from ISIS militants who want to create a pure Islamic state in Iraq. Such attacks of members of one religion on another, he told them, was 'a blasphemy'.

'The Apostle Paul who went from being a persecutor to being persecuted encourages us to be steadfast in faith,' he continued.

> And, at this most agonising time we have to struggle not to forget that Our Lord called upon us to love our enemies and to pray for those who persecute. As you and your families know only too well, that is easier said than done.

> But by being with you this Christmas time I wanted to assure you of my constant thoughts and sympathy, and those of my family. As you know, the story of the Nativity ends with the Holy Family fleeing for refuge from persecution. You and your families are quite literally following in the footsteps of the Holy Family.[68]

In December 2015 came a further gathering, this time in Archbishop's House, hosted by Cardinal Vincent Nichols, where the Prince once more met Christian refugees from countries such as Syria, after expressing a desire to stand in solidarity with them.

Then, for the fourth year in a row, Charles turned his attention once more to persecuted Christians but using a particularly prominent platform. For the second time in his life, he used the 'Thought for the Day' slot on BBC Radio 4's *Today* programme to highlight what was happening in the Middle East. The programme regularly has an audience of seven million and is viewed as one of the BBC's main agenda-setting programmes. The Prince pulled no punches, warning that the attacks on Christians were akin to the Nazi persecution of the Jews in the 1930s.

He began his 'Thought for the Day' by recalling a conversation with a Syrian Jesuit priest in London who warned him that in five years Christians could have disappeared completely from the lands described in the Bible, the lands where Christianity was founded. 'The scale of religious persecution around the world is not widely appreciated,' Prince Charles said, adding that attacks were also increasing on Yazidis, Jews, Ahmadis, Bahá'ís and many other minority faiths. He continued:

> All of this has deeply disturbing echoes of the dark days of the 1930s. I was born in 1948 – just after the end of World War II in which my parents' generation had fought, and died, in a battle against intolerance, monstrous extremism and an inhuman attempt to exterminate the Jewish population of Europe. That, nearly seventy years later, we should still be seeing such evil persecution is, to me, beyond all belief.[69]

The Prince trod into more politically sensitive territory with his call for the refugees to be made welcome – an issue that has divided communities and politicians over whether people are fleeing attacks and possible death or whether they are economic migrants. The Prince, however, focused on the need for welcome and hospitality.

In recent years, Charles has become close to the Catholic charity Aid to the Church in Need, supporting its work in the Middle East and with refugees here in Britain. It is evidence of his ecumenical approach, which has surprised some Catholics who thought him not so sympathetic to Rome. They believed he took the view, as certain Anglicans do, that Catholicism can be found in the Church of England, if people prefer that kind of liturgical and theological approach. But evidence suggests that he has grown in sympathy to the Church that first gave the title Defender of the Faith – which has become such a controversial matter for him – to an English monarch.

The King has made several visits to Rome in the past forty years, visits which, like his mother's to the Vatican, are as much about diplomacy as spiritual matters. Members of the Royal Family are among the key assets of the Foreign Office when it engages with other states, including the Holy See. This was apparent in 2017 when the Prince of Wales visited Rome to see Pope Francis, with whom he shares several passions, including the environment and the persecution of Christians. Pope Francis' encyclical on the environment, *Laudato Si'*, was emphatic that climate change is real, and he has accused sinful humankind of turning the planet into a 'polluted wasteland full of debris, desolation and filth', while the Prince in his foreword to a book on climate change he co-authored has called it the 'wolf at the door' and urged that action must be 'urgently scaled up, and scaled up now'.[70]

Both of them have also regularly expressed deep concerns about the plight of Christians in the Middle East: in January 2017, the Pope complained that the media doesn't speak about the persecuted because they are not newsworthy, while a few weeks later the Prince told guests at a Lambeth Palace reception that people cared more about Brexit than the plight of those fleeing ISIS in the Middle East.[71] He continued to press the plight of Christians the following year at a special service in Westminster Abbey where he gave his own personal reflections, heard by four patriarchs of Middle East churches, Coptic Church leaders, the Archbishop of Canterbury and Jewish, Muslim and Roman Catholic leaders from Britain.[72]

The speech was notable for its theological discourse, exploring Christian notions of forgiveness, after being inspired by persecuted people who manage to forgive their persecutors:

> Forgiveness, as many of you know far better than I, is not a passive act, or submission. Rather, it is an act of supreme courage; of a refusal to be defined by the sin against you; of determination that love will triumph over hate.
>
> It is one thing to believe in God who forgives; it is quite another to take that example to heart and actually to forgive, with the whole heart, 'those who trespass against you' so grievously.[73]

The importance that Prince Charles gives to people of different faiths and Christian denominations coming together was also evident in the article which he wrote for the Vatican newspaper, *L'Osservatore Romano*, about John Henry Newman, published on the eve of Newman's canonisation on 13 October 2019, which Charles attended as part of a substantial British delegation. The Anglican priest who converted to Roman Catholicism, later being made a cardinal, won praise from the Prince for his faith, intellect and honesty. The article covered the dominant themes of Charles' own writing: he noted Newman's description of the divine vision in his poem 'The Dream of Gerontius' as 'a grand mysterious harmony', and went on to tell *L'Osservatore Romano* readers, 'Harmony requires difference. The concept rests at the very heart of Christian theology in the concept of the Trinity.' He also used the article to comment once more on wisdom, praising Newman for his recognition of his own flaws and understanding of the mercy of God.

Then, like many others over the years, Charles turned to Newman for his insights on conscience:

> Individual Christians have found their personal devotion challenged and strengthened by the importance he attached to the voice of conscience. Those of all traditions who seek to define and

> defend Christianity have found themselves grateful for the way he reconciled faith and reason. Those who seek the divine in what can seem like an increasingly hostile intellectual environment find in him a powerful ally who championed the individual conscience against an overwhelming relativism.[74]

For King Charles himself, as with previous British monarchs, there are occasions when a tussle of conscience is complicated by an issue being not only about what one believes to be right or wrong, but also about what one's duty is to the country and to the Crown. One such occasion for Charles occurred on a visit to Rome in April 1985 when he and Diana, the Princess of Wales, met Pope John Paul II. The visit mostly followed the usual pattern of such visits, with the Prince and Princess ushered into a vast, high-ceilinged room where the Pope sat behind a desk and they sat some distance away on spindly chairs. There was a moment of confusion when Diana attempted to ask the Pope about his recovery from an assassination attempt two years earlier, patting her stomach to indicate she was asking about his stomach wound. The Pope took this to mean she was talking about being a mother and blessed her tummy.

But there was another issue regarding the visit which became a matter of controversy – Charles' desire to attend Mass celebrated by the Pope. Three years earlier, Pope John Paul had visited Britain on a pastoral visit which had almost been abandoned owing to Britain being at war with the devout Catholic nation of Argentina over the Falkland Islands. One of its highlights had been an ecumenical service at Canterbury Cathedral, and the Archbishop of Canterbury, Robert Runcie, invited Charles to attend. He had readily agreed but the invitation had led to a discussion between the Prince of Wales' private secretary and the Queen's as to whether he should do so, given her standing as Supreme Governor of the Church of England. Although she herself greeted John Paul at Buckingham Palace, it was the matter of the Prince attending a religious service that was the issue, and how it would be received by Protestants. Runcie, like his predecessor Michael Ramsey, was a fervent ecumenist, and keen for the Prince to be involved in the cross-denominational service, the like of which, with a pope participating in an ancient Anglican Cathedral that had been Roman Catholic until the Reformation, had never happened before. The Queen took the view that Charles could attend but not participate – a sort of royal religious equivalent of being seen but not heard.

This, however, was not enough to placate the tough-minded Protestants, and when it was announced that the Prince of Wales would attend, there was an outcry. The Moderator of the Free Church of Scotland wrote to Charles, denouncing his plan to attend the Canterbury Cathedral service, called A Celebration of Faith, saying, 'We fear that the false and blasphemous claims of the Papacy may be given more credence by Your Royal Highness' attendance at this service.'[75] Charles went ahead anyway, but such aggressive language may well have caused his mother to think that caution must be the order of the day, if even attending something organised by the Church of England, involving Roman Catholicism, would cause such outrage.

Charles himself was keen to do more for ecumenical relations, and when the visit to Rome was under discussion, he wanted to find a way of further symbolising warmer relations between Anglicans and Roman Catholics. Getting this right proved tricky. Archbishop Runcie, who was consulted by Charles' office, thought the Prince's attendance at a service in St Peter's Basilica would be a suitable gesture of reconciliation. There were fears that his active involvement would again upset the Wee Frees and other evangelical Protestants and it might be seen as the future Supreme Governor accepting the authority of Rome. But if he were merely to attend, it could upset his Vatican hosts.

The solution, agreed by Charles and Runcie and their officials, was for the Prince and Princess to attend a private Mass in the Pope's chapel, although they would not receive Holy Communion. There was concern about how this might be viewed at home, although Runcie wrote to the Prince's private secretary, Edward Adeane, to reassure him that only 'the lunatic fringe' would object. The visit to see the pontiff on his home territory had seen much huffing and puffing from some, even without a Mass; the Free Presbyterian Church of Scotland wrote to Charles' office, to say that 'we most vehemently protest'.[76]

The decision was made, given these opinions, that there would be a news blackout. The Vatican, of course, knew, but until two weeks before the visit and the planned Mass, the Queen did not. When she learned of the plan, she and her son had a long discussion about it. The Canadian Prime Minister, Brian Mulroney, who was a Catholic, happened to be visiting Britain at the time and later recalled that the Queen asked him if it was a good idea for the Prince of Wales to attend Mass. He thought it was not a problem but he could tell she was concerned that it might risk Charles' accession to the throne. Mulroney thought the Queen a tolerant person, but this did not run to approval of 'any position that might undermine the monarch's integrity as head of the Church of England'.[77] These fears became the order of the day, and the Mass was called off. Word of the plan, however, leaked on the actual day of the Prince and Princess' audience with the Pope. What might have been an historic moment of reconciliation, with news of it released after the event, instead became an embarrassment, with the Vatican put out and Charles annoyed.

The Queen herself remained resolute that relations with Rome could only go so far, although her meetings with popes were warm, as was their admiration for her. The one time she herself attended a Mass was the Requiem for her friend, King Baudouin of the Belgians, in 1993. Just as it was planned that Charles would not receive Communion at the aborted private Mass, she did not do so either. For a monarchy that still denounced the Catholic belief in transubstantiation in accession oaths until the twentieth century, this still seems impossible.

Charles, however, had been keen to understand more of Catholic spirituality, reading devotional literature before his audience with John Paul, and receiving a rosary from the Pope which he kept at his bedside. Rosaries are gifts often offered by Catholics: the Princess of Wales was given one by Mother Teresa of Calcutta, which her butler, Paul Burrell, said was entwined in her hands after she was laid out following her death in a car crash in Paris in 1997. She was also attended by a Catholic priest, Fr Yves-Marie Clochard-Bossuet, who prayed beside her body for ten hours following her death, after being summoned to the hospital. He later made contact with Diana's mother, Frances Shand Kydd, who was a Catholic convert and who asked him to celebrate Mass some three weeks later in the room where her daughter had died, together with other parents who had lost their children in accidents.[78]

On occasions, rumours persisted that Diana might convert to Catholicism, just as there were rumours of her interest in Islam. But, like her former husband, she remained an Anglican while being open to the insights and consolations of other faiths and denominations. For Charles, though, it remained more difficult, and more formal, given the role he would inherit from his mother.

As Prince of Wales, his role was frequently one of official representation of the Queen, and while eyebrows were raised in 1985 about his possible attendance at Mass, he returned to Rome in April 2005 for the funeral of John Paul II. The Requiem was in danger of being the cause of a row between Downing Street and Buckingham Palace: when the late Pope's funeral was announced, the Vatican had chosen the same day as the Prince of Wales' planned wedding to Camilla Parker-Bowles. The Prime Minister, Tony Blair, let it be known that he would choose the funeral over the wedding. The Archbishop of Canterbury, Rowan Williams, was also due to attend the pontiff's obsequies – the first time that a British Prime Minister and an Archbishop of Canterbury would do so. It emphasised both the stature of John Paul, whose papacy lasted twenty-six years, and the thawing of relations between Protestant Britain and Rome.

The sheer scale of the funeral indicated that something had to change – two hundred world leaders were to attend, including a hundred heads of state. Charles bowed to the inevitable and postponed his marriage by a day – but not before one of those world leaders, Robert Mugabe of Zimbabwe, who had become a Commonwealth pariah, managed to shake the heir to the throne's hand during the funeral.[79]

Charles' second wedding, this time to Camilla, the following day, combined a register office ceremony in Windsor's Guildhall with a blessing at St George's Chapel. It had been a matter of controversy for some years, but clerics, both Roman Catholic and Anglican, told me at the time it was best to regulate the situation rather than have Mrs Parker-Bowles remaining a *maîtresse en titre*. Some thought it should be a quiet, private event, but a marriage in the UK is a public event, and clerics close to it advised it was better to have it all out in the open.

For some years it was thought that a second marriage was not possible for the Prince, given that he was a divorcee and that a divorced man could not be crowned, nor be Supreme Governor. A steady, unremitting PR campaign by the Prince's advisers ensured that Mrs Parker-Bowles was slowly accepted by the public. I have been told that Charles believed they should be allowed a full wedding in the Church of England, and given that General Synod had changed the Church's rules in 2002 to allow the remarriage of divorced people in church, his view was understandable. It also said this was only possible in exceptional circumstances and the heir to the throne's remarriage was presumably an exceptional event.[80]

Charles was annoyed at the Church of England holding fast against a full second church wedding for him – another moment when there was tension between the clerics and the heir to the throne. Instead, he had to make do with his Guildhall civil ceremony and a blessing in St George's Chapel.

Even the civil ceremony proved controversial, with some constitutional experts saying that it was not possible for a member of the Royal Family to marry in a civil ceremony. Under section 45 of the 1836 Marriage Act, civil marriages for royals were banned. The 1949 Marriage Act also includes the clause that nothing in it should affect 'any law or custom relating to the marriage of members of the Royal Family'. At the time of the controversy over Princess Margaret wishing to marry the divorced Peter Townsend in the 1950s, the then Lord Chancellor, Lord Kilmuir, advised that civil marriages for royals were not possible, while records from the time also show that the Archbishop of Canterbury, Geoffrey Fisher, was confident the 1949 Act did not change the practice legislated for by the 1836 Act.

But in 2005, Lord Falconer, Lord Chancellor in Tony Blair's Labour government, said the exact opposite – that the 1949 Act did mean that members of the Royal Family could have civil ceremonies. How Lord Falconer reached that decision, we will not know for many years. When a Freedom of Information application was made five years after the wedding to see details of Lord Falconer's thinking, the Justice Secretary Jack Straw blocked it, and the Information Commissioner later refused an appeal against that decision.[81]

The St George's Chapel service followed the norms of a blessing, with the press noting that the pair chose the act of penitence from the 1662 Book of Common Prayer rather than a more modern form of words: 'We acknowledge and bewail our manifold sins and wickedness, Which we, from time to time, most grievously have committed, by thought word and deed, Against thy Divine Majesty, Provoking most justly thy wrath and indignation against us.'[82] Eight hundred guests attended the service, with a former Archbishop of Canterbury, George Carey, reading a lesson, the Dean of Windsor writing a prayer, and the Archbishop of Canterbury, Rowan Williams, officiating. It seemed that the Church of England fully endorsed the marriage of the royal couple.

And yet it did not entirely, given it was only a blessing. Charles may have thought that he was entitled to a full Anglican marriage service because, while divorced in 1996, his former wife Diana was killed in a car crash the following year, so he was in fact a widower when he remarried. The sticking point, then, must have been Camilla's first marriage to Andrew Parker-Bowles which had ended in divorce as well, in 1995. The couple had married in Wellington Barracks chapel on 4 July 1973; as a Roman Catholic, Parker-Bowles had invited one of his teachers from Ampleforth, Dom Jerome Lambert, a Benedictine monk and priest, to marry them in a Catholic service, and the pair went on to have two children, who were raised as Catholics.

When Charles and Camilla had been married for four years, they went to Rome, where they had an audience with John Paul's successor, Benedict XVI. The Vatican likes to research who comes to visit, even a Prince and his wife. I am reliably informed that when they looked into Camilla, knowing she had had a Catholic wedding, church records showed that this marriage had been annulled (Clarence House did not respond to a query about this). The details of annulments are kept in diocesan marriage tribunal archives, but if the Vatican wants to know, it can easily find out. Could this mean that Charles and Camilla now might in fact be eligible for a second full marriage in the Church of England?

There is also a clear irony about the whole matter of the Prince of Wales, a divorcee, later wishing to marry again. The monarchy remains inextricably linked to the Church of England, the Church first created by Henry VIII because of that monarch's desire to have his marriage annulled and be free to remarry. But at the time that Charles' first marriage crumbled, it would have been more likely that he could have found a solution had his first marriage been a Roman Catholic one, through current canon law and its understanding of nullity. Concerns about his full desire to enter into a lifelong union with Diana, in what Archbishop Runcie assessed was an arranged marriage, given his love for Camilla Parker-Bowles, might have suggested Charles could have had the marriage made void. This declaration of the sacrament of marriage being null would not, though, have made his children, William and Harry, illegitimate, as legitimacy is linked to the legal marriage contract, not the sacrament. In the Church of England, nullity is recognised if it is declared by the civil courts, but happens less frequently, given the Church of England's willingness to at least offer a blessing to the divorced who wish to remarry.[83]

Pulling together the canon law of the Roman Catholic Church and the Church of England and how it affects the heir to the throne is a challenge only the most experienced ecclesiastical lawyers would undertake. And it would raise again sensitive issues about Roman Catholicism and its proximity to the throne. Fortunately for Camilla, the Queen Consort, she was never tempted to convert to the faith shared by her first husband and her children, which in 2005 would have blocked her from marrying Charles. But since then, the Succession to the Crown Act of 2013 has allowed a royal to marry a Catholic – a change to a law that had existed since 1701, although the ban on the monarch being a Roman Catholic remains in place.

Another change is the growing toleration for divorcees to marry in the Church of England; while Charles was thwarted in 2005 and only allowed a blessing, by 2018 the Church of England was ready to marry Prince Harry in a full marriage service to the divorcee Meghan Markle. That Meghan, now the Duchess of Sussex, had previously been married only two years and had no children by that marriage might have made the decision simpler. The Archbishop of Canterbury, Justin Welby, appeared to have had no qualms, given the 2002 reforms, and in St

George's Chapel – the same place where he and Camilla had had their wedding blessed thirteen years earlier – the future Supreme Governor walked Meghan down the aisle for her marriage to his younger son.

For fifty-three years following his investiture as Prince of Wales, Charles attempted to bring together people of different faiths and Christian denominations. The longevity of his mother's reign was frequently commented on, not least in the run-up to the record-breaking Platinum anniversary of her accession, but it also meant that Charles was the longest-serving heir to the throne – a difficult role which he attempted to use, he said, to build bridges. At times that role proved controversial and at others fruitful. Who would envy someone being like a plane, circling again and again, waiting so long to be given the go-ahead to finally land? Yet in an era of growing secularism as well as faith diversity, he managed to carve a distinct role for himself.

In the early 1990s he caused consternation among some with his interest in using the title Defender of Faith, rather than the conventional Defender of the Faith. Then in 2015, revisiting the topic, he said that he would use Defender of the Faith. In the interview on Radio 2, previously mentioned, in which he talked about his concerns about radicalisation, he once more talked about building bridges. He also said that he felt that he could be a protector of faith: 'You have to come from your own Christian standpoint – in the case I have as Defender of the Faith – and ensuring that other people's faiths can also be practised.'

The influential Anglican blog, Archbishop Cranmer, provided an insightful commentary on how Charles can be both protector of various faiths and defender of a particular one:

> It is not possible to defend generalised faith when those faiths represent a plurality of mutually-exclusive theological propositions and conflicting dogmata. But it is ecclesially possible and entirely theologically coherent to be simultaneously Defender of the Faith and protector of faiths: the latter role involves general exhortation; the former a particular mission. It is missiologically possible to defend the Protestant freedom to believe (or not) as the individual wishes, while making them aware of the uniqueness and 'particular mission' of Christianity.[84]

In that sense, the then Prince of Wales set himself a particular mission as a bridge-builder – what some might call a pontifex, to use the old Latin name for a pope. One cleric close to the Royal Family told me some months before the King's accession: 'Charles is essentially in line with what he says about the title of Defender of the Faith with what the Queen has been doing during her reign. By committing yourself to the particular you then understand the general.'[85]

In the decade leading up to Charles' accession to the throne, leading Anglican clerics told me that they noticed a change in his relationship with the Church of England. Dr John Hall, who retired as Dean of Westminster in 2019 and met the Prince at countless services there over the years, said, 'The Prince had some awkward times when people like George Austin [the Archdeacon of York] sounded off. But since then he has been a very faithful Christian.'[86]

Justin Welby, the Archbishop of Canterbury charged with crowning Charles, has observed, 'Every indication is that for him his personal faith is something of immense importance,' and then noted that the King – perhaps unusually for someone in twenty-first-century public life – 'has a deep appreciation of the mystical, of the inner life in a way that is very challenging'. Welby also pointed out that this spirituality leads the King to go on retreats 'from time to time, to reflect and be with God, to be quiet'.[87]

Welby's predecessor as Archbishop of Canterbury, Rowan Williams, who officiated at Charles' wedding to Camilla Parker-Bowles, spotted like other clerics a thawing in Charles' relationship with the Church of England. He commented to me about Charles, some months before Elizabeth II died, 'His Christian faith has been a bit of a multicoloured fabric over the years. But his destiny now awaits. He is coming back into the fold.'[88]

On 8 September 2022, that moment of destiny finally happened. Charles, Prince of Wales, became King Charles III. The weeks following his accession seemed to set a pattern for the reign of a new monarch, a new Supreme Governor and a Defender of the Faith.

# 9

# The changing of the guard: the accession of Charles III

THERE IS ONE moment when the heir to the throne becomes the monarch: at the moment of the death of their predecessor. But ceremony by ceremony, speech by speech, their claim to the throne is endorsed, as the people, Parliament and the Church recognise a new reign is underway. When Charles III became King, succeeding his mother, Elizabeth II, it was as if Britain stepped back in time. Officials that few knew existed – the Garter King of Arms, the Lord President of the Privy Council, the Clarenceux King of Arms – stepped into the twenty-first-century spotlight for their role in the accession and proclamation of the new sovereign.

Yet this was an accession that also combined the modern with the ancient, from the King speaking to the nation for the first time with a television address the night after his mother died, to the public being able to witness the Accession Council for the first time in history through the mediums of television and live-streaming, to the King and Queen Consort travelling across the UK in the immediate days following the accession. There was the pomp and ceremony the world expects from British royal occasions, but there was informality too. It was an occasion where the medieval met the modern age.

The crowd that gathered outside St James's Palace on Saturday 10 September for the first proclamation of the new King, following the Accession Council, saw the Garter King of Arms, David White, step forward, amid state trumpeters in elaborate hats, and announce the new King, in elaborate language. Below the balcony were members of the Coldstream Guards in red jackets and bearskin hats, calling hip-hip-hoorah as White cried, 'Three cheers for His Majesty the King.' The crowd, some clothed in tracksuits and trainers, held their mobiles aloft to record the moment, an ancient ceremony captured by the latest technology. The *Mail on Sunday* reported, 'There is another fanfare of trumpets and a rendition of the national anthem, which, as thousands join in, swells to a roar. So determined are the people to salute their new King that their three cheers ring out a dozen times.'[1]

For historians, royal commentators and the public, the first few months of the Carolean era were, in many ways, surprising. Many over the years had wondered whether the country would struggle when the old Queen died. They thought the mood might be akin to that of Britain when it last lost a long-serving monarch: Queen Victoria. On the day she died in 1901, after sixty-three years on the throne, the novelist Henry James was staying at his London club, the Reform. He wrote to friends about the atmosphere in London and his own 'unexpected emotions': 'I mourn the safe and motherly old middle-class Queen, who held the nation warm under the fold of her big, hideous Scotch-plaid shawl and whose duration has been so extraordinarily convenient and beneficient . . . She was a sustaining symbol . . . the wild waters are upon us now.'[2]

There was certainly plenty of emotion when Victoria's great-great-granddaughter, Elizabeth II, died, some of it expressed in formal ways that Henry James would recognise – his club, the Reform, hung black drapes on its Pall Mall building – and in ways he would not – the piles of flowers and Paddington Bears outside the royal palaces. Yet there was no sense that the wild waters were upon us when it came to the monarchy, in sharp contrast to the political situation in the country, with Liz Truss taking over as Prime Minister just days before the Queen died, and out of office within a few weeks.

Instead, there was a strong sense of continuity, with the longest-serving heir to the throne already one of the most familiar figures in Britain. His words in his first few days as monarch were reassuring, offering commitment and honouring his mother and what she stood for. The days of mourning included walkabouts to meet the public, formal events full of tradition that also suggested continuity, and indications of what the new reign might be like.

Much of what happened in the first days of Charles III's reign had long been devised through Operation Spring Tide, an accession plan forged by government officials, members of the Royal Household and Church leaders. But there was nevertheless a question mark hanging over what might happen. Given that Charles had once said he wanted to if not completely ditch then amend the traditional monarchical title of Defender of the Faith and become Defender of Faith, to reflect the diverse nature of Britain and the many different beliefs held by its people, would he do so? The answer came quickly and definitively.

On Friday 9 September, the day after the death of Queen Elizabeth, the new King addressed the nation in a speech, recorded in the Blue Drawing Room of Buckingham Palace, from where his mother had broadcast many of her Christmas messages. It was shown on television before the first commemorative service for the late Queen, held in St Paul's Cathedral. Newspaper reports the following morning noted the King's hint of tears, but he made the speech without faltering in a firm, decisive voice.[3]

During the broadcast, in which he paid tribute to his 'darling Mama', he referred to the promise she made in her 1947 pledge on her twenty-first birthday to commit her entire life to Britain and the Commonwealth.[4] His message was about duty, sacrifice and commitment to Britain – words used to describe Elizabeth II frequently in the days after her death and leading up to her funeral ten days later. They were qualities with which the new King associated himself and made it clear, in this first address, that he would be a constitutional monarch, a king with a Christian faith, and a particular connection to the Church of England. Those who had fretted about his Anglican loyalties over the years and had questioned whether he understood the particular responsibility for impartiality – other than that Anglican partisanship – that a monarch holds, would have been reassured:

> The role and the duties of Monarchy also remain, as does the Sovereign's particular relationship and responsibility towards the Church of England – the Church in which my own faith is so deeply rooted. In that faith, and the values it inspires, I have been brought up to cherish a sense of duty to others, and to hold in the

> greatest respect the precious traditions, freedoms and responsibilities of our unique history and our system of parliamentary government. As The Queen herself did with such unswerving devotion, I too now solemnly pledge myself, throughout the remaining time God grants me, to uphold the Constitutional principles at the heart of our nation. And wherever you may live in the United Kingdom, or in the Realms and territories across the world, and whatever may be your background or beliefs, I shall endeavour to serve you with loyalty, respect and love, as I have throughout my life.[5]

And he went on:

> My life will of course change as I take up my new responsibilities. It will no longer be possible for me to give so much of my time and energies to the charities and issues for which I care so deeply.[6]

This was a king confirming both continuity and change. The following morning, the crowds that gathered outside St James's Palace for the historic occasion of the Accession Council and the proclamation of King Charles III were also reminded of the balancing act between tradition and modernity. While the Council and the proclamation followed the same format as previous occasions, what was truly historic was that people at home could watch: for the first time ever, the business of the Accession Council was televised, allowing the public to see the workings of state and the transfer of power from one head of state to the next. Declarations and swearings of oaths have never captured the public imagination as the grand spectacle of coronations have done. But the solemnity, the choreography and the sense of watching history in the making that morning of 10 September made for gripping television viewing.

The first part of the Council took place in St James's Palace's picture gallery, without the King, overseen by Penny Mordaunt MP, appointed as Lord President of the Council by the new Prime Minister, Liz Truss, just three days earlier.

Amid portraits of previous monarchs, the great and good of the nation – two hundred members of the Privy Council, chosen out of the total body of 718 – gathered for the historic occasion. There were politicians, including six former Prime Ministers. Tony Blair, then Gordon Brown, alongside Boris Johnson, edged out of Number 10 in the previous week, then his fellow Etonian, David Cameron, and next to him Britain's second female Prime Minister, Theresa May, alongside Sir John Major, stood before the dais awaiting the arrival of what was called the platform party: royal members of the Privy Council, together with leading Anglican clergy and officials.

Of the six Prime Ministers, only Major is old enough to be able to remember a previous King; he would have been almost nine when George VI died, while Brown was just a year old when Elizabeth II acceded to the throne. All the rest were fully Elizabethan – born during the Queen's reign.

Alongside them were the Speaker of the House of Commons, Lindsay Hoyle, and Church leaders, including Lord Carey, who had been Archbishop of Canterbury during the most difficult years of Charles and Diana's marriage and the fallout from his affair with Camilla, now the Queen Consort.

After the Cabinet Secretary, Simon Case, urged those attending to switch off their mobile phones, Mordaunt announced, 'My Lords, it is my sad duty to inform you that her most gracious majesty, Queen Elizabeth the Second, has passed away on Thursday the 8th September 2022 at Balmoral Castle.'

Not one phone beeped. Mordaunt then called upon the Clerk of the Privy Council, Richard Tilbrook, to read the proclamation to the packed room. It fell silent as he announced that Charles, on 'the Tenth day of September, in the year of Our Lord Two thousand and twenty-two, is now become our only and rightful liege lord, head of the Commonwealth, Defender of the Faith'.

The gathering repeated his final phrase – for most of them, the first time in their lives that they would have said it: 'God Save The King.'

Then the platform party, including Prince William as the newly appointed Prince of Wales, Camilla as the newly appointed Queen Consort, Liz Truss, the newly appointed Prime Minister, Justin Welby, the Archbishop of Canterbury, Stephen Cottrell, the Archbishop of York, the Lord Privy Seal, the Lord Great Chamberlain and the Earl

Marshal, who had stood listening on a raised dais, came forward one by one and signed the proclamation.

It meant that the title, Defender of the Faith, which had been first bestowed by a pope on a Tudor king in 1522, was given once more to a king, this time the fifth monarch of the House of Windsor, despite all the question marks that had existed over Charles using that title ever since he had first queried its use and relevance thirty years earlier.

An hour after the proclamation was read to the Accession Council, it was read to the people outside St James's Palace, as the Garter King of Arms announced from the balcony to those below in Friary Court:

> Whereas it has pleased Almighty God to call to His Mercy our late Sovereign Lady Queen Elizabeth the Second of Blessed and Glorious Memory, by whose Decease the Crown of the United Kingdom of Great Britain and Northern Ireland is solely and rightfully come to The Prince Charles Philip Arthur George: We, therefore, the Lords Spiritual and Temporal of this Realm and Members of the House of Commons, together with other members of Her late Majesty's Privy Council and representatives of the Realms and Territories, Aldermen and Citizens of London, and others, do now hereby with one voice and Consent of Tongue and Heart publish and proclaim that The Prince Charles Philip Arthur George is now, by the Death of our late Sovereign of Happy Memory, become our only lawful and rightful Liege Lord Charles the Third, by the Grace of God of the United Kingdom of Great Britain and Northern Ireland and of His other Realms and Territories, King, Head of the Commonwealth, Defender of the Faith, to whom we do acknowledge all Faith and Obedience with humble Affection; beseeching God by whom Kings and Queens do reign to bless His Majesty with long and happy Years to reign over us.
>
> Given at St. James's Palace this Tenth day of September in the year of Our Lord Two thousand and twenty-two.[7]

Between the announcement to the Accession Council and to the people, the Privy Councillors made their way to the throne room to greet King Charles III. It was, stated *The Times*:

> a notably more diverse group than the one that greeted Queen Elizabeth on her accession in 1952, and it was a less overwhelming affair, with far less Tudor flummery. Then a tearful 25 year old Elizabeth told the assembly that her heart was 'too full' with grief and emotion to say more than she would work, as her father had, to 'advance the happiness and prosperity of my peoples'.[8]

It was there that the new King made his Accession Declaration. This is, by tradition, a deeply personal statement which usually includes a tribute to the new monarch's predecessor, a request for support and a commitment to the monarch's new role. It can be used to announce a regnal name – Edward VII announced that he would not use his own Christian name, Albert, leaving that to one side as he felt that only his father, the Prince Consort, should be known by that name. Another Albert, the Duke of York, became George VI, when he succeeded his abdicating brother, Edward VIII. On this occasion, it was already known before the Accession Council that Charles would be known as Charles III: that had been made clear on the day that he had acceded to the throne.

Declarations of monarchs are also studied to give some sense of where their priorities lie. George III, one of the German Hanoverians, stressed his Englishness, while Elizabeth II voiced particular grief regarding her father's death, and talked about her religious belief.

The Declaration of Charles III had been superseded by the statement the King had made the night before on television, and the Declaration followed a very similar pattern to that speech, although, following tradition, the King announced the death of his mother to the Council, even though they had heard it announced minutes earlier by the Lord President, Penny Mordaunt. But tradition was making the running on this occasion.

Then, like the TV address, the King paid tribute to his mother's long reign and service, and spoke of the 'irreparable loss we have all suffered'. But the focus was less than the night before on the old Queen and more on the responsibilities of the new King. There was an almost imperceptible shift – a slight turn of the page. That shift had been symbolised by the change in flags as the Accession Council began: across Britain and Northern Ireland, flags that had been at half-mast since the Queen died were now raised for the Council and the proclamation of the new monarch. They were then returned to half-mast the following day, until after the Queen's funeral.

The King therefore slightly adjusted gear and turned to face what he described as 'the duties and heavy responsibilities of Sovereignty which have now passed to me. In taking up these responsibilities, I shall strive to follow the inspiring example I have been set in upholding constitutional government and to seek the peace, harmony and prosperity of the peoples of these Islands and of the Commonwealth Realms and Territories throughout the world.'[9]

As well as Britain's current government and Church leaders, and past ones too, representatives of those Commonwealth Realms and Territories – fourteen of them, including Australia and Canada, but mostly Caribbean islands – listened intently to the new King. What they heard was very conventional, with nothing that would rock the Establishment boat. And yet, amid the talk of peace and prosperity was mention of harmony – that Platonist ideal beloved of the first King Charles, upheld by the new King's mentor, the late Kathleen Raine, and the word that had peppered his speeches as Prince of Wales for decades.

Charles III moved on again, referring to the support of his 'beloved wife', the new Queen Consort, and the people he was to reign over, as well as the importance of their elected parliaments – this was, after all, a constitutional monarch. There was practical detail – a confirmation that he would do a deal with the government, just as his mother had during her reign: he would surrender the hereditary revenues of the monarchy, including the Crown Estate, and in return, he would get back the Sovereign Grant. In 1952, Elizabeth II had not mentioned money at all, focusing far more on faith: 'I pray that God will help me discharge worthily this heavy task that has been laid upon me so early in my life.'[10]

Yet Charles III's final words – for all the previous focus on hard cash – proved he was very much his mother's son, with almost a replica of her words: 'In carrying out the heavy task that has been laid upon me, and to which I now dedicate what remains to me of my life, I pray for the guidance and help of Almighty God.'[11]

The previous evening Charles had put faith at the centre of his commitment as King with a confirmation of his own Christian beliefs and the centrality of his role regarding the Church of England. But the meeting of the Accession Council on the Saturday morning was not only about personal faith but also about statutes; it also included a statutory oath to uphold the Church of Scotland. The oath was the result of negotiations between the English and Scottish Parliaments that had led to the Acts of Union of 1706/1707, and it was a means of providing Scotland with something similar to the coronation oath whereby the sovereign promises to uphold the Church of England.

The oath that Charles took said:

> I, Charles the Third, by the Grace of God of the United Kingdom of Great Britain and Northern Ireland and of My other Realms and Territories, King, Defender of the Faith, do faithfully promise and swear that I shall inviolably maintain and preserve the Settlement of the true Protestant Religion as established by the laws made in Scotland in prosecution of the Claim of Right and particularly by an Act intituled 'An Act for Securing the Protestant Religion and Presbyterian Church Government' and by the Acts passed in the Parliament of both Kingdoms for Union of the two Kingdoms, together with the Government, Worship, Discipline, Rights and Privileges of the Church of Scotland.
>
> So help me God.[12]

It was exactly the same legal terminology as the oath taken by his mother seventy years earlier, bar the change from Queen 'of Great Britain, Ireland and the British dominions beyond the seas' to King 'of the United Kingdom of Great Britain and Northern Ireland and of My other Realms and Territories' – a move that reflected the changing fortunes of Britain as it attempted to move further away from its colonial past.

Above all, though, this was a Scottish moment rather than the old Empire transformed to a modern Commonwealth. It was an endorsement from the monarch of the importance of the Presbyterian version of Protestantism. Those who stepped up to sign, stopped in their tracks by a sudden kingly tantrum about a pen tray getting in his way, were not only Camilla and William and the Lord Chancellor but also the Secretary of State for Scotland, the First Minister of Scotland Nicola Sturgeon, the Lord Advocate of Scotland Dorothy Bain KC, and the Lord President of the Court of Session Lord Carloway. One copy of the signed document was kept in the Books of the Privy Council in London, and another was delivered to Scotland to be kept among the papers of the Court of Session.

Legally speaking, the oath is not needed. The Church of Scotland Act 1921 gave full parliamentary recognition to the Church of Scotland as a national church. And Charles III is not Supreme Governor of the Church of Scotland – he has no means of enforcing the Protestantism of Scotland. Yet it did indicate a certain privileging of Protestantism, something that is reflected in the other two oaths of the monarch – the second, under the Accession Declaration Act, to be a faithful Protestant, which is usually made at the new monarch's first State Opening of Parliament, and then through his third oath, due to be made at the coronation when he will swear to uphold the rights and privileges of the Church of England.

All three oaths in 2023 appear to be following the same legislative pattern as the oaths taken by Elizabeth II, George VI, Edward VIII (although he never took the coronation oath) and George V, despite calls from some, including The Constitution Unit, for them to be revised and updated, given both the increasing religious diversity of Britain and its growing secularisation. There was no such updating evident in the proclamation of the King, either.

The title Defender of the Faith – the one about which there had been so much controversy for nearly thirty years – was used countless times that day, in the signed proclamation, the public one to the Accession Council and then finally across the country in the proclamations made in towns and cities. There could be no further doubt that it would stay the same as it has been for 502 years.

The reading of the proclamation around the country was a moment for more people with grand and little-known titles to emerge from the shadows. First, it was read at noon that Saturday in the City of London from the steps of the Royal Exchange by Clarenceux King of Arms, Timothy Duke; he processed from the Mansion House accompanied by heralds, the Lord Mayor and other

City office-holders. Trumpets were sounded at the Royal Exchange, their calls echoed by another four trumpeters at the Mansion House. Not to be outdone, in Northern Ireland the proclamation was given by the Norroy and Ulster King of Arms, on the terrace at Hillsborough Castle, while in Scotland the Lord Lyon King of Arms made the first proclamation in Scotland at the Mercat Cross in Edinburgh, before the party of heralds and other Scottish officials made their way to Edinburgh Castle to make the proclamation a second time. In Wales, it was a little more subdued, with the Lord-Lieutenant for South Glamorgan, Morfudd Meredith, and Wales Herald, making the proclamation for Wales in Welsh in the grounds of Cardiff Castle in the presence of representatives of the country's civil and military establishments.

Crowds turned out at every proclamation, following in the footsteps of those of previous eras who had no telephone, no ticker tape, no text message with which to share glad tidings – only the human voice. There were proclamations across Britain, read out by High Sheriffs, Lord Mayors and Mayors as well as in the Commonwealth realms and British Overseas Territories and dependencies.[13]

The combination of the old and the new was particularly evident in the City of London, where the sight of the Clarenceux King of Arms and the Lord Mayor, surrounded by pikemen and musketeers of the Honourable Artillery Company, the oldest regiment in the British Army, was overshadowed by the glass-walled skyscrapers of the twenty-first-century business district. John May, a lawyer and the upper warden of the Paviors, a livery company in the City, summed up the mix of ancient and modern: 'It's the thing that makes the City such a living and successful place. Like the Royal Family itself, there's constant change and yet, at the same time, continuity.'[14]

The continuity was evident in the following days. Two days after the Accession Council, Declaration and proclamation, it was the turn of Parliament, with the King attending Westminster Hall to hear condolences offered by both Houses and for him to address MPs and peers. It was the first time as King that he had addressed Parliament, and as he stood at a gilded lectern beneath the medieval hammer beam roof, he admitted, 'I cannot help but feel the weight of history which surrounds us.'[15] The parliamentarians felt it too. Members of both Houses pledged loyalty to the King – the first time any of them had ever done so, given the length of Elizabeth II's reign.

'There is nobody in either House who has taken an oath of allegiance to anybody other than Queen Elizabeth,' Conservative peer and former MP Lord Cormack told the BBC's political editor, Chris Mason. 'I've been here 52 years, I've taken the oath 14 times. On Saturday for the first time to the new King.'[16]

The address from the King followed what was, by now, a familiar formula, with a tribute to his mother followed by a promise to reign as she had done: 'She set an example of selfless duty which, with God's help and your counsels, I am resolved faithfully to follow.'[17] Note the reference to 'your counsels': this was a King consolidating the relationship between monarch and Parliament, rather than being separate or above it, in the very place, Westminster Hall, where his namesake, Charles I, had been put on trial in 1649 for governing outside the law and waging war on Parliament.

This King promised to the MPs and members of the House of Lords that he would 'maintain the precious principles of constitutional government'. It reflected the sentiment expressed in his personal Accession Declaration two days earlier when he had pledged 'upholding constitutional government'. The two chief purposes of the monarch – being an upholder of the British Constitution and being Defender of the Faith – are considered so essential that in these first few days of the new King being both proclaimed and endorsed, they were repeated several times.

On 15 September, after the final stop of his devolved nations tour and just in advance of the weekend before his mother's funeral, the King hosted an unexpected landmark event, not mentioned in the Operation Spring Tide accession plan, when he invited thirty faith leaders to a reception. Leaders of the Church of which he was now Supreme Governor and representatives of other Christian denominations joined rabbis, saffron-robed Brahmins and Sikhs and Buddhists gathered in the Bow Room of Buckingham Palace – a less formal place than the state apartments, through which thousands pass each summer on their way to the Royal Family's garden parties.

It gave the King and the faith leaders a chance to converse and for them to offer their condolences on the death of his mother. It was also the setting for a brief, landmark speech which set out how Charles sees his role in diverse, multi-faith Britain. The country, he said, is 'a community of communities'.

He explained his particular role:

> I am a committed Anglican Christian, and at my Coronation I will take an oath relating to the settlement of the Church of England. At my Accession, I have already solemnly given – as has every Sovereign over the last 300 years – an Oath which pledges to maintain and preserve the Protestant faith in Scotland.

Then he moved to a more general responsibility – and a more contemporary one:

> the Sovereign has an additional duty – less formally recognized but to be no less diligently discharged. It is the duty to protect the diversity of our country, including by protecting the space for Faith itself and its practise through the religions, cultures, traditions and beliefs to which our hearts and minds direct us as individuals . . . By my most profound convictions, therefore – as well as by my position as Sovereign – I hold myself bound to respect those who follow other spiritual paths, as well as those who seek to live their lives in accordance with secular ideals.[18]

While King Charles suggested that this role protecting diversity and other faiths was a duty, it was not one that was recognised through title, legislation or previous pledges at the time of the monarch's accession, as are his duties regarding the Protestant religion or constitutional government. As he put it, it is 'less formally recognized'. But it was a duty that his mother, Elizabeth II, had expressed late in her reign, when she said the Church of England, of which she was then Supreme Governor, had a duty to protect the free practice of other faiths.[19] It also chimed with what Charles, when Prince of Wales, had said about other faiths when he made his famous comments about the title, Defender of the Faith, back in 1994 and had then caused such controversy as well as consternation among Anglican clerics. Now, the new King had managed to square the circle: to both keep the old title, Defender of the Faith, as proclaimed just six days earlier, and present himself as a protector of all faiths.

His interest in different faiths, expressed in this speech, which was so personal – it was confirmed to me that he wrote the address himself[20] – delighted the faith leaders who attended the reception.

Among them was Bishop Kenneth Nowakowski, bishop of the Ukrainian Catholic Eparchy of the Holy Family, London, who is based at the Ukrainian Catholic Cathedral in London's Duke Street. 'For me, hearing these words from His Majesty the King, to express himself as a guarantor of faith – that coming from the sovereign – that was extraordinary,' he said. 'I expected him to speak about faith, but to say that was a particular delight. It means such a lot to those of us who have seen people of faith not protected.'[21]

To Dr Hisham Hellyer, from the Centre of Islamic Studies at the University of Cambridge, the King's thoughts expressed at his faith reception were the culmination of many decades of studying religions and encounters with people of different faiths:

> You have politicians and public figures who say we have to celebrate diversity, but this is not really what the King is talking about. He has this other world view; he senses that religions are in some way united – that there is almost a meta religion with common truth. It is akin to perennialism – that the religions are basically the same.

Perennialism is one of the topics that courses at the Temenos Academy explore. The King's association with the Academy may cause some Anglican alarm bells to ring, but for the government, the King's interest in religion, while esoteric, likely to pay dividends in today's diverse Britain, and ministers made some suggestions about guests at the Buckingham Palace reception.

'The reception was important,' said Hellyer, 'because it showed the King genuinely believes in this engagement with different people of faith in the UK and it is likely to be a prominent feature of his reign.'[22]

It was certainly a feature of his first few weeks as King, when he undertook a series of engagements involving faith. They were a mixture of the highly conventional and the more unusual and showed that while in the past Charles' interest in faith was quite cerebral, his focus is increasingly on supporting faith in action.

The more conventional visits included a trip to York Minster to unveil a statue of his late mother, the Cenotaph service on Remembrance Sunday, and a service in the Chapel Royal at St James's Palace for members of the Order of Merit. Trips to different parts of the country, to mark places being given city status, took in church visits. But even one of the conventional, Anglican trips – to Westminster Abbey for a carol service, later televised on Christmas Eve – came with a twist. Amid all the traditional readings and carols was a more radical choice – the poem 'Refugee', by Malcolm Guite. The order of service said, 'Dame Kristin Scott-Thomas DBE reads, at his Majesty The King's suggestion', and the lines included:

> We think of him as safe beneath the steeple,
> Or cosy in a crib beside the font,
> But he is with a million displaced people
> On the long road of weariness and want.[23]

The King's more unusual visits, focusing on faith in action, saw him engaging with several projects to help refugees. On 30 November, he opened The Ukrainian Welcome Centre, at the Ukrainian Catholic Cathedral, off London's Oxford Street, where refugees from the war in Ukraine can visit for advice, get help with items such as clothing, and find a listening ear. It was the second time that he had visited since the war began; the first trip to the cathedral was in early March. Bishop Kenneth Nowakowski, who had been at the September Buckingham Palace reception for faith leaders, hosted Charles on both occasions. 'That first time we were all a little frayed around the edges after what had just happened in Ukraine,' he said, 'and it was a comfort to have him come and talk to us. This latest time he spoke to every single person there, including mothers from Ukraine and our volunteers.'[24]

The King also met refugees during his visit to the JW3 community centre in north London, which is a focus for both the Jewish community and its outreach work. The centre runs a bakery where asylum seekers help with the baking for food bank deliveries. Among those he met were people from Sudan and Nigeria who help in the bakery, while donations for JW3's food bank were handed over to the centre from the boot of the King's car. As part of the visit, the King also took part in the centre's pre-Hanukkah reception for Holocaust survivors, and participated in traditional Jewish dancing. Among his dancing partners was Anne Frank's stepsister, Eva Schloss, aged ninety-three, who endured years of incarceration in concentration camps and has since worked for peace.

The King's visit, according to Oliver Marcus, marketing manager of JW3, was important because it endorsed the approach of the centre. 'We are very much open to all, Jewish and non-Jewish,' he said. 'We are inward-looking to our own community but also outward-looking so we run a local food bank and he was very interested in that.'

According to Marcus, the visit was also vital at a time when anti-Semitism is still a problem: 'The visit was affirmative. The highest power in the land was saying that we are welcome and part of this country, that we are as much a part of Britain as anybody else.'[25]

Other visits to social action projects taken by the King since he acceded to the throne included one to King's Cross Church in London, where he opened its King's House centre, and the nearby Ethiopian Fellowship Church. There were conversations with the volunteers at King's Cross Church, which hosts a variety of community programmes, including meetings for parents, carers and children, as well as work with refugees, through a café, and debt relief and prison chaplaincy. King's Cross Church looks more like a welcoming shop than a church, and is a 'plant church', which was set up in the tough neighbourhood surrounding King's Cross Station by St Mary's Bryanston Square twelve years ago. King's Cross Church is an Anglican church with a strong evangelical flavour, and the King was joined on his visit by the Archbishop of Canterbury Justin Welby, and the Bishop of London Dame Sarah Mullally. With Archbishop Anba Angaelos, the Coptic Orthodox Archbishop of London, they all adjourned to the Ethiopian Fellowship Church nearby for an Advent service.

Marking Advent with different Christian communities, and often focusing on the plight of persecuted Christians, had become a tradition of the then Prince of Wales. But during his first Advent as King, he focused on other religions too. There was a visit to a Sikh temple in Luton in early December, where he met representatives of different religions in the Bedfordshire town. As well as the newly built Guru Nanak Gurdwara's religious spaces, he saw the community food hall and heard about the vaccination programme that the Gurdwara ran, targeting the local Black, Asian and Middle Eastern population during the Covid pandemic.

During the pandemic, the King was seen frequently using the traditional Sat Sri Akal gesture as an alternative to shaking hands, and he used it again during his visit, when he also wore a traditional Sikh headdress as a gesture of humility and respect.

But none of these events was awaited with the huge anticipation surrounding the King's first Christmas message. There was certainly a poignancy around it, and a sense of history too. Not only was it the first time for seventy years that the nation would not be addressed by Elizabeth II, but it was also the first time ever that a Christmas message from a king would be televised: George V, who began the Christmas message tradition, and his son, George VI, spoke only on the wireless. There was genuine interest, too, in what King Charles would say.

If you can gauge the impact of something by what soap operas make of it, then this Christmas message was huge: characters on both the BBC's *EastEnders* and *The Archers* mentioned they would be listening to 'the first King's speech', as they called it. And when it was broadcast, substantial numbers of viewers put aside their pudding and mince pies to tune in: 10.6 million viewers watched the broadcast, which was a record for a monarch's Christmas address, as well as making Charles' eight-minute programme the most watched of Christmas Day, outstripping festive favourites such as the *Strictly Come Dancing Christmas Special* and *Call the Midwife*.

So why did so many people tune in? It might have been, as it was for the lying-in-state of Elizabeth II, her funeral and the Accession Council and proclamation, a desire to see history in the making. It might have been a certain kind of voyeurism – the speech came in the wake of revelations from Prince Harry and his wife Meghan about the Royal Family in their Netflix documentary series, and people might have thought the King would mention them (he didn't). It might have been habit, given the Queen's Christmas message had long been a part of the festive season for many families. Or maybe it was curiosity – what would this new monarch say? Whatever the reasons, the audience was considerable.

The late Queen certainly featured strongly in this year's message, from where it was filmed – St George's Chapel, Windsor, where she was laid to rest – to the tribute the King made to his mother. It was a neat way for him both to praise her for her commitment to service and to her faith and to confirm that he shared them. There was also a further expounding of his own faith, with mention of his visit some years ago to the Church of the Nativity in Bethlehem and to stand in the Chapel of the Manger. 'It meant more to me than I can possibly express to stand on that spot,' said the King, 'where, as the Bible tells us, "The light that has come into the world" was born.'[26]

That idea of light overcoming darkness – so often used in Hebrew and Christian Scriptures, as well as those of other faiths – enabled King Charles to mention the many faiths of Britain today, and to pay tribute to the work people of faith do in solidarity with others, from feeding the hungry to housing the homeless. There was a reference, too, to those without belief who also serve others.

But there was something missing. Like his mother, Elizabeth II, this monarch's first Christmas message came just a few months before the coronation. In December 1952, the new Queen asked that people pray for her on her coronation day to ask that God grant her the wisdom and strength to fulfil her promise to serve him. For 1953, it was a very progressive request; the Queen asked, 'I want to ask you all, whatever your religion may be, to pray for me on that day.' This was long before the days of regular interfaith dialogue, yet the Queen reached out well beyond her fellow Anglicans to ask for spiritual help.

King Charles has made it known since he ascended to the throne that he is a committed Anglican, but has also pledged to help protect all faiths. So it would have been entirely natural for him to make a similar request to that of his mother. Yet he didn't do so. Perhaps in twenty-first-century Britain there is a nervousness about asking for prayer. Charles' message attempted to embrace the entire nation, with its mention of his faith, others' faith and those of no faith at all. But as he could not ask non-believers to pray, maybe he thought better of asking anyone.

Christmas 2022's message gave an insight into the King's thinking. It was also an indication of what a fine balancing act a believing monarch has to perform in secular Britain, especially when he is not just sovereign of the entire nation but also has a specific role for one Christian denomination – that of Supreme Governor of the Church of England. That is the role I will look at before discussing the moment when the King and that Church come together for what is likely to be the most dramatic – and certainly the most liturgical – occasion of his reign, and a moment of mutual endorsement.

# 10

# Supreme Governor: or a future patron?

If you look through photographs of Elizabeth II's seventy-year-long reign, the same groups of people accompanied her time and time again. The individuals around her may have changed, while she remained constant, but the groups remained the same. One, of course, was her family. Once there was her mother and her sister; later Princess Diana, and until the last year of her life, her husband, Prince Philip. Death removed them. Others over the years took their place: alongside her children, grandchildren and eventually great-grandchildren were sometimes pictured with her.

Then there were those who held the greatest office of state: Churchill, Wilson, Thatcher, Blair – all fifteen of her Prime Ministers appeared with her on different official occasions.

But perhaps even more than politicians, the Queen was photographed time and time again with the clergy of the Church of England. Pictured with her were Archbishops of Canterbury, Archbishops of York, diocesan bishops and cathedral deans from around the country whom she would meet at Maundy Thursday services. There were Deans of Westminster and Windsor who oversaw great ceremonial occasions, as well as royal weddings and funerals that were also national occasions. These photographed events are not just a reminder of the Queen's personal faith – although that was considerable, and she was a devout attender of Sunday service – but also of her role as Supreme Governor of the Church of England and of the Church of England's pre-eminent position in this country as the established Church. It is a role that Charles III inherited immediately on his accession to the throne in September 2022.

The Queen was a beacon of stability throughout her seventy-year reign. Much of the British population almost took it for granted that she would always be the monarch. You have to be well into old age to remember the time her father, George VI, was on the throne, and the day it was announced – 6 February 1952 – that the King had died and that his elder twenty-five-year-old daughter succeeded him as Elizabeth II. On that day, many people might have turned to their Anglican faith for succour. But did they seek out the Book of Common Prayer and a Church of England service for comfort and consolation when Elizabeth II died, or even celebration of her Platinum Jubilee some months earlier?

While the monarchy has been a go-to institution for a sense of permanence, the Church of England has not. Its buildings continue to have a hold on people; the ancient village church has a special place in many a heart, and cathedrals attract plenty of tourists and are decently filled with worshippers. But statistics show that the Church of England itself is in sharp decline. The British Social Attitudes Survey which examined religion in 2016 showed that just 15 per cent of people considered themselves Anglican, half the proportion that had said this in 2000. Young people are particularly underrepresented. Just 3 per cent of those aged eighteen to twenty-four described themselves as Anglican, compared to 40 per cent of those aged seventy-five and over.[1]

At the same time, the country is far more religiously diverse than it was in 1953: we have a sizeable Muslim population of 3.3 million, as well as Jews, Hindus, Sikhs and others. Roman Catholic churches attract around one million Massgoers a week, with another four million still defining themselves as Catholic: all of them remain barred, of course, from becoming monarch on account of their faith, according to the 1701 Act of Settlement.

The even greater change in the seventy years of Elizabeth II's reign is that a substantial number of people profess no religious belief: 53 per cent in 2016, a number that is inexorably growing: it was 31 per cent in 1983.[2] The 2021 Census figures, released in November 2022, showed that 46.2 per cent of people identified themselves as Christian, compared with 59.3 per cent ten years earlier, while 22.2 million said they had no religion, up by 8.5 million in a decade.[3]

Given this diverse religious affiliation and the fact that a quarter of the population of England and Wales says it has no religion, can the Church of England retain its position as the established Church?

And should the head of state have this special connection to the Church of England, as its Supreme Governor, in such a country?

That the monarch of this country is Supreme Governor is down to Elizabeth I. Following the break with Rome caused by the marriage of her parents, Henry VIII and Anne Boleyn, Henry put himself in charge of the Church of England with the 1534 Act of Supremacy, declaring himself Supreme Head of the Church of England. The first Elizabeth then amended the title in 1559, taking into consideration the opposition of those who argued that only Christ could be called head of the Church. Since then, all monarchs have called themselves Supreme Governor, even those such as James II, who was Roman Catholic, and Charles II, who harboured a fondness for the old Roman ways and converted on his deathbed.

The clearest definition of the monarch's role in relation to the Church of England states that royal supremacy in regard to the Church is 'in its essence the right of supervision over the administration of the Church, vested in the Crown as the champion of the Church, in order that the religious welfare of its subjects may be duly provided for'.[4]

Essentially, the monarch acts with the advice and consent of Parliament, according to the coronation oath to uphold the Church of England and the Protestant religion, and gives or withholds assent to the Church's legislation and the appointment of its senior figures.

Being Supreme Governor is therefore linked to the status of the Church of England as *the* Church in England that had barred Roman Catholicism, post-Reformation. It was a Church that helped shape the identity of the English nation – Christian, but not Roman Catholic – and where English thrived as the chosen language of religion. Church and society were twinned, the monarchy the glue that held them together. Unlike 'La Marseillaise', the national anthem of republican France with its call to arms of its citizens, or 'The Star-Spangled Banner', urging Americans to look out for the flag that waves over 'the land of the free and the home of the brave', the national anthem of Britain is a prayer urging that 'God Save the King', inextricably linking monarch, nation and faith.

The national anthem might no longer be played in cinemas at the end of the programme or at the end of the night's BBC television programmes, but it is still sung lustily at sporting occasions as England or Great Britain supports its national teams and athletes. A similar combination of a more relaxed approach with a certain retained enthusiasm illustrates the position of the Church of England: falling attendance at ordinary Sunday parish church services but a constant keen interest in the national occasions at which it officiates, from Remembrance Sunday at the Cenotaph to great occasions of state, such as services of thanksgiving and memorials. This engagement with the Church of England was most evident on the occasion of Elizabeth II's funeral, when around 28 million people in the UK watched the ceremony at Westminster Abbey, as it was broadcast simultaneously by an unprecedented fifty UK channels. The numbers could be even higher as they do not include the people who watched it on big screens outdoors and in pubs, cinemas and churches.[5]

This Christian denomination at the heart of the nation, called the established Church, also has a particular role in every town and village. It continues to declare itself the Church for everyone in the country; it will bury you, regardless of your religion, and welcome you to its altars.

Being established also gives its other status: it has twenty-six bishops – the Lords Spiritual – in the House of Lords. The Archbishop of Canterbury is second in precedence after the Royal Family at state occasions, such as banquets for visiting heads of state. And it crowns the monarch.

This intertwining of monarch and religion, and in particular the Church of England, is evident from the moment of accession. The announcement of the start of Elizabeth II's reign came the same day that her father, George VI, died. The Lords Spiritual and Temporal and the Privy Council proclaimed that after 'it hath pleased Almighty God to call to his mercy our late Sovereign Lord King George VI', they announced that Princess Elizabeth had become Elizabeth II as 'Queen of this Realm' and Defender of the Faith – the title bestowed, pre-Reformation, on Henry VIII by the Catholic Church, and used ever since by this country's monarchs.

The Queen's own thoughts on her accession came two days later, after her return from Kenya where she had been on tour when her father died. Her declaration to the first Privy Council of her reign was, as it always is for monarchs, deeply personal, and she told them, 'I pray God will help me discharge worthily the heavy task that has been laid upon me so early in my life.' There was then, according to tradition, a pledge to preserve the 'True Settlement of the Protestant Religion and Presbyterian Government' of Scotland, although given she was not head of that Church it was not something she could actually enforce.

Then, at the first Parliament of her reign, came her accession oath: 'I do solemnly and sincerely in the presence of God profess, testify and declare that I am a faithful Protestant', and that she would uphold and maintain that faith – a form of words that did not include the earlier version of the oath's damnings of the liturgy of the Roman Catholic Church as 'superstitious and idolatrous'.

When Charles III acceded to the throne upon the death of his mother, the situation was less complicated, in that he was in Britain at the time. Indeed, he was at his mother's bedside. There was no delay, as there had been in 1953, while the new monarch arrived back in Britain from Africa. Instead, Charles III came down from Scotland to London for a meeting of the Accession Council that officially proclaimed him King, and he then held his first Privy Council meeting where he made his personal declaration on becoming sovereign. (For more details of King Charles' accession, see chapter nine.)

In 1953, it was the coronation oath that made the Queen's link with the Church of England most overt when she was asked:

> Will you maintain and preserve inviolably the settlement of the Church of England, and the doctrine, worship, discipline and government thereof, as by law established in England? And will you preserve unto the Bishops and Clergy of England and to the Churches there committed to their charge, all such rights and privileges, as by law do or shall appertain to them or any of them?

To which she answered, 'All this I promise to do.'

A similar oath is expected at King Charles' coronation.

This powerful relationship between monarch and Church is reinforced by the work that goes on as part of the role as Supreme

Governor, particularly formally appointing bishops, on the advice of the Prime Minister.

The arrangements are similar for the appointment of the highest church official, the Archbishop of Canterbury. The Crown Nominations Commission was formed in 1974 as the Crown Appointments Committee, when the Prime Minister agreed to its creation as a way of supplying him with the names of candidates. The Commission is made up of members of General Synod and six members elected by the diocese where there is a vacancy. When it comes to the See of Canterbury, three votes are given to the Anglican Communion's representatives and three to the Diocese of Canterbury. The name of the person nominated is then passed by the Commission to the monarch.

Given the Archbishop of Canterbury's status, there are regular formal encounters between the office holder and the monarch. The relationship behind the scenes can be likened to that between the sovereign and the Prime Minister – the monarch provides a listening ear, remains impartial, sometimes warns and, as was the case for Elizabeth II and her long reign, offers a certain historical perspective. According to the former Archbishop of Canterbury, Rowan Williams, the connection between the Queen and the Archbishop was 'a comparable relationship in a scaled-down way', in that 'there would be a one-to-one meeting a couple of times a year' rather than the PM's weekly audiences. There were also, he said, unscripted conversations at more informal events, citing a dinner they had at Lambeth Palace on one occasion: 'At the meetings we would always talk about church matters in a general way and my sense was of her support. This is somebody who had weathered a fair number of storms herself so she could be very sympathetic; at times she could be motherly.'[6]

Closer relationships exist between the monarch and the churches and chapels called royal peculiars, which are outside the jurisdiction of the dioceses and subject to the direct jurisdiction of the monarch. As well as the Chapels Royal of St James's Palace, Hampton Court and the Tower of London, the most notable of them are Westminster Abbey and St George's Chapel, Windsor, and its affiliated church, All Saints in Windsor Great Park. They are independent and symbolise the strong link between the monarch and the Church of England.

The Deans of Westminster and Windsor are also churchmen with whom the sovereign has considerable contact. It was the Dean of Windsor, rather than the Archbishop of Canterbury, who was Queen Elizabeth's first port of call if she were in need of spiritual guidance. At times she consulted the Archbishop of Canterbury on personal matters involving her family – such as controversies over divorce – if there might have been wider implications for the position of monarchy. In January 2023 it was reported that the King had turned to the Archbishop of Canterbury, Justin Welby, for help regarding the continuing tensions between the Duke and Duchess of Sussex and the rest of the Royal Family, and asked the Archbishop to act as a peacemaker.[7]

The official position of Supreme Governor is, however, altogether different from this. John Habgood, then Archbishop of York, made a distinction between the monarch's personal position and the official role of Supreme Governor in the 1990s when there was a debate over whether the Prince of Wales – now Charles III – might be able to fulfil the role on his accession to the throne, given his marital difficulties at that time:

> Is the Supreme Governor of the Church of England required to be at least as morally sober as an archbishop? If supreme governorship were the same as spiritual leadership the answer might be yes. But this would represent a serious misunderstanding. A monarch's personal involvement in the Church is welcome. The role of Supreme Governor, however, is not personal but institutional.
>
> The monarch is the visible representative of the unity and identity of the nation, and it is the Church's commitment to the nation, and responsibility for its spiritual welfare, which is symbolized by Supreme Governorship. It would be theoretically possible to hold the symbol even if in personal terms the monarch only fulfilled the minimum requirement of belonging to the Protestant succession.[8]

Some have argued that the powers of the monarch as Supreme Governor should be expanded and should have a more hands-on role. Thirty years ago, a committee chaired by William van Straubenzee and commissioned by the Church of England's General Synod examined the monarch's role in the appointment of archbishops, diocesan bishops and deans. It found that this involvement was valued, and recommended that senior church appointments should be made by the monarch, rather than the system of the time – by the Prime Minister and through his or her office and the Crown Appointments Committee. Straubenzee's committee thought this would enhance the role of the sovereign as Supreme Governor and would end the political aspects of the process. But it was shot down, with General Synod accepting that, under the unwritten British Constitution, the sovereign can only act on the advice of a minister, and this applies as much to the role of Supreme Governor as to being head of state.[9]

In 2007, reforms were made to the system – not by handing more power to the monarch, but by more power being given to the Church. Prime Minister Gordon Brown – son of a Church of Scotland clergyman – produced a Green Paper arguing for a new system. Instead of the Prime Minister being given two names of candidates for a bishopric, the Crown Nominations Commission would in future provide only one, and this would be passed along to the monarch, unless the first named person could not take up the post. Political involvement more or less came to an end – and the head of state's remained the same.

This role of Supreme Governor has also been expressed more overtly since 1970 owing to reforms made fifty years ago in the Church of England with the creation of General Synod replacing the Church Assembly. From that moment, Queen Elizabeth inaugurated and addressed the opening session every five years after diocesan elections, until 2021 when she sent Prince Edward to represent her, owing to her ill-health.

General Synod is also a reminder that the government of the Church of England takes place according to royal authority and is, being the established Church, part of the government of the country. It meets according to a writ issued by the monarch, and measures and canons passed by General Synod, once they have received royal assent, are part of the country's laws.

There is a less well-known aspect to the monarch's role in the Church of England that particularly distinguishes it from the head of other churches. The presence of the monarch at Synod, with its three houses of bishops, clergy and laity, is a reminder that in the Church of England, laity play a key role. After all, the sovereign, while a particular individual, is a lay person, not a cleric, and as Supreme Governor is a lay person at the apex of the Church.

Paul Avis, a former General Secretary of the Church of England's Council for Christian Unity, points out that royal supremacy is a constitutional fact, expressed in the Church of England's Canon A7, which is part of English law, outlining that the monarch 'is the highest power under God in the kingdom'. He argues that this means that the sovereignty exercised by the Queen – and now the King – in Parliament under God extends to all institutions, even other Churches – something that would no doubt be utterly rejected by the Roman Curia. But at the same time as noting the sovereign's constitutional position as a supreme power, Avis noted that the monarch, being a layperson, is of immense importance. There is a remarkable tension holding the two together here: the individual who is chosen to symbolise sovereignty and majesty and is dressed like a priest and anointed in a coronation that is effectively an ordination, is also playing a part because they remain part of the laity.

Avis explained:

> It is no embarrassment to a church profoundly touched by the Reformation that a lay person should hold large responsibilities in the Church. It is simply an outworking of the doctrine of the universal royal priesthood of the baptized. But it also signals symbolically that in the Church of England lay people have major responsibilities and significant privileges. A church that recognizes the spiritual competence of lay persons is likely to be a broad and tolerant church.[10]

Simon Sarmiento, who runs the Thinking Anglicans website, which has long been a centre of discourse for members of the Church of England, believes that Elizabeth II played a highly significant role as Supreme Governor, and commented before she died, 'In my personal opinion, it's a very good thing that she is not a cleric. It makes a difference. People of all stripes in the Church of England have a high regard for the Queen,' he said. 'She embodies the still small voice of calm.'[11]

According to Fr Marcus Walker, Rector of Great St Bartholomew's in London and an Anglican commentator, the fact that those 'people of all stripes' stay together in the Church of England has much to do with the role of the sovereign as Supreme Governor: 'Anglicans in the Church of England stumbled into tolerance, with the aim of having as many people as possible as members of the Church. The Sovereign is fundamental to the identity of the national church, as the binding force. The Queen is its unifying figure.'[12]

This is clearly one of the challenges of kingship that Charles III now faces.

The tolerance of the Church of England was certainly tested during the reign of Elizabeth II. In the 1950s it was a conservative, and even Conservative, Church, with most people in England filling in hospital forms with CofE when asked for their religion, even if they were not actively observant. Writers such as T. S. Eliot and C. S. Lewis evoked a vibrant Anglican religion that offered spiritual counsel and intellectual stimulation, and its traditional liturgies inspiration for the imagination. But as the 1950s wore on, the divisions in the Church of England became more apparent. One faction was vocal in its opposition to nuclear weapons, with clerical collars appearing among the marchers at Aldermaston, and were also alarmed by the Suez Crisis. The CofE could no longer be described as the Tory Party at prayer.

Then there was in-house factionalism. The Anglican Settlement had created a Church that was a reaction against the extremes of Roman Catholicism and Puritanism. The Church of England was a bulwark against excess, fanaticism, superstition, even passionate enthusiasm. It was where religion met reason. But by the 1950s, evangelicals, enthused by the missions of preachers such as Billy Graham, began to assert themselves. Anglo-Catholics, meanwhile, argued for the Church of England to be a more sacramental, worshipping community with the Eucharist at its heart. The Church of England, since then, has struggled to be a *via media*, with these two groups still at times at loggerheads. The divisions between them were particularly apparent during the Covid-19 lockdown over the closure of churches so that Anglican vicars could not celebrate at their altars. The more evangelical wing, including the current Archbishop of

Canterbury, Justin Welby, seemed comfortable at their kitchen table, livestreaming Sunday service. Others, for whom the sacred space of church and the altar mattered profoundly, were horrified that the Church of England closed its doors completely so not even a solitary priest could cross the threshold to livestream the Eucharist from a consecrated building.

Meanwhile, the Church of England has made every effort to be an inclusive Church, encouraging families through the services called Messy Church, and many parishes welcoming anybody who wants to receive Holy Communion regardless of whether they have been baptised or confirmed. These sincere gestures of hospitality haven't been entirely successful: congregation numbers continue to slide. Nor have attempts to liberalise alongside an increasingly liberal, secular nation. Efforts, for example, to be more tolerant of homosexuality have infuriated the traditional wing, while liberals have been angered that the Church has not gone far enough, especially now that the state has legalised same-sex marriage. Women priests and bishops now seem the norm for most members of the Church of England, but still a small faction continues to be offered pastoral care by so-called flying bishops, again infuriating those who want further progress, while feminists outside the Church find it objectionable and sometimes laughable. Pleasing all of the people all of the time has proved impossible; the *via media* of the Church of England in the late twentieth and twenty-first centuries has been at times a *via dolorosa*.

In the twenty-first century, then, what does an established Church headed by the monarch stand for, and can it continue? While the Church of England is undeniably in decline in terms of observance and attendance, it is still seamlessly woven into the life of the nation. Richard Harries, the retired Bishop of Oxford who is known for his liberal views, is nevertheless an advocate for Establishment. In 2003 he gave a lecture on Church and state at St Bride's, Fleet Street, pointing out signs of Establishment: the Church of England's involvement in civic ceremonies, prayers said before Parliamentary sessions, the appointment of bishops to the House of Lords. It gave the Church a bigger voice in society; people listened when bishops had something to say.

That seems to put the Church on the side of officialdom and convention, but in recent times the Church's influence – and in this the Church of England is not alone, but is joined by other denominations and other faiths – is felt by most people, not because of what it does in the House of Lords but by its activities within the parish and at the grassroots. The National Churches Trust 2020 report, 'The House of Good', identified that churches generate at least £12.4 billion a year of social and economic value.[13]

This is the social gospel writ large, something that has long been associated with the Church of England. But it is not exclusive to it. The Roman Catholic Church, for example, has a plethora of charitable organisations serving the homeless, the sick, young people, old people, those with disabilities, prisoners, seamen and more. Opposition to the Church of Rome was once the very reason for the Church of England's existence, and it was banished from these shores, finally returning after emancipation in 1829. It now matches the Church of England in philanthropy and beats it in the numbers games of Sunday church attendance. It now seems outlandish, therefore, that part of the Church of England's *raison d'être* should be to keep Romish ways at bay. When Elizabeth II, as Supreme Governor, swore to uphold the Protestant religion when she acceded to the throne, this certainly did not include holding her nose when it came to Roman Catholicism. She visited popes in Rome and welcomed them to Britain; she invited Archbishops of Westminster to stay with her. Above all, her subjects included loyal Roman Catholics – and Methodists, Muslims, Jews, Sikhs, Buddhists, a cornucopia of religious adherents and a sizeable population of non-believers. This is the Britain that the new Supreme Governor, Charles III, is concerned about and spoke about soon after his accession (as recounted in chapter nine).

As head of the Commonwealth, the Queen was aware, perhaps long before many of her politicians, of the plethora of religions to which those who called her Queen belong. She met those varied believers across Africa, in Asia and in the Indian subcontinent. As the decades of her reign wore on, she met them too in Birmingham, Manchester, Leeds and many other towns and cities where migrant communities live. As Supreme Governor of the Church of England – of the denomination that oversaw her crowning and therefore sacralised her standing – but also as head of state, she came up with a rethink of what being the established Church means.

'The concept of our established Church is occasionally misunderstood and, I believe, commonly under-appreciated,' she told a multi-faith gathering at Lambeth Palace in 2012, the first event to mark her Diamond Jubilee. 'Its role is not to defend Anglicanism to the exclusion of other religions. Instead the Church has a duty to protect the free practice of all faiths in this country . . . Woven into the fabric of this country, the Church has helped to build a better society.'

If the Church has helped to build a better society – and there is much evidence that it has done so, thanks to the contribution at parish level – then few seem to believe that is because of its established status. Giles Fraser, the Anglican priest and commentator, has criticised the Establishment for making the Church of England complacent and has said that it needs to transform its Christian message: 'We've been turned into flunkies of the Establishment, seduced by pomp and circumstance. Disestablishment would require the C of E to reinvent itself. We need to be less concerned with those in power, and more concerned with the poor and marginalized. We need to exercise influence, not executive power; be radical, not pull our punches.'[14]

The representatives of other faiths at the Lambeth gathering liked her words. Rowan Williams, then Archbishop of Canterbury, had given them the nod in the dialogue between Buckingham Palace and Lambeth prior to the event.

Reform Rabbi Jonathan Romain said that Jewish people and those of many faiths and none used to listen attentively to Elizabeth II 'because she was our Queen, as much as anybody else's. It was still a powerful message because she was a unifying force.'[15]

In 2003, at the start of Williams' tenure at Lambeth, a polemic against the Establishment of the Church of England by Theo Hobson was published. Its cartoon cover showed Elizabeth II with Williams on a lead. But rather than depict the Welsh-born Archbishop as a Welsh corgi – curious, snappy, burrowing away – he was a smiley poodle.

This was a curious choice: after all, the Archbishop of Canterbury's role is not to submissively do the bidding of the finger-wagging monarch and Supreme Governor. The role of Supreme Governor does not include the spiritual sphere – this belongs to the Church's prelates, once appointed. It is they who administer the sacraments and preach the word – although Elizabeth II's increasing role as an advocate for the Christian faith has been noted in this volume.[16] The classic apologist for the sixteenth-century settlement of the Church of England, Richard Hooker, made it clear that there was a distinction to be made between the monarch being directly responsible for spiritual welfare and ensuring that those needs are catered for by the Church which the monarch empowers. It was 'a gross error,' said Hooker, 'to think that regal power ought to serve for the good of the body, and not for the soul,' as if, he so memorably put it, 'God has ordained kings for no other end and purpose but only to fat up men like hogs.'[17] But this regal power serves the soul, he advised, by ensuring the Church performs its spiritual tasks properly.

That cartoon of Williams and the Queen hardly reflected the character of the two individuals. Williams at one time was someone who questioned Establishment, and when he was Archbishop of the disestablished Church in Wales, he said that the role of Supreme Governor 'had outlived its usefulness'.

In 1998, when serving in that role, he wrote, 'If there is a case for the Church's Establishment it must be cast in terms of the Church's witness to a community without boundaries other than Christ – not the Church's guardianship of the Christian character of a nation (which so easily becomes the Church's endorsement of the de facto structures and constraints of the life of a sovereign state).' And he went on to warn that Establishment could be seen as 'privileging one of a number of religious groupings within the state'.[18]

That was the issue that the Supreme Governor seemed particularly aware of in her Lambeth Palace speech.

Her desire to break away from the privileging also became apparent in her comments to the Opening of the eleventh General Synod in 2021, delivered by Prince Edward owing to her absence caused by illness, which urged reconciliation. 'St Paul reminded us that all Christians are entrusted with the ministry of reconciliation,' she wrote, and praised ecumenism.

Critics of the monarchy, however, do not seek reconciliation.

The monarch's position as a religious head of state has been criticised by secular organisations, including the National Secular Society.

Its president, Keith Porteous Wood, says, 'The position of the head of state should not be reserved for members of one particular faith. The British monarch's coronation reinforces the privileged position of the Church of England and risks alienating the non-Christian and non-religious majority.'[19]

According to the current Archbishop of Canterbury, Justin Welby, disestablishment would not be a disaster – 'Nothing's a disaster with God' – but removing privileges of the Church of England should be 'a decision for parliament and people'. Separating Church and state would be, he said, 'a complicated process'.[20]

Rowan Williams, too, has talked about disestablishment involving 'a great deal of constitutional unscrambling',[21] and he wonders if there is much appetite for it. Another reason he is now disinclined to support it, he told the left-leaning *New Statesman*, is that the drive for disestablishment among politicians is to do with 'trying to push religion into the private sphere and that's the point where I think I'd be bloody-minded and say, well, not on that basis'.[22]

Others in the Church of England have proffered a more radical alternative. David Edwards, a former provost of Southwark Cathedral and a former leader writer for the *Church Times*, who shook up the Church of England by publishing John Robinson's million-selling *Honest to God*, suggested some years ago that the monarch might be called Senior Member of the Church of England. It would be a move akin to the relationship between the monarch in Sweden and the Lutheran Church of Sweden; in that country there is a separation between Church and state.[23] Such a change of title would suggest a connection, just as there is between the monarch and the Church of Scotland, of which they are a member but over which they have no jurisdiction, although they promise on accession to preserve it. Or a future monarch might consider, in a restructuring of the Church of England and the sovereign's role, being recognised as its patron, rather like the patronages of other charities by the monarch, providing a royal imprimatur which attracts others to it. The unscrambling, as Rowan Williams has put it, would be complicated, and fraught with legal difficulties. Those who passionately advocate change, such as the polemicist Theo Hobson, say that out of the Church of England's decline, and even disintegration, will come a new way: 'the *via media* is not the solution, but the space in which the new will emerge'.[24]

The current British set-up, when it comes to the place where religion and monarchy collide, is beset with anomalies. Not only is there an established Church to which the vast majority of people in the country feel little allegiance, or at best a nostalgic connection, but also its membership is now outnumbered by membership of the very institution – the Roman Catholic Church – it sought to replace in this country. And then there are the occasions on which the Church of England – the national Church of one of the four nations that make up Great Britain and Northern Ireland – acts as if it is the national Church of the entire United Kingdom. The majority of the occasions on which it does this are royal – funerals, including Prince Philip's and Queen Elizabeth's, and weddings, such as that of the Duke and Duchess of Cambridge in 2011 – but above all it takes this role as its own at coronations. This will become even more apparent – and bizarre – at the coming coronation, the first since devolution.

According to Alan Wilson, the Bishop of Buckingham, 'the great genius of the monarchy has been its capacity to adapt', during an era when 'the CofE has become more churchy and the state has become more secular'.[25]

What sort of coronation, then, will we have in 2023, when Charles III is crowned? Many people seem to believe that the rituals surrounding a coronation have never changed through the centuries, but history proves otherwise. These are not hand-me-downs but adaptations that can be used to express the spirit of the age as well as eternal verities.

So what might King Charles, who, after all, during his time as the longest-serving heir, indicated that changes need to be made, yet is also a lover of tradition, wish for? What influence might a declining Church of England bring to bear on such a ceremony, or indeed might a government, whether it be one that wishes to rule a country that stands for heritage and traditional values or one that advocates modernity and progress? It is the coronation – that era-defining moment – that I will now consider.

# 11

## *Vivat! Vivat! Vivat Rex!*
## The coronation of Charles III

THERE IS A lot at stake. The coronation of King Charles III on 6 May 2023 is being planned as an opportunity for national unity, a moment to confirm the British people's support for the monarchy, and a chance for Britain to assert itself on the world stage. Coronations have always been about endorsement, but the challenges this time are even greater. The coronation comes at a time of controversy over the Royal Family, following the scandal surrounding the Duke of York and his involvement with paedophile Jeffrey Epstein, and the soap opera of the fallout between Prince Harry and his wife and the King, the Queen Consort and the Prince and Princess of Wales, laid bare in Harry's memoir, *Spare*.[1] Then there is the position of the Queen Consort, who will be crowned alongside her husband. The former Camilla Parker-Bowles, once the third person in the failed marriage of Charles and Diana, is now far more accepted by the public, especially following her late mother-in-law's endorsement in her seventieth anniversary accession statement of February 2022, when she said it was her wish that her son and heir's wife be known as Queen Consort when he acceded to the throne. (She did not, however, state overtly that she wished Camilla to be crowned.)[2]

These various dramas may well cause people, as the coronation comes ever closer, to question what the monarchy is for and what it stands for. And they may also ask, in 2023, what has God got to do with it? The coronation will certainly place the Church of England well within the public spotlight – an institution that remains the established Church, yet its numbers of worshippers are dwindling, its beliefs on contemporary mores such as same-sex marriage are criticised, and even its own members are in revolt over its finances. There will be those who ask why it should have the key role in endorsing the monarch, while some secularists, opposed to religion in the public square, remain critical of the place of religion at all in the coronation. In November 2022, the National Secular Society wrote to Prime Minister Rishi Sunak to complain that the 'overwhelmingly Anglican' coronation would be 'deeply incongruent with the increasingly pluralist and secular society that is 21st century Britain'.[3]

Certainly, the King has listened to commentary about whether the coronation should be modernised or remain a traditional ceremony, while the government, keen to offer a message about Britain to the world through the event, has its own ideas. Given that Britain is the only European country with a monarchy that still has a coronation ceremony, cameras will certainly be turned towards Westminster Abbey on 6 May, for what will be a momentous occasion. Week by week, newspapers have been revealing titbits about it, including plans for major celebrations surrounding the actual coronation service.

But it is the religious ceremony itself that has the capacity to capture the public's imagination with its music, its liturgy, and its ceremonies unseen for seventy years. Simplifying it and supposedly making it more relevant to people today has its dangers. As the King's friend, Lord (Richard) Chartres, the former Bishop of London, put it, 'You don't want to Disneyfy it, but you do need drama.'[4] Much of that drama will be provided by the creation of what is always called at the time of a coronation the 'theatre' within Westminster Abbey, a raised area beneath the lantern where the coronation rites will be performed, and also the music that will be included – the King has been closely involved in choosing it. Among the music will be Handel's spine-tingling 'Zadok the Priest', heard at every coronation since George II's, and which more than any other composition suggests the solemnity and history of the coronation ceremony. There will also be twelve new compositions from contemporary composers, including Andrew Lloyd Webber, responsible for a coronation anthem, Patrick Doyle, with a coronation march, and Iain Farrington, with an organ work including coronation themes. Some choral music will be sung in Welsh, and there will be also Greek Orthodox chant, in tribute to

Prince Philip but also reflecting the King's love of orthodoxy (see chapter nine).

That the most important of the Crown Jewels to be used in the coronation, St Edward's Crown, needs to be altered for Charles' crowning is a suitable metaphor for the whole of the ceremony on 6 May, for there has been speculation for years about the extent to which Charles' coronation will be different from previous ones. Made of solid gold, permanently set with semi-precious jewels and based on the design of the original crown of St Edward the Confessor, the St Edward's Crown is only ever used once in a monarch's life, for the crowning ceremony that is the climax of the coronation. In December last year, it was removed from the Tower of London, where it is usually kept with the rest of the coronation regalia. Buckingham Palace announced that it had been sent off for modifications in advance of the coronation of King Charles III. This isn't surprising: the crown, at 5lbs, is remarkably heavy and may well need to be adjusted to be worn by a man in his seventies during the coronation. Although the crown was made to be used at coronations – after the original St Edward's Crown was melted down in 1649 during the republic of Oliver Cromwell, Charles II had this one made in 1661 – not all monarchs have used it because of its weight. The last former Prince of Wales to be crowned, Edward VII, was considered too weak to wear the heavy object after recovering from appendicitis at the time of his coronation.

The coronation service, like the crown, can be altered and modified on each occasion. Yes, the coronation is an ancient, traditional ceremony, but it is not set in stone. There have been changes over the years, from rearranging the order of service, to its length, and to the numbers attending. Some have been impossibly grand – that of George IV – and some much more humble – that of his brother, William IV.

Despite being seventy years ago, the last coronation – that of Charles' mother, Elizabeth II – looms large because of the extensive film footage that exists of it. It is easy now to assume that it was free of controversy and that it was steeped in tradition. But in its time it was controversial: the very thing that now suggests a ceremony hidebound by tradition – the footage – was a revolution, for the whole thing was televised after a power struggle between the Duke of Edinburgh, charged by his wife to organise it, and the Establishment. Debate also surrounded the role of the Duke during the ceremony itself, and it was not always accepted that he should be the first peer to kneel before his wife and pay homage, nor were the words he used readily agreed upon.

One thing that was very different from today was that the Queen acceded to the throne unexpectedly and at a very young age, when her father suddenly died. As she was in her early twenties and had not been expected to become sovereign for another twenty to thirty years, speculation and planning about the next coronation had been minimal. But with Elizabeth II on the throne for seventy years, there has been plenty of time to plan the ceremony of her successor.

Operation Golden Orb has been the codename for the coronation plans, worked on for decades by the then Prince of Wales' office at Clarence House, government representatives, Lambeth Palace and Westminster Abbey. But following the death of Elizabeth II, organisation revved up to another level. In the late autumn of 2022, the Duke of Norfolk, who, like his forebears, holds the title of Earl Marshal and so is responsible for organising the coronation, wrote to me of his role: 'I'm flat out already!'[5]

However dramatic this coronation will be, it is not likely to match the shock of 1953 when Britain and the world watched such a young woman take on the heavy burden of queenship. Three of Britain's longest-serving monarchs – Elizabeth I, Victoria and Elizabeth II – all communicated the sacrificial aspect of monarchy in a way that eludes male monarchs, not least through the garb used to dress them in – a simple white shift for the most intimate and sacred moment of anointing. While the thinking was that such a garment would suggest that the young Queen had divested herself of all earthly vanity as she stood before God, it also evoked something akin to virginal sacrifice and a suffering servant, like Isaiah's lamb led to the slaughter. And being young, these women's crownings also seemed to herald a new age, something different.

It clearly won't be the same with a man who has served for so many decades as Prince of Wales, waiting in the wings. Dr John Hall, former Dean of Westminster, who was involved in planning for Charles' coronation, likened the difference between his ceremony and that of his mother's as akin to a sacrament of initiation and one for a more mature Christian: 'The next coronation will be more like a confirmation, rather than the Queen's which was more like a baptism,' he said.[6]

The idea that there will be at least some changes or modifications was confirmed just a fortnight after the announcement about alterations to St Edward's Crown, when the Cabinet Office announced that it was seeking certain people to carry out particular tasks or roles at the coronation. This was a surprising announcement because it had been mooted for some time that this time the coronation would be simplified, with smaller roles disappearing, such as the holder of the royal glove. In 1953, an institution was set up, called the Court of Claims, which assessed people's right to carry out certain roles. However, this time round, the Cabinet Office announced, 'In line with His Majesty's wish for the event to be rooted in tradition but reflective of today, and in accordance with Government advice, a Coronation Claims Office has been created within the Cabinet Office to consider claims to perform an historic or ceremonial role.'[7]

While the announcement went on to explain that those who might be considered for the role would have to prove a connection with someone who had held the role at previous coronations, the statement's real importance was its confirmation that the King wanted a ceremony that was rooted in tradition while reflecting the present. Oliver Dowden, Chancellor of the Duchy of Lancaster, went even further: 'His Majesty The King's Coronation will be a momentous occasion in the history of our country. The new Coronation Claims Office will ensure we fulfil The King's wish that the ceremony is rooted in tradition and pageantry but also embraces the future.'[8]

A ceremony that reflects how the world is today and embraces the future – these ideals of the King were matched by the desires of the government. At its last Cabinet meeting before Christmas, about three weeks before the Claims Office announcement, the government discussed the coronation with the Prime Minister Rishi Sunak, who said it would be a 'unique moment for the country'. Number 10 also let it be known that Oliver Dowden had told ministers that the ceremony would be a 'moment of constitutional significance which will allow us to showcase the very best of the United Kingdom'.[9]

Ever since Queen Elizabeth's death there were claims that the new King's coronation would be a scaled-down ceremony, with journalists reporting Buckingham Palace sources as saying that he was mindful of the cost-of-living crisis and so thought a shorter, smaller service would be appropriate.

According to the source quoted, 'The King is very aware of the struggles felt by modern Britons so will see his wishes carried through that although his coronation ceremony should stay right and true to the long held traditions of the past, it should also be representative of a monarchy in a modern world.'

They added, 'The King has long been an advocate of a streamlined or slimmed down monarchy and this project could certainly be said to fit with his vision. He has already spoken of his wish to continue his mother's legacy and this includes continuing to recognise what the people are experiencing day by day.'[10]

But within three months, around the same time that the government was saying the coronation should be a showcase for Britain, newspapers had changed tack, saying the King refused to countenance a 'cut-price coronation'.

According to Victoria Ward, royal correspondent of *The Daily Telegraph*, the King wanted the coronation to be a showcase for the UK, and organisers had been persuaded of the ceremony's potential, given the extent to which the Queen's funeral had proved to be, in Ward's words, 'a great advertisement for Britain'.[11]

Certain characteristics of this coronation, then, have emerged: grandeur, pomp, colour, PR for brand UK. And while it might no longer be thought to be wise to make it 'cut-price', all the thinking is that it will be shorter than previous coronations and involve far fewer guests than ever before.

There is certainly no chance of Westminster Abbey hosting a coronation service with eight thousand people crammed into every nook and cranny, as happened in 1953. Health and safety regulations have put paid to that, and the numbers of people are expected to be up to three thousand, including people with roles to play, from clergy to choristers to cameramen, with guests numbering around two and a half thousand.

But as to its length: if a coronation is to include all the aspects of the ancient sacred service – retaining the tradition that the King is so keen to honour – then it cannot last less than an hour and probably will be close to at least an hour and a half.

Coronations have changed over the years, in mood, in order of service, in who is involved. But they always include three essentials: oath-taking, anointing and crowning. As earlier chapters have demonstrated, these various aspects of the coronation can be dated to the earliest recorded coronation in this country, that of Edgar in 973. After the oath-taking – the first of the three crucial elements – the anointing and the crowning take place within a service of Holy Communion. For the Constitution and the Crown, the oaths might be the essential part of the coronation service, but advocates of the religious character of the ceremony say that the anointing and the receiving of Communion matter most because they are the moments that bring the sovereign closest, symbolically, to God. To use the words of the old Penny Catechism of the Roman Catholic Church, anointing is a sacrament – an outward sign of inward grace, the grace needed to serve. The anointing is also the moment that connects the coronation with not just the crowned monarchs of Britain that have gone before but also with the ideas of kingship derived from Scripture, as the Archbishop of Canterbury intones the words 'as Solomon was anointed King by Zadok the priest and Nathan the prophet' – and the words are also heard set to Handel's music. The oil, placed on hands, breast and head, is used to make signs of the cross – a link to the kingship and sacrifice of Christ.

Although some oil left over from the 1953 coronation has been kept in Westminster Abbey, new oil has been made, with some of the olive oil used coming from the olive groves in Jerusalem where the King's grandmother, Princess Alice is buried (see chapter six for details of her life). The oil is perfumed with sesame, rose, jasmine, cinnamon, neroli, benzoin and amber and orange blossom and no animal products such as civet oil or ambergris were included as is traditional. It was consecrated at the Church of the Holy Sepulchre in Jerusalem by the city's Anglican Archbishop and the Orthodox Patriarch of Jerusalem – an historic ecumenical innovation.

Holy Communion, too, is another outward sign of inward grace, a confirmation of God's blessing bestowed. The idea that the timing could be cut and the service be made less religious – or, at least, less Anglican – by Communion being removed, has been rejected. The clergy of Westminster Abbey themselves have stressed they would consider the coronation meaningless if it were not within the context of a Communion service.[12] The Eucharist reflects the theme of service and sacrifice running through the coronation: that just as Christ sacrificed himself, so must a monarch follow his example of service. Like the current Chapter, previous Deans of the Abbey have been vehemently in favour of retaining Holy Communion. Wesley Carr, Dean from 1997 to 2006, said removing the Eucharist would be a massive break from history,[13] while his successor, Dr John Hall, told me, 'It would be a tragedy to remove it; it is a sacramental occasion.'[14]

In fact, removing it would have a precedent: James II, being a Roman Catholic when he was crowned, did not receive Communion during the Anglican service. That exception aside, Holy Communion has always been part of the coronation service, with the new monarch kneeling at the altar to receive the consecrated bread and wine from the Archbishop of Canterbury. The coronation chalices, patens and Last Supper altar dish, all kept with St Edward's Crown at the Tower of London, are testimony to the importance of the Eucharist within the ceremony.

The ceremony is above all an endorsement of the monarch from the highest possible level – that of God, and his representatives on earth, in this case the Church of England and its most senior prelates. Anointing the monarch is a sign of God's grace being given to help the monarch with their duties and their office. Rowan Williams, who was involved in planning discussions about the coronation during his time as Archbishop of Canterbury, was quite clear when he talked to me about the coronation ceremony: 'If you have a coronation, then, in the course of it, the monarch is anointed. That is the bottom line.'[15]

Next in order of importance within the ceremony – but actually the first key element to take place – are the oaths, the promises made by the monarch to uphold the laws of the United Kingdom.

Finally, in the order of the ceremony but also in importance, comes the crowning. Its lesser significance may surprise some, given it is the most visual sign of the monarch's majesty.

All these aspects have many purposes, but it should be remembered that they are not needed for a monarch to be recognised as sovereign. Edward VIII was never crowned, yet he was recognised as King from the moment his father, George V, died on 20 January 1936 until he abdicated on 11 December 1936. Charles III has been recognised as King since Elizabeth II breathed her last, and he was formally endorsed through the Accession Council and the proclamations around the country and the Commonwealth.

But the coronation imparts a particular message about monarchy – particularly through the orb and the crown, with their crosses atop them – that all earthly power bows down before a greater, divine power. Then there will be the moment, through the oaths, that Charles will vow to uphold British laws and the Protestant religion – in effect the status quo. Again, the message is about the monarch bowing down to greater powers – this time, of the people and of the Church.

Despite debate over the years as to whether the ceremony will be modernised, and the King's recent messages, imparted through his staff and government ministers, that he wants his coronation to embrace the present and the future, time has run out for truly significant and major changes.

One of the more anachronistic oaths, in a country with a sizeable Roman Catholic population and an even more sizeable agnostic and atheist one – not to mention members of other faiths – is the pledge to uphold the Protestant religion. The Constitution Unit, based at University College, London, has offered various proposals over the years for reworkings of the oaths. But going by the oath taken by the King on the day of the Accession Council, to preserve and maintain the Protestant religion in Scotland, the oaths at this coronation will be as they were in 1953.

Bob Morris, The Constitution Unit's leading expert on oaths, told me that there appears to be no appetite at all for changing the oaths made at the coronation. He said of the King, 'He has made it known in Anglican circles that he does not wish change.'

> Then there were the discussions held in the Lord Chancellor's Department in the early years of the last decade when they asked [Buckingham Palace] to look at the oaths. Michael Peat (principal private secretary to the then Prince of Wales) told them it was a waste of time; Charles is going to swear the oaths.[16]

With previous reigns, there has often been a much bigger gap between the accession of the new monarch and the coronation. Elizabeth II, for example, became Queen in February 1952 but her coronation was not held until sixteen months later in June 1953. So between accession and crowning, the oath under the Accession Declaration Act 1910 was taken at the State Opening of Parliament on 4 November 1952, well before her coronation. The wording is:

> I [monarch's name] do solemnly and sincerely in the presence of God profess, testify and declare that I am a faithful Protestant, and that I will, according to the true intent of the enactments which secure the protestant succession to the throne of my realm, uphold and maintain the said enactments to the best of my powers according to law.[17]

This oath is a reformulation of a previous oath which, by the start of the twentieth century, was deemed deeply offensive to Roman Catholics. Edward VII, who had several Catholic friends and was friendly to the Catholic Church to the extent that some maintain he converted on his deathbed (see chapter three), objected to the wording, but no change was enacted. His son George V also objected and threatened to not open Parliament if changes were not made. The Prime Minister, Herbert Asquith, was backed into a corner and, realising that it would do well to avoid alienating Irish nationalists at that time, relented. Out went the wording regarding rejection of the Roman Catholic Church's teaching on transubstantiation – the moment at the consecration of the bread and wine at Mass when they are believed to become the body and blood of Christ – as well as denunciation of 'adoration of the Virgin Mary or any other saint and the Sacrifice of the Mass, as they are now used in the Church of Rome' because they were 'superstitious and idolatrous'.

Now, even the mention of being a faithful Protestant might seem odd in the context of twenty-first-century Britain. When Charles III made his remarks to religious leaders at his faith reception in Buckingham Palace on 16 September, he used the softer term, 'I am a committed Anglican.' But there will no testing of the water regarding the King's role of protecting Protestantism before the coronation. The short amount of time between accession and the date set for the coronation, as well as the Government's legislative business, means that there will be no State Opening of Parliament until the autumn, well after the coronation in May, according to Baroness Morgan, speaking on BBC Radio 4 in January.[18] So the oath under the Accession Declaration Act will not precede the coronation.

If the oaths of the coronation follow the formats of 1937 (George VI) and 1953 (Elizabeth II) – and it is likely that they will, bar some tweaking – they will be like this:

> Archbishop of Canterbury: 'Sir, is your Majesty willing to take the Oath?'
>
> And the King answers, 'I am willing.'
>
> The Archbishop of Canterbury will then ask several questions in turn: 'Will you solemnly promise and swear to govern the Peoples of the United Kingdom of Great Britain and Northern Ireland, Canada, Australia, New Zealand, and of your Possessions and other Territories to any of them belonging or pertaining, according to their respective laws and customs?'
>
> King: 'I solemnly promise so to do.'
>
> Archbishop: 'Will you to your power cause Law and Justice, in Mercy, to be executed in all your judgements?'
>
> King: 'I will.'
>
> Archbishop: 'Will you to the utmost of your power maintain the Laws of God and the true profession of the Gospel?
>
> 'Will you to the utmost of your power maintain in the United Kingdom the Protestant Reformed Religion established by law?
>
> 'Will you maintain and preserve inviolably the settlement of the Church of England, and the doctrine, worship, discipline, and government thereof, as by law established in England?
>
> 'And will you preserve unto the Bishops and Clergy of England, and to the Churches there committed to their charge, all such rights and privileges, as by law do or shall appertain to them or any of them?'
>
> King: 'All this I promise to do.'

> Then the King will go to the altar and will kneel and lay his right hand on the Bible, saying, 'The things which I have here before promised, I will perform, and keep. So help me God.'

Then the King will kiss the Bible and sign the oath.

With this oath comes the statutory requirement for the monarch to be in communion with the Church of England, something that Charles undoubtedly is, and has gone out of his way to confirm since becoming King, with his address to the nation the night after his mother died and his remarks at his faith leaders' reception. But some will wonder about this promise to preserve inviolably the Church of England, arguing that it is broken as an established Church, with half of Britons saying they have no religion and the numbers belonging to non-Christian religions at 6 per cent. At the end of 2022, the 2021 Census results were published, showing for the first time that less than half the population described themselves as Christian (see chapter 10).[19]

Even thirty years ago there were murmurings from within the Church of England about its involvement in the coronation. Paul Bradshaw, an Anglican theologian, marked the fortieth anniversary of Elizabeth II's coronation by arguing that the oath needed to be amended so that it did not sound 'so exclusive of other Churches and faiths . . . is there not something rather distasteful about the spectacle of the Archbishop of Canterbury exacting a commitment from the monarch to secure the interests of the Church before proceeding to anoint him/her?'[20]

It concerns The Constitution Unit too, which argues that 'it seems odd that the longest part of the oath should be exclusively preoccupied with the preservation of the interests of the Church of England', as if 'religious approval of the monarch is conditional upon continued state support for a particular religious denomination'.[21] This issue seems even more pertinent when one considers that the Church of England is the national Church of England and not Scotland, Wales and Northern Ireland, and yet will play a key role in the coronation of a monarch of all the nations.

But there is precedent for a change. When the last king, George VI, was crowned, he promised in Westminster Abbey to maintain the

Protestant Reformed Religion, but in the dominions he promised to uphold the Gospel of whatever Communion they adhered to.[22] This indicates that King Charles could somehow, during the coronation, promise to protect different denominations and other faiths – confirming what he pledged to do at his faith reception.

Should the King and his advisers – and those involved in planning the coronation including the government, the Church of England, Buckingham Palace and the Earl Marshal – have a late change of heart, they might consider The Constitution Unit's alternative oath: 'Will you to your power maintain tolerance and freedom, including religious tolerance, and will you seek to uphold the rights of all your peoples to observe their different religions and beliefs without fear or persecution?'[23]

This certainly would chime with the sentiments expressed by the King at his faith leaders' reception in September 2022. But what seems much more likely is that the old oath will be used – matching his desire for tradition – and contemporary Britain will be reflected in the ecumenical and interfaith guests who will be invited not only to attend the coronation but also to participate in some way. This will no doubt be acceptable to the Church of England and to the Dean and Chapter of Westminster Abbey, given the ecumenical events they have frequently hosted[24] and the annual Commonwealth Day services that have long had an interfaith character, supported by Elizabeth II and her heir, the then Prince of Wales, and other members of the Royal Family. However, the involvement of other faiths will be limited: Church of England canon law does not allow joint prayer with other faiths. Westminster Abbey as a royal peculiar, has more flexibility for interfaith engagement in its Commonwealth Day services but at the coronation, the Archbishop of Canterbury is in charge of liturgy, so is more restricted.

While the roles of others might be limited, it does not mean that they will be ineffective. That was apparent during the funeral of Queen Elizabeth, where leaders of other denominations were involved in saying prayers and representatives of other faiths participated in the procession. It was even more apparent during the services of reflection held at cathedrals in Edinburgh, Cardiff and Belfast during the days of mourning for the Queen in September 2022 (see chapter seven). And given that the King is not just King of Great Britain and Northern Ireland but also of other realms and territories, it is likely that some of those involved in the liturgy of the coronation will be from the Commonwealth.

The impact on the coronation service of including for the first time a procession of additional Christian denominations and other faiths will add time to the proceedings, just when the common view appears to be that the coronation, if it follows the example of 1953's three hours, will be too long. Involving other denominations in the service, however, might not take more time: their representatives could easily be responsible for reading the Epistle and the Gospel. Even if prayers from previous coronations are not considered to work well as interfaith intercessions, the Cardiff service of reflection in September, with its interfaith contribution, showed that suitable prayers can be found.

Keeping the coronation shorter than on previous occasions will ultimately require the discarding of elements. The homage of peers of the realm, for example, could easily be cut.

What else might be excised from the service? One element that could be removed is the Investing of the Armills – or bracelets – and the Stole and the Robe – items of decoration and clothing in which the monarch is dressed before the crowning. A portrait of George VI, in his coronation robes, painted by Frank O. Salisbury and commissioned by the Prime Ministers of Canada, Australia, New Zealand and South Africa to commemorate the coronation of King George VI and Queen Elizabeth, shows him in a cope and stole of gold cloth. As previous monarchs before him, George wore garments more usually associated with clergy than monarchy, for on coronation day, the clothing worn by English monarchs over the years has been almost always ecclesiastical, symbolising a link between kingship and priesthood.

In January, it was reported that the King would not wear breeches at his coronation[25] – as his grandfather did – but the key issue here is not the type of trousers but the potential discarding of ecclesiastical clothing. Instead of the breeches, the King could wear a ceremonial uniform linked to his military and naval service. That might seem more modern and more acceptable to the public, but it introduces a new element into the coronation – a connection with the martial world. It seems unlikely that a robe akin to a cope would be placed on top of military uniform, so the decision to wear the dress of, say, an admiral, would surely require a break in the service if the King were to then wear more priestly garments at one point.

Of far more significance is the fact that the 2023 ceremony will differ distinctly from 1953 and mirror instead that of 1937 in one key element: it will include a second anointing and crowning, that of Camilla, the Queen Consort. The acceptance of her as Consort owes much to her late mother-in-law, Elizabeth II, and her seventieth anniversary accession statement about her wish for Camilla to be Queen Consort. Certainly the country has moved a long way in a few years: in 2017 the *Daily Mirror* ran the headline 'Everyone relax – this is why Camilla may never become Queen',[26] regarding the controversy over whether her civil marriage to Charles was lawful (see chapter eight). There is certainly no constitutional requirement that a king's consort should be crowned. Charles I's Catholic Queen, Henrietta Maria, declined to participate in the Anglican coronation, while George IV had his estranged wife, Caroline, barred from Westminster Abbey. But the acceptance of Camilla by the public, despite the claims of her stepson, Prince Harry, that she had gone after the Crown, and the thinking of growing numbers of senior clergy that not including her in the coronation would be bizarre, has meant there is no question now of her not having a crown placed upon her head.

But there will be more to Camilla's involvement than a crowning. If this coronation follows the pattern of 1937, after the oath-taking, anointing, crowning and inthroning of her husband, Camilla will not only be crowned but also anointed.[27]

Her two ceremonies will take place before the altar of the Abbey, and will likely begin with this prayer, or similar words:

> Almighty God, the fountain of all goodness: Give ear, we beseech you, to our prayers, and multiply your blessings upon this your servant, Camilla, whom in your Name, with all humble devotion, we consecrate our Queen; Defend her evermore from all dangers, ghostly and bodily; Make her a great example of virtue and piety, and a blessing to the kingdom; through Christ our Lord, who

lives and reigns with you, Father, in the unity of the Holy Spirit, world without end. Amen.

As with that of the King, the anointing ceremony, where the Queen Consort is anointed and blessed with holy oil, is considered the most sacred moment of all. Once it is completed, the Queen Consort will receive a ring (as the monarch does during a coronation) as a sign of the bond of faith, and then she will be crowned.

This will not be the first time that a church congregation and a TV audience will have seen Camilla kneeling before an altar. She did so, together with her new husband, Charles, during the church blessing of their marriage, held at St George's Chapel, Windsor, in 2005.

While Charles' faith and interest in religion has been well documented, Camilla's has not. Her first marriage to Andrew Parker-Bowles took place in a Catholic church and their two children were raised as Catholics (see chapter eight), and while she was happy with that arrangement, Camilla considered herself a communicant member of the Church of England. I am told that as she has grown older, faith has become more important to her, and that during difficult times, such as controversies over her relationship with the King, somehow her faith has got her through.[28]

Crowns used for Queen Consorts have often included some of the most expensive jewels in the royal collection.[29] Among them is the Koh-i-Noor diamond, mined in the Golconda diamond mines of southeast India. It passed from Indian rulers to the Persian ruler Nadir Shah when he sacked Delhi in 1739. When he first saw it, Shah exclaimed that it was Koh-i-Noor, meaning a mountain of light. It passed through various owners, then returned to India before being acquired by the British as part of the treaty signed to end the Anglo–Sikh Wars in 1849, and it was agreed that it would be handed to Queen Victoria. At the time it was the centrepiece of an armlet, but Victoria had it removed and wore it within a brooch. Upon her death, the Koh-i-Noor, cut as a cushion-shaped brilliant of 105.6 carats, was set in the coronation crown of Queen Consort Alexandra in 1902. It was reset again for the crown of Queen Mary in 1911 and then used to adorn the crown of Queen Elizabeth in 1937.

Other major pieces in the Crown Jewels collection which adorn items to be used in the coronation are St Edward's Sapphire, once believed to have been in the saint's ring, and the Black Prince's Ruby (which is actually a semi-precious balas), both set in the Imperial State Crown, which the King will wear later in the proceedings, although it is not used for crowning – the St Edward's Crown is used for that purpose.

Additional important stones used in the Crown Jewels are cut from the Cullinan Diamond which, when mined in the Transvaal colony of South Africa in 1905, was the biggest ever found. The diamond known as Cullinan I (530.2 carats) was inserted into the Sovereign's sceptre on the order of George V in 1910, and Cullinan II (317.4 carats) was set in the front band of the Imperial State Crown – the two of them the largest flawless cut white diamonds in the world. But, like the Koh-i-Noor, the Cullinan is now linked to colonialism. Using items in the coronation associated with Britain's imperial past, and its rule and military occupation of parts of Africa and India, may well seem inappropriate, however keen the coronation organisers are for a show-stopper coronation. The spoils of colonialism surely do not pass the modernity test and so Camilla will be crowned with Queen Mary's crown, used when she was crowned alongside her husband George V in 1911, but without the Koh-i-Noor diamond. Yet some of the Cullinan diamonds will be used despite their colonial heritage. Using an old crown has been portrayed by Buckingham Palace as 'in the interests of sustainability and efficiency' - yet it will hardly make the new Queen Consort a second hand rose. Queen Mary's crown, with Cullinan diamonds, is serious bling.

Another potentially contentious issue could be the use of the Stone of Scone. Otherwise known as the Stone of Destiny, the twenty-four-stone oblong block of pink buff sandstone is an ancient symbol of Scotland's monarchy and was used in ceremonies marking the inauguration of the country's new kings. In 1296, Edward I of England – the same king who conquered Wales and created the title of Prince of Wales for his own son, much to Welsh fury – seized the stone from the Scots and transferred it to London, where it was built into a throne for English monarchs. It has been used ever since in the coronations of first English and later British monarchs.

The stone was taken from Westminster Abbey on Christmas Day

1950 by four Scottish students, who made off with it in a Ford Anglia. They were dismayed when it broke in half, but this was owing to the impact of a bomb that had been planted by suffragettes in the Abbey in 1914 and damaged it. The stone was later found on the altar of Arbroath Abbey in April 1951, and returned to Westminster Abbey and repaired. In 1996, seven hundred years after it was first taken from the Scots, the British Government decided to hand it back to Scotland. There, the Commissioners for the Keeping of the Regalia, who are also responsible for the Scottish Crown Jewels, are entrusted with it, and it is kept in the Crown Room at Edinburgh Castle. Some Scottish nationalists, including former Scottish National Party leader, Alex Salmond, say the Stone should not be handed over for the coronation in protest at Scotland being denied another independence referendum – making the Stone a sort of giant bargaining chip.[30]

These possible controversies highlight how much of a balancing act is involved in creating a spectacular, traditional service, yet one that reflects diverse twenty-first-century Britain. Not keeping the coronation as long as before seems a no-brainer, yet to cut it too short, as one senior cleric commented, is risky. 'The danger,' he said, 'is that you strangulate it.'[31] Then there are the decisions to be made about what should go and what should stay; if tradition seems to offer a sense of timelessness, then the decision is probably to keep it, but if it seems anachronistic, then cut it. Rowan Williams, who was party to the discussions on the coronation during his time as Archbishop of Canterbury, told me that 'the Gilbert and Sullivan elements will go' – think of those acres upon acres of aristocracy in their ermine attire, although gold copes of the clergy are likely to still be on show.[32] In an effort to modernise further, the guest list is unlikely to even have many MPs, but instead will include more representatives of charities whose patrons are the King and other members of the Royal Family.

Modernity will be part and parcel of the events surrounding the coronation. In January, it was announced that the ceremony will take place during a whole weekend of celebration that will include a laser and drone lightshow, a concert at Windsor Castle with global stars, and a coronation choir drawn from members of other choirs including ones for NHS workers, refugees, and LGBTQ+.

Will these events, though, satisfy people who feel that the religious ceremony of the coronation is too distant from them, unconnected from their lives? Some of those who have clamoured for a more secular celebration of the new monarchy might not be satisfied by the inclusion of a laser lightshow but by something more solemn.

For King Charles, his advisers, the Church of England and the government, the difficulty is that there is little else in the world to offer inspiration and alternative ideas. The remaining European monarchs do not have coronations. The one place that comes close to a Western coronation is Japan, and in 2019 the then Prince Charles attended the enthronement of its new emperor, Naruhito. Like the British coronation, the Japanese enthronement is an ancient ceremony – the same family has held the Chrysanthemum Throne for fifteen hundred years. The Japanese emperor also retains strong connections to the Shinto religion; some Japanese still claim that he is a god; others that he is the symbol of the nation.

As with Britain, Japan holds three ceremonies for its new monarch; two immediately after accession and the third months later, to allow plenty of time for planning. The first usually takes place immediately after the death of the previous emperor, but Naruhito's father, Akihito, abdicated, following a special law being passed to enable this to happen. It consists of a special ceremony acknowledging the accession, and then is followed by the new Emperor meeting political leaders and citizens' representatives – somewhat akin to the new British monarch meeting the Accession Council.

It is the enthronement which is the most spectacular occasion, and Naruhito's attracted royalty from around the globe, as well as dignitaries and diplomats from 183 countries. What may well have intrigued Prince Charles and given him some ideas for his own coronation was that the enthronement effectively consisted of two ceremonies, a more secular one and a religious one.

The first was a series of ancient rituals known as Sokuirei-Seidenno-gi. They took place in the Matsu-no-Ma state room at the Imperial Palace, where the Emperor, clothed in a traditional rust-coloured robe, stood on the twenty-one-foot Takamikura throne. Naruhito, who also wore a black headdress decorated with an upright tail, appeared as a pair of black-robed chamberlains opened the purple curtains of the throne at the sound of a bell. His wife Masako stood nearby, on a shorter throne, where she was wearing a multi-layered kimono as tradition also dictates.

Naruhito made his oath as he stood inside the Imperial Throne:

> I hereby swear that I will act according to the constitution and fulfil my responsibility as the symbol of the state and of the unity of the people of Japan, while always praying for the happiness of the people and the peace of the world as I always stand with the people.

A sword and a jewel – two of the three items that symbolise the Imperial status – were placed on a table close to him.

His pledges were followed by a speech of congratulation by the Prime Minister, Shinzo Abe, and 'banzai' cheers from the attendees, including Prince Charles.[33]

Then, a month later, came the highly religious ritual of the Grand Harvest. Known as the Daijosai, it is considered the most important ritual of the imperial succession and involves giving thanks, prayers and connection to the Imperial Family's ancestral gods.

Some aspects of the first stage of the Grand Harvest ritual bear comparison with the coronation's most sacred moments of anointing and Communion. It is held in private, just as previous British coronations have kept this sacred moment private; only certain assistants are privy to what happens to the Emperor, just as only a very few clergy are witness to the coronation anointing beneath the canopy. There are prayers in both rituals. There is Communion in the coronation ceremony using the traditional bread and wine of the Anglican Eucharist, and in the Japanese one the Emperor partakes in a communion of offerings of rice, sake, vegetables and seafood, used to honour the harvest.[34]

A major similarity between the Japanese ceremony and the British coronation is that it is funded by the state and, despite some debate as to whether it should be, the Japanese government insists that it is important to keep backing it because it is an important succession for the hereditary monarchy, written in the constitution, and so serves the public interest.

The then Prince of Wales' interest in the Japanese enthronement can be measured by who else was in Japan. The court circular for that day notes the Prince's presence and that his wife Camilla was meanwhile in Britain visiting a cheese farm. But I am told that also in Tokyo that day was one of the Prince's most trusted aides, Michael Fawcett. Fawcett, who began his royal career as the Prince's valet, was by the time of the Naruhito enthronement chief executive of The Prince's Foundation (from which he later resigned amid controversy over cash for honours) as well as running his own events company. One person, who has observed the Royal Family at close quarters for years, claimed, 'Fawcett was there because he was doing a recce, finding out how the Japanese did an event like that.'[35]

The Japanese model shows that in a modern country there is still space for tradition: if the coronation is a dramatic spectacle, it will appeal to a contemporary culture where the visual is all. The Japan experience also shows that two ceremonies, one religious, one secular, can co-exist. But if a secular ceremony were also to take place, such as transferring the first part of the coronation, what is called the Recognition, to Westminster Hall, it may well struggle to match what Westminster Abbey offers to people watching around the world. However much organisers want something for the twenty-first century that is shorter and simpler, the coronation surely needs to tug on the heartstrings by being a feast for the senses.

Television companies realised from the numbers around the globe who watched Elizabeth II's funeral and committal that there is an appetite for watching ceremonial. The government also knows the tremendous soft power of a royal occasion, and will want to repeat the opportunities – as the funeral offered – for receptions for international world leaders who will flock to London in May. It will want to use the occasion of the coronation to communicate what Britain is – a place of tradition – but also that it is not a failed power, living on its laurels, but a modern, multi-ethnic, multicultural country, forging a new post-Brexit, post-Elizabethan role.

But the toughest challenge of all will be: can the coronation, full of religious meaning, speak to a secular, cynical majority, weary of our nation's leaders and suspicious of extravagance – or at least a majority that is not so much cynical but sceptical. One way would be to help them find it more relatable by having a monarchy patterned less on power and more on justice, wisdom, sacrifice and humility – in other words, a biblical notion of kingship.

The coronation, then, is a moment when the country will consider values and meaning. According to Richard Chartres, there is a key element that should always be remembered about monarchy: 'the important thing about it is that it is there to cheer us up. It's also part of crafting our narrative'.[36] Roxanna Panufnik, one of the twelve composers commissioned to create new works, said: 'There has been a lot of discussions, to-ing and fro-ing about the music. Above all, we are committed to making this a truly joyful occasion'.[37]

In other words, the coronation needs a liturgy that affords structure, drama and meaning, and a moment when hearts and souls are lifted by voices calling: *Vivat! Vivat! Vivat Rex!*

# Conclusion

LIKE HER LONG-LIVED, long-reigning great-great grandmother, Queen Victoria, Elizabeth II was a sustaining symbol of Britain. Her being on the throne for seventy years gave the nation stability and a sense of what its values were: duty, stoicism, patriotism, service. As Lord (Richard) Chartres, the former Bishop of London, whom I quoted in chapter eleven of this book, put it, 'the monarchy is part of the crafting of narrative'.

Now that Queen Elizabeth is gone, what has been always bubbling away beneath the surface seems just that bit more evident. The country is far from what it was when she came to the throne seventy years ago: the death of deference – some might even go as far as to say respect – together with a decline in Anglican church attendance, a lost Empire and lost influence, uncertainty about Britain's place in the world, a country with a sometimes dizzying number of different cultures and religions are apparent. Yet among the upsides, there have been efforts, not entirely successful, to create a more equal society, with more opportunities for far more people. Women especially in the Elizabethan age made great advances. The increasingly disparate nation can still come together, whether united by hosting the Olympics or joining forces to combat Covid, or to stand in solidarity with another democratic nation, Ukraine, in its adversity. So how does the monarchy help craft the narrative in 2023?

If Queen Elizabeth's success in representing and symbolising the nation owed much to her longevity, then Charles III's years of service, as the longest-ever-serving Prince of Wales, should help him do the same. In that sense he is not burdened with convincing the public about who he is or his commitment: it is well known already. But there are other problems, other issues to tackle.

One is reassuring the nation that he follows in his mother's footsteps, something that the King focused on doing as soon as he acceded to the throne, praising her for her duty and aligning himself with that sense of public service. But, at the same time, things cannot stay the same, and people know that. So there have been hints that this monarch will be different, with his visits to different parts of Britain to take in smaller venues, such as the Aboyne Community Shed in Aberdeen or the JW3 community centre in north London, where he happily danced with the crowd and filled the boot of his car with donations for the centre's food bank. There will be plenty of pomp and circumstance in his reign – and it will be evident at his coronation – but the signs are there that there will more informality too.

Many of the more casual encounters so far have been with charitable organisations, and patronage of charities remains one of the monarchy's abiding purposes. The difficulty is whether there are enough members of the Royal Family to support the different organisations that have come to rely on royal endorsement. As Prince of Wales, the King was often referred to as wanting a slimmed-down monarchy when he acceded to the throne – and that is what he now has, even though he did not plan it.

The year 1986 can be described as Peak Royalty. Then, there were both the newlyweds and the old guard: the Queen; Prince Philip; the Queen Mother; Princess Margaret; as well as Charles and Diana, the Prince and Princess of Wales; Andrew and Sarah, the Duke and Duchess of York; Princess Anne and Prince Edward. There was also the solid, dependable second tier, with all of them, like the top tier, carrying out engagements: the Kents, the Gloucesters and Princess Alexandra. In all, fifteen members of the Royal Family were part of this postwar welfare monarchy, providing patronage and encouraging philanthropy for charitable concerns, as well as opening hospitals, schools and other public places.

Today, the number to carry out those same official duties has halved. So the duties have to be shared between the King and Queen Consort, the Prince and Princess of Wales, the Princess Royal, and Prince Edward and the Countess of Wessex. A slimmed-down monarchy will inevitably mean that it can no longer carry out the same number of engagements and support as many good causes.

This has greater implications than just patronage. As Dr Craig

Prescott, a constitutional expert on the monarchy, has pointed out, 'Retrenching to being a London-based monarchy goes against the tide when there are efforts to boost the rest of Britain. But that will happen without large numbers of royals. The problem is that monarchy does have a function as a point of unity and it can't be successful without being present.'[1]

Prescott's analysis is an academic version of what Elizabeth II used to say – that she had to be seen to be believed. One reason for the lack of numbers, making the presence less obvious, is the death of members of the Royal Family, and the old age of most of the second tier. But it is also owing to other members stepping aside from public life, notably the Duke of York and the Duke and Duchess of Sussex.

That move away from royal duties has caused a light to be shone on the House of Windsor and its family strife and turmoil. For a Royal Family that previously made the embodiment of stability and family values such a key part of its image and purpose, this forensic examination of dysfunction is a disaster. It also places even more burdens on the remaining royals to stand for reliability and domestic rectitude. In such a situation, the monarchy may have to retreat and make its focus tighter, on constitutional, ceremonial and religious roles, and its soft, diplomatic power at home and abroad. But even diplomacy might be contentious. The role of the King and the Royal Family will also be under the spotlight abroad as greater scrutiny takes place of Britain's connections with colonialism, so any visits they make, especially to Commonwealth countries, are likely to be tricky, as was the visit of the then Duke and Duchess of Cambridge, now the Prince and Princess of Wales, to Jamaica in March 2022.

Yet the signs are that the King and his heir, the Prince of Wales, and their wives are not yet going down the path of more narrow focus, with their mutual interest in social action, from mental health to domestic violence, and other concerns that might take them into more neuralgic issues for the government, such as dealing with climate change. Though the King indicated the day after his accession that he would no longer be involved in some of his causes of the past and that he would pass that baton on to Prince William, the visits that he has made around the country since becoming monarch have very much been about grass-roots projects.

Many of them in the early days of his reign were to faith organisations. While Elizabeth II was known for her deep Christian faith, her interest in interfaith dialogue was something that often went unrecognised by the general public. Her son has for many years been better known for his interest in other faiths, rather than his Christian beliefs. Yet, just as they did for his mother, for him the two go hand in hand. As the King's friend, Lord Chartres, put it, 'You can't support other faiths unless you are rooted in a faith yourself.'[2]

The Carolean era is, given the King's age – he is seventy-four – bound to be shorter than the Elizabethan one. Attention will inevitably turn to his son, William, and his wife, Catherine. William, in time, will succeed his father not only as King but also as Supreme Governor of the Church of England. Baptised as and raised an Anglican, confirmed at St George's Chapel, Windsor, by Lord Chartres in March 1997, William has yet to follow in his grandfather Philip's and father Charles' footsteps with cerebral musings in public on faith and spirituality. His connections with faith seem more practical, especially through his keen interest in The Passage, the Catholic organisation for homeless people, to which he was introduced by his mother, Diana, Princess of Wales, and which he has frequently visited. In 2019 he was named its royal patron and has been involved in serving meals and engaging with young people at its base in London's Victoria. In January this year he also spent time with Depaul UK, another Catholic charity that works with the homeless, praising it for its 'tailored, long-term support'.[3] A similar interest in faith in action took William and Catherine to Burnley, Lancashire, in September 2022 to meet Pastor Mick, a drug-dealer-turned-lifesaver, who runs the Church on the Street, which not only provides a space for prayer and worship but also helps people struggling to survive through its own food and clothes banks, and a private space where qualified counsellors provide much-needed mental health support.[4]

This, then, is a modern monarchy that is going out to the people, with royals who are not always dressed in their best, and where everything around them is not polished and sparkling, but where there is pain and difficulty too. In many ways it is a reworking for the modern age of the medieval idea of the monarch bringing healing – a royal touch that can make the difference. It is certainly something that William and Catherine believe is their responsibility. At their wedding, Lord Chartres, then the Bishop of London, read a prayer during his homily that the couple had composed:

> *God our Father, we thank you for our families; for the love that we share and for the joy of our marriage.*
>
> *In the busyness of each day keep our eyes fixed on what is real and important in life and help us to be generous with our time and love and energy.*
>
> *Strengthened by our union help us to serve and comfort those who suffer. We ask this in the Spirit of Jesus Christ. Amen.*[5]

While previous eras might have understood this pledge, it is not quite what the British have been used to in the last few decades. As the constitutional expert Professor Vernon Bogdanor said in a television documentary to mark the accession of King Charles, 'When the Queen came to the throne in 1952, we had a fairly mystical monarchy and in a survey around that time around a third of the people thought she had been chosen by God . . . people don't think that way now. They ask instead of every institution what use is it.'[6]

One of the biggest challenges for both the King and the Prince of Wales is to shape the monarchy in such a way that it is more than what some members of the Royal Family are tempted to make it become: a form of celebrity. Celebrity is faddish. People fall in and out of favour and fashion. The monarchy needs to be a constant, offering more than a style guide but reflecting the nation, perhaps helping it to believe in itself and what it stands for, beyond the confines of politics and being more than that utilitarian attitude of the public, that Bogdanor alludes to.

In her lifetime, Queen Elizabeth was described as the Servant Queen, a woman who interpreted her role through the prism of biblical ideas of the servant, especially Christ the Servant King. In a ceremony in 2015, to mark publication of the two-volume set of Prince Charles' speeches by two Welsh universities and the University of Maryland, Professor Medwin Hughes, vice-chancellor of the University of Wales and University of Wales Trinity Saint David, pinpointed something else. The Prince, he said, 'has placed the concept of stewardship at the heart of his commitment to service'.[7]

Stewardship is another theological idea, a creed that sees humanity as having a particular care and responsibility. There is not quite the humility of the servant, but the steward is prepared to step up, not for himself, but for others and for God.

Stewardship fits with the role that the four main principals of the Royal Family – Charles, Camilla, William and Catherine – seem to be carving for themselves with their particular interest in social action. It certainly takes them further away from the searchlight of celebrity that they find so intrusive, yet to which some members of their family have been attracted, like moths to a flame. And yet monarchy, if it is to survive, surely needs to be something more than worthy acts and speeches full of empathy, something less utilitarian.

It will be hard for the septuagenarian in his double-breasted suit to pull this off without the glamour of youth that his mother had in 1953 and his son William and his wife still retain for the moment. But it is possible. After all, this country has always got along with a combination of ancient and modern – an approach that seems to suit the philosophy and temperament of the new Defender of the Faith. Whether he has the wisdom – that gift he puts such store by – to bring the harmony he craves so much and speaks of so often, this disparate nation will soon find out.

Monarchy is not rational. If we were to invent Britain today, no family would be chosen for such an hereditary role. And yet, within a democratic constitutional system, it can work, if it still appeals to something deep within us, connecting us to our history, acting as a signpost to something greater, more meaningful, transcending the everyday. King Charles has understood that aspect of the human psyche, what he once called 'a sense of the sacred',[8] to be found deep down in the recesses of the heart.

That appetite for something almost indescribable, for something sublime, something mysterious, can be sated for some by the transcendence of music, for others through faith. If monarchy points to something greater than ourselves, then the key moment when it can do so is during a coronation. The government may have the reductive hope that it can help sell brand UK through the global, televisual arena, but it is also a ceremony that is about connecting with the past, understanding the present and thinking about the future. It may even point the way to God. It will certainly shape this country's narrative for years to come.

# *Acknowledgements*

I AM INDEBTED TO many people for their help with this book: for their conversation, advice, encouragement, suggestions and insights. Particular mention must go to Robert Hazell and Bob Morris of The Constitution Unit, to Lord Williams of Oystermouth – Rowan Williams, former Archbishop of Canterbury – and to the Very Rev. Dr John Hall, former Dean of Westminster, for their time and guidance over some particularly complicated matters.

I have also greatly benefited from conversations both recently and over the years with Professor Lord (Peter) Hennessy, Francis Campbell, Lord (Chris) Patten, Andrew Brown, Ruth Peacock, Richard Kay, Rev. Marcus Walker, Rev. Giles Fraser, Simon Sarmiento, Martin Palmer, Christopher Lamb, Brendan Walsh, Rabbi Jonathan Romain, Rev. Dr Jamie Hawkey, Richard Bailey, Nicholas Pyke, Edward Stourton, Robert Mendick, Rev. Lucy Winkett, the late Cardinal Cormac Murphy-O'Connor, the late Lord Camoys, Lord (Richard) Chartres, Geoffrey Lean, Bishop Kenneth Nowakowski, Zaki Cooper, Dr Hisham Hellyer, Father Dragos Herescu, Ernie Rea, Steve Richards, Nigel Baker, Sally Axworthy, Stephen Bates, Michael McCarthy, Chris Blackhurst, Keith Porteous Wood, Paul Clements, Ruth Hughes, Richard Palmer, Kate Mansey and Rhiannon Mills.

Some people who spoke to me would prefer not to be named but were enormously helpful, and their contributions have greatly benefited this volume. I am also indebted to Grahame Davies of the King's staff for guidance on sources, and to Simon Blundell, librarian of the Reform Club. The British Library is invaluable for any researcher, but having another rich collection of books in a place where you can read in great comfort and even take them home is even better, and Simon sourced many books for me, including some not on the club's shelves.

Particular thanks must also go to the team at Hodder Faith who have worked so hard to produce this revised edition of my original book in time for the coronation of King Charles III, including Jessica Lacey and Nicki Copeland, and especially to Andy Lyon, my commissioning editor, whose enthusiasm and encouragement never wavered. Nor did that of my husband, Kevin, whose support has been invaluable as I strove to meet yet another extremely taxing deadline. The pleasure in writing this book has been enormous, and I hope my delight and curiosity did not override attention to detail. Any errors remaining are mine.

# *Timeline*

| | |
|---|---|
| *April 1509* | *Henry VIII succeeds his father, Henry VII, as King, at the age of seventeen* |
| June 1509 | Henry marries Catherine of Aragon, widow of his elder brother, Arthur, Prince of Wales |
| *1516* | *Their daughter Mary is born* |
| 1519 | Henry writes *In Defence of the Seven Sacraments* as a riposte to Martin Luther |
| *1521* | *Pope Leo XI awards Henry the title of* Fidei Defensor, *Defender of the Faith* |
| 1527 | Church hearing held into Henry's marriage to Catherine and its legitimacy, given she was his brother's widow |
| *1531* | *Henry recognised in England as sole protector and Supreme Head of the Church of England* |
| January 1533 | Henry marries Anne Boleyn; their daughter Elizabeth is born in September |
| *1533* | *Pope Clement VII orders Henry to take Catherine back as his wife* |
| 1534 | Act of Royal Supremacy: declares Henry and his heirs as Supreme Head of the Church of England, replacing the pope |
| *1535* | *Oath of Supremacy – any person holding public office has to swear allegiance to Henry as Supreme Head of the Church of England; John Fisher and Thomas More refuse and are executed* |

| | |
|---|---|
| 1536 | Royal Injunctions Act – Henry instructs all parish churches to display William Tyndale's English translation of the Bible |
| *1543* | *All lessons in matins and evensongs have to be read in English* |
| 1547 | Henry is succeeded by his son, Edward VI, born in 1537 |
| *1549* | *Thomas Cranmer's Book of Common Prayer published* |
| 1553 | Mary succeeds Edward: the first Queen to reign in her own right. Restores Roman Catholicism |
| *1558* | *Mary succeeded by Elizabeth; Anglicanism restored* |
| 1559 | Act of Settlement: Monarch now described as Supreme Governor of the Church of England |
| *1570* | *Pope Pius V declares Elizabeth a heretic and excommunicates her. Any Catholic obeying her would also be excommunicated* |
| 1571 | Challenging the Queen's position as Head of the Church of England is declared treason |
| *1587* | *Execution of the Catholic Mary, Queen of Scots, perceived as a threat to the Protestant Elizabeth* |
| 1598–99 | James VI of Scotland, son of Mary, Queen of Scots but raised Protestant, writes his treatise on the divine right of kings |
| *1603* | *James VI of Scotland becomes James I of England* |
| 1605 | Gunpowder Plot of Guy Fawkes and fellow Catholic conspirators is thwarted |
| *1611* | *Authorised King James Version of the Bible is published* |
| 1626 | Succession of Charles I; his Catholic wife Henrietta Maria refuses to participate in the coronation |
| *1649–60* | *Execution of Charles I, followed by the Commonwealth interregnum; Anglicanism disestablished* |
| 1660 | Restoration of the monarchy; Anglicanism restored |

| | |
|---|---|
| *1661* | *Charles II crowned with new regalia, still in use today for coronations* |
| 1673 | Test Act bans Catholics from public office |
| *1678* | *Titus Oates' Popish Plot* |
| 1685 | James II, Catholic convert, inherits the throne |
| *1688–99* | *Glorious Revolution: James II deposed and flees to France; William of Orange, married to James' daughter Mary, lands in Britain* |
| 1689 | Parliament declares James II has abdicated; his daughter Mary and her husband William of Orange rule jointly; Bill of Rights bans Roman Catholics from the throne |
| *1701* | *Act of Settlement confirms the ban on a Catholic or anyone married to a Catholic succeeding to the throne; rules that without issue of William III and his successor Anne, the crown will go to Electress Sophia of Hanover and her Protestant descendants. Fifty Catholics with stronger claims excluded* |
| 1702 | Queen Anne succeeds William; at her coronation she declares that she rejects the Roman Catholic doctrine of transubstantiation |
| *1714* | *Anne dies with no surviving children; succeeded by Prince George of Hanover, son of Electress Sophia* |
| 1715 | Old Pretender James III, son of deposed James II, makes abortive attempt to claim his throne |
| *1727* | *Handel's 'Zadok the Priest' sung for the first time at the coronation of George II* |
| 1746 | Young Pretender Bonnie Prince Charlie, son of James III, defeated at Culloden as he attempts to claim the throne |
| *1772* | *George III pushes through the Royal Marriages Act to prevent any member of the Royal Family under twenty-five marrying without the monarch's permission* |

| | |
|---|---|
| 1778 | George III agrees to the Catholic Relief Act, allowing Catholics to join the army and acquire land if they swear an oath of allegiance; no longer punishable to be a Catholic priest |
| *1780* | *Gordon Riots – violent response to the Catholic Relief Act* |
| 1785 | Prince of Wales (born 1762, later George IV) marries in secret Maria Fitzherbert, a Catholic widow, breaking the terms of the Act of Settlement and the Royal Marriages Act |
| *1791* | *Catholic Relief Act allows freedom of worship* |
| 1795 | Prince of Wales marries Caroline of Brunswick |
| *1801* | *Act of Union comes into force, uniting Britain and Ireland* |
| 1820 | Death of George III; accession of George IV with his estranged wife Caroline banned from the coronation at Westminster Abbey |
| *1829* | *George IV, opposed to further Catholic freedoms, finally relents and signs the Catholic Relief Act* |
| 1830 | Waterloo Chamber decorated in Windsor Castle, with portraits of Britain's allies, including Pope Pius VII |
| *1830* | *William IV becomes King; his wife Queen Adelaide focuses on philanthropy – a new innovation* |
| 1837 | William IV succeeded by Victoria, aged eighteen. St Edward's Crown considered too heavy for her to wear at her coronation |
| *1850* | *Pius IX restores the Catholic hierarchy of England and Wales* |
| 1861 | Death of Prince Albert, after twenty-one years of marriage to Queen Victoria, leading to a cult of mourning |
| *1872* | *Service of thanksgiving at St Paul's Cathedral after the Prince of Wales recovers from typhoid* |

1874 Victoria supports the Public Worship Regulation Act, limiting Catholic practices in Anglican services

*1887 National service of thanksgiving for Victoria's Golden Jubilee*

1897 National service of thanksgiving for Victoria's Diamond Jubilee

*1902 Coronation of Edward VII, who succeeded Victoria in 1901. Repudiation of transubstantiation removed from the service*

1903 Edward makes a private visit to Pope Leo XIII

*1910 Edward visits the Catholic pilgrimage town of Lourdes; dies weeks later in London; continuing speculation that he made a deathbed conversion to Catholicism*

1932 First Christmas broadcast by a monarch; George V speaks to Britain and the Empire

*1932 George V reintroduces the custom of the monarchy distributing Maundy money*

1936 The year of three kings: death of George V; accession and abdication of Edward VIII; accession of George VI

*1936 Archbishop of Canterbury Cosmo Lang indicates that the Church of England cannot accept the marriage of Edward VIII to twice-divorced Wallis Simpson*

1937 George VI's coronation broadcast on the ministry of kingship

*1939 George VI's first wartime Christmas broadcast, quoting prayer*

1947 Princess Elizabeth makes her pledge to the Commonwealth and Britain with her 'God make good my vow' speech

*1947 Prince Philip of Greece leaves the Greek Orthodox Church and is received into the Church of England by the Archbishop of Canterbury in advance of his marriage to Princess Elizabeth*

1949 Marriage Act Confirms civil marriages for royals are banned

*1952* *Princess Elizabeth succeeds her father George VI as monarch and asks people – 'whatever your religion may be' – during her first Christmas broadcast to pray for her during her coronation*

1953 Coronation of Elizabeth II – the first to be televised

*1955* *Princess Margaret announces that she will not marry Peter Townsend, a divorcee, because of church teaching*

1961 Elizabeth II visits Pope John XXIII in Rome

*1962* *Founding of St George's House by Prince Philip and the Dean of Windsor, Robin Woods*

1963 Commonwealth Day service held for the first time in Westminster Abbey

*1965* *Commonwealth Day multi-faith services moves to the Guildhall but Queen later asks for it to return to the Abbey*

1969 Investiture of Prince Charles as Prince of Wales

*1970* *Creation of Church of England's General Synod; Queen addresses opening session every five years*

1980 Elizabeth II meets Pope John Paul II in Rome

*1981* *Marriage of Prince Charles to Lady Diana Spencer*

1982 John Paul II meets Elizabeth II at Buckingham Palace; the first time a British monarch meets a Pope in the United Kingdom

*1986* *Prince Philip invites faith leaders to an inter-faith event in Assisi to discuss the environment*

1992 Divorced Princess Anne marries again, in the Church of Scotland's Crathie Church; Charles and Diana separate

*1994* *Prince Charles announces in a TV documentary that he would prefer the title Defender of Faith to Defender of the Faith*

1995 Prince Philip founds the Alliance of Religions and Conservationists

*1996 Divorce of Prince Charles and Diana, Princess of Wales*

1997 Death of Diana, Princess of Wales

*2000 Elizabeth II talks about her personal faith in a Christmas Day Millennium broadcast*

2005 Prince of Wales marries Camilla Parker-Bowles in a register office ceremony; marriage blessed at St George's Chapel, Windsor

*2010 Elizabeth II and Prince Philip greet Pope Benedict XVI in Scotland at the start of his state visit to the UK*

2011 Marriage of Prince William, second in line to the throne, to Catherine Middleton

*2012 Elizabeth II marks her Diamond Jubilee with a major speech on the Church of England's role in Britain*

2013 Succession to the Crown Act, relaxing restrictions on royalty marrying Roman Catholics; monarch must still be an Anglican

*2014 Elizabeth II meets Pope Francis in Rome*

2015 Charles confirms he will use full Defender of the Faith title when King

*2018 Church of England allows full church wedding for Prince Harry and divorcee Meghan Markle in St George's Chapel, Windsor*

2021 Death of Prince Philip with his wife, Elizabeth II, photographed at his funeral, masked and alone owing to Covid restrictions

2022 6 February: Elizabeth II marks the seventieth anniversary of her accession to the throne with her hope that the Duchess of Cornwall will in time be Queen Consort

*2022* *14 April: Queen withdraws from Maundy Service owing to mobility issues; Prince of Wales instead distributes the traditional Maundy money on behalf of the monarch*

2022 2–5 June: Britain celebrates the Platinum Jubilee of Elizabeth II who appears for the last time on the balcony of Buckingham Palace

*2022* *8 September: Elizabeth II dies at Balmoral Castle; Charles III accedes to the throne*

2022 10 September: Accession Council and proclamation of King Charles III

*2022* *15 September: King meets faith leaders to pledge to be a protector of faiths*

2022 25 December: King's first Christmas message

*2023* *6 May: Coronation of King Charles III due to take place at Westminster Abbey*

# Bibliography

## Online sources

Elizabeth II's speeches and Christmas messages
www.royal.uk

The Prince of Wales' speeches
www.princeofwales.gov.uk

The King's Accession, Accession Council and Proclamation, recent speeches
www.royal.uk

The coronation service
www.oremus.org/liturgy/coronation/cor1953b.html

The coronation: history and ceremonial
David Torrance, House of Commons library 2023
www.commonslibrary.parliament.uk/research-briefings/cbp-9412/

The Constitution Unit
www.ucl.ac.uk/constitutionunit

Politico think tank
www.politico.eu

The Church of England
www.churchofengland.org

The Church of Scotland
www.churchofscotland.org.uk

The Vatican
www.vatican.va

Hansard: UK Parliament
hansard.parliament.uk

United Kingdom Legislation – The Act of Settlement 1700
www.bailii.org/uk/legis/num_act/1700/1565208.html

The Perth Agreement
en.wikipedia.org/wiki/Perth_Agreement#Published_content_of_the_official_announcement.2C_Perth.2C_October_2011

*The Times*
www.thetimes.co.uk

*The Times* archive
www.thetimes.co.uk/archive

BBC News
www.bbc.co.uk/news

*The Telegraph*
www.telegraph.co.uk

*The Independent*
www.independent.co.uk

*The Guardian*
www.theguardian.co.uk

*Daily Mail*
www.dailymail.co.uk

*Church Times*
www.churchtimes.co.uk

*The Tablet*
www.thetablet.co.uk

*L'Osservatore Romano*
www.vaticannews.va

Bradford *Telegraph and Argus*
www.thetelegraphandargus.co.uk

*Yorkshire Post*
www.yorkshirepost.co.uk

*The New York Times*
www.nytimes.com

*UnHerd*
www.unherd.com

Religion Media Centre
www.religionmediacentre.org.uk

*Prospect*
www.prospectmagazine.co.uk

*The Spectator*
www.spectator.co.uk

*The New Statesman*
www.newstatesman.com/uk

Archbishop Cranmer blog
archbishopcranmer.com

Westminster Abbey
www.westminster-abbey.org

St George's Chapel
www.stgeorges-windsor.org

*Irish Legal News*
www.irishlegal.com

The Sociological Review
thesociologicalreview.org

Enoch Powell life and views
www.enochpowell.net

The website of John Major
johnmajorarchive.org.uk

Alliance of Religions and Conservation
www.arcworld.org

Evangelical Alliance
www.eauk.org

Temenos Academy
www.temenosacademy.org

## *Printed sources*

Altrincham, Lord. *Is the Monarchy Perfect?* London: John Calder, 1958.

Aspinal, A. (ed.). *The Later Correspondence of George III: Volume two, 1783–1793*, Cambridge: Cambridge University Press, 1963.

Avis, Paul. *Church, State and Establishment*, London: SPCK, 2001.

Barnes, D. G., *George III and William Pitt, 1783–1806: A New Interpretation Based upon a Study of Their Unpublished Correspondence*, Stanford: Stanford University Press, 1939.

Bedell Smith, Sally. *Prince Charles: The Passions and Paradoxes of an Improbable Life*, London: Penguin Michael Joseph, 2017.

The Bible.

Bible Society. *The Servant Queen and the King She Serves*, London, 2016.

Bonney, Norman. *Monarchy, Religion and the State: Civil Religion in the United Kingdom, Canada, Australia and the Commonwealth*, Manchester: Manchester University Press, 2013.

Borg, Marcus J. and Crossan, John Dominic. *The Last Week LP: A Day-by-Day Account of Jesus's Final Week in Jerusalem*, London: HarperCollins, 2007.

Borman, Tracy. *Crown & Sceptre: A New History of the British Monarchy From William The Conqueror to Elizabeth II*, London: Hodder and Stoughton, 2021.

Bower, Tom. *Rebel Prince: The Power, Passion and Defiance of Prince Charles*, London: William Collins, 2018.

Bradley, Ian, *God Save The Queen: The Spiritual Heart of the Monarchy*, London: Continuum, 2021.

Brandreth, Gyles, *Elizabeth II: An Intimate Portrait*, London: Michael Joseph, 2022.

Bridgett, T. E. and Lennon, James, *Life of Blessed John Fisher: Bishop of Rochester, Cardinal of the Holy Roman Church, and Martyr Under Henry VIII*, London: Burns, Oates & Washburne, 1922.

Broughton, Lord, *Reflections of a Long Life, With Additional Extracts from his Private Diaries*, London: John Murray, 1909–11.

Bulloch, Rev. Charles, *Wedding Bells: Prince George and Princess May: With Glimpses of Royal Weddings*, London: Home Words, 1893.

Cannadine, David (ed.). *Westminster Abbey: A Church in History*, New Haven: Yale University Press, 2019.

Carpenter, Humphrey. *Robert Runcie: The Reluctant Archbishop*, London: Hodder and Stoughton, 1996.

Chadwick, Owen. *The Victorian Church Part Two: 1860–1901*, London: A&C Black, 1980.

Coggins, R. J. and Houlden, J. L., (eds). *A Dictionary of Biblical Interpretation*, London: SCM Press, 1990.

Colley, Linda. *Britons: Forging the Nation 1707–1837*, New Haven: Yale University Press, 2009.

Colville, John. *The Fringes of Power: Downing Street Diaries 1939–1955*, London: Hodder and Stoughton, 1985.

Davie, Martin. *A Guide to the Church of England*, London: Bloomsbury, 2019.

Dempster, Nigel. *HRH Princess Margaret, A Life Unfulfilled*, London: Quartet, 1981.

Dennison, Matthew. *The Queen*, London: Head of Zeus, 2021.

Dimbleby, Jonathan. *The Prince of Wales: A Biography*, London: Little Brown, 1995.

Doran, Susan (ed.) *Elizabeth and Mary: Royal Cousins, Rival Queens*, London: The British Library exhibition catalogue, 2021.

Eade, Philip. *Young Prince Philip: His Turbulent Early Life*, London: Harper Press, 2011.

Edel, Leon (ed.). *The Letters of Henry James, Volume 4, 1895–1916*, London: Macmillan, 1984.

Filby, Eliza. *God and Mrs Thatcher: The Battle for Britain's Soul*, London: Biteback Publishing, 2015.

Fisher, G. F., *I Here Present Unto You . . . Addresses Interpreting the Coronation of Her Majesty Queen Elizabeth II*, London: SPCK, 1953.

Fraser, Antonia. *The King and the Catholics: The Fight for Rights 1829*, London: Weidenfeld and Nicolson, 2018.

Gibson, Edgar C. S. *The Thirty Nine Articles of the Church of England*, sixth edition, London: Methuen, 1908.

Glenconner, Anne. *Lady in Waiting: My Extraordinary Life in the Shadow of the Crown*, London: Hodder, 2020.

Gwynn, Denis, *The Struggle for Catholic Emancipation, 1750–1829*, London: Longmans, 1928.

Hadlow, Janice. *The Strangest Family: The Private Lives of George III, Queen Charlotte and the Hanoverians*, London: William Collins, 2014.

Harris, Kenneth. *The Queen*, London: Weidenfeld and Nicolson, 1994.

Harry, Prince. *Spare*, London: Bantam, 2023.

Hartley, T. E. (ed.). *Proceedings in the Parliaments of Elizabeth I, Volume III: 1593–1601*, Leicester: Leicester University Press, 1981–95.

Hartnell, Norman. *Silver and Gold*, London: Evans Brothers, 1955.

Haynes, Samuel, *A Collection of State Papers Relating to Affairs in the Reigns of King Henry VIII, King Edward VI, Queen Mary, and Queen Elizabeth From the Year 1542 to 1570*. Left by William Cecil, Lord Burghley, at Hatfield House, London, 1740.

Hennessy, Peter. *Having It So Good: Britain in the Fifties*, London: Penguin Allen Lane, 2006.

Hibbert, Christopher. *King Mob: The Story of Lord George Gordon and the Riots of 1780*, London: Longmans, 1958.

Hobson, Theo. *Against Establishment: An Anglican Polemic*, London: Darton, Longman and Todd, 2003.

Hodder, Edwin. *The Life and Work of the 7th Earl of Shaftesbury, KG, Volume 2*, London: Cassell, 1886.

Howard, Anthony. *Basil Hume: The Monk Cardinal*, London: Headline, 2005.

*King James Bible*, London: Harper Perennial, 2004.

Kynaston, David. *Austerity Britain, 1945–51*, London: Bloomsbury, 2007.

Ledger-Lomas, Michael. *Queen Victoria: This Thorny Crown*, Oxford: Oxford University Press, 2021.

Lockhart, John Gilbert. *Cosmo Gordon Lang*, London: Hodder and Stoughton, 1949.

Longford, Elizabeth. *Elizabeth R: A Biography*, London: Weidenfeld and Nicolson, 1983.

Longford, Elizabeth. *Queen Victoria: Born to Succeed*, London: Harper, 1964.

McBride, Denis (ed.). *Your Sunday Missal*, Chawton, Hampshire: Redemptorist Publications, 2011, p. 693, with material copyright International Commission on English in the Liturgy Corporation.

MacCulloch, Diarmaid. *A History of Christianity: The First Three Thousand Years*, London: Allen Lane, 2009.

MacCulloch, Diarmaid. *Reformation: Europe's House Divided 1490–1700*, London: Penguin, 2004.

Martin, Kingsley. *The Magic of Monarchy*, London: Thomas Nelson, 1937.

Mayer, Catherine. *Charles: The Heart of a King*, London: Penguin Random House, 2022.

Morrah, Dermot. *Princess Elizabeth*, London: Odhams, 1947.

Morrah, Dermot. *To Be a King*, London: Hutchinson, 1968.

Murphy, Clare. The Crown Jewels Souvenir Guidebook, Historic Royal Palaces, 2018.

Murphy, Deirdre. *The Young Victoria*, New Haven: Yale University Press, 2019.

Murphy-O'Connor, Cormac. *An English Spring: Memoirs*, London: Bloomsbury, 2015.

Nicolson, Adam. *Power and Glory: Jacobean England and the Making of the King James Bible*, London: Harper Perennial, 2004.

Pepinster, Catherine. *The Keys and the Kingdom: The British and the Papacy from John Paul II to Francis*, London: T&T Clark, 2017.

Pimlott, Ben. *The Queen: A Portrait of Elizabeth II*, London: Harper Collins, 1996, 2001.

Plowden, Alison. *Caroline and Charlotte: Regency Scandals*, London, 2005.

Potter, John, Bishop of Oxford. 'A Sermon Preach'd at the Coronation of King George II', C. Ackers for R. Knaplick, London, 1727.

Prince of Wales, His Royal Highness, *Speeches and Articles, 1968–2012*, selected by David Cadman and Suheil Bushrui, Cardiff: University of Wales Press, 2014, in two volumes.

Prochaska, Frank. *Royal Bounty: The Making of a Welfare Monarchy*, New Haven: Yale University Press, 1995.

Quenell, Peter (ed.). *A Lonely Business: A Self-Portrait of James Pope-Hennessy*, London: Weidenfeld and Nicolson, 1981.

Quennell, Peter (ed.). *Memoirs of William Hickey*, Routledge and Kegan Paul, 1975.

Radzinsky, Edvard. *The Last Tsar: The Life and Death of Nicholas II*, London: Doubleday, 1992.

Rappaport, Helen. *Magnificent Obsession: Victoria, Albert and the Death That Changed the Monarchy*, London: Hutchinson, 2011.

Ridley, Jane. *Bertie: A Life of Edward VII*, London: Chatto and Windus, 2012.

Robinson, Brian. *The Royal Maundy*, London: Kaye and Ward, 1977.

Rose, Kenneth. *King George V*, London: Weidenfeld and Nicolson, 1983.

Royal Academy of Arts. *Charles I: King and Collector* catalogue, London: Royal Academy of Arts, 2018.

St John-Stevas, Norman (ed.). *The Collected Works of Walter Bagehot*, Volume V, London: *The Economist*, 1965–74.

Schama, Simon. *A History of Britain, Volume 2: The British Wars 1603–1776*, London: BBC, 2003.

Schillebeeckx, Edward. *Jesus: An Experiment in Christology*, New York: Seabury, 1979.

Sedgewick, Romney (ed.). *Letters from George III to Lord Bute, 1756–66*, London: Macmillan, 1939.

Seward, Ingrid. *My Husband and I: The Inside Story of the Royal Marriage*, London: Simon and Schuster, 2017.

Shlapentokh, Dmitry. *The French Revolution and the Russian Anti-Democratic Tradition: A Case of False Consciousness*, Transaction Publishers, 1997.

Skidmore, Chris. *Edward VI: The Lost King of England*, London: Weidenfeld and Nicolson, 2007.

Smith, E. A. *George IV*, New Haven: Yale University Press, 1999.

Starkey, David. *Crown and Country: A History of England through the Monarchy*, London: Harper Collins, 2011.

Starkey, David. *Elizabeth*, London: Vintage, 2001.

Starkey, David. *Monarchy*, London: Harper Perennial, 2007.

Stead, W. T. *Her Majesty The Queen: Studies of the Sovereign and the Reign*, London: Review of Reviews Office, 1897.

Streitberger, W. R. *Court Revels 1485–1559*, Buffalo: University of Toronto Press, 1994.

Strong, Roy. *Coronation: From the 8th to the 21st Century*, London: Harper Perennial, 2006.

Stuart, C. *The Reith Diaries*, London: Collins, 1975.

Talbot, William, Bishop of Oxford, 'A Sermon Preach'd at the Coronation of King George I', W. Wilkins for John Church, London, 1714.

Townsend, Peter. *Time and Chance*, London: William Collins and Son, 1978.

Tremlett, Giles. *Catherine of Aragon: Henry's Spanish Queen*, London: Faber and Faber, 2010.

Vickers, Hugo. *Alice: Princess Andrew of Greece*, London: Hamish Hamilton, 2000.

Weir, Alison. *Elizabeth of York: The First Tudor Queen*, London: Jonathan Cape, 2013.

Weir, Alison. *The Life of Elizabeth I*, New York: Ballantine, 1998.

Windsor, Duke of. *A King's Story: The Memoirs of HRH the Duke of Windsor, KG*, Cassell & Co, 1951.

Whitelock, Anna. *Mary Tudor: England's First Queen*, London: Bloomsbury, 2009.

Worden, Blair. *The English Civil Wars, 1640–1660*, London: Weidenfeld and Nicolson, 2009.

Ziegler, Philip. *King Edward VIII: The Official Biography*, London: Collins, 1990.

Ziegler, Philip. *King William IV*, London: Harper and Row, 1971.

# Notes

## Introduction

1. His Majesty The King's Declaration, 10 September 2022, www.royal.uk/his-majesty-kings-declaration (accessed 21 January 2023).
2. Geoffrey Fisher, *I Here Present Unto You: Six Addresses Interpreting the Coronation of Her Majesty Queen Elizabeth II* (London: SPCK, 1953), pp. 15–29.
3. Interview with the author.
4. Norman St John-Stevas (ed.), *The Collected Works of Walter Bagehot*, Volume V (London: The Economist, 1965–74), p. 235 .
5. Queen Victoria in a letter to Lady Waterpark, from the diaries of Lady Waterpark, quoted by Michael Ledger-Lomas, *Queen Victoria: This Thorny Crown* (Oxford: Oxford University Press, 2021), p. 111.
6. Kenneth Harris, *The Queen* (London: Weidenfeld and Nicolson, 1994), p. 373.
7. Frank Prochaska, *Royal Bounty: The Making of a Welfare Monarchy* (New Haven: Tale University Press, 1995).

## 1 *When Zadok the Priest anointed Solomon King*

1. Matthew 19:24.
2. Philippians 2:7.
3. Zechariah 9:9.
4. Psalm 72:1–2.
5. 2 Samuel 5:2.
6. 2 Samuel 7:12–13.
7. 1 Kings 3:1–15.
8. Wisdom of Solomon 6:24.

9. Exodus 29:7–8; Leviticus 8:10–12.
10. 1 Samuel 10:1.
11. 1 Samuel 16:13.
12. For a full account of the ancient English coronations, see Roy Strong, *Coronation: From the 8th to the 21st Century* (London: Harper Perennial, 2006).
13. Strong, *Coronation*, p. 5.
14. John Eaton, 'Kingship', in R. J. Coggins and J. L. Houlden (eds), *A Dictionary of Biblical Interpretation* (London: SCM Press, 1990), p. 381.
15. See 1 Kings 10 and 2 Chronicles 9.
16. John 1:45–50.
17. Mark 11:10; Luke 19:38.
18. Edward Schillebeeckx, *Jesus: An Experiment in Christology* (New York: Seabury, 1979).
19. Matthew 21:1–11.
20. Marcus J. Borg and John Dominic Crossan, *The Last Week LP: A Day-by-Day Account of Jesus's Final Week in Jerusalem* (London: HarperCollins, 2007), p. 5.
21. Matthew 21:12.
22. John 6:1–14.
23. Leviticus 16.
24. John 18:36–38.
25. Matthew 27:29.
26. John 19:12.
27. Ian Bradley, *God Save the Queen: The Spiritual Heart of the Monarchy* (London: Continuum, 2021), p. 49.
28. Graham Kendrick, 'The Servant King', 1989.
29. H. M. The Queen, foreword to *The Servant Queen and the King She Serves* (London: Bible Society, 2016).
30. Denis McBride (ed.), *Your Sunday Missal* (Chawton, Hampshire: Redemptorist Publications, 2011), p. 693, with material copyright International Commission on English in the Liturgy Corporation.
31. John 18:37; Luke 23:32–43.
32. Matthew 25:31–46.
33. Fr Robert Gay OP, 'Feast of Christ The King', 23 November 2009, www.english.op.org/godzdogz/feast-of-christ-the-king (accessed 3 March 2022).
34. Romans 13:1.
35. 1 Peter 2:13–17.
36. John 13:13–15.
37. Brian Robinson, *The Royal Maundy* (London: Kaye and Ward, 1977), pp. 29–31.

## 2 *The home-grown pope*

1. Tracy Borman, *Crown & Sceptre: A New History of the British Monarchy from William the Conqueror to Elizabeth II* (London: Hodder and Stoughton, 2021), p. 186.
2. Alison Weir, *Elizabeth of York: The First Tudor Queen* (London: Jonathan Cape, 2013), p. 374.
3. Leviticus 20:21.
4. Giles Tremlett, *Catherine of Aragon: Henry's Spanish Queen* (London: Faber and Faber, 2010), p. 258.
5. Tremlett, *Catherine of Aragon*, p. 267.
6. Deuteronomy 25:6.
7. David Starkey, *Crown and Country: A History of England through the Monarchy* (London: Harper Collins, 2011), p. 289.
8. Rebecca Larson, 'The Plight of Katherine of Aragon (21 June 1529)', Tudors Dynasty, 21 June 2017, https://tudorsdynasty.com/plight-of-katherine/ (accessed 3 March 2022).
9. Quoted in Tremlett, *Catherine of Aragon*, p. 317.
10. Samuel Haynes, *A Collection of State Papers Relating to Affairs in the Reigns of King Henry VIII, King Edward VI, Queen Mary, and Queen Elizabeth From the Year 1542 to 1570*. Left by William Cecil, Lord Burghley, at Hatfield House, London, 1740, Volume vii, p. 262.
11. Cranmer was going against Roman Catholic canon law, according to canon lawyer Dr Helen Costigane of St Mary's University. The sacrament of marriage is nullified, not its legal standing.
12. T. E. Bridgett and James Lennon, *Life of Blessed John Fisher: Bishop of Rochester, Cardinal of the Holy Roman Church, and Martyr Under Henry VIII* (London: Burns, Oates & Washburne, 1922), p. 355.
13. Borman, *Crown & Sceptre*, p. 193.
14. John 14:28.
15. Tracy Borman, 'Henry VIII: confident young king or insecure son?' BBC History Extra, 18 August 2020, www.historyextra.com/period/tudor/henry-viii-like-father-like-son/ (accessed 3 March 2022).
16. David Starkey, *Monarchy* (London: Harper Perennial, 2007), p. 55.
17. 'Proclamations of Accession of English and British Sovereigns (1547–1952): Edward VI, www.heraldica.org/topics/britain/brit-proclamations.htm (accessed 14 March 2022).
18. For a more detailed account of the coronation of Edward VI, see Strong, *Coronation*, pp. 198–201.

19. 2 Kings 22.
20. Bradley, *God Save the Queen*, p. 122.
21. Calendar of State Papers Spanish, Volume IX, p. 419, as quoted by Anna Whitelock, *Mary Tudor: England's First Queen* (London: Bloomsbury, 2009), p. 138.
22. W. K. Jordan (ed.), *The Chronicle and Political Papers of Edward VI* (London: George Allen & Unwin, 1966), p. 56.
23. Chris Skidmore, *Edward VI: The Lost King of England* (London: Weidenfeld and Nicolson, 2007), p. 260.
24. Letter of Simon Renard to Prince Philip, 3 October 1553, 'Spain: October 1553, 1–5', in Royall Tyler (ed.) *Calendar of State Papers, Spain, Volume 11, 1553* (London, 1916), pp. 261–72. *British History Online*, www.british-history.ac.uk/cal-state-papers/spain/vol11/pp261-272 (accessed 14 March 2022).
25. For more details of Mary I's coronation, see Strong, *Coronation*, pp. 205–8.
26. W. R. Streitberger, *Court Revels 1485–1559* (Buffalo: University of Toronto Press, 1994), p. 219.
27. 'The Royall Passage of her Maiesty from the Tower of London, to her Palace of White-hall, with al the Speaches and Deuices, both of the Pageants and otherwise, together with her Maiesties seuerall Answers, and most pleasing Speaches to them all' (sic) (London, 1604), The British Library, www.bl.uk/treasures/festivalbooks/BookDetails.aspx?strFest=0231 (accessed 3 March 2022).
28. Strong, *Coronation*, p. 225.
29. For more details of Elizabeth I's coronation, see Strong, *Coronation*, pp. 210–11.
30. Starkey, *Crown and Country*, pp. 314–15.
31. David Starkey, *Elizabeth* (London: Vintage, 2001), p. 292.
32. Alison Weir, *The Life of Elizabeth I* (New York: Ballantine Books, 1999), p. 201.
33. Letter from Sir Nicholas Throckmorton, ambassador to Elizabeth I, following a conversation with Mary, then wife of Dauphin Francis, 22 August 1560, The National Archives, Kew, SP70/17, f.81v.
34. John Guy, Introduction to *Elizabeth and Mary, Royal Cousins, Rival Queens*, edited by Susan Doran (London: The British Library exhibition catalogue, 2021). See also Sir William Cecil, 'British Unity and the Problem of Mary Queen of Scots', 31 August 1559, British Library, Lansdowne manuscripts, MS 4, f. 26r.
35. T. E. Hartley (ed.), *Proceedings in the Parliaments of Elizabeth I, Volume III: 1593–1601* (Leicester: Leicester University Press, 1981–95), p. 118.

36. From *The Political Works of James I*, quoted by Strong, *Coronation*, p. 237.
37. Quoted by Bradley, *God Save the Queen*, p. 137.
38. *The Political Works of James I*, quoted by Strong, *Coronation*, p. 239.
39. Eyewitness quoted by Strong, *Coronation*, p. 256.
40. Diarmaid MacCulloch, *Reformation: Europe's House Divided 1490–1700* (London: Penguin, 2004), p. 515.
41. Adam Nicolson, *Power and Glory; Jacobean England and the Making of the King James Bible* (London: Harper Perennial, 2004), p. xviii.
42. Simon Schama, *A History of Britain, Volume 2: The British Wars 1603–1776* (London: BBC, 2003), p. 60.
43. The indictment of the King, quoted in Schama, *A History of Britain*, p. 137.
44. 'The Trial of Charles I, King of England, Scotland and Ireland', European Royal History, 29 January 2020, europeanroyalhistory.wordpress.com/2020/01/29/the-trial-of-charles-i-king-of-england-scotland-and-ireland (accessed 3 March 2022).
45. Blair Worden, *The English Civil Wars 1640–1660* (London: Weidenfeld & Nicolson, 2009), p. 101.
46. Quoted in Schama, *A History of Britain*, p. 139.
47. MacCulloch, *Reformation*, p. 529.
48. George Morley, 'A Sermon Preached at the Magnificent Coronation of the Most High and Mighty King Charles the IId', quoted by Strong, *Coronation*, p. 340.
49. *The London Gazette*, 15 July 1685, p. 1.
50. 'James Francis Edward Stuart', www.englishmonarchs.co.uk/stuart_10.htm (accessed 4 March 2022).
51. Linda Colley, *Britons: Forging the Nation 1707–1837* (New Haven: Yale University Press, 2009), p. 48.
52. Quoted by Colley, *Britons*, p. 47.

## 3 *From turmoil to stability*

1. Quoted by Strong, *Coronation*, p. 359.
2. William Talbot, Bishop of Oxford, 'A Sermon Preach'd at the Coronation of King George I', W. Wilkins for John Church, London, 1714.
3. John Potter, Bishop of Oxford, 'A Sermon Preach'd at the Coronation of King George II', C. Ackers for R. Knaplick, London, 1727.
4. 'George II and Caroline', Westminster Abbey, www.westminster-abbey.org/abbey-commemorations/royals/george-ii-and-caroline (accessed 4 March 2022).

5. Janice Hadlow, *The Strangest Family: The Private Lives of George III, Queen Charlotte and the Hanoverians* (London: William Collins, 2014), p. 101.
6. Hadlow, *The Strangest Family*, p. 115.
7. Romney Sedgewick (ed.), *Letters from George III to Lord Bute, 1756–66* (London: Macmillan, 1939), p. 168.
8. Strong, *Coronation*, p. 386.
9. Peter Quennell (ed.), *Memoirs of William Hickey* (Routledge and Kegan Paul, 1975), pp. 18–19.
10. Quoted by Hadlow, *The Strangest Family*, pp. 234–5.
11. Prochaska, *Royal Bounty*.
12. Richard Abbott, 'Brighton's Unofficial Queen', *The Tablet*, 1 September 2007, p. 12.
13. Christopher Hibbert, *King Mob: The Story of Lord George Gordon and the Riots of 1780* (London: Longmans, 1958), p. 161.
14. A more detailed account of this encounter is to be found in Antonia Fraser, *The King and the Catholic: The Fight for Rights 1829* (London: Weidenfeld and Nicolson, 2018), pp. 42–5.
15. D. G. Barnes, *George III and William Pitt, 1783–1806: A New Interpretation Based upon a Study of Their Unpublished Correspondence* (Stanford: Stanford University Press, 1939), pp. 377–8.
16. A. Aspinal (ed.), *The Later Correspondence of George III: Volume two, December 1783–1793* (Cambridge: Cambridge University Press, 1963), p. xiv.
17. *The Times*, 26 October 1809, quoted by Bradley, *God Save The Queen*, p. 150.
18. William Thomas Fitz-Gerald, 'Ode for the Royal Jubilee', *The Gentleman Magazine*, Select Poetry, November 1809, p. 1053.
19. Alison Plowden, *Caroline and Charlotte: Regency Scandals* (London: Sutton, 2005), p. 264.
20. Strong, *Coronation*, p. 395.
21. Denis Gwynn, *The Struggle for Catholic Emancipation, 1750–1829* (London: Longmans, 1928), pp. 244–5.
22. Quoted by Fraser, *The King and the Catholic*, p. 233.
23. E. A. Smith, *George IV* (New Haven: Yale University Press, 1999), p. 239.
24. Smith, *George IV*, p. 239.
25. Fraser, *The King and the Catholics*, p. 254.
26. Starkey, *Crown and Country*, p. 452.
27. Philip Ziegler, *King William IV* (London: Harper and Row, 1971), pp. 193–4.
28. Deirdre Murphy, *The Young Victoria* (New Haven: Yale University Press, 2019), p. 187.

29. For more details of Victoria's coronation see Strong, *Coronation*, and Roy Strong, 'Queen Victoria's Coronation', Queen Victoria's Journals, www.queenvictoriasjournals.org/info/QueenVictoriasCoronation.do (accessed 4 March 2022).
30. Elizabeth Longford, *Queen Victoria: Born to Succeed* (London: Harper, 1964), p. 279.
31. W. T. Stead, *Her Majesty The Queen: Studies of the Sovereign and the Reign* (London: Review of Reviews Office, 1897), p. 92.
32. Lord Broughton, *Reflections of a Long Life, With Additional Extracts from his Private Diaries* (London: John Murray, 1909–11).
33. Rev. Charles Bulloch, *Wedding Bells: Prince George and Princess May: with Glimpses of Royal Weddings* (London: Home Words, 1893), pp. 7–8.
34. Ledger-Lomas, *Queen Victoria*, p. 43.
35. Bradley, *God Save the Queen*, pp. 156–7.
36. Bradley, *God Save the Queen*, p. 157.
37. For further details see Ledger-Lomas, *Queen Victoria*.
38. Owen Chadwick, *The Victorian Church Part Two: 1860–1901* (London: A&C Black, 1980), p. 336.
39. Queen Victoria's Journals, 10 December 1859, p. 206.
40. Edwin Hodder, *The Life and Work of the 7th Earl of Shaftesbury, KG, Volume 2* (London: Cassell, 1886), p. 331.
41. 'Irish Legal Heritage: Maud Gonne and The Famine Queen', *Irish Legal News*, 8 March 2019, www.irishlegal.com/articles/irish-legal-heritage-maud-gonne-and-the-famine-queen (accessed 4 March 2022).
42. Quoted by Ledger-Lomas, *Queen Victoria*, p. 90. Simon Jeffery, 'Park life', *The Guardian*, 30 January 2003, www.theguardian.com/politics/2003/jan/30/antiwar.uk (accessed 4 March 2022).
43. Letter from Miss Ella Taylor, 7 January 1872, held in the Royal Archives and quoted in Helen Rappaport, *Magnificent Obsession: Victoria, Albert and the Death That Changed the Monarchy* (London: Hutchinson, 2011), p. 83.
44. Rev. George Albert Rogers, *The Royal Lament: A Sermon on the Death of HRH the Prince Consort, December 22, 1861* (London: Macintosh and Hunt, 1861), pp. 12–14.
45. *The Illustrated London News*, 21 December 1861, p. 616, quoted by Rappaport, *Magnificent Obsession*, p. 97.
46. Rappaport, *Magnificent Obsession*, p. 107–8.
47. Ledger-Lomas, *Queen Victoria*, p. 119.
48. 2 Timothy 4:7.
49. Ledger-Lomas, *Queen Victoria*, p. 11.

50. Diary of the Life at Court of Eliza Jane, Lady Waterpark, 1864 to 1893, British Library MSS 60750, ff.137.
51. Quoted by Borman, *Crown & Sceptre*, p. 489.
52. Proclamation of Queen Victoria, read at Allahabad, India, 1 November 1858, British Library collection, BL MSS EUR D62D.
53. Queen Victoria's Journal, 14 December 1878, quoted by Jane Ridley, *Bertie: A Life of Edward VII* (London: Chatto and Windus, 2012), p. 213.
54. Ridley, *Bertie*, p. 368.
55. Notes, *The Tablet*, 14 May 1910, p. 764.
56. Ridley, *Bertie*, p. 456.
57. Ridley, *Bertie*, p. 458.
58. Shane Leslie, Patron of the plutocracy, review of *King Edward the Seventh* by Sir Philip Magnus, *The Tablet*, 21 March 1964, p. 323, reader.exacteditions.com/issues/71588/page/11 (subscription required).
59. Letters, *The Tablet*, 4 March 1978, p. 214, reader.exacteditions.com/issues/69654/page/22 (subscription required).

## 4 *God make good my vow*

1. Elizabeth II, 'Christmas Broadcast 1952', 25 December 1952, www.royal.uk/queens-first-christmas-broadcast-1952 (accessed 5 March 2022).
2. Interview with the author by a source, October 2021.
3. Elizabeth II, 'Christmas Broadcast 2000', 25 December 2000, www.royal.uk/christmas-broadcast-2000 (accessed 5 March 2022).
4. Elizabeth II, 'A Speech by the Queen on Her 21st Birthday, 1947', 21 April 1947, www.royal.uk/21st-birthday-speech-21-april-1947#:~:text=I%20declare%20before%20you%20all,to%20which%20we%20all%20belong (accessed 5 March 2022).
5. Ben Pimlott, *The Queen: A Portrait of Elizabeth II* (London: Harper Collins, 1996), p. 115, claims Sir Alan Lascelles as the author but family members have since revealed it was Morrah. Tom Utley, 'Grandad's words made Churchill and the Queen cry. How sad Beardy misquoted them this week . . .', *Daily Mail*, 8 June 2012, www.dailymail.co.uk/debate/article-2156173/Grandads-words-Churchill-Queen-How-sad-Beardy-misquoted-week-.html (accessed 5 March 2022). Notebook, The Queen's Speech, *The Tablet*, 12 September 2015.
6. Pimlott, *The Queen*, p. 117.
7. See Philip Ziegler, *King Edward VIII: The Official Biography* (London: Collins, 1990).

8. Ziegler, *King Edward VIII*, p. 250.
9. Lord Wigram, memo, 15 February 1936, Royal Archives, King Edward VIII papers, Box 4.
10. John Gilbert Lockhart, *Cosmo Gordon Lang* (London: Hodder and Stoughton, 1949), pp. 396–401.
11. Duke of Windsor, *A King's Story: The Memoirs of HRH the Duke of Windsor, KG* (London: Cassell and Co., 1951), pp. 331.
12. Mike Priestley, 'Not-so-blunt words that stopped a coronation', *Bradford Telegraph and Argus*, 1 December 2006, www.thetelegraphandargus.co.uk/display.var.1053791.0.notsoblunt_words_that_stopped_coronation.php (accessed 5 March 2022).
13. King Edward VIII abdication broadcast.
14. Lockhart, *Cosmo Gordon Lang*, pp. 404–5.
15. *King George VI to His Peoples, 1936–51, Selected Broadcasts and Speeches* (London: John Murray, 1952), p. 3.
16. Matthew Dennison, *The Queen* (London: Head of Zeus, 2021), p. 122.
17. Dermot Morrah, *Princess Elizabeth* (London: Odhams, 1947), p. 126.
18. Dennison, *The Queen*, p. 130.
19. Prochaska, *Royal Bounty*, p. 230.
20. C. Stuart, *The Reith Diaries* (London: Collins, 1975), p. 197.
21. *King George VI to His Peoples*, p. 21.
22. 'Andrew Vine: The Queen and the abiding influence of "Grandpa England"', *Yorkshire Post*, 23 January 2016, www.yorkshirepost.co.uk/news/opinion/columnists/andrew-vine-queen-and-abiding-influence-grandpa-england-1805590 (accessed 5 March 2022).
23. Quoted in Kenneth Rose, *King George V* (London: Weidenfeld and Nicolson, 1983), p. 364.
24. David Cannadine (ed.), *Westminster Abbey: A Church in History* (Yale: Yale University Press, 2019), p. 7.
25. Kingsley Martin, *The Magic of Monarchy* (London: Thomas Nelson, 1937), p. 107.
26. Geoffrey Dennis, *Coronation Commentary* (New York: Dodd, Mead and Co, 1937), p. 217.
27. Elizabeth Longford, *Elizabeth R: A Biography* (London: Weidenfeld and Nicolson, 1983), p. 72.
28. Her Royal Highness Princess Elizabeth, 'The Coronation', 12 May 1937, kept in the Royal Library.
29. Pimlott, *The Queen*, p. 52.
30. Jock Colville, *The Fringes of Power: Downing Street Diaries 1939–1955* (London: Hodder and Stoughton, 1985), pp. 165–6.

31. Norman Hartnell, *Silver and Gold* (London: Evans Brothers, 1955), p. 113.
32. Pimlott, *The Queen*, p. 135.
33. Prince Philip, however, did not altogether abandon the Greek Orthodoxy of his youth. See chapter six.
34. Quoted by *The Times* the next day. See also Pimlott, *The Queen*.
35. Pimlott, *The Queen*, p. 205.
36. Robert Piggott, 'Archbishop: Not everyone appreciates how funny Queen is', BBC News, 1 June 2012, www.bbc.co.uk/news/uk-18289442 (accessed 5 March 2022).
37. Geoffrey Fisher, *I Here Present Unto You*, (London: SPCK, 1953), pp. 15–29.
38. Anne Glenconner, *Lady in Waiting: My Extraordinary Life in the Shadow of the Crown* (London: Hodder, 2020), p. 71.
39. Edward Shils and Michael Young, 'The Meaning of the Coronation', *The Sociological Review*, 1953, issue 1, volume 2, pp. 68–9, onlinelibrary.wiley.com/doi/abs/10.1111/j.1467-954X.1953.tb00953.x (accessed 5 March 2022; log-in required).
40. Shils and Young, 'The Meaning of the Coronation'.
41. Shils and Young, 'The Meaning of the Coronation'.
42. Shils and Young, 'The Meaning of the Coronation'.
43. Shils and Young, 'The Meaning of the Coronation', p. 69.
44. 'The Form and Order of Service that is to be performed and the Ceremonies that are to be observed in The Coronation of Her Majesty Queen Elizabeth II in the Abbey Church of St. Peter, Westminster, on Tuesday, the second day of June, 1953', An Anglican Liturgical Library, www.oremus.org/liturgy/coronation/cor1953b.html (accessed 5 March 2022).
45. 'The Form and Order of Service', An Anglican Liturgical Library.
46. 'The Form and Order of Service', An Anglican Liturgical Library.
47. From *Church Times*, 14 April 2000, quoted by Bradley, *God Save the Queen*, p. 109.
48. Glenconner, *Lady in Waiting*, p. 70.

## 5 *The framework of her life*

1. Lord Altrincham, *Is the Monarchy Perfect?* (London: John Calder, 1958), p. 11.
2. Altrincham, *Is the Monarchy Perfect?*, p. 11.
3. *The Times*, 12 March 1964, quoted by Pimlott, *The Queen*, p. 336.

4. Quoted by Pimlott, *The Queen*, p. 386.
5. Peter Townsend, *Time and Chance* (London: William Collins and Son, 1978), p. 309.
6. Nigel Dempster, *HRH Princess Margaret, A Life Unfulfilled* (London: Quartet, 1981), p. 23.
7. Quoted by Pimlott, *The Queen*, p. 236.
8. *The Times*, 26 October 1955.
9. Longford, *Elizabeth R*, p. 177.
10. Peter Quenell (ed.), *A Lonely Business: A Self-Portrait of James Pope-Hennèssy* (London: Weidenfeld & Nicolson, 1981), p. 242.
11. Recorded by Cabinet minister Richard Crossman in his diaries following a meeting of the Privy Council, 28 July 1967, quoted by Pimlott, *The Queen*, p. 374.
12. 'Frequently Asked Questions (marriage)', Church of Scotland archived material, web.archive.org/web/20160404195306/http://www.churchofscotland.org.uk/__data/assets/pdf_file/0019/2449/guide_marriage.pdf (accessed 5 March 2022).
13. Cited in Peter Stanford, 'One Year On: Memorials and what they say about us', *The Independent*, 29 August 1998, www.independent.co.uk/life-style/one-year-on-memorials-and-what-they-say-about-us-by-peter-stanford-1174709.html (accessed 5 March 2022).
14. Quoted by Cannadine, *Westminster Abbey*, p. 358.
15. H. M. The Queen, 'Her Majesty's Reply', address to Parliament, 30 April 2002, Hansard, hansard.parliament.uk/Lords/2002-04-30/debates/74145ecc-f0b3-4402-a8c5-7db244b36394/LordsChamber (accessed 5 March 2022).
16. Interview with the author, December 2021.
17. Elizabeth II, 'A Speech by the Queen at Lambeth Palace', 15 February 2012, www.royal.uk/queens-speech-lambeth-palace-15-february-2012 (accessed 5 March 2022).
18. Interview with the author, December 2021.
19. Interview with the author, December 2021.
20. Interview with the author, December 2021.
21. 'Queen says the Church of England is misunderstood', *The Guardian*, 15 February 2012, www.theguardian.com/uk/2012/feb/15/queen-says-church-misunderstood (accessed 5 March 2022).
22. Comment from a source in an interview with the author, October 2021.
23. Elizabeth II, 'Christmas Broadcast 1963', 25 December 1963, www.royal.uk/christmas-broadcast-1963 (accessed 5 March 2022).
24. Elizabeth II, 'Christmas Broadcast 1970', 25 December 1970, www.royal.uk/christmas-broadcast-1970 (accessed 5 March 2022).

25. Elizabeth II, 'Christmas Broadcast 2000', 25 December 2000, www.royal.uk/christmas-broadcast-2000 (accessed 5 March 2022).
26. See chapter eight for a longer discourse on the relationship between the monarchy and the Church of England.
27. Interview with Dr John Hall by the author, December 2021.
28. Interview with Dr John Hall by the author, December 2021.
29. Interview with Lord Williams by the author, December 2021.
30. Interview with Richard Kay by the author, December 2021.
31. Elizabeth II, 'Christmas Broadcast 2021', 25 December 2021, www.royal.uk/christmas-broadcast-2021 (accessed 5 March 2022).
32. Interview with Rabbi Jonathan Romain by the author, December 2021.
33. Elizabeth II, 'Christmas Broadcast 2000', 25 December 2000.
34. Interview with Rabbi Jonathan Romain by the author, December 2021.
35. Elizabeth II, 'Christmas Broadcast 2004', 25 December 2004, www.royal.uk/christmas-broadcast-2004 (accessed 5 March 2022).
36. Comment made to the author in Rome in 2015.
37. Comment from a source in an interview with the author, October 2021.
38. Interview with Nigel Baker by the author, October 2015.
39. Interview with the then Dr Rowan Williams, July 2015.
40. 'Address of John Paul II to the Queen of England', 17 October 1980, www.vatican.va/content/john-paul-ii/en/speeches/1980/october/documents/hf_jp-ii_spe_19801017_regina-elisabetta.html (accessed 5 March 2022).
41. Queen Elizabeth II, 'Papal Visit 2010: Queen's Speech to Pope Benedict – full text', *Catholic Herald*, 16 September 2010, catholicherald.co.uk/papal-visit-2010-queens-speech-to-pope-benedict-full-text (accessed 5 March 2022).
42. See Catherine Pepinster, *The Keys and the Kingdom: The British and the Papacy from John Paul II to Francis* (London: T&T Clark, 2017) for more details on this issue.
43. Pepinster, *The Keys and the Kingdom*, p. 135.
44. 'Speech by the Rt. Hon. J. Enoch Powell, MP, to the East Grinstead Young Conservatives at East Court, East Grinstead, Sussex. at 8 pm, Friday, 5th December, 1980', 5 December 1980, enochpowell.info/wp-content/uploads/Speeches/Sept-Dec%201980.pdf (accessed 5 March 2022).
45. 'The Thirty Nine Articles', Anglican Church League, acl.asn.au/the-thirty-nine-articles (accessed 5 March 2022).
46. Cabinet papers for 25 May 1982, the Thatcher archive.
47. Elizabeth II, 'A Speech by The Queen at the Inauguration of the General Synod, 2015' 24 November 2015, www.royal.uk/queens-speech-inauguration-tenth-general-synod-24-november-2015 (accessed 5 March 2022).

48. 'Message of His Holiness Pope Benedict XVI to Her Majesty Queen Elizabeth II on the Occasion of the Diamond Jubilee of Her Reign', 23 May 2012, w2.vatican.va/content/benedict-xvi/en/messages/pont-messages/2012/documents/hf_ben-xvi_mes_20120523_queen-elizabeth-ii.html (accessed 5 March 2022).
49. Miguel Cullen, 'Pope sent greetings to the Queen straight after his election, says cardinal', *Catholic Herald*, 12 September 2013, www.catholicherald.co.uk/news/2013/09/12/pope-sent-greeting-to-queen-straight-after-his-election-says-cardinal (accessed 5 March 2022).
50. Anthony Howard, *Basil Hume: The Monk Cardinal* (London: Headline, 2005), p. 287.
51. Howard, *Basil Hume*, p. 288.
52. Howard, *Basil Hume*, p. 290.
53. Footage of the funeral of King Baudouin with The Queen, 'Partial Funeral of King Baudouin', YouTube, 7 August 1993, www.youtube.com/watch?v=1hQC7Jd19Yo (accessed 5 March 2022).
54. Reported to the author by a witness to the meeting.
55. 'Act of Settlement 1700', www.bailii.org/uk/legis/num_act/1700/1565208.html (accessed 5 March 2022).
56. Thomas Norton and Hugh Farmer, 'Queen's grandson and Catholic fiancée revive Act of Settlement row', *The Tablet*, 4 August 2007, p. 36.
57. Pepinster, *The Keys and The Kingdom*, p. 131.
58. Adrian Hilton, 'The Price of Liberty', *The Spectator*, 8 November 2003.
59. Nicholas Watt and Andrew Sparrow, 'Gordon Brown committed to ending anomaly of Royal ban on Catholics', *The Guardian*, 27 March 2009, www.theguardian.com/politics/2009/mar/27/gordon-brown-royal-succession (accessed 6 March 2022).
60. 'Perth Agreement', en.wikipedia.org/wiki/Perth_Agreement#Published_content_of_the_official_announcement.2C_Perth.2C_October_2011 (accessed 6 March 2022).
61. *The People*, 30 October 1966, quoted by Dennison, *The Queen*, p. 331.
62. Reuters, 'Newspaper Says Queen Is Upset by Thatcher', *The New York Times*, 20 July 1986, www.nytimes.com/1986/07/20/world/newspaper-says-queen-is-upset-by-thatcher.html (accessed 6 March 2022).
63. For further details of Margaret Thatcher's theology, see Eliza Filby, *God and Mrs Thatcher: The Battle for Britain's Soul* (London: Biteback Publishing, 2015).
64. Filby, *God and Mrs Thatcher*, p. 159.
65. Humphrey Carpenter, *Robert Runcie: The Reluctant Archbishop* (London: Hodder and Stoughton, 1996), p. 258.

66. Philippians 2:7.
67. Giles Fraser, 'Our Queen's finest moment', *UnHerd*, 28 October 2021, unherd.com/2021/10/why-the-queen-must-suffer/?tl_inbound=1&tl_groups%5b0%5d=18743&tl_period_type=3&mc_cid=c6ef7fa9a0&mc_eid=b28daeofd9 (accessed 6 March 2022).
68. Catherine Pepinster, 'Thought for the Day', *Today* programme, BBC Radio 4, 22 November 2021.
69. Interview with a source by the author, October 2021.
70. According to a source interviewed by the author.

## 6 *Her strength and stay*

1. From the Mountbatten papers, University of Southampton, quoted in Philip Eade, *Young Prince Philip: His Turbulent Early Life* (London: Harper Press, 2011), p. 18.
2. For more information about the life of Princess Alice, see Hugo Vickers, *Alice: Princess Andrew of Greece* (London: Hamish Hamilton, 2000).
3. For more details of the political turmoil in Russia at this time see Edvard Radzinsky, *The Last Tsar: The Life and Death of Nicholas II* (London: Doubleday, 1992).
4. Dmitry Shlapentokh, *The French Revolution and the Russian Anti-Democratic Tradition: A Case of False Consciousness* (New York: Transaction Publishers, 1997), p. 266.
5. Eade, *Young Prince Philip*, p. 86.
6. Pimlott, *The Queen*, p. 95.
7. Pimlott, *The Queen*, p. 104.
8. Pimlott, *The Queen*, p. 204.
9. Mentioned in unpublished diaries of Jock Colville, quoted by Pimlott, *The Queen*, p. 185.
10. Quoted by Eade, *Young Prince Philip*, p. 274.
11. According to clergy who knew him, in conversation with the author.
12. Quoted by Ingrid Seward, *My Husband and I: The Inside Story of 70 Years of the Royal Marriage* (London: Simon and Schuster, 2017), p. 264.
13. HRH Prince Philip's Address to the General Assembly of 1969, The Church of Scotland, 14 April 2021, www.churchofscotland.org.uk/news-and-events/news/2021/articles/hrh-prince-philips-address-to-the-general-assembly-of-1969 (accessed 6 March 2022).
14. HRH The Duke of Edinburgh and The Rt Rev. Michael Mann, *A Windsor Correspondence* (Norfolk: Michael Russell Publishing, 1984).

15. 'Advent Sermon. HRH The Prince Philip, St George's Chapel, Windsor, 27th November 1988. Theme: The Coming of Christ – The Creator Made Created', www.arcworld.org/downloads/HRH_Advent_Sermon.pdf (accessed 6 March 2022).
16. 'Beyond Belief on Prince Philip', BBC Radio 4, 12 April 2021, www.bbc.co.uk/sounds/play/m000v1nx (accessed 6 March 2022).
17. Andrew Brown, 'The Duke listened quietly as faith leaders and scientists made sense of the world', Religion Media Centre, 9 April 2021, religionmediacentre.org.uk/news/prince-philip-listened-quietly-as-faith-leaders-and-scientists-made-sense-of-the-world (accessed 6 March 2022).
18. Martin Palmer speaking on 'Beyond Belief', BBC Radio 4, 12 April 2021.
19. 'Advent Sermon. HRH The Prince Philip, St George's Chapel, Windsor, 27th November 1988'.
20. HRH The Duke of Edinburgh and Rt Rev. Michael Mann, *Survival or Extinction: A Christian Attitude to the Environment* (Wilby, Norfolk: Michael Russell Publishing, 1989). Quoted in Seward, *My Husband and I*, p. 269.
21. Recalled by Rabbi Jonathan Romain.
22. Anna Della Subin, 'How Prince Philip was turned into a god', *Prospect*, 28 December 2021, www.prospectmagazine.co.uk/arts-and-books/how-prince-philip-was-turned-into-a-god (accessed 6 March 2022).
23. Della Subin, 'How Prince Philip was turned into a god'.
24. Della Subin, 'How Prince Philip was turned into a god'.
25. As explained to me by a source close to the Royal Family.
26. Giles Milton, 'A Prince Among Priests', *The Spectator*, 14 March 1992, archive.spectator.co.uk/issue/14th-march-1992 (accessed 6 March 2022).
27. Cormac Murphy-O'Connor, *An English Spring: Memoirs* (London: Bloomsbury, 2015), p. 199.
28. 'Beyond Belief', BBC Radio 4, 12 April 2021.

## 7 *Demise*

1. Alfred, Lord Tennyson (1809–92), 'The Brook'.
2. As witnessed by the author, present in the BBC Television newsroom on the afternoon of 8 September 2022.
3. Caroline Davies, 'Queen Elizabeth died of "old age", death certificate says', *The Guardian*, 29 September 2022, www.theguardian.com/uk-news/2022/sep/29/queen-elizabeth-died-of-old-age-death-certificate-says (accessed 25 January 2023).
4. Comments from sources to the author, October 2022.

5. According to a source, interviewed by the author, November 2022.
6. Gyles Brandreth, 'The Queen knew her time was running out and accepted it with good grace', *Daily Mail*, 26 November 2022, extracted from Gyles Brandreth, *Elizabeth: An Intimate Portrait* (London: Michael Joseph, 2022).
7. Molly Moss, 'Huw Edwards recalls emotional reaction while reporting the Queen's death', *Radio Times*, 18 October 2022, www.radiotimes.com/tv/current-affairs/huw-edwards-queen-death-reaction-newsupdate (accessed 25 January 2023).
8. Allison Pearson, 'The Queen's own words of wisdom provide comfort in our moment of sorrow', *The Telegraph*, 9 September 2022, www.telegraph.co.uk/royal-family/2022/09/09/queens-words-wisdom-provide-comfort-moment-sorrow (accessed 25 January 2023).
9. 'Announcement of the death of The Queen', The Royal Family, www.royal.uk › announcement-death-queen (accessed 25 January 2023).
10. 'His Majesty The King's Address to the Nation and the Commonwealth', 9 September 2022, www.royal.uk/his-majesty-king%E2%80%99s-address-nation-and-commonwealth (accessed 25 January 2023).
11. 'Britain mourns', *The Guardian*, 10 September 2022, p. 4.
12. Daniel Boffey, 'No hysteria, just quiet respect as crowds gather in remembrance', *The Guardian*, 10 September 2022, pp. 4–5.
13. Janice Turner, 'Ritual isn't rational but it tempers our grief', *The Times*, 17 September 2022, p. 29.
14. Quentin Letts, 'Queen's journey from Balmoral: Extraordinary respect in every village', *The Times*, 12 September 2022, pp. 1, 3.
15. Valentine Low, 'The Queen's oak coffin was ready 30 years ago', *The Times*, 12 September 2022, www.thetimes.co.uk/article/the-queens-oak-coffin-was-ready-30-years-ago-3lmqb58qs#:~:text=When%20the%20Queen's%20coffin%20appeared,more%20than%2030%20years%20ago (accessed 25 January 2023).
16. Reported by a source to the author, November 2022.
17. 'Order of Service for a Service of Thanksgiving for the life of Her Majesty the Queen', 11 September 2022, www.royal.uk/order-service-service-thanksgiving-life-her-majesty-queen (accessed 25 January 2023).
18. 'Order of Service from St. Anne's Cathedral Service of Reflection', 13 September2022www.gov.uk/government/publications/order-of-service-from-st-annes-cathedral-service-of-reflection (accessed 25 January 2023).
19. 'A speech by the Queen at the Irish State Banquet, 2011', www.royal.uk/queens-speech-irish-state-dinner-18-may-2011 (accessed 25 January 2023).
20. 'Order of Service for A Service of Prayer and Reflection for the Life of

The Queen', 16 September 2022, www.royal.uk/order-service-service-prayer-and-reflection-life-queen (accessed 25 January 2023).

21. Steve Richards, Twitter, 13 September 2022, twitter.com/steverichards14/status/1569771093249908740 (accessed 25 January 2023).
22. David Brown, Neil Johnson, Charlotte Wace, Lucy Bannerman, 'Queen's lying in state: They said the line was closed. It didn't make a difference', *The Times*, 17 September 2022, p. 6.
23. Charlie Parker, 'This will warm your cockles. Queen didn't want a dull funeral', *The Times*, 19 September 2022, p. 9.
24. Linda Molina-Whyte, 'Queen's funeral estimated to be watched by 37.5 million in the UK – 4 billion worldwide', *Radio Times*, 21 September 2022, www.radiotimes.com/tv/current-affairs/queen-funeral-tv-viewers-worldwide-newsupdate (accessed 25 January 2023).
25. Charles Moore, 'I sat in the same spot for Diana's funeral but the Queen's was quite different, it went deeper', *The Telegraph*, 20 September 2022, pp. 2–3.
26. The Most Revd Justin Welby, 'The Archbishop of Canterbury's Sermon for The State Funeral of Her Majesty Queen Elizabeth II', 19 September 2022, www.archbishopofcanterbury.org/speaking-writing/sermons/archbishop-canterburys-sermon-state-funeral-her-majesty-queen-elizabeth-ii (accessed 25 January 2023).
27. Hannah Furness, 'An outpouring of love', *The Telegraph*, 20 September 2022, p. 1.
28. 'Order of Service for Committal of Her Majesty the Queen', 19 September 2022, www.royal.uk/order-service-committal-service-her-majesty-queen (accessed 25 January 2023).
29. Simon Schama, 'Elizabeth II became the personification of our national identity', *The I*, 10 September 2022, p. 16.
30. Schama, 'Elizabeth II became the personification of our national identity', p. 16.

## *8 Defender of Faith*

1. An interview with the author, October 2021.
2. HRH The Prince of Wales, 'A Time To Heal', from the *Temenos Academy Review*, Number 5, Autumn 2002, reprinted in *Speeches and Articles, 1968–2012, His Royal Highness The Prince of Wales, volume two*, selected by David Cadman and Suheil Bushrui (Cardiff: University of Wales Press, 2014), p. 613.

3. Confidential letter written by HRH Prince Charles, 8 February 1964, quoted in Jonathan Dimbleby, *The Prince of Wales: A Biography* (London: Little Brown, 1995), p. 71.
4. See chapter six for an account of the friendship between Prince Philip and Robin Woods.
5. 'Trinity College Chapel, Memorial Service for Harry Williams, 13-v-2006, Rt Revd and Rt Hon Richard Chartres', Trinity College Chapel, Cambridge, 13 May 2006, trinitycollegechapel.com/media/filestore/sermons/Chartres HarryWilliams130506.pdf (accessed 7 March 2022).
6. In an interview with the author, 23 November 2022.
7. Paul Vallely, 'The cost of the royal snub to Carey', *The Independent*, 10 March 1997, www.independent.co.uk/voices/the-cost-of-the-royal-snub-to-carey-1272137.html (accessed 5 March 2022).
8. Aaron James, 'Prince Charles and Archbishop Welby send Bishop of London off in style', *Premier Christian News*, 9 February 2017, https://premierchristian.news/en/news/article/prince-charles-and-archbishop-welby-send-bishop-of-london-off-in-style (accessed 7 March 2022).
9. Dimbleby, *The Prince of Wales*, p. 113–14.
10. Dermot Morrah, *To Be a King* (London: Hutchinson, 1968), p. 132.
11. HRH The Prince of Wales, speech for the twenty-fifth anniversary reception for the Prayer Book Society, St James's Palace, London, 29 April 1997, reprinted in Cadman and Bushrui, *Speeches and Articles, 1968–2012*, p. 603.
12. HRH The Prince of Wales, 'A Deep Sense of the Sacred', Foreword written for the 2011 version of the King James Bible, 20 March 2011, reprinted in Cadman and Bushrui, *Speeches and Articles, 1968–2012*, p. 665.
13. Dimbleby, *The Prince of Wales*, p. 250.
14. Dimbleby, *The Prince of Wales*, p. 252.
15. Comment made to the author, October 2021.
16. Dinitia Smith, 'Master Storyteller or Master Deceiver', *The New York Times*, 3 August 2002, www.nytimes.com/2002/08/03/books/master-storyteller-or-master-deceiver.html (accessed 7 March 2022).
17. Carpenter, *Robert Runcie*, p. 223.
18. Carpenter, *Robert Runcie*, p. 222.
19. Carpenter, *Robert Runcie*, pp. 224–5.
20. Carpenter, *Robert Runcie*, p. 221.
21. Carpenter, *Robert Runcie*, p. 224.
22. Carpenter, *Robert Runcie*, p. 221.
23. 'Clerics concerned about Prince Charles' fitness to be king', UPI Archives, 12 December 1993, www.upi.com/Archives/1993/12/12/Clerics-concerned

-about-Prince-Charles-fitness-to-be-king/5954755672400 (accessed 14 March 2022).

24. 'Obituary: The Ven George Austin', *Church Times*, 8 March 2019, www.churchtimes.co.uk/articles/2019/8-march/gazette/obituaries/obituary-the-ven-george-austin (accessed 7 March 2022).
25. 'Clerics concerned about Prince Charles' fitness to be king', 12 December 1993.
26. HRH The Prince of Wales in conversation with Jonathan Dimbleby, 'Prince Charles: his children, the paparazzi & marriage to Diana', YouTube, www.youtube.com/watch?v=EHzHMhtZ7h4 (accessed 30 January 2023).
27. Harriet Sherwood, 'Prince Charles kept in touch with ex-bishop later jailed for abuse', *The Guardian*, 20 July 2018, www.theguardian.com/uk-news/2018/jul/20/prince-charles-kept-in-touch-with-ex-bishop-jailed-for-abuse-peter-ball (accessed 14 March 2022).
28. 'Executive Summary', Independent Inquiry into Child Sexual Abuse, Anglican Church Case Studies: Chichester/Peter Ball Investigation Report, www.iicsa.org.uk/reports-recommendations/publications/investigation/anglican-chichester-peter-ball/executive-summary (accessed 14 March 2022).
29. Dimbleby, *The Prince of Wales*, p. 528.
30. Dimbleby, *The Prince of Wales*, p. 528.
31. Dimbleby, *The Prince of Wales*. pp. 531–2.
32. 'Faith and Nation: Report of a Commission of Inquiry to the UK Evangelical Alliance', Evangelical Alliance, www.eauk.org/current-affairs/publications/upload/Faith-and-Nation.pdf (accessed 7 March 2022).
33. Dimbleby, *The Prince of Wales*, p. 532.
34. Cadman and Bushrui, *Speeches and Articles, 1968–2012*.
35. Temenos Academy, www.temenosacademy.org (accessed 7 March 2022).
36. 'A Message From Our Patron', Temenos Academy, www.temenosacademy.org/message-patron (accessed 7 March 2022).
37. Janet Watts, 'Kathleen Raine' obituary, *The Guardian*, 8 July 2003, www.theguardian.com/news/2003/jul/08/guardianobituaries.books (accessed 7 March 2022).
38. HRH The Prince of Wales, 'Kathleen Raine – Address given at the Memorial Service for Kathleen Raine', Queen's Chapel, London, 4 December 2003, reprinted in Cadman and Bushrui, *Speeches and Articles, 1968–2012*, p. 616.
39. HRH The Prince of Wales, 'Kathleen Raine', in Cadman and Bushrui, *Speeches and Articles, 1968–2012*, p. 619.

40. *Charles I: King and Collector* catalogue (London: Royal Academy of Arts, 2018).
41. See chapters four and five.
42. 'Prince Charles's Thought for the Day' text, *The Guardian*, 1 January 2000, www.theguardian.com/uk/2000/jan/01/ruralaffairs.millennium (accessed 7 March 2022).
43. 'BBC Reith Lectures 2000, A Royal View', news.bbc.co.uk/hi/english/static/events/reith_2000/lecture6.stm (accessed 7 March 2022).
44. HRH The Prince of Wales, 'Cranmer's Prayer Book', 25th Anniversary Reception for the Prayer Book Society, St James's Palace, London, 29 April 1997, reprinted in Cadman and Bushrui, *Speeches and Articles, 1968–2012*, p. 603.
45. For a full account of Prince Philip and his mother, Princess Alice, see chapter six.
46. Boris Kálnoky, '"It's in my blood": Prince Charles's love of Transylvania', *The Spectator*, 18 June 2022, www.spectator.com.au/2022/06/letter-from-transylvania/ (accessed 25 January 2023).
47. Interview with the author, November 2022.
48. Interview with the author, November 2022.
49. Sally Bedell Smith, *Prince Charles: The Passions and Paradoxes of an Improbable Life* (London: Michael Joseph, 2017), p. 355.
50. Bedell Smith, *Prince Charles*, p. 356.
51. Interview with the author, November 2022.
52. 'Prince Charles succeeds Queen Elizabeth as patron of Holocaust Memorial Day Trust', International March of the Living, 12 January 2016, www.motl.org/prince-charles-succeeds-queen-elizabeth-as-patron-of-holocaust-memorial-day-trust (accessed 25 January 2022).
53. Victoria Murphy, 'Portraits of Holocaust Survivors Commissioned by Prince Charles to Be Displayed in Buckingham Palace', *Town and Country*, 12 January 2022, www.townandcountrymag.com/society/tradition/a38739031/prince-charles-buckingham-palace-portraits-of-holocaust-survivors (accessed 25 January 2023).
54. Cnaan Liphshiz, 'Prince Charles at 30 days ceremony: Rabbi Sacks "a light unto this nation"', *Jerusalem Post*, 7 December 2020, www.jpost.com/diaspora/prince-charles-at-30-days-ceremony-rabbi-sacks-a-light-unto-this-nation-651355 (accessed 25 January 2023).
55. Interview with the author, December 2022.
56. 'Remarks by HRH The Prince of Wales at the Bridge Awards, Hosted by the Council of Christians and Jews at Spencer House', 23 June 2021, www.princeofwales.gov.uk/speech/remarks-hrh-prince-wales-bridge-

awards-hosted-council-christians-and-jews-spencer-house (accessed 25 January 2023).

57. 'A speech by HRH The Prince of Wales titled "Islam and the West" at the Oxford Centre for Islamic Studies, The Sheldonian Theatre, Oxford', 27 October 1993, www.princeofwales.gov.uk/speech/speech-hrh-prince-wales-titled-islam-and-west-oxford-centre-islamic-studies-sheldonian (accessed 7 March 2022).
58. 'A speech by HRH The Prince of Wales', 27 October 1993.
59. 'A speech by HRH The Prince of Wales', 27 October 1993.
60. Ronni L. Gordon and David M. Stillman, 'Prince Charles of Arabia', Middle East Forum, September 1997, www.meforum.org/356/prince-charles-of-arabia (accessed 7 March 2022).
61. Jonny Dymond, 'Prince Charles and Camilla: Why diplomats love it when royalty visits', BBC News, 20 November 2021, www.bbc.co.uk/news/uk-59351372 (accessed 7 March 2022).
62. Richard Wollffe and Simon Targett, '$33 m gift to Oxford Islamic Centre', *Financial Times*, 30 May 1997.
63. Jamie Grierson and Vikram Dodd, 'Prince Charles could be called as witness in cash-for-honours investigation', *The Guardian*, 16 February 2022, www.theguardian.com/uk-news/2022/feb/16/prince-charles-could-be-called-as-witness-in-cash-for-honours-investigation (accessed 5 March 2022).
64. 'A speech by HRH The Prince of Wales at the Oxford Centre for Islamic Studies', 16 May 2017, www.princeofwales.gov.uk/speech/speech-hrh-prince-wales-oxford-centre-islamic-studies (accessed 7 March 2022).
65. Andrew Alderson, 'Prince Charles to plead Islam's cause to Bush', *The Telegraph*, 29 October 2005, telegraph.co.uk/news/uknews/1501789/Prince-Charles-to-plead-Islams-cause-to-Bush.html (accessed 7 March 2022).
66. Brian Whitaker, 'Prince Charles, the Islamic dissident', *The Guardian*, 27 March 2006, www.theguardian.com/commentisfree/2006/mar/27/princecharlestheislamicdis (accessed 7 March 2022).
67. 'Prince Charles says radicalization of young people "alarming"', BBC News, 8 February 2015, www.bbc.co.uk/news/uk-31199692 (accessed 7 March 2022).
68. 'London: Prince Charles meets Chaldean Catholic community', *Independent Catholic News*, 9 December 2014, www.indcatholicnews.com/news/26228 (accessed 7 March 2022).
69. 'Prince Charles speaks out for freedom of religion or belief', The APPG for International Freedom of Religion or Belief, 22 December 2016,

appgfreedomofreligionorbelief.org/prince-charles-speaks-freedom-religion-belief (accessed 7 March 2022).

70. HRH The Prince of Wales, Tony Juniper and Emily Shuckburgh, *Climate Change*, A Ladybird Expert Book (London: Michael Joseph, 2017). Kate Pickles, 'Climate change is "wolf at the door" says Charles: Prince urges world leaders to do more to tackle the issue in foreword of Ladybird book he co-authored', *Daily Mail*, 20 January 2017, www.dailymail.co.uk/news/article-4138736/Climate-change-wolf-door-says-Prince-Charles.html (accessed 14 March 2022).
71. Robert Mendick, 'Prince Charles complains Brexit "obsession" has stifled debate on Christian persecution', *The Telegraph*, 27 January 2017, www.telegraph.co.uk/news/2017/01/27/prince-charles-complains-brexit-obsession-has-stifled-debate (accessed 7 March 2022).
72. Catherine Pepinster, 'Prince Charles to call for Middle East peace at service for persecuted Christians', *National Catholic Reporter* online, 4 December 2018, www.ncronline.org/news/world/prince-charles-call-middle-east-peace-service-persecuted-christians (accessed 7 March 2022).
73. 'Address by HRH The Prince of Wales at a service to celebrate the contribution of Christians in the Middle East', 4 December 2018, www.princeofwales.gov.uk/speech/address-hrh-prince-wales-service-celebrate-contribution-christians-middle-east (accessed 7 March 2022).
74. HRH Prince of Wales, 'John Henry Newman: The harmony of difference', *L'Osservatore Romano*, 12 October 2019, www.vaticannews.va/en/vatican-city/news/2019-10/newman-canonization-prince-charles-editorial-britain.html (accessed 7 March 2022).
75. Letter from the Prince's archive, quoted by Dimbleby, *The Prince of Wales*, p. 350.
76. Dimbleby, *The Prince of Wales*, p. 351.
77. Bedell Smith, *Prince Charles*, p. 180.
78. Richard Pendlebury and Stephen Wright, 'The priest, the princess's mother and a friendship forged from grief: How a French cleric who prayed over Diana's body formed a lifelong bond with Frances Shand Kydd', *Daily Mail*, 25 June 2021, www.dailymail.co.uk/news/article-9726885/Princess-Dianas-days-French-cleric-forged-bond-mother.html (accessed 7 March 2022).
79. Stephen Bates and Steven Morris, 'Charles puts Rome first and postpones wedding', *The Guardian*, 5 April 2005, www.theguardian.com/uk/2005/apr/05/monarchy.catholicism (accessed 7 March 2022).
80. Church of England, Marriage in Church after divorce, www.churchofengland.org/sites/default/files/2017-10/marriage%20in%20church%20after%20divorce.pdf (accessed 30 January 2023).

81. Andy McSmith, 'Charles' civil ceremony may not be legal', *The Independent*, 20 February 2005, www.independent.co.uk/news/uk/this-britain/charles-s-civil-ceremony-may-not-be-legal-484143.html (accessed 7 March 2022). Simon Walters, 'The wedding secret Charles must take to his grave: legal advice on Camilla marriage sealed until after his death', *The Mail on Sunday*, 10 April 2010, www.dailymail.co.uk/news/article-1265095/Charles [sic] Camilla-marriage-Legal-advice-sealed-Princes-death.html (accessed 7 March 2022).
82. 'Royal couple to acknowledge "sin"', BBC News, 9 April 2005, news.bbc.co.uk/1/hi/uk/4421481.stm (accessed 7 March 2022).
83. Church of England, advice to clergy concerning marriage and the divorced, https://www.churchofengland.org/sites/default/files/2017-11/MarriageAFTERdivorceFORM.pdf (accessed 14 March 2022).
84. 'Charles confirms he will be anointed and crowned "Defender of the Faith"', Archbishop Cranmer, 9 February 2015, archbishopcranmer.com/charles-confirms-he-will-be-anointed-and-crowned-defender-of-the-faith (accessed 7 March 2022).
85. Interview with the author, October 2021.
86. Interview with the author, December 2021.
87. Justin Welby interviewed in *Charles: Our New King*, transmitted on ITV, 2 November 2022, 9 p.m.
88. Interview with the author, December 2021.

## 9 *The changing of the guard*

1. Ian Gallagher and Sarah Oliver, 'After 70 years in the wings . . . the moment Charles became our King', *Mail on Sunday*, 11 September 2022, p. 6, www.pressreader.com/uk/the-mail-on-sunday/20220911/281556589665676 (accessed 26 January 2023).
2. Leon Edel (ed.), *The Letters of Henry James, Volume 4*, 1895–1916 (London: Macmillan, 1984).
3. Rebecca English and Sam Greenhill, 'Tearful Charles's tribute to his darling Mama', *Scottish Daily Mail*, 10 September 2022, p. 1, www.pressreader.com/uk/scottish-daily-mail/20220910/281492165155040, (accessed 26 January 2023).
4. See chapter four.
5. 'His Majesty The King's address to the Nation and the Commonwealth', 9 September 2022, www.royal.uk/his-majesty-king%E2%80%99s-address-nation-and-commonwealth (accessed 26 January 2023).

6. 'His Majesty The King's address to the Nation and the Commonwealth', 9 September 2022.
7. 'Accession Proclamation', 10 September 2022, www.college-of-arms.gov.uk/2-coa/75-proclamation (accessed 26 January 2023).
8. Josh Glancey and Nicholas Hellen, 'King Charles III: A new era begins with the most gloriously elaborate piece of box-ticking', *The Times*, 10 September 2022, p. 1.
9. 'His Majesty The King's Declaration', 10 September 2022, www.royal.uk/accession-council-and-principal-proclamation-0 (accessed 12 January 2023).
10. 'Her Majesty The Queen's Declaration', *London Gazette*, 12 February 1952, quoted in 'Swearing In The New King: The Accession Declarations and Coronation Oaths', Constitution Unit, University College London, May 2018, p. 6.
11. 'His Majesty The King's Declaration', 10 September 2022.
12. 'His Majesty The King's Oath relating to the security of the Church of Scotland', St James's Palace, 10 September 2022, www.royal.uk/his-majesty-kings-oath-relating-security-church-scotland (accessed 26 January 2023).
13. 'Accession Proclamation', College of Arms, www.college-of-arms.gov.uk/2-coa/75-proclamation (accessed 26 January 2023).
14. Gallagher and Oliver, 'After 70 years in the wings . . .'
15. 'His Majesty The King's reply to addresses of condolence at Westminster Hall', 12 September 2022, www.royal.uk/his-majesty-kings-reply-addresses-condolence-westminster-hall (accessed 26 January 2023).
16. Chris Mason, quoted in James Gregory, 'King Charles III promises to follow Queen's selfless duty', BBC News, 12 September 2022 www.bbc.co.uk/news/uk-62874346 (accessed 26 January 2023).
17. James Gregory, 'King Charles III promises to follow Queen's selfless duty'.
18. 'The King's Remarks to Faith Leaders', 16 September 2022, www.royal.uk/kings-remarks-faith-leaders (accessed 26 January 2023).
19. See chapters five and ten.
20. Confirmed by staff during an informal gathering, 27 October 2022.
21. Interview with the author, 9 December 2022.
22. Interview with the author, 25 November 2022.
23. Malcolm Guite, 'Refugee', January 2012, malcolmguite.wordpress.com/2012/01/07/refugee (accessed 26 January 2023).
24. Interview with the author, 9 December 2022.
25. Interview with the author, 18 December 2022.
26. 'The King's Christmas Broadcast 2022', 25 December 2022, www.royal.uk/kings-christmas-broadcast-2022 (accessed 26 January 2023).

## *10 Supreme Governor*

1. British Social Attitudes, National Centre for Social Research, 2016, www.bsa.natcen.ac.uk/media-centre/archived-press-releases/bsa-34-record-number-of-brits-with-no-religion.aspx (accessed 8 March 2022).
2. British Social Attitudes Survey, 2016.
3. Pamela Duncan, Carmen Aguilar García and Lucy Swan, 'Census 2021 in charts: Christianity now minority religion in England and Wales', *The Guardian*, 29 November 2022, www.theguardian.com/uk-news/2022/nov/29/census-2021-in-charts-christianity-now-minority-religion-in-england-and-wales (accessed 26 January 2023).
4. Henry Offley Wakeman, *Introduction to the History of the Church of England*, quoted in Edgar C. S. Gibson, *The Thirty Nine Articles of the Church of England*, sixth edition (London: Methuen, 1908), p. 771.
5. 'The Queen's funeral watched by 29 million viewers in the UK', BBC News, 20 September 2022, www.bbc.co.uk/news/entertainment-arts-62966616 (accessed 26 January 2023).
6. Interview with the author, December 2021.
7. Glen Owen, 'King to Welby: I want Harry at Coronation', *Mail on Sunday*, 29 January 2023, p. 1.
8. Bradley, *God Save the Queen*, p. 233.
9. Bradley, *God Save the Queen*, p. 232.
10. Paul Avis, *Church, State and Establishment* (London: SPCK, 2001), pp. 29–30.
11. Interview with the author, February 2022.
12. Interview with the author, February 2022.
13. 'The House of Good', National Churches Trust, 2020, www.houseof-good.nationalchurchestrust.org (accessed 8 March 2022).
14. Harriet Sherwood, 'Church and state – an unhappy union?' *The Observer*, 7 October 2018, www.theguardian.com/global/2018/oct/07/church-and-state-an-unhappy-union (accessed 14 March 2022).
15. Interview with the author, December 2021.
16. For details of Establishment and the role of the Supreme Governor, see Martin Davie, *A Guide to the Church of England* (London: Bloomsbury, 2019).
17. Richard Hooker, *The Laws of Ecclesiastical Polity, Book VIII*, iii.3, quoted in Davie, *A Guide to The Church of England*, p. 65.
18. Rowan Williams, *On Christian Theology* (Oxford: Blackwell, 2000), pp. 233–4.
19. Interview with the author, December 2021.

20. Harriet Sherwood, 'Justin Welby: separation of church and state not a disaster', *The Guardian*, 18 May 2018, www.theguardian.com/world/2018/may/18/justin-welby-separation-of-church-and-state-not-a-disaster (accessed 8 March 2022).
21. Interview with the author, December 2021.
22. 'Archbishop's New Statesman magazine interview', Dr Rowan Williams, 22 December 2008, rowanwilliams.archbishopofcanterbury.org/articles.php/609/archbishops-new-statesman-magazine-interview.html (accessed 14 March 2022).
23. David Edwards, 'Defender of the Faith – a title still with meaning', *The Tablet*, 2 February 2002, p. 19.
24. Theo Hobson, *Against Establishment: An Anglican Polemic* (London: Darton, Longman and Todd, 2003), p. 134.
25. Sherwood, 'Church and state – an unhappy union?'

## 11 *Vivat! Vivat! Vivat Rex*

1. Prince Harry, *Spare* (London: Bantam, 2023).
2. 'The Queen's Accession Day message', 5 February 2022, www.royal.uk/queens-accession-day-message (accessed 26 January 2023).
3. 'NSS calls for a more secular and inclusive coronation', National Secular Society, 3 November 2022, www.secularism.org.uk/news/2022/11/nss-calls-for-a-more-secular-and-inclusive-coronation (accessed 26 January 2023).
4. Interview with the author, November 2022.
5. Email exchange between the author and the Earl Marshal, November 2022.
6. Interview with the author, December 2021.
7. 'Coronation Claims Office to look at historic and ceremonial roles for King Charles III's Coronation', Cabinet Office, 5 January 2023, www.gov.uk/government/news/coronation-claims-office-to-look-at-historic-and-ceremonial-roles-for-king-charles-iiis-coronation (accessed 26 January 2023).
8. Rt Hon Oliver Dowden CBE MP, cited in 'Coronation Claims Office to look at historic and ceremonial roles for King Charles III's Coronation', 5 January 2023.
9. David Hughes, 'Coronation will show off the "best of Britain", ministers pledge', *Evening Standard*, 20 December 2022, www.standard.co.uk/news/politics/rishi-sunak-cabinet-king-prime-minister-oliver-dowden-b1048465.html (accessed 26 January 2023).

10. Liam James, 'King Charles "vows to have slimmed down coronation" amid cost of living crisis', *The Independent*, 21 September 2022, www.independent.co.uk/news/uk/home-news/king-charles-coronation-cost-crown-b2171646.html (accessed 26 January 2023).
11. Victoria Ward, 'The King rejects cut-price coronation in favour of "glorious" pomp and pageantry', *The Telegraph*, 21 December 2022, www.telegraph.co.uk/royal-family/2022/12/21/king-rejects-cut-price-coronation-favour-glorious-pomp-pageantry (accessed 26 January 2023).
12. According to Westminster Abbey sources.
13. Wesley Carr, 'This Intimate Ritual: The Coronation Service', *Political Theology*, 21 April 2015, https://www.tandfonline.com/doi/abs/10.1558/poth.v4i1.11 (accessed 26 January 2023), pp. 11–24.
14. Interview with the author, December 2021.
15. Interview with the author, December 2021.
16. Interview with the author, October 2021.
17. 'Swearing in the new King: The Accession Declaration and Coronation oaths', The Constitution Unit, University College London, www.ucl.ac.uk/constitution-unit/sites/constitution-unit/files/180_swearing_in_the_new_king.pdf (accessed 30 January 2023).
18. *Woman's Hour*, BBC Radio 4, 16 January 2022.
19. 'Religion', Office for National Statistics, 2021 Census results www.ons.gov.uk/peoplepopulationandcommunity/culturalidentity/religion (accessed 26 January 2023).
20. Paul Bradshaw, 'On Revising the Coronation Service', *Theology*, 1 March 1993, Sage publications (log-in required to view full article) journals.sagepub.com/doi/abs/10.1177/0040571X9309600205 (accessed 19 January 2023).
21. 'Swearing in the New King: The Accession Declaration and Coronation Oaths,' The Constitution Unit, University College, London, May 2018, www.ucl.ac.uk/constitution-unit/sites/constitution-unit/files/180_swearing_in_the_new_king.pdf (accessed 8 March 2022).
22. Longford, *Elizabeth R*, p. 72.
23. The Constitution Unit, May 2018.
24. Westminster Abbey has hosted events during the annual Week of Prayer for Christian Unity and annual lectures for the ecumenical organisation at the Anglican Centre in Rome.
25. Matt Wilkinson, 'Charles told to drop his breeches', *The Sun*, 21 January 2023, p. 1.
26. 'Everyone relax – this is why Camilla may never be Queen', *Daily Mirror*, 23 August 2017, www.mirror.co.uk/news/uk-news/everyone-relax-camilla-never-queen-11025881 (accessed 30 January 2023).

27. 'Order of Service of the Coronation of King George VI and Queen Elizabeth', www.oremus.org/coronation/1937/ (accessed 26 January 2023).
28. According to a well-placed source interviewed by the author in January 2023.
29. For full details of the Crown Jewels collection, see Clare Murphy, The Crown Jewels, Historic Royal Palaces, 2018.
30. 'Stone of Destiny will be moved for King Charles' coronation', Stone World, 19 September 2022, www.stoneworld.com/articles/92616-stone-of-destiny-will-be-moved-for-king-charles-coronation (accessed 27 January 2023).
31. Interview with the author with a well-placed source.
32. Interview with the author, December 2021.
33. Robert Jobson and Jonathan Prynn, 'Japan's Emperor Narahito ascends throne in traditional ceremony as he becomes country's 126th emperor, *Evening Standard*, 22 October 2019, www.standard.co.uk/news/world/japan-s-emperor-naruhito-ascends-throne-in-traditional-ceremony-a4267361.html (accessed 27 January 2023).
34. Mari Yamaguchi, 'Japan emperor's harvest is his 1st communion with gods', *Associated Press/The Detroit News*, 14 November 2019, www.detroitnews.com/story/news/world/2019/11/14/japan-emperor-secret-daijo-sai-ritual/40612869 (accessed 27 January 2023).
35. Interview with a source by the author, October 2021.
36. Interview with the author, November 2023.
37. Interview with the author, February 2023.

## *Conclusion*

1. Dr Craig Prescott, speaking at a webinar on the coronation and the accession oaths, The Constitution Unit, University College, London, 1 November 2022.
2. Interview with the author, November 2022.
3. 'The Prince of Wales visits de Paul UK in London', 19 January 2022, www.royal.uk/prince-wales-visits-depaul-uk-london (Accessed 27 January 2023).
4. 'Prince William and Kate meet Burnley's Pastor Mick', BBC News, 20 January 2022, www.bbc.co.uk/news/av/uk-60062262 (accessed 27 January 2023).
5. 'The Royal Wedding Homily by Dr. Richard Chartres, Anglican Bishop of London', 29 April 2011, www.patheos.com/blogs/thedudeabides/2011/04/29/the-royal-wedding-homily-by-dr-richard-chartres-anglican-bishop-of-london (accessed 27 January 2023).

6. Professor Vernon Bogdanor, speaking in *Charles: Our New King*, ITV, 2 November 2022.
7. 'Speeches and Articles, 1968–2012, His Royal Highness The Prince of Wales', University of Wales Press, 2 April 2015, www.uwp.co.uk/speeches-and-articles-1968-2012-his-royal-highness-the-prince-of-wales (accessed 10 March 2022).
8. 'BBC Reith Lectures 2000, A Royal View', news.bbc.co.uk/hi/english/static/events/reith_2000/lecture6.stm (accessed 27 January 2023).

# Index